THE SECRET COLLECTOR:
THE LOST ART COLLECTION OF ERICH ŠLOMOVIČ

LEON POGELŠEK AND SLAVKO PREGL

ARCA PUBLICATIONS

The Secret Collector:
The Lost Art Collection of Erich Šlomovič

By Leon Pogelšek and Slavko Pregl
Translated from Slovenian by Irena Duša Draž

All rights reserved. No part of this publication may be reproduced, stored in a retrieval system, or transmitted in any form or by any means, without prior permission in writing of ARCA Publications, or as expressly permitted by law, or under terms agreed with the appropriate reprographics rights organization. Inquiries concerning reproduction outside the scope of the above should be sent to ARCA (Association for Research into Crimes against Art) via its website, www.artcrimeresearch.org.

Disclaimer: The authors, editors and publisher (ARCA Publications) will not accept any legal responsibility for any errors or omissions that may be made in this publication. The publisher makes no warranty, express or implied, with respect to the material contained herein. ARCA accepts no responsibility for the content published herein. The opinions expressed by the author in this publication do not represent the official opinions of ARCA and its staff.

ARCA is a registered Associazione Culturale in Italy. Profits from the sale of this book go directly to support ARCA's activities in promoting the study of art crime and cultural heritage protection. Support for this publication series was raised by a 2019 Kickstarter campaign. Support for the translation of this book came from the Slovenian original came from JAK (The Slovenian National Book Agency).

Title in the original language: *Skrivnost se imenuje Erich Šlomovič* (Mladinska knjiga Založba, 2019)

Translated from Slovenian by Irena Duša Draž
Cover design and interior design and layout by Urška Charney
ISBN: 978-1-7343026-4-6

TABLE OF CONTENTS

Summary	7
About the Authors	9
Prologue	11
(Who is Erich Šlomovič?)	
Could you love me?	15
Come out, I'm going to smash your face and head in	25
At your service, fair lady	27
You know what they say, dignity is lost on account of rushing	33
To hell with jokes if you can't take them	41
A marvellous piece, my sweet boy, just look at it	48
I'm not being difficult, I just want a decent beefsteak	50
Fuck it, son, money is everything	55
We have a treasure here! Don't just stand there like a dummy	67
I need a man, my stud	71
It's not about the coffee. It's about the system	76
You're throwing money out the window while I'm dying	78
I am the only one who knows what needs to be said	83
Have another whiskey! I need to think about this	87
Did the sabre hack like it was supposed to?	95
If I may, dear madam, I'd like to ask you for this dusty little old notebook	99
And what are you doing here, young man?	103
That's very noble of you. It's one of the reasons I like you	108
We're not going to shoot. Are we?	114
Don't ask questions, learn with your eyes and keep your mouth shut	121
Everyone wants white bread but no one wants to hoe the land	134
You're a genius. Geeenius	144
You must have gone mad. Go see some psychiatrists	148

Don't take me for a fool. I've come to get the money or the stuff	153
Not a move on your own	160
What kinds of misfortunes made you come and remember your mother?	164
Well, half a million, only half a million	166
I have solid connections at the Interpol section. The chief is a friend of mine	173
Those guys at Sotheby's are annoying	178
This is not a quick scam. It's not like throwing a rock and then running	180
You're laughing, are you? Do you even know what this is?	186
How in the world? Nothing for a hundred years, and now three world class authors in one week	191
Is this what you want? Ha? Is this what you want?	197
Of course, you screwed the silver deal and pushed me in the gutter	199
Modigliani, I'm holding a real Modigliani	205
There are days when I hide my pain...	213
Citizen of this state, shut up and open the trunk, as the competent authority of the state tells you to	216
What the hell have you done this time?	223
The business must go on regardless	229
Your house was ransacked by default	234
I'm not having this. If you do this, I will leave with him right now	242
Being a commoner, I would prefer a double whisky	249
These are truly stunning pieces of art	253
The eagle will land at noon tomorrow	258
There are millions at stake and this is how you two act...	261
Get out of my sight! You won't put your balls on the table	267
You were brilliant: strict and steadfast. You'll have them eating out of your hand now	271

Even God would do better to rest in this heat	282
But it can't be possible, it can't be, how could it appear out of nowhere...	291
I used to be an ardent dissident back in the day	295
You own nothing. The stuff was bought by my investors	299
No. There are too many crooks and swindlers in this business all over the world	309
The old man is interested in business. He saw there was a ton of money involved	316
I was sure they would find my stash and then half a million would go to hell	320
What price would you set at the beginning, according to your own judgement?	326
Is there something in the air here? Are they leaving me high and dry?	334
Is this how you do businesses worth millions?	342
Will you kindly put away the money?	352
This is really not enough. I want nineteen million	360
Am I still on the team?	365
And what do you plan to do with this money?	376
I have to do everything myself	385
In the end, I was duped by that deceitful professor of yours!	392
Would you mind if I took down the painting so I can check the back?	399

Summary

There are countless stories of buried, hidden, lost and then "exhumed" artworks, preserved thanks to having been hidden. The Croatian Jew Erich Šlomovič possessed an art collection of around 600 paintings, including works by Picasso, Chagall and Matisse, which he acquired while working in Paris in his early twenties as the protégé of the art dealer Ambroise Vollard. When Šlomovič fled Paris in anticipation of the Nazi invasion, he placed 190 paintings in a bank vault, while the rest were boxed up and smuggled across Nazi-occupied territories with the assistance of the Yugoslav Embassy, eventually to be brought to Belgrade. Šlomovič was arrested shortly after and was killed in a concentration camp, aged 27.

His art collection survived far longer. In 1981, the 190 works in the vault in Paris were set to be auctioned off, in lieu of unpaid banking expenses. This prompted Šlomovič's descendants into legal action, in opposition to Vollard's heirs, who claimed that Šlomovič stole the works from the renowned dealer. The auction of the vault's contents, which were eventually divided among Šlomovič's and Vollard's heirs, finally went ahead at Sotheby's in 2010, and the 190 works earned around $30 million. But the 400 or so that made their way back to Belgrade were hidden behind a false wall, in anticipation of the rounding up of Belgrade's Jews, and remained undiscovered throughout the war. After the war, Šlomovič's relatives recovered the artworks but died in a train crash while carrying them to Belgrade; the art was described in one account as being scattering across "a muddy field in central Serbia." The works were retrieved and eventually arrived at the National Museum of Belgrade, where they have remained ever since.

But there are other versions of this story. It is all ostensibly true, but varies depending on which historical account you read, and who you ask. One alternate version is told in a novelistic style here by Leon Pogelšek, a Slovenian art dealer who personally knew some of the characters involved in the Yugoslav chapter of the story and, indeed, was involved himself—he appears in this story under the pseudonym Leon Sattler. He related his version of the Šlomovič story, which remains one of the great mysteries of lost art, to multi-award-winning Slovenian author, Slavko Pregl. The result is the book in your hands.

It's a true story to the best knowledge of the authors, but it reads like a novel. Can the lost collection be found?

About the Authors

Slavko Pregl (born in 1945 in Ljubljana, Slovenia), completed the Faculty of Economics. He is a journalist, editor, publisher and writer, who has published 50 books in the Slovene language, with translations into 14 languages (Croat, Serbian, Bosnian, Macedonian, Bulgarian, Albanian, Slovak and Czech languages, Polish, Russian, Kazakh, Uzbek, Italian, English), with his short stories (fables) translated into Greek, Swedish, German and Latvian languages.

He received many prizes for the best novel for young adults in Slovenia (in 1976, 2004, 2005, 2010 and 2014), as well as a lifetime achievement for literature for children and young adults prize (2015). He is also recipient of the Premio Jugra (Russia, 2016) for the best novel for young adults translated into Russian from Slavic languages (*Geniuses without Pants*, translated into Albanian, Bosnian, Bulgarian, Russian and English).

His satirical texts have also received prizes (in 1972 in Slovenia, 1973 in Belgrade, 1978 in Trieste and in 2003, the Grand Prix Aleko, Bulgaria).

Leon Pogelšek (born in 1963 in Brežice, Slovenia) is an art historian, painter and gallerist, and appears as a character in this book. He is the owner of the oldest commercial gallery in Ljubljana. His story, based on real facts and events, is the basis for the book.

Prologue
(Who is Erich Šlomovič?)

According to one of the versions, Erich Šlomovič (pronounced Shlomoveech) was born into a wealthy Jewish merchant family, to his father Bernard and mother Roza, on March 10th, 1915, in Vinkovci, Croatia, then part of the Austro-Hungarian Monarchy. The second (and less plausible) version states that he was born in 1901, in the Jewish-friendly Bosnia, then part of the Ottoman Empire. One version has him shot on January 1st, 1943, despite the official date of death being May 9th, 1945, for all hostages and victims of German violence, for whom there are no undisputed documents available. According to another version, he met his end in a mobile gas chamber.

No matter what the case, Erich Šlomovič arrived in Paris at a very young age, and was offered a job in a gallery on Rue Laffitte by the renowned, at the time seventy-year-old gallery owner and art collector Ambroise Vollard. Vollard was known to support yet unestablished artists - Cezanne, Renoir, Monet, Gauguin, Van Gogh, Picasso, and others - and exhibit their works. The two men got quite close; Šlomovič was expected to become his secretary, while Vollard was to introduce the young art enthusiast to the society of French Impressionists and European vanguard. Šlomovič also collected artwork for himself, he bought some, some he received as gifts, a few were given to him by Vallard, and some he acquired through exchange. It was his desire to establish museum of French Impressionists in Belgrade, and a museum of the (then) contemporary Yugoslav art in Zagreb. Vollard trusted his young friend to occasionally take his paintings to Belgrade, where he would try to sell them in the elite circles.

Ambroise Vollard died in a car accident, aged seventy-three, on July 21st, 1939, on his way back to Paris from his summer residence in Le Tremblay-sur-Mauldre in the central part of France. His driver lost control of the vehicle on the wet road, it flipped over twice; they were both found dead the following morning. Vollard kept ten thousand works of art in his apartment on Rue Martignac.

In the looming atmosphere of the German invasion and approaching war, Erich Šlomovič stored two hundred paintings in a safe at the Société Générale in Paris, covering the rent costs until 1943, while he sent his own collection - six hundred works of art by one version, four hundred and twenty-one by another, and three hundred by a third - to Yugoslavia via diplomatic postal service. Back then it seemed the war would not reach as far. He exhibited his collection for the first (and last) time in the round Meštrović pavilion in Zagreb, on November 24th, 1940, before sending it off to Belgrade. There, he held a long and unsuccessful negotiation on the construction of a museum with the heir to the throne, Pavel Karadjordjević.

When Hitler attacked Yugoslavia, the Šlomovič family retreated to Bačina village in South-West Serbia. Erich concealed his collection behind a double wall in a village house. During one of the German pogroms - a hundred hostages for each fallen soldier - the father Bernard Šlomovič and his sons Erich and Egon were captured and executed. Despite Hitler's, or rather Göring's organised efforts to find the collection, which he knew existed; they never came close to finding it. Erich's mother Roza lived to see the end of the war. She made an arrangement with Dr. Ivan Ribar, a friend of the family, for the collection to be transferred to the National Museum in Belgrade, in exchange for which she was promised life annuity.

The night train, which drove Roza Šlomovič and the collection to Belgrade on December 31st, 1944, collided with an oncoming train and Roza died in the crash. The paintings scattered among deceased passengers and train wreckage. Many artworks supposedly disappeared at that point, with only fifty-eight paintings making it to Belgrade (among others works by Cezanne, Degas, Gauguin, Matisse, Derain, and others), as well as two hundred and sixty-eight drawings and graphics.

Since the rent wasn't paid for such a long time, Société Générale opened the safe in 1979 in order to cover due cost by selling its contents. The debt amounted to five thousand dollars. They stumbled upon a treasure: paintings by Picasso, Cezanne, Van Gogh, Derain...Sotheby's auction house raised thirty-seven million dollars at two auctions - one in London and another one in Paris. Before the auctions there was a dispute about the ownership of the artworks. The court granted the majority of the works to Vollard's heirs, with the exception of those explicitly inscribed to Erich Šlomovič.

There are many things in the short life and work of Erich Šlomovič which will forever remain shrouded in mystery. Imagination is perhaps most stirred by the fact that the number of pieces of art which the young curator and art lover was supposed to have collected doesn't match the number of hitherto found and recorded works. Had they gotten lost on their way from Zagreb to Belgrade, how many had really disappeared in the train crash?

Countless articles have been published in both domestic and foreign press on secrets and difficulties associated with Erich Šlomovič's art collection. Veljko Bulajić filmed his story in *Donator* (*Donor*, 1989), Momo Kapor wrote the book *Dosije Šlomovič* (*The Šlomovič Dossier*, 2004).

Occasionally, like some years ago in Bavaria, pieces "from the lost collection" of Erich Šlomovič find their way to the art market.

One of such finds, discovered and wittingly launched into the world by masters of their profession from a small village in the middle of Panonnia plain, in the vicinity of Pančevo, Serbia, is the subject of this work of narrative, modestly-speculative non-fiction. It is written like a novel but is based on fact, first-hand account and scholarly research.

Could you love me?

First, a thought came over him: "I'm dreaming!"

Next to him on his bed, a beautiful woman lay on her back, naked, leaning slightly to her right, even in the dark, her full breasts with perfect nipples spoke of long hours spent in the tanning bed, her folded and raised left knee covered the triangle where her rousingly slender legs met. Her breathing was calm and deep, her elongated face sunk into sumptuous golden hair, like a Modigliani masterpiece. The pale morning light, pushing its way in through heavy drawn curtains, obscured the image in an almost mysterious and make-believe fashion.

A collie by the name of Šeri lifted her head at the foot of the bed and observed him faithfully.

"Ha!" his now awakened brain began to check in as the memories of the passionate night came to him. "Did the bitch witness the romantic welcome, as Kristina and I fell naked among the sheets in the middle of the night?"

He sat on the edge of the bed, a bit too soft, stretched slightly and slowly got up. The door from the bedroom to the living room was open. He picked his clothes off the floor along the way, while the bitch snuggled lovingly against his legs, before turning to her usual spot under the window, and then joining him once again. He shut the bedroom door carefully. Still naked he sat in the sofa next to the small Bidermeier table.

"So, it happened!" he nodded to himself.

Leon Sattler, the eternal third-year art and history student and occasional peddler of antiques at the flea market, after a month of heavy flirting and a week of making love, gathered his essentials yesterday, put them in a large travel bag, and moved out of his parents' house and in with his ten years older woman, beauty and former model, Kristina Pirc. Nowadays she rarely walked the catwalk, but her connections and charm led her increasingly into organisation of star-studded events and paving the way for up-and-coming music bands. These included first recordings for radio and records in a private studio owned by a very wealthy man. She had a fascinating history, of course. But since her primary job was being beautiful, she put a lot of effort into it and indeed looked much younger than her actual years. All those men who tried so hard, devoured her with their eyes and pushed to come close to her were once again left, presumably, envious bystanders. All they could thoroughly do was compete in interpretative gossip, speculating that the woman, a sex enthusiast, brought the necessary quality and quantity home with her, as enjoying youthful pleasures allowed her to sift through her long-term possibilities in peace. No-one, not even Leon himself, could hardly believe that he made it into her life, being the youngest of the competition. It is true that he had established somewhat of a name for himself among the ladies; many seductive eyes tried and succeeded in inviting him over into their moist bodies. But to him, Kristina was a trophy, obscuring all others. He didn't waste time thinking about tomorrow or the direction this unusual liaison would take; he was overwhelmed by the triumph of the present. *"Ima šuma, ima voda, ima zemlja za oranje* (There is forest, there is water, there is land to plough)," the lines from Vuk Karadžić's *Crven Ban* (The Red Ban) wantonly flooded his body.

He didn't lose much sleep over his studies. Although he was fond of art history, he had no desire to practice it directly, on the market, so he rarely took any exams at the university. He felt there would always be time for this, while time for carousing would eventually run out. He became somewhat estranged from his generation, substituting them with other circles, antique dealers and art peddlers, and since he had money, he was also well acquainted with all city bars and suburban pubs. This is how he stumbled upon the beauty who made the blood flow through his veins, Kristina Pirc. He wanted to conquer her, whatever the cost, and he finally made it.

There was at the same time a small problem, but it was the last thing he would worry about right now. The woman had lately been the lover of Janko Ferkolj, an older general salesman, also dealing in antiques, with whom Sattler had carried out many a deal in the past. But Ferkolj, who was never married and made good money selling antiques, which younger women living the good life happily helped him spend, eventually started leaning towards established business, slow, reliable and risk-free. While he honourably settled for fifty-fifty split in partnership with Sattler, he always insisted on having the first and last say in everything. In addition to official reading lists, the young student continuously devoured books on painting, old furniture, silver and porcelain; he was becoming a great expert and gradually entitled to his own opinion. At the same time, he came from a wealthy family; his mother and father were decently situated in high managerial positions at various prominent companies. In addition to occasional tiring and reproachful lectures on the necessity of full-time study and settled life, which were prompted by his rather relaxed attitude toward spending his youth, they had no problem supplying him with additional funds when need arose. His wallet also bulged comfortably with cash earned by the occasional deals he made. In combinatory discussions about business ideas with Ferkolj, and especially in the presence of a beautiful lover, Sattler relished in flaunting his knowledge. Statuesque, with dark wavy hair, dark eyes, gallant and young, not even twenty-five, and of course smart, he could not escape experienced female observations, whenever the three of them ventured into one of Ljubljana's pubs or popular discotheques.

And then, not long ago, in a nice bar, as Ferkolj slumped under the table following a very long series of double whiskies, and he needed a ride home, Kristina subsequently instructed the obliging driver to proceed to her weekend house near the forest in the suburbs. Once there, she didn't leave him outside her door. The wild night proved that the beautiful woman was able to recognize and appreciate the difference between a placid older man and a fiery younger one, while the younger man couldn't care less about the ten-year age gap between him and the older and very hot woman, highly experienced in matters of love. With her slightly parted luscious lips and widely spread lower part, he was entranced enough to forget about the entire world and some less passionate details which were about to surface in their relationship and its immediate reality.

A few repetitions on, one morning Kristina got up before her lover, went to the bathroom to make herself up, and then sat back naked on the bed with Sattler, waking him. She sweetly batted her long eyelashes over her very deep green eyes a few times, leaned over to his ears and gently whispered:

"Leon, could you love me?"

The boy drew her to him and dispersed any doubts with his actions.

It later transpired that her question was more broadly set: would he move in with her and would he at the same time provide enough money to allow her to continue with the life she wanted and had gotten used to.

And this is how Leon ended up sitting naked in her armchair, in the living room of an agreeably furnished apartment in Ljubljana, an immigrant in the home of a prestigious model, the prey so many men ran after in their erotic fantasies, while he was the one who caught her in reality. His gaze travelled along the beautiful, old furniture.

He patted Šeri lightly with his right hand, as she lay dutifully at his feet. Slowly he started waking up and arranging the more relevant thoughts.

"Kristina is mine! So this is where I am now!"

He thought about Ferkolj, who would in all likelihood go berserk. There will be no more joint ventures. From now on, people will expressively put their heads together and slander him in pubs and discotheques they used to frequent together. Would there be admiration? Would men, very wealthy stalkers of beautiful women among them, repose? Would they chuckle benevolently and wait compassionately for the beauty to have her fill of young flesh while he runs out of money?

Money?

He needs to speed up his business, to expand it and find something new, something big; his occasional deals so far yielded only small change. He did meet many people though, masters among them, who secretly turned large sums of money. He would have to push his way into their circle now.

He got up, went to the bathroom, took a shower and got dressed. He opened the door quietly and saw through the narrow crack that Kristina slept on. Of course, her days started later. He ventured toward the front door and the bitch ran after him.

"I can't walk you now," he dismissed her. "Work is calling. Our lady is very demanding."

He should check the flea market's temperature and try to sell off the stock he acquired from antique dealers in Belgrade last week. His old Quatrelle held quite a few interesting things in its boot. It should certainly suffice for this one time, so he could fork over a wad of cash on the table of now his and ex-Ferkolj's lover. He was certain the profit could buy a six months' worth of a decent life. And then... it'll work out somehow!

He drove to Novi trg and parked his car on the bank of the Ljubljanica River. He found a nice shady spot under a horse chestnut tree. It was still early.

He loved Ljubljana in late spring mornings. Damp mists over the river disintegrated quickly, disappearing in the rising sun, while people on both sides of the river walked to their work or to run some errands; random ramblers were yet to appear. Costermongers rushed their carts toward the marker on Trnovo side, providing fresh vegetables to mostly regular customers. The pigeons were taking off and landing. The Minster church bells rang the passing of time over the city. Waiters were noisily arranging tables and chairs, setting up parasols on the sidewalks in front of their riverbank cafes.

It's about time to serve the first morning coffees.

Coffee!

Leon was suddenly caught up with a memory of an antique dealer from Belgrade, whom everyone called Pera "the Horse" and who filled the boot of his Quatrelle just a few days ago. A tall man of fifty-four, already grey-haired, of ascetic appearance, always wearing one of his grey pants and a chequered flannel shirt, never holding a real job, despite his degree from business school. In the courtyard of his ground floor house in the vicinity of Kalinić market, you could find just about anything. His business area was delimited by the cities of Belgrade, Skopje, Sarajevo and Novi Sad. He never set foot over the national border. He was a renowned wholesale antique dealer; everyone would bring their mostly valuable artefacts to him first. He would haggle at length, seemingly unable to make up his mind, just to pull a wad of banknotes from his pocket at the end, accompanied by a price tag and a cry of "My last price!" Take it or leave it. You came to me, not the other way around. One could always leave Pera "the Horse's" place with cash, as long as they didn't dream too big; at the same time, he always relented a little when selling stuff to end sellers. I know you have to make something, too. The chosen few were honoured by coffee he used to prepare himself. The first-time acquaintances referred Leon to him, he was greeted in a friendly manner:

"Quite a distance you covered from Ljubljana, my little friend! Here, have some coffee to wake you up!"

He limped to the kitchen and put on the coffee, as he was taught by his father, a member of a powerful Beg family from Sarajevo. As a competent prospect, he was routinely sent off from the province to Belgrade. His ancestry could be traced all the way back to Sephardic Jews, who had immigrated to Sarajevo from Spain. Pera's coffee was made by his wife early in the morning, before she left for the market. If a guest worthy of a coffee appeared before the wife made it back, the coffee making was therefore left to Pera.

He started by roasting the still green coffee beans on the "smederevac," a firewood stove manufactured in a stove factory in Smederevo, and then ground them in a brass hand mill. Coffee fats were released into the air and there was the first strong aroma. He then put a teaspoon of sugar into a copper coffee pot on the hot stove, roasting it and waiting for the sugar to melt and caramelize, pouring some water over the pretty dark brown mass and waiting for it to boil. He then removed the coffee pot from the heat, waited for the water to calm down, and added two and a half teaspoons of freshly ground coffee; he waited for the coffee to sink, stirring it slightly, careful for it not to spill over, and brought the mixture to a boil once more. Then the second strong coffee aroma came. Some more time later, he served it and "the finest Turkish coffee in the world, in Belgrade, and in this street," an explosion of aroma and taste, finally arrived.

Patient and careful preparation were worth the while; the drinker was blessed with slurps of concentrated energy, enjoyment, and the right to a moment of peaceful and quiet reflection.

Leon's mouth started to water at the image in his mind and he sat down at the first table in Zlata ladjica Bar. The waiter nodded hello, put down the chairs he was arranging, and disappeared inside the bar. After a while he re-emerged with Turkish coffee.

"The usual, right?" he grinned, jerking his head to get his long black hair out of the way, bowed slightly and went back to his chairs. He was a regular waiter, who brought Leon's coffee countless times, so he knew exactly how he took it. Besides, Leon was a good tipper. He was well aware of what it means to be served by a happy waiter.

He took a sip of his coffee and looked in the direction of Artes Gallery. It was officially still closed, but he saw Metoda, the boss, a short brown-haired, early middle-aged lady, looking at him through the large display window, waving to him. He lifted his cup of coffee, as if to invite her to have some with him, but she shrugged her shoulders and pointed at her watch. There's still so much to do before we open, he read her gesture. The Artes Gallery, Metoda the boss and her girls were an urban legend in the old part of the town. Artists, musicians, film makers and writers from all over the country used to come over for coffee, a friendly chat and of course strict business. Sometimes court appointed appraisers came to sit under one of the large Bernik's canvases, sharing their wise thoughts on the price-restless younger generation, they would tell an interesting story or two about forgeries, dropping hints on whose collections might soon appear on the market. Old ladies sometimes entered, kind and fragile, trying to help resolve their grandchildren's housing needs by dismantling a Jakopič painting from the walls of their homes, or taking a piece of old and valuable jewellery from their silver plated boxes; and plain-spoken womanizers, among all the beautiful things in the gallery warming up to the young sales-ladies, and gentlemen who decided to remelt an antique piece of furniture into more urgent and common needs. Last but not least, there were young designers, both male and female, testing their products on the market, everything from jewellery to artisan chairs. Various peddlers were also trying to sell all sorts of things, but Metoda's competent managerial eye always assessed the correct price. Even Leon sometimes ventured there with a nice silver dish or two on his own account, but for the most part, he brought old trunks there with Ferkolj, ones they collected over the countryside and then embellished and "aged" with the help of various craftsmen.

From the gallery's façade, writer Jurčič cast a bronze gaze on the small square, endowing it with his name. Opposite the Zlata ladjica Bar were the homes of old picture frames repairer and new frames manufacturer, and a shoemaker, both exceptional craftsmen in their respective artisan fields. Having coffee in this square was always enhanced by a subtle bonus of old times.

Right there on Cobblers' Bridge, antique dealer and master of general book sales, the vivacious Peter Kovač, started to arrange his stands, wide planks on woodworking trestles, covered with plastic tablecloths, and piling on heaps of all sorts of books. His makeshift bookstore on the bridge proved an excellent temptation for the passers-by, and later on, when diligent city security chased him off the bridge, he would often boast gloomily about the bridge earning him three times more than your average bookstore. He was an expert lady flatterer and rarely did a woman leave his sight without a book. When elderly professors hardly made it to him, aided by their walking canes, and lamented about not knowing what to do with their affluent libraries, he would propose enthusiastically:

"No worries, young man, we will take everything off your hands for a small fee!"

The many people asking themselves how it was possible for him to sell books at such low prices could never imagine that the wholesale price of most of his stock had been zero, so any kind of sale was of course a profit. At the same time, such extensive libraries always contained a good number of extremely rare books, suitable for connoisseurs, who didn't mind reaching deep in their pockets.

After finishing his coffee, Leon was greeted by him from a distance: "Come, come, Dr. Sattler, come over. I have a marvellous book for you. A cheap one, too!"

He was already digging through his boxes of books and pulled out one titled *Silver*. Still warm, a hard cover with a shiny dust jacket, he explained with pride, just left the printer's. He knew what Leon was into and would often have precious books prepared for him. He acquired them in a variety of ways, most of which the buyers were happily unaware of. His regular suppliers, hobos and junkies among them, were able to provide the freshest releases, angering the city's booksellers. Leon flipped through the offered book and saw it was indeed unused, a Serbian translation of an English original, printed in Ljubljana. It contained a host of data, useful to both collectors and amateurs. Following a haggling match, which was more theatre than anything else, he bought the edition for a third of the recommended price, stated on the jacket.

Leon checked his watch and noticed it was almost opening time for the flea market on Vodnik Square. He returned to his car, crossed Karlovški Bridge and drove through the tunnel under the castle hill to the ramp closing the road just in front of Vodnikov Hram Tavern. The security officer waved to him from afar, indicating that the parking lot was full, but let him through nonetheless, seeing that he was a vendor. Leon rented two canopied stands in order to properly present everything he set out to sell, as well as stay protected from potential rain or scorching sun, before checking out the rest of the offer.

Beside him, two other people displayed folk antiques, postcards and old books. They were almost friends of the family, a married couple, Mrs and Mr. Ulčar. The latter was often also selling old firearms. The grey-haired man with a history of Partisan resistance once sold Leon a Walther P 38 handgun, following the boy's unendurable exhortation. Leon had to promise to keep it in the deepest drawer, wherever that might be, and to use it only for theoretical boost to his abstract feeling of safety. Ulčar of course would have never ventured in such a deal if he hadn't been a close friend of Leon's father ever since the time of war. A short distance away, the art critic Stane Čolnik was selling proofs of graphics, often given to him by different artists. Further on, numerous older ladies offered colourful artisan textiles, tablecloths, napkins, bedspreads, embroidered cotton sheets, wall "home happiness," crocheted hats and scarves, while sometimes pieces of old clothing, national costumes and more could also be found on their stalls. Josip imported paintings from Sombor and beat up furniture from Hungary, a wide range of "imported goods" from Czech Republic and Slovakia was offered by Marko from Sisak: glass, crystal and silverware, candlesticks and assorted miniatures which he also collected himself. Azra, the wife of antique dealer Fehim from Belgrade, sold all kinds of jewellery and silver bits and bobs. The flea market in Ljubljana was visited by many a solvent buyer and was therefore an attractive destination for vendors from near and far. Numerous stands buckled under masses of goods; many vendors were regulars, many more were there occasionally, like Leon.

He spread his Belgrade harvest on the red plush tablecloth; he had a splendid offer. All items - rugs, candlesticks, crockery, cutlery, silver and porcelain - were a premiere, which was immediately noticed by other vendors, mingling among the first buyers. They were searching for interesting items to bring home, clean, repair, restore and polish, and later offer for sale themselves at an increased price. Leon sold off most of his stock surprisingly quickly, fully returning his investment. Immediately after this he raised prices of some of the nicer items and was no longer prepared to haggle, as he was in no hurry to sell. He was waiting for better buyers; he would take the more expensive items he was left with to Tabernakelj on Mestni Square. They will be sold there whenever, and he would be able to take Katarina on a vacation in the meantime. He cleared his stand, packed the unsold items and left the market.

He drove to Tabernakelj. Antiques were kept on the first floor of a mighty classicistic building as part of a business performed by the otherwise state-run company Dota, dealing mostly in selling Slovenian folk products. As an important company, it received goods confiscated from smugglers by numerous customs authorities over the country: paintings, sculptures, furniture, crockery, precious cutlery, antique clocks and whatnot, which all ended up in Tabernakelj in search of official buyers and for the alleged profit of the state. With appropriate skills, mastered beautifully by the boss, Tone Blažič, many items from less reliable sources got mixed in with the official merchandise, while the most valuable state confiscated pieces quickly and discreetly disappeared at friendly prices. The store was therefore also well aware of what potential buyers and sellers were looking for, and it made everybody happy, as the paperwork was in order and everything was official. Tone the boss, a fifty-year-old man of average build, with lush curly white hair, not unlike Einstein's, squinted his eyes behind thick glasses and knew how to stir confidence in his customers, and doubt in his buyers, never letting them be sure as to where they stand. It was rumoured that he had good connections with merchants abroad, and close, yet discreet relations with the police. After all, he had to pay for his business freedom somehow.

Come out, I'm going to smash your face and head in

"What's up?" Tone said in lieu of a greeting as Leon appeared in the store, adding, "We made a nice deal for you on the two candlesticks. Come to my office so I can give you your money."

"Excellent," Leon thought to himself, "great sales at the flea market and now money here as well. What an amazing day!"

They went up the stairs and into the main office. Tone carefully closed the door behind them, walked to the built-in metal cabinet, opened it using first the combination lock and then a key, and pulled a pretty hefty white envelope from the oblong brown box.

"Four thousand, like we agreed," he explained persuasively and laid the envelope down on the table. "Silver candlesticks are always in demand. If you have some more..."

Leon put the envelope away with a smile, then took three long parcels from his travel bag.

"How did you know?" he asked merrily. "This is exactly what I've brought. I have reliable sources. The silver needs a bit of polishing and you're good to go. The marks are clearly visible as it is. There is no rush to sell them, I have plenty of time; go ahead and set an appropriate price."

Tone started to slowly unfold the soft wrapping paper and suddenly stopped.

"What's up with you and Ferkolj? He spent the entire morning fulminating at the door, asking whether you were coming, threatening to kill you, and boozing at the Town hall across the street the whole time, every time he came by he was more drunk... Did you really steal his woman?" Tone asked with a raised squinted look, and Leon could not decide if he meant this as a question or maybe a reproach or a slight ridicule.

Leon shook his head.

"You don't steal women. They come on their own," he retorted self-confidently, smiling ambiguously in his turn, out of pride or as a hint that he was unwilling to discuss private matters.

"You should know," Tone murmured.

They descended to the ground floor and headed toward the main entrance. The moment they stepped in the street, a drunken shriek came their way from across the road, accompanied by the sound of shattering glass off the overturned table.

"So you crawled out of your hole, you deceitful snotty brat! You think you can go after my broads and steal my business just like that, you weren't even born yet, and I mentored you!" Ferkolj screamed, staggering toward them on unsteady legs with an almost flaming red face, brandishing a small axe in his hand. "Come out, you little shit, come out in the open, I'm going to smash your face and head in..."

In the midst of all the screaming he suddenly swung and flung his axe. Tone and Leon jumped off to the side and ducked. The sharp blade dug into the wooden frame of the store window. Leon went pale and almost froze, while Tone grabbed his arm, seizing the spectacles on his nose, pulled him back into the store and slammed the heavy door shut and bolted it with a metal lever.

"You see?" he said to Leon, almost reproachfully.

Outside, Ferkolj kept banging on the door and yelling:

"Come out, you cowards, if you have any guts, let's talk about this like men, you thieves, robbers, you sons of bitches..."

"Let's go up to the office," Tone ordered, "we'll have a drink to summon our courage, wait a bit for the lad to calm down, and then you can leave through the back door. You'll be able to handle it from there, right? I'll call security if I have to; but I don't want any unnecessary fuss. There is a bunch of spectators in front as it is."

Leon felt bad. He knew things would get rough and difficult with his former partner, his almost friend, but he never imagined such a bestial reaction. He didn't think that after all the women he had had, he'd fly off the wall like this over just one. If he'd ducked just a bit less... He downed the generous shot of whiskey which Tone offered him.

"You'll have to settle this somehow," he said after pouring another one. "There's enough room in this business for all. But you need to get your hormones straight, why, there are more than enough women in this world, for God's sake."

"Right," Leon nodded and kept quiet for quite a while. Then he got up slowly and said: "Where's that back door you were talking about?"

He carefully crossed the interior yard and walked to the corner of Town Square, looked around, briskly almost ran to his car and drove off. Ferkolj was nowhere to be seen.

At your service, fair lady

As soon as the bitch heard the key grate the lock on his front door, she greeted him joyfully and ran with him to the kitchen, where Kristina stood in the centre of a small cloud of pale vapour, preparing lunch. He walked up to her, hugged her from behind and kissed her bare shoulder. Her hair was tied up and her long neck reigned with devastating seductiveness above the low-cut back of her dress.

"What took you so long, master?" she turned to him, flirting, and gave him a hug, ready for a kiss. Then she noticed the sweat on his forehead and pushed him away lightly in surprise: "Oh, you're completely wet! Is it this hot outside?"

"It is," he lied, "and I rushed home. Good news. I took the stuff I got in Belgrade to the flea market. It wasn't bad."

They walked to the living room, still hugging. Leon reached into his pocket and brazenly threw a wad of money and an envelope on the table.

"Oooh!" Kristina squealed with joy, grabbed the money and started counting. "This will cover us for a month or two. There's a heap of bills over there."

She pointed in the direction of the dresser and added quickly:

"Plus, we really should take care of the weekend house now, you know."

"I ran into Ferkolj," Leon cut her off. He could not keep quiet, so he dumped the nasty burden off his shoulders. "He was drunk, throwing a fit."

"It's not like we didn't expect it," Kristina shrugged with indifference, as if listening to the weather report, and continued counting the money. "He'll cool off eventually. You are better anyway and you're going to run your own business, aren't you? We wouldn't want his money anyway!"

A whiff of something burning came from the kitchen.

"Oh my," Kristina flinched, "I'll burn the sauce."

"Ok, you get the stove under control, I have to hit the shower. After lunch we'll go to the antique collectors' meeting at Ilirija Hotel; I'll hook up with some new partners there, hopefully. You're going to help, right? It's good that people see you with me," Leon continued on his way to the bathroom.

As jets of water gushed down his body, he felt as if they were washing away foul remains of his meeting with Ferkolj earlier that day, as well as clarifying his plans to start something new with the money he acquired in the morning. He closed his eyes, delighted. Suddenly he felt the touch of hands on his back, followed by a tight embrace of the beloved, beautifully formed naked body.

"It's good that people see me with you now. Sometimes I long to be just yours," Kristina said. "The pots await safely at the side of the stove."

They caused a minor flood in the bathroom, but Leon hardly noticed it. He was overflown not with water, but with victorious enthusiasm brought on by the lusciousness of boundless coupled pleasure. They were driven by savage energy, from their toes to the tips of their hair, and all over their skin, finally erupting under their tightly wedged bellies. Moments such as these made Leon completely impervious to the outside world.

After making love, they sat at the kitchen table, wrapped in towels. As several times before, Leon once again realised that while Kristina was sufficiently confident in the kitchen to satisfy basic needs and appease hunger, he would still have to turn to trusted chefs in fancy restaurants for debauchery of his taste buds and silent joy in his stomach. He took a good portion of the steak over to Šeri's bowl, and she followed him reluctantly.

"It's time," Leon said, "we should get going."

He threw an off-white summer jacket over his unbuttoned light blue shirt with no tie, he was wearing dark blue jeans and brown loafers on his bottom half, and he spread himself out on the sofa. He was getting drowsy, just as Kristina stepped out of the bathroom. Her hair was pinned up high; she wore gold earrings, a heavy gold necklace around her neck, a bright red dress ending half way down her thighs, and open shoes with gold ribbons and very high heels.

"Oops," Leon whispered. "This was worth the wait."

Kristina smiled confidently.

"Well, you did say that we were going to find some new partners and that I should help," she said playfully and slipped her hand through his arm. "Shall we?"

"Certainly," he nodded and pressed his nose into her neck. "Even your perfume is one big flowering summer. I reckon the collectors will forget what they came for."

Tables were already arranged amidst the greenery and flowers in Ilirija Hotel's conservatory. The tables were laden with much more valuable pieces than the ones found at the flea market. Seated behind them were collectors and vendors, all in one. They knew the prices and values of exhibited items; most of them were kept under glass bell jars, old coins and banknotes of every kind among them, antique jewellery of European aristocracy and decorative valuables from Africa and Asia, heavy rings for warding off evil eyes and spells, pendants carrying secret spiritual messages, figurines of deities, a few exceptional smaller items of furniture, mainly from Baroque, Empire and Biedermeier periods, exquisite grandfather clocks, Gothic statuettes, even some silver dinnerware baring Faberge marks... Buyers were roaming around the place, they seemed to exude expertise and issued thunderous remarks at exhibited items, others were picking up items with caution and whispers, swiftly reaching in their jackets and getting the money from their inside pockets, filled with banknotes they had prepared back home, closing deals which had often been arranged in advance and only double-checked and finished at this point. There were no customary busybodies as there was a handsome entry fee just to get through the door.

When Kristina and Leon entered they aroused some interest from the crowd, just as Leon had suspected. Naturally, beautiful women are wonderful promenades for looks, although at this particular gathering of collectors, the focus was nevertheless largely on deals and older hand-made items.

"I'm going out for a smoke," Kristina said after a short walk among the laid out tables, and she stepped toward the door leading to the open terrace. She reached into her purse as a charming and sharp male baritone caught her by surprise:

"Would you like a cigarette?"

Standing in front of her was a man of average build, around thirty five years of age, with thick, long black hair covering his ears and reaching over the left side of his face, covered in slight burn scars. The scar spread downwards to the back of his neck, where it disappeared under his shirt. He had a pensive, almost sombre look in his black eyes, his face was covered with a few days of neatly trimmed grey and black beard. The connoisseur she was, she quickly recognised the navy blue sports coat covering the relatively full torso as originating from an expensive foreign store. The unfolded white handkerchief was neatly tucked in the upper left outside pocket. Both blended nicely with the dark blue silk shirt, a crimson tie was secured by a platinum pin with a miniature enamel coated post stamp. He had his feet stuck in black patent-leather shoes made of snake skin. He was leaning slightly forward, thus hiding a budding belly. As she lifted her gaze to his hand, offering Davidoff cigarettes, she noticed a gold Patek Philippe watch with a blue clock face on his wrist, and an antique diamond encrusted women's engagement ring on his little finger.

"Yes, please," she said, took a cigarette, waited for the gold lighter to flash in his rich palm, and then sighed: "Thank you."

She inhaled two deep puffs of smoke, exhaled, turned her big eyes to the stranger, and before she could utter a word, he gently took hold of her hand with his own, bent at the elbow, bowed, kissed her fingers, never breaking eye contact, not even once he had already let go of her hand.

"Milorad Živković, at your service, fair lady," he said.

"I knew it," Kristina almost shrieked. A learned captivating smile flashed across her face. "A Serbian man. You know your chivalry."

Then she added: "Kristina Pirc."

She felt Leon appear close to her shoulder. She turned to him and then back to Živković.

"This is..." she said, pausing, "this is... let me introduce you. This is my... my Leon."

The two men shook hands and muttered their nice-to-meet-yous.

"I've never seen you here before," Leon said quickly. He was caught off guard. He knew that he should say something, just to be polite, and this was the first thing he could come up with.

"Of course," the stranger replied, "this is my first time here. I live and work in Belgrade and I need a serious business connection in Ljubljana to conduct business throughout Europe."

"Oh," Kristina said, took another drag on her cigarette and gave Leon a meaningful look. "But," she smiled flirtatiously, "allow me, mister Živković, we women are so silly and curious: what is this tiny emblem on your tie pin?"

Živković smiled:

"It's ok, fair lady, you women are the most wonderful creatures in the world, just looking at you makes this absolutely obvious to me once again."

He then unpinned the needle and offered it to her for inspection:

"This is a small tribute to my Serbian heritage, a miniature of the Order of the White Eagle, first class. It was awarded to my grandfather and now I'm flaunting it. How wonderful of you to notice such a detail."

They chatted some more, stopped a waiter and asked him to bring some champagne - no, no, not for me, I'll have a double whisky, Živković instructed - and then Kristina said, it's stifling in here, we should have coffee at our place, it would be my pleasure, Živković said, but I have a plane to catch in the evening, no problem, Leon assured him, I'll take you to the airport, and so they left.

In the living room of Kristina's apartment, in deep armchairs under the Venetian chandelier, they had coffee, the guest and Leon had no problems emptying a bottle of aged Jack Daniels while they were at it, leading an increasingly sober conversation despite everything. Kristina chirped and kept adjusting her tight skirt which seemed to run up her thighs all the time. The chance meeting was turning into a chatter among old friends. During the conversation, Živković noticed a book titled *Old Silver* sitting on the table.

"Oh," he said delightedly, "are you into old silver?"

"Of course," Leon nodded, "among other things."

Živković flipped through the book, then became pensive, closed it and abruptly and almost elatedly announced:

"If you would be willing to collaborate with me, young man, I shall make a master out of you, and afford you experience you are unlikely to get anywhere else in the world."

Leon shot right back, as if he were just waiting for this to happen:

"It would be my honour, Mr. Živković, it would be my honour."

"I'm older than you," he laughed broadly, loudly for the first time, lifting his glass, "call me Bata."

"Leon," Leon reciprocated.

They both drank up. Bata turned to Kristina.

"I will take your Leon on as my apprentice, if you don't mind, fair lady, and I will make a master out of him," he said solemnly.

"I don't mind, Bata," Kristina said. "I'm Kristina. Call me Kristina."

The most charming of her smiles floated onto her cheeks, while her eyes danced in flirtatious joy.

Živković got up, saluted, gestured kissing her hand while saying "I kiss your hand," grabbed his very elegant suitcase, and off to the airport he went with Leon.

You know what they say, dignity is lost on account of rushing

Bata, a great authority among antique dealers, known in professional circles as Bata the Beard, and Siniša, known to his friends as Siniša the Heart (he lived through two heart attacks, never letting this detail get in his normal ways), antiquarian buddies from Belgrade, rented a suite in the beautiful classicistic Esplanade Hotel in Zagreb, in the early morning hours of Saturday, March 24, 1984.

Siniša was the younger of the pair and had spent a few years prior as an insignificant pickpocket in Germany, amassing enough by the time he turned thirty to allow him to return to his homeland in a low slung, olive green, outrageous Datsun sports car, and blending slowly among local antique dealers. He was a short man with closely cut brown hair, all muscle, and accustomed to German fashion tastes, trying hard all the time to present himself in very expensive items of clothing. He was a gambler and so he came upon Bata on a particularly strenuous night. The loud braggart and the reserved know-it-all bonded in drunken brotherhood, they felt as if destiny had brought them together. After that, they often carried out some business endeavour or another together, a habit which also brought them to the Esplanade.

The hotel's beauty and service could match the most prestigious European hotels and was the best in the city, naturally. The porter took their car to the underground parking garage, while the two of them wasted no time and entered the aperitif bar in the conservatory on the first floor. They had a great view of the city throb from their table among the greenery and flower arrangements, set against the giant glass wall; the road led from the hotel entrance to the main train station and farmers' market, which made the selection of people passing by interesting in itself, as supplies were distributed around the city in these early hours, while ladies and pretty girls of course started on their way past the famous hotel and through its door somewhat later.

They were regulars; they had spent a lot of money in the cosmopolitan, but also sinful hotel. The waiters, receptionists and other hotel staff knew who they were, some of them were like friends of the family. This time around they were lured to the city by an antique dealers' convention, a once-a-year event of great importance for the most prominent collectors and dealers from the entire country. With its aristocratic bourgeois background and its history, Zagreb was a great treasure trove of miscellaneous valuable goods. A special, direct way of dealing was adopted for the convention. There was no superfluous chatter, showing off photos and delaying tactics; the goods were on display, readily available. Have a look, haggle, pay, take away.

They ordered Turkish coffee; a very dignified older waiter brought it over in Rosenthal porcelain cups coupled with a sugar bowl full of brown sugar, and a couple of crispy walnut croissants dusted in powdered almond sugar on a small silver platter. One could not help but be overwhelmed by memories of late grandmother's cookies. They sipped their coffee, nibbled on the croissants and dug into Vjesnik daily and its Buying-Selling section with professional vigour, despite them knowing full well that they would encounter everything worth anything at the grand hall of the university campus that afternoon.

"Where have you been, gentlemen, it's been ages since we had you as our guests? What have you been up to, how are your wives, your children, your health? I see that you are as elegant as ever." They were startled by the thunderous voice of the hotel chef, Stevan Karapandža, who popped up by the table unannounced. A tall black-haired man nearing his forties with a giant chef's hat laughed merrily and rubbed his hands in delight.

"You haven't been doing too bad yourself," Siniša returned his greeting with a grin, got up and shook his hand vigorously. "One can tell you're not too busy working, there isn't a stain on your white uniform! The great *chef*, aren't you!"

The chef swiftly got down to business:

"Is everything ok? Have my people taken good care of you two? Do you have everything? What about breakfast?"

On this note, Bata laid down his paper as well, spread his hands and gave the chef a friendly slap on the back, without so much as getting up from his chair.

"You really have to ask, when it's clear: some of your famous salmon, and some smoked trout, and a few of your house pates, and, to start off a good day, some Dom Perignon, of course. Check if you happen to have a bottle from 1981 laying around, that year was the best in the last decade," he almost dictated.

"Of course," the chef nodded. "Would you like to have your table extended? There are probably more antique dealers coming?"

"No, no," Bata shook his head, "I'm expecting my assistant from Ljubljana to arrive about now, the young Leon, we'll do just fine with the table as it is. First meetings are not until this afternoon. You know what they say, there is no dignity in a hurry. And you can't get anything done in Zagreb without putting on a show. This is the way you are, Stevo my friend."

"Your wish is my command," the chef chuckled. "So, the classics. I'm off."

"Come back when you're done, have breakfast with us," Siniša tried to stop him. "You can tell us everything that this paper won't say."

The chef ran off and soon after another refined waiter appeared, wheeling his elegant cart with a glitzy champagne bucket; it was made from Maillechort and filled with ice, with a protruding neck of a bottle. The waiter fished the bottle out and offered the label for Bata's inspection. Bata leaned towards the bottle, simply nodded negligently, and then, amidst the pronounced sentence of "We only have a few bottles from that year, but there will always be one for guests like yourselves!" - opened it in one skilful move. No later than the bottle gave off a discreet pop and a puff, the liquid was already being poured into crystal glasses made by the renowned Rogaška Glassworks. Elite company always called for Dom Perignon and Bata was one to observe labels with great care in important moments.

The champagne went down well and offered a pleasant additional refreshment after the strong coffee. They were now ready to start with the serving cart with two young waiters in tow, and Karapandža closely supervising behind their backs, keeping a watchful eye over the correct placement of cutlery, overseeing the positioning of plates and making sure that the morning pleasures were had appropriately. When all the delicacies, which oozed freshness, were neatly assembled and available, he pulled a chair from the adjacent table and sat with his friends.

"I'm not eating, I already had breakfast. I'll have a glass of champagne, though," he said.

A loud inquiry sounded from the door then; "Are they here?" and just a moment later Leon joined their group. He didn't seem tired, but his eyes flashed in gluttony at the sight of the laden trays.

"Come, my boy! You've chosen the best moment," Bata got up

from the table, gave him a hug and three pecks on the cheeks, put his arm around Leon's shoulders and introduced him to his friends, "This is my Leon from Ljubljana, he joined me as apprentice a year ago, so I would mould him into an antique dealer the whole Europe will bow to!"

"You could have taken me, I'm closer to you," Siniša grinned, "what does this kid have that I don't?"

Leon greeted the men at the table somewhat hesitantly but without any redundant humility.

"You have your business and I have mine, and besides, you're too old for me to teach you anything," Bata rejected Siniša and turned back to Leon. "Sit down and eat. I bet you drove here straight from some famous Ljubljana club, just making enough time to lay your beautiful Kristina to bed, right?"

Leon grinned and reached for the cutlery the waiter brought over instantly, without saying a word. The pleasant ambience at the table was accompanied with clinking sounds made by heavy silver knives and forks. Leon put together a salmon toast with connoisseur precision, and one with smoked trout right after that one. The heavenly harmony of butter and delicate fish meat in light pink, with a hint of yellow, practically demanded an immediate sip. But the bottle was empty.

"Could I get a glass of Radgona sparkling wine?" Leon asked after the first few bites, turning to the waiter who was standing silently at the next table.

"Do you see him, my man? He wants champagne," Bata shouted with a gesture of his hand, as if he needed to emphasize his words.

"I'm sure not going to have tea with salmon," Leon said curtly and matter-of-factly. But," he turned to the chef, "now that our mouths are full and we need to work, spill it, tell us what's new in the city? Is there a good painting, a nice tabernacle, a brilliant piece in silver, a porcelain collection, some exquisite bourgeois jewellery? Speak!"

Karapandža pulled his chair a bit closer and started to explain:

"Two well-known dealers from Vienna came around last week already, at Dr. Valka's invitation, you know him, don't you? There were heavy pieces of old jewellery laid out on the table, fantastic stuff. Valka must have gotten them from some highly esteemed Zagreb family. There were even original packages of the manufacturers, first class goods, I'm telling you. There was serious money involved. I've never before seen such diamonds and rubies on our tables as I did when I went over to ask the gentlemen if they were happy with the food."

"Don't spoil our appetite," Bata grumbled. "Stop talking about things that are not here. Tell us if there's anything left anywhere. A nice piece of furniture, perhaps?"

Bata was in the process of setting up another house for himself in Belgrade and he was on the lookout for the best possible furniture to complete his interior design. He was not interested in modern design, of course.

"You know I like Biedermeier. Have you heard about some tabernacle, a chest of drawers, a divan?" he continued in mock offendedness. "Never mind, I know you're saving such things for yourself, not thinking about your friends."

The chef shook his head and wrinkled his forehead.

"Now that I think about it, I did hear a while ago about a villa in Pantovčak, from the beginning of the century. There's supposed to be a grand bookcase on offer there, complete with a bird cage and made entirely of walnut roots. I could never afford anything like it. It might suit you, though; if I wanted anyone to have it that would be you. I also hear the owner is a very beautiful woman, in her best years, and blond, just like the women you usually bring to your suite down here."

Bata started to pay attention, mumbled something in his beard, leaned idly towards Siniša and looked at him askance, calculatingly.

"And would you give your friend this beautiful woman's phone number or do you have another master plan for her?"

"Don't worry," the chef said, chuckling and getting up, "her number will await you in an envelope at the reception desk. Well, gentlemen, I must leave you now. I know you have to make your plans for this afternoon. I hope to see you at lunch."

"Of course," Siniša nodded. "You've got your work cut out for you."

Once they finished their meal, Bata rubbed his belly and declared that they should urgently get some rest from the road and the food. One should always approach business rested and clear-headed.

They took the lift to their suite. Not a moment later, a room attendant in uniform brought their luggage from the wardrobe next to the reception desk and Bata put a hundred Deutchmark note in his hand.

The boy was lost for words as he had never in his life gotten a tip like this, let alone in a foreign currency. Bata knew from experience that generosity, when performed at the right moment, can work wonders, even late at night, when everyone else is asleep, or in the hotel kitchen, or in a remote bar. He glanced around the premises and handed his clothes over to the attendant to have them ironed. He needed to appear at the fair in all his glory, his competition, undoubtedly numerous on a day like this, had to instantly feel his supremacy.

Bata chose a bedroom for himself, Siniša took the other one, while Leon lingered hesitantly at the door. Was he going back home in the evening or would the business drag on? Should he rent an expensive room in the hotel now and immediately start spending his money, the money he brought for other purposes? Bata noticed the boy's unease and cordially offered him the couch in the living room, if it was not beneath him, of course, if the need arose, as the maid could easily arrange it into a bed.

"Only if I didn't disturb you," Leon objected tentatively, happy on the inside, but appearing considerate.

"Don't be silly. We'll be occupied with women, not with you!" Siniša hollered wantonly from his bedroom.

Leon rested his travelling bag against the armchair and declared that he was off to the fair right away, since he would like to check out the offer, and would meet them there later. Bata murmured something about the spurring quality of youth, and intellectual prowess of old age, and waved him good-bye. For himself, he promptly arranged a bath featuring every scent from the bottles lining the rim of the tub, relegating Siniša to a shower sometime later.

After the refreshing soak he slumped into the leather armchair, dressed in a bathrobe, and turned on the TV. He didn't even follow the telecast, he only needed a sound backdrop to help him think.

He needed to finish his house, furnish it, the craftsmen were waiting to get paid, they refused to continue, they had been dropping by every night, claiming what they were owed, while he had no real money on him, this had been dragging on for too long, his wife was on the verge of a nervous breakdown, the two of them and their daughter spent the last three years crammed into a single bedroom in his mother's place in an apartment complex, accusations had reached boiling point...

He brought this on himself when he gave in to this wild, savage passion, losing his head, trusting his lucky stars. One of his great gambling expeditions in the past cost him everything: his money, his house, even his wife's jewellery. They gambled for three days and three nights straight, without any sleep, luck moved on to others and left his side forever. The blow was horrendous, sobering. He hadn't played the dice for a long time and moved on to other things. His mother, a descendant from a Serbian family of wholesalers in London, a sophisticated lady, obscurely instilled other forms of love in him early on. Despite graduating from economics, he remained a life-long admirer of culture, trying to see himself in it, from theatre to opera, from films to museums and their collections. He started with antiques. He knew that they could be much more profitable than gambling. He was slowly getting back on his feet after the gambling debacle. And now he had his hard-saved five thousand Deutschmarks in his pocket, meant to do business with, and he was in Zagreb. He needed to find his treasure, truly marvellous stuff which he could resell in Frankfurt or Brussels. If a good opportunity presented itself, he could borrow around ten thousand; this was why he was staying in a suite at the Esplanade hotel, potential lenders needed to be sure that money was not a problem when it came to him, that he had just encountered an incredibly good investment, which he needed a whole lot of money for.

Siniša emerged from the bathroom.

"Duty calls," he almost chirped, clean shaven and fragrant. "Off to the fair and later on to the club. I organised everything. There'll be some company awaiting us there, that is to say, some comely young babes, just waiting to get into the hands of us masters. Shall we?"

Bata put on his freshly ironed clothes and stuck his usual pin in his tie. Siniša sported a bow-tie under his neck. They descended to the first floor.

The receptionist arranged a big black Mercedes for them. Their arrival to the fair had to be victorious and magnificent. Loafers gathering in front of the entrance had to be blinded by their splendour, and these small fish needed to let the slightly bigger fish know about them, and they to those even bigger and so on until the greatest of all knew:

"Dealers with big bucks have arrived!" Everyone would swarm around them, the kings of the event, offering their goods, wanted to get next to them at the bar and have the most expensive drinks on offer.

Indeed, they headed straight for the bar and ordered some Chivas Regal 12. The boy at the bar got confused:

"What do you mean, twelve, are you expecting more people?"

"It's a brand, dumbass!" Siniša boasted. "Make mine a double!"

To hell with jokes if you can't take them

Marko from Sisak came rushing towards them, he was a regular at the fairs, even the ones in Ljubljana. He was akin to a general public announcement system; if anyone had any new information that would be him. He was always on the prowl, like a tracking dog, and never took any risks; he knew that midmarket was his field, and within it, the very best items. First he greeted Siniša loudly and then turned to Bata almost like a subject would to a duke. Marko came from Glina in Serbian Krajina, a place with a constant atmosphere of famous history. Later he moved to Sisak, got married, took over his father-in-law's painting company and gained considerable wealth. For a talented part-time antique dealer, this was a dream job: he had access to almost every house in town and registered every family treasure. Once he completed his work, he could simply round the price up, and because people were generally broke, he then calmly asked:

"You don't happen to still use this porcelain bowl, and the candlestick standing up there on the cupboard? I'll take it as part payment."

He succeeded almost every time. Moreover, he sometimes got his hands on additional merchandise on account of his lively character and the fact that the housewives often felt lonely at home. He then happily showered his envious antiquarian pals with his stories.

"So," Siniša was obliged to ask out of sheer politeness, "how are the widows doing, are there any more around?"

"Whew," Marko radiated, "I was just about to tell you about a housewife from a village near Sisak, she was so willing, and the bed was a real country one, with high sides, the feather pillows freshly made, and she was there smiling among them, a bit plump, she was, like they should be, she spread her legs, waiting for my harambasha, and I drove it in, she was so happy she was practically squealing, and then I toiled and I toiled, it must've been about five times, but she just couldn't get enough, I barely escaped."

Bata couldn't help himself and teased him:

"If your brushwork was half as good as you say you are in bed, you'd be the greatest craftsmen out there, you'd be buying from us instead of peddling this mediocre junk."

"Bata, do I ever lie about these things? If I say I did it five times, I did it five times," Marko defended himself crossly.

"Alright, alright," Bata waved it off, "let's leave it alone. Did you spot anything good at the fair? Tell me everything!"

Marko pondered; he knew to carefully skip the things he had marked for himself. If there was another buyer he could just forget about them; and it was vital that his sources didn't dwindle, as this could put his business in jeopardy. So he reached higher.

"I saw an incredibly beautiful silver chalice, a Nürnberg, I would say, at least eight hundred grams, the doctor has a marvellous silver Diana, oh, and of course, I've almost forgotten, there's also a charming silver dish with multiple cast and hand finished figurines, about three kilos, I'd say, an Augsburg, around 1870, a truly majestic piece," he itemized with radiant eyes.

Bata kept his poker face on, but his mind was racing: this was something for Hans from Frankfurt; he was likely to pay good money for it. This was his opportunity! He finished his whiskey and, with his glass still raised, saw the old dealer Gvido from Trieste appear at the door. Oops, he would need to act swiftly. Gvido Belen was an exile and he was in wholesale timber trade; he imported timber from Yugoslavia. He was spending a portion of his substantial profit on antiques, so he visited Ljubljana and Zagreb regularly. He refused to go to Belgrade anymore, as the good food and drink made him succumb to Serbian charm too many times in the past, resulting in him spending a lot and getting too little. Now they would start approaching the Doctor's stand each from their respective side and it was important who got there first.

Doctor Valka was an expert in silver trade. His stand was laden with beautiful items. The doctor worked at a large clinic and was well liked by old bourgeois families; practically everyone needed a doctor after they hit sixty, one that they knew was kind, refined and good, and had a noble way with words. The affection the patients in need of a speedy operation or those who recovered in his care was very tangible, especially because everyone knew what the doctor liked. He only occasionally sold something at the antique fairs; his vanity and stinginess caused him to more or less just showcase his possessions on his stand. When he did sell something, he spiced the price so high that the onlookers gasped for breath.

He noticed Bata approaching and he knew an important moment was imminent. He had decided on selling the silver bowl and it was clear to him that Bata was the only one who'd know the value of the piece and also the only one who'd be willing to pay a decent price. He watched him slowly proceed toward his stand, but in that moment was approached by the chatty Mrs. Weržinski, a regular, who started a conversation on the candle piece that caught her eye. She had one just like this at home and would like to add another one. She never negotiated his prices, as no amount of money she spent ever presented a problem for her successful tradesman husband. She talked and talked to Valka, eager to prove all her knowledge in an avalanche of words; so many words, and not nearly as much substance. Valka struggled to keep up his forced politeness, and at the same time by all means trying to track the great Bata's movements. Bata also noticed the woman standing next to Valka, she kept talking and talking, so he stopped by a man selling icons a few stands to the side; he felt the doctor's gaze on him so he clearly signalled his intent to buy something by waving his arms around and inspecting icons up close and from various different angles. This sent a chill down Valka's spine. He knew the woman wouldn't buy the precious bowl, and he also knew that Bata was the only one who could sell it to Europe through his connections. What if he spent his money on icons? Bata knew how to get the doctor riled up; he agreed to buy the icons but arranged it to have them delivered to Belgrade, where he'd pay for them on the spot. The seller knew him, so he trusted him and agreed, while Bata withdrew from Valka's sight and kept secretly watching him, hidden next to a wall. Valka clearly saw him purchase the icons but he didn't know how much he paid for them. He had trouble containing his composure as he wrapped up the conversation with the plump woman, the price he put on the candlestick was in the range of Dorotheum in Vienna. The woman paid and left, but Bata was nowhere to be seen. Where was he? Did he spend all of his money and leave the fair? Nervously he ordered his assistant to watch the stand, while he rushed toward the bar. Bata saw what was going on and smiled. He had won the first battle. He, too, slowly walked along the wall toward the bar.

There, Siniša and Marko were still cracking their stories. They could discuss women till kingdom come. Bata turned to the waiter:

"I'll have a double Chivas. I've earned it. Plus I have to concentrate for my next deal."

"Anything new?" Siniša asked, as he was interested in the views and appraisals of the guileful antique dealer. Marko, too, fell silent. Bata only shook his head, because he saw Doctor Valka race to the bar, where he finally caught sight of the most likely buyer for his bowl.

"Did you see that wonderful bowl?" Marko began complaisantly, to call attention to himself, but the newly arrived doctor promptly cut him off: "What would you know about it? You better stick to your second-rate stuff instead of talking about things you know nothing about!"

Only now did Bata acknowledge the doctor's presence and asked in a merry tone:

"Oh, hello there, Doctor! What's up?"

Valka gallantly offered his hand and spoke, with a scornful gaze aimed at Marko:

"These petty peddlers are always trying to get into other people's business."

"What are you talking about, dear Doctor?" Bata asked innocently. "What's with this bowl he mentioned?"

"It's a very beautiful bowl. I'm not even sure I want to sell it, I'm thinking maybe I should keep it in my private collection. It belonged to a well-known Zagreb family, with German ancestors and some Jewish blood, also, they used to be important merchants before World War One, even held shares in the Russian imperial railways...That's what it is," Valka uttered in almost one single breath.

Bata calmly took another sip of his whisky and asked:

"What shall we do then, dear Doctor? Shall we have a drink to celebrate our new deal and then take a look at the thing, or shall we make the deal first and drink later?"

"No, no, dear Bata," Valka quickly shook his head, starting his negotiating game, "I need to get back to my stand, it's crowded with customers, you stop by later, take your time and enjoy your drink."

Once the doctor left, Siniša turned to Bata:

"So, are we going to go and have a look at this wonder together? I'm starting to get interested myself."

Bata noticed the silver bowl long before he reached the stand. It glimmered under the portable spotlight which Valka had turned on in the middle of the day to emphasize the effect and enhance the radiance of figurines attached to it. Bata approached, asked for permission to pick it up, and once he held the heavy bowl in his hands, he first looked for the hallmark. He took a 20x magnifying glass from his pocket and inspected the hallmark to see which master manufactured it and, of course, if the hallmark was genuine, not stamped into the silver at a later time. There were a lot of forgeries on the market, he should know.

"This is all really nice," he nodded in approval and smacked his lips, "I'm just a bit sceptical about the hallmarks. They seem too nice, too sharp and precise. And there's no patina. I have a little bit of a problem with this."

"Don't degrade the goods, that's so inappropriate," Valka retorted with outrage and strong determination. He was aware of how valuable the silver piece was, and he was also aware of the strength of his position in this negotiation, "after all, you can walk away, you don't have to buy the bowl. But don't insult me! We really don't need to go there."

"Come on, don't get all worked up. To hell with jokes if you can't take them," Bata said reassuringly and coupled his words with his signature look, the one no one could ever decipher his thoughts from. "The piece is alright. So, what's the asking price?"

"For you, fifteen thousand Deutschmarks," Valka quickly hissed through his teeth, to get the information to Bata only and not to disturb the passers-by.

"God Almighty," Bata sighed, averted his eyes to the ceiling and slightly raised his voice, "You Zagreb people have gone a bit mad lately, who's going to agree to these prices, I could get this cheaper even in Germany. Have a seat, think it over, doctor, and give me a realistic, fair offer if you'd like to do business with me and get anything done."

"Alright then," the doctor said hurriedly, looking Bata in the eye, as if they had just entered an intimate world of collegial trust, "but I can't let you have it for less than ten thousand."

Bata shifted in his seat. He knew now was the time to introduce some hard arguments into the conversation.

"And what am I supposed to do?" he asked. "I'll have to travel to Germany if I want to make a profit, you know there's no way I can sell this around here, so: travel expenses, hotel, food, and so on, plus my profit, you know I can't sell this for more than three marks per gram, and you're asking for three and a half as it is, which means I'd be trading at a loss from the get-go."

"You never trade at a loss," Valka chortled abruptly, letting him know the calculation was more complex than that, "and you're not going to in this case either. Just look at these nymphs on the rim, they're almost lifelike, once you remove the patina they will shine and positively come to life."

"So why didn't you clean it off?"

"You know it's better to keep the original patina on."

"But how can I buy something if I can't see the details?" Bata objected, licked his thumb and rubbed it over the face of a small nymph, reclining and supporting a pillar on the upper part of the bowl. The miniature girl's face shined through, hinting at the beauty of the piece.

"Alright, then," he attempted a lower figure to make it harder for the price to go up during negotiations, "take five thousand, doctor, and we have a deal. I don't have more than that, I've just bought several beautiful icons and I'm running dry."

"No, no," Valka replied firmly, almost wearily, "eight thousand is my final price. I won't part with it for less. I just won't. There's no deal for less than that. I'll take you to lunch to make up for your lost time, but you can't have it for less than eight."

"Seven and a half, and a lunch at Karapandža's," proposed Bata. "Here, let's shake on it!"

Valka propped his head up, frowned, brought his right hand over his eyes, paced a few steps back and forth, gazed into the distance, then turned back around and shook Bata's extended hand.

"You Serbs always rip us off. Alright, you can have it," he gave up.

Bata took out his wallet and began forking banknotes over on the table. Five times one thousand.

"Here's five thousand, I'll get you the rest when I return from Germany."

"No, no," Valka rebelled nervously, practically jumping to his feet, "no way. The piece is beyond beautiful, it'll be worth at least fifteen thousand in Germany. Pieces like this are always paid for on the spot and in full."

Bata now turned to Siniša who'd been silently observing the negotiation, asking him to lend him three thousand so he could pay this Jew out. Siniša groaned about only having ten thousand, which he planned to buy some golden necklaces he reserved at Fehim with. You can explain it to him, Bata proposed as if it was a self-evident thing, he's a softie, and he likes you, too, give me the three grand, I don't want this deal to fall through! Siniša kept shaking his head, thinking, shuffling his feet, and at last gave him the money with a heavy heart: three thousand, and Valka paid back the five hundred difference. Bata promptly stashed the money in his pocket and exclaimed:

"Well, now that we settled this, let's have some lunch, some *gablec*, as you say in Croatia. Let's meet at the Esplanade in one hour!"

A marvellous piece, my sweet boy, just look at it

Valka wrapped the bowl in some paper and Bata took it to the bar, which Leon was already leaning against.

"Well, well," he called as he snatched the parcel from Bata's hands and started to unwrap it. They sat down at a table. "What have you got?"

"A marvellous piece, my sweet boy, just look at it," Bata said somewhat absorbed in thought, carefully watching Leon's face which grew more radiant with every part of paper that came off the bowl. Like him before, Leon first went for the hallmark; he examined it closely and then moved on to admire the figurines on the bowl. His enthusiasm grew by the minute. Unbelievable, he was saying, a capital, museum piece! Bata feverishly searched his memory; he couldn't pinpoint the name of the master featured in the hallmark, but he was certain that he had seen it before and that it surely belonged to a prestigious supplier to European courts. In the meantime, Leon finished unwrapping the bowl and gaped. He raised it so it sparkled for everyone to see, and the waiter at the bar was left with his mouth open. He held the precious item in his hands; if this is what I think it is, the silver is worth a small apartment in Ljubljana. Sensational! I'm in the right company now, he thought to himself and looked Bata in the eyes gaily, with admiration. I have the right mentor, a grand master, his eyes were saying.

"This is something," was all he could say. His voice almost let him down.

Bata continued to regard him somewhat absentmindedly, clearly going over something in his head, and then he twitched and said decisively:

"Would you be willing to take me to Belgrade tomorrow, and from there on to Germany?"

"But why to Belgrade, let's just go straight to Germany," Leon fervently suggested in astonishment. "Why delay?"

No, no, I have to get home, I need to go through my books of sterling silver hallmarks, Bata began explaining, I need to be sure what it is that I have. I believe this one on the bowl is a genuine one, Leon gave his confident appraisal. Of course it's genuine, Bata affirmed almost angrily, but I need to figure out exactly which master and firm this was made by first, and whether it was an imperial workshop, of course. I need to know, I need to, Bata kept almost mumbling while already flipping numbers in his head. When selling in high circles, you need to be absolutely certain of what you've got! This will surely be something for Fritzl from Hofbahnstrasse in Frankfurt, just as he had thought in the first instant.

Leon was on cloud nine. For the first time in his life, he was holding something almost magical in his hands, and besides, Bata, a grand master, excited at the prospect of great business, would take him along. True, his role would be limited to one of an interpreter, as Bata spoke almost no foreign languages, but he would be right there, learning the art of the trade at a high level, and some of the profits were bound to land in his pocket, as well. He shuddered at the thought that he would be gone from home longer than he promised Kristina, but this was an unmistakeable first step up, which she, too, would undoubtedly appreciate. He would make good money. He clenched his teeth.

"Alright," he said, "I'll take you, first to Belgrade, and then to Germany. But first, I'll stop by at home, for a change of clothes and to tell Kristina what's going on."

In the meantime, Bata downed another double whisky and he was becoming increasingly playful.

"And now, if you don't mind, my sweet boy, wrap my treasure back up, take it to the car, and we can drive to the hotel. Doctor Valka is taking us to lunch, and you'll see what my friend Karapandža is capable of. You better fill up, because Siniša has some wild clashes with the local elite female stock planned, and it's nothing short of excellent, you can take my word for it. We triumphant antique dealers enjoy good food, good drinks, and...guess what!" he grinned, unable to conceal his joy.

It was obvious that he planned to let go completely, as he was certain that the troubles of his financial despair were about to come to an end.

I'm not being difficult, I just want a decent beefsteak

A special table awaited the antique dealers at the Esplanade Hotel for a late lunch, and no sooner did they take their seats around the table than the serving carts came rolling out of the kitchen, laden with starter dishes as chef Karapandža envisioned them for his esteemed guests. He knew their preferences in detail. Even the discreet noise coming from the surrounding tables temporarily died down to allow the special atmosphere to slowly flourish through the space under the high ceiling, with slightly veiled windows, lined with luxurious drapes. The antique dealers, happy with the deals made, started spreading white napkins over their knees, releasing gastric juices in jovial anticipation, rubbing their hands and individually pondering what to spice the conversation with while having magical creations by the famous chef ladled from heavily laden trays to their large dinner plates.

The starter was a mix of cured meats and mild pâtés. The transparency and colour of the Karst prosciutto was an enticing reminder of the Karst bora wind which cured it, and of the various kinds of noble plants which percolated through it from the meagre soil. The spicy *kulen* sausage next to it, dyed red by the sharp paprika from the fields of Vojvodina, caused a serious stir to their taste buds. They were only soothed by fresh cottage cheese which erased the spicy taste and brought to mind the undulating grassy hills of Medžimurje. The game terrine was a symphony of tastes, accentuated with Istrian white truffle. The base consisted of carefully selected wild boar meat cuts, cooked in garlands of different vegetables from nearby gardens. It was coarsely minced, enriched with butter and olive oil from Dalmatian islands, and sprinkled with Horgoš paprika; unrefined salt from Pag Island called for frequent sips of golden yellow Silvanec wine from the hills of Zagorje. The pâté spread perfectly over the white bread, baked in special loaf pans and reminiscent of foam, yet resisting to yield under pressure. Temporary relief was provided by the hard cheese, aged in stone Istrian cellars, and embalmed in oil made from tiny grey olives, infused with rosemary and bay leaf. The antiquarians each had to brag a little about the deals they made that morning, some were more loquacious, others brief and ambiguous, but all simultaneously badmouthed their competition, in line with the ancient antiquarian tradition, trashing both their goods and their limited knowledge.

After a short breather, three serving carts appeared simultaneously at the table, carrying main courses on dinner plates and in accompanying pots. It was time for the diners' digestive tracts to tackle the main task.

Siniša got a giant beefsteak Florentine style; this was his favourite dish. He was known to occasionally waver between tenderloin and rib, but then came up with the elegant solution of ordering both in one. Although blasphemously thick and somewhat heavily burnt at the appropriate parts, to the point that it hinted at the taste of freshly baked bread, it was juicy and soft, just as the most demanding eaters want it, and in just the right hues of blushing meat, which only the best chefs are able to capture.

Bata loved game. Carefully selected pieces of deer, buck and wild boar lay in a deep copper pan, bathed in a sauce made from their own juices, cognac and fresh cream. Štruklji from Zagorje awaited in the side dish section, their mild taste delicately balanced with the meat. The renowned chef of the prestigious hotel used well established wholesale sources: forest rangers, who carefully kept up the natural balance in Kopački Rit national park, the site of some of the best flat hunting grounds in Europe, were also its managers and they always put the Esplanade Hotel on the very top of the list when distributing prime pieces of hunted game.

Marko was "never difficult," he just "wanted a good beefsteak"; this time was no exception, he got a magnificently thick piece of aged baby beef, beautifully browned on butter, slightly caramelised at the edges and red-raw in the middle, generously doused in green pepper sauce; with a side dish of steamed thin carrots and small round potatoes.

Doctor Valka, a connoisseur and convinced proponent of the stipulation that the amount of fish in a healthy diet should increase with one's age, was served a scorpion fish "lesso," a white fish boiled in clear broth with a lot of vegetables, carrots, leeks, potatoes, cauliflower, fennel and parsley, with the addition of bay leaf and garlic. Placed in a serving dish, the fish gave the impression of still floating in the seawater somewhere between the islands of Krk and Cres, where the fishermen caught it the previous night. The flesh was soft, yet firm, and came nicely off the multitude of tiny bones; it looked like a masterfully processed piece of Carrara marble. Several shrimp scampi and vongole clung beautifully to its sides. One could imagine a grandma observe the sight with a sigh of how even the angels would eat this if they had bottoms, and remember the times when this dish was served to heal the very sick in Dalmatia.

Leon has never before found himself in such company, in the midst of such a luxurious feast. He devoured every conversation, hint and comment, and of course looked forward to having a window into this world opened to him by Bata. It was obvious that the men sitting around the table had known each other for a long time, and it was also clear that such meals were not something they weren't well accustomed to. Their conversations spoke of mutual respect and occasional trickery, and of course of the fact that experience and certain skills in the field of dealing with antiques could yield fine profit. And because the meals always end with a check, which would cause many a person to faint, this also meant that seated around this table were men who knew how to enjoy themselves and wanted to enjoy themselves, and therefore exercised no frugality when it came to dining. Leon was an offal lover; he ordered sweetbreads, which he liked prepared in various ways: grilled, roasted, like scrambled eggs and brains, or cooked in a pan with butter, flambéed with Armagnac. This time he went for the baked version from a pan, made on butter and doused in Hollandaise sauce, with the side of tagliatelle and roasted breadcrumbs, at the same time generously sprinkled with parsley and coriander.

Most of them transitioned from Silvanec to Pošip wine for the main course, a heavy black wine coming from the islands, which goes well with both light and heavy food. The sometimes a bit overbearing aroma unobtrusively brought to mind the merciless summer heat in the midst of stone vineyards of the Adriatic.

They finished off with a sweet wine, a Muscat from the cellars of Radgona, which was served quite chilled to accompany the Slavonian dessert. Crumbly on the outside, creamy on the inside, almost runny and juicy, it was unable to hide shades of the best Hungarian traditional heritage.

The almost pleasantly exhausted company at the table then summoned chef Karapandža and hoarsely sang him praises for his past work and recommendations for the future. They followed this with several hugs and handshakes, well-wishing in terms of health and good business, accompanied by an occasional uncontrolled yawn. Words of parting were spoken. Prior to this, Doctor Valka was discreetly called to the side to settle the bill, which he did without batting an eyelid, adding a generous tip which made the otherwise dignified waiter pick his nose in an almost undignified manner.

At Bata's explicit demand, the company retreated shortly to his suite, where they stood in the reception room and completed the culinary story with a cognac, named over a hundred and fifty years ago after Alexandre Bisquit, years after Napoleon had been defeated and Europe opened to French delights. After some sniffing and knowledgeable smacking of lips at the round snifter glasses, Marko, Siniša, and the doctor went back to the fair, while Bata slipped on his bed without removing the covers, and Leon stretched out on the couch.

Leon was initially drawn into sweet idleness by vague triumphant thoughts; Bata took him under his wing, he completed an unbelievable acquisition in the morning, tomorrow they'll be doing business in Germany, a small stack of money is bound to end up in his pocket, too...and he'll continue from there. Ever since they first met they've been mutually helping each other out with smaller things. Now, Leon thought, things will really take off. His Kristina will have as much money as she likes, these questions will now subside and give way to the perfect, crazy love, no need to worry about the whole world anymore, now he has arrived to conquer it and start living his new life. No more petty deals at the flea market and haggling for peanuts. Mastery, love, success...He fell asleep.

Bata needed to make some space in his belly so he turned from his stomach onto his back and stared at the ceiling. At first, sleep wouldn't come. Images of the glorious silver bowl he had bought were too vivid in his mind. He suspected that he had acquired something which would push away his financial troubles with craftsmen and his expanding house for a good while. He wondered how much he could make on the silver beauty. He would need perfect negotiation skills and it would be excellent to have Leon there with his knowledge of German. Ha, Leon! He thought of his beautiful woman, exuding lust from her eyes and every part of her body. Kristina! She's playing with a youngster and he's lost his head, no wonder. But there comes a time when a young man needs this, too. Once he runs out of money, she'll leave. This is certain.

But it's not my problem, Bata smiled to himself. I have a fine assistant, I can see that he's knowledgeable; he speaks several languages and is full of energy. I will make a master out of him, my Ljubljana subsidiary, and together we'll be able to make a lot of things happen. Well, they'll have to. Something really big, big money needs to happen, he simply needs it to. But it'll be easier for him to think about this after he completes the deal with the silver bowl, he thought and finally dozed off.

Fuck it, son, money is everything

"Get up, soldiers! You've been sleeping while I've been working," Siniša noisily entered the suite a little over an hour later. "I got us a job to do over the night. Come on, let's go!"

"Don't count on this night," Bata mumbled, still groggy, coming out of his room all wrinkled up from his late afternoon slumber, "Leon and I are leaving early in the morning, first to Belgrade and then on to Frankfurt, maybe even Brussels."

"Stop it with this nonsense! It's been ages since we had a proper night out; I need to find me a luscious Croatian woman and get it on... Stop whining, Bata. This has never been a problem for you. You have a driver, he'll take you. You can sleep like a baby the entire time. Don't be a party pooper. Let's go!"

"Hold your horses, Siniša!" Bata kept resisting, but it was obvious that his resolve was weakening, "don't be a fool, are you looking for a third heart attack? Haven't you had enough?"

"Stop it, Bata! Shut up! I'll take being ten centimetres inside a woman over two meters under the ground any day. I'll go as far as I can go. But it'll be under my terms!" Siniša cut him off and turned to Leon, "How about you?"

"I don't have a problem," Leon stretched himself, "I can manage a couple of sleepless nights."

"Now you're talking!" Siniša spoke at the top of his voice again. "Let's go, let's go!"

It was getting dark outside, lights of the city were flickering on in the dusk, hinting at its quite remote outer limits; the remains of the sunset were still visible to the West, the upper floor of the hotel offered a nice view of light lines, drawn by cars along the roads.

Bata and Siniša started changing into their luxurious public attire; they were complementing their sophisticated clothes with flashy accessories.

A small heap of gold jewellery which Siniša had acquired at the fair rested on the table. Some of it he bought, some he traded for items he brought along to the fair.

"Take something, Bata, give your classics a rest, add something modern; we need to flourish tonight. Not only material girls, gold diggers are waiting for us tonight, too. Come on, show off a little!"

"No," Bata shook his head. "I swear by the classics. That's final!" he said while putting on his standard Patek Phillipe wristwatch in white gold.

"Then at least you take something, Leon. A leather jacket is alright, but it's not enough. Put this Cartier gold chain on, and this Rolex will match it nicely," Siniša insisted.

Leon did like the watch and quickly slipped it on. The blue clock face and stop watch practically screamed of the highest rank, somewhere in the range of thirty-five thousand Deutschmarks. He was among the more discreet wearers of gold jewellery, so he quickly located a ruby encrusted money clip in the heap of other gold items.

"How about this?" he asked, as this was something he'd always wanted.

"Of course," Siniša nodded. "We need to slay it tonight, slay everything in our path!"

Leon reached for the wallet in his pocket, but the few banknotes he had were not even enough to fit firmly in the clip. He mumbled something about going down to the reception, and waiting for his buddies in the lobby. A beautiful blond greeted him obligingly at the reception desk. She asked him what she could help him with. She accommodated him and exchanged ten thousand notes for a bunch of thousand ones. Now the clip looked the way it was supposed to: nice and full.

"You share the suite with the gentleman from Belgrade, am I right?"

"Right," Leon nodded.

The receptionist reached under her desk and handed him an envelope.

"The chef left a note for mister Živković," she said kindly. "Is there anything else I can do for you?"

"Not right now, while you're working," Leon answered teasingly.

"Another time then," the girl smiled, acting seductive and trying to hide the fact that she felt a bit embarrassed.

Once outside the hotel door, Leon lit a cigarette.

"Oh shoot!" Bata became upset when he came down from his suite and read the note, "Of course, the villa in Pantovčak, a bookcase and a beautiful mistress, and here I am, with no money. How can I show my face there?"

"Don't you count on me this time," Siniša grinned, "I burnt everything I brought along to spend on new acquisitions."

"Too bad," Bata said, shoved the envelope containing the message in his inside pocket and waved it off. "Let's not talk about it now. Call a taxi. Life awaits!"

They drove off in a black Mercedes toward the discotheque. They noticed a long line of boys and men in front from a long way away; they were aged sixteen to sixty. They all wanted to experience the magic of the famous place: the younger ones were after dancing and fun, selected drinks which you couldn't get elsewhere, the latest music, and the older were also there for the sophisticated food. Of course, both were very attentive to women, and there were a lot of them, as the place was letting them in for free. The modern and slightly decadent touch stirred imagination to reach all sorts of conclusions. Love affairs were forming and dying, the short-lived and longer lasting ones, which resulted in an occasional fist fight. When that happened, two men from Hercegovo stepped in, like two ogres, and they sorted things out in no time.

At the moment, they were standing in front of the door, guarding the entrance. Siniša, Bata, and Leon ignored the line and approached them directly. They were met there by Marko, who greeted them.

"Finally, my friends, finally!" he spread his arms and fleetingly pointed at one of the bouncers for Siniša to discreetly put a hundred Deutchmark note in his hand. They entered quickly to loud complaints from those waiting in line, as the second bouncer gallantly pushed back the golden rope for them.

The disco was packed full, the air thick with alcohol vapour and cigarette smoke, large revolving chandeliers made from tiny mirrors were tirelessly tossing stars of light all over the floor, which practically groaned under the savage music. Sweaty bodies were milling tightly on the dancefloor. Before they even managed to get a good look around, the waiter assigned for the job obligingly took them to one of the tables which were always reserved for esteemed and important guests. The mass of people parted before them, simultaneously wondering who they were, as their arrival in the tails of the employee of the discotheque spoke of adequate excellence. Girls especially showered them with looks, since many of them came with the intention to spend a nice and luxurious night with a rich man of importance, partially financing their studies with the night's profit. It was a well- known fact that some of them, who were unwilling to do so before, were more than willing to sacrifice their central charms later on with an acquaintance they met here, in exchange for a suitable compensation.

Siniša was in a playful mood and shot obvious glances at the women on offer, choosing among them with reservations; his behaviour was clearly sending a message that he was an alfa male, beautiful and loaded, looking for company to spend a wild night with. Bata stretched lazily over the leather bench and lit up a Drina cigarette, no filter. He sometimes liked to choose someone to spend the night with, but never in such a show-offy, Siniša way. But Siniša was the master of the night and he dictated the game. Leon wiped his sweaty forehead and rubbed his itchy eyes; the smoke almost blinded him.

A uniformed waiter approached their table and placed a bottle of Chivas down in front of the trio, accompanied by three glasses and an ice bucket.

"The boss sends his regards," he said with a bow.

Siniša looked around and saw the owner standing at the end of the bar. He raised a glass of whisky in greeting and the man respectfully returned the gesture. Siniša was the king of discotheques, a loose man of the best kind, cheeky and full of swagger, and at the same time sincere and kind to his friends. There was a cool and demanding charm about his appearance. He always knew what he wanted; and he got it, too, by simply taking what he felt he was entitled to.

They emptied the bottle in less than an hour and Bata ordered another one.

"This one's on me, for us and the Gods! I bought the most beautiful piece at the fair."

They emptied more glasses and were slowly becoming overwhelmed with warmth on the inside. The slight intoxication sent their minds racing.

"It's time for girls and fun," Siniša stated self-evidently, "so let's look for what we're entitled to. I'm going to see the boss."

The owner at the bar shook his hand.

"How's Belgrade?" he asked merrily.

"How's the sea?" Siniša answered with a joyous question, "Any fish?"

"Well, my friend, you can see for yourself. We have everything, from calm waters to tropical cyclones. You just have to choose, just choose," the owner responded.

"I can see that, I can see, but I need a little help from you anyway. I don't want any hookers, give me something, something quick, something fresh, but adept, I don't have the time to school anyone... And, of course, I want them here right away," Siniša demanded.

"OK, my friend, OK, I promised you, didn't I. Look at the five down there by the podium," the boss pointed. "I told them I'm expecting some special guests tonight, and I hinted to them that the gentlemen are walking the fine line of the law. Women are always roused by this, as you know. Well," he added after a short pause, "I also let them know that you're staying at the Esplanade. They were taken by this, too."

He underlined his words with suggestive winks and a nod of his head in the direction of the subjects of their conversation.

Five girls were sitting at a small booth next to the turntables, swaying gently to the rhythm of the music. They were looking at their boss, not at all embarrassed as they clearly saw the conversation was about them.

"Yes, I've noticed them already," Siniša nodded, "nice. What are they having?"

"It's cocktail night; we have the European champion over here and they've started drinking a while ago," the owner bragged.

"Alright," Siniša ordered, "have the waiter take over five cocktails. Let's begin."

He returned to Bata and Leon.

"Look over to that table," he chuckled, "and greet them nicely."

The waiter was just putting the drinks down in front of the girls and then pointed in Siniša's direction. They all followed his finger with their eyes. Siniša smiled, bowed and raised his glass.

Leon appraised the girls meticulously from afar, they were beautiful, smiling, slightly provocative and full of expectation. He was especially drawn to a slender black-haired girl, although he also found interesting the not so slender brunette sitting next to her. He always wanted to explore in detail if there was anything substantial hiding in a woman he felt attracted to at first sight.

"I have to take a leak," he said and got up promptly. When he came close to the women's table, he ran his hand through his hair, once more checking out the girls from under his upper arm. He was stunned by an instant realisation that the black-haired one was indeed the queen of the bunch. He spent some more time adjusting his hair and then headed past them to the restroom. There was a long waiting line there, too, so he simply stepped out and relieved himself in the darkness among the parked cars. There were some expensive ones in the parking lot, confirming the fact that the place was also frequented by wealthy and prestigious customers. The fresh, almost cold air felt really good, as it was much too hot for him inside. He breathed in all the freshness he could and returned to the entrance.

The bouncer let him back in the hot, smoky room with a slight bow and no problem. When he managed to make his way to their table, the girls designated for them by the owner of the place were already there; he could hear their laughter and Bata's and Siniša's thunderous comments from way off. The wanton noise coming from the table, freshly laden with cocktails and a new bottle of Chivas, announced that it became the centre of exciting action. Numerous envious men's looks had to revert from the most attractive girls and start their search anew, not without hope, of course, as the few women who had hoped to win the spot of companions to the obviously rich blokes were forced to offer their charms to those still available and unwilling to nurse their drinks in solitude.

A spacious leather armchair and every chair at the table were already taken; the black-haired woman who had attracted Leon's attention before was of course sitting next to Siniša, the king of the group. Leon looked around for a chair, when the black-haired woman pulled him close and got up.

"Come here, come here," she suggested with a deep look, "I can sit in your lap."

"Oh!" Siniša exclaimed almost offendedly, "He hasn't even sat down yet and he's already taken the best for himself!"

Leon pretended not to hear the comment, sat down and the girl immediately climbed into his lap. She put her left arm around his neck and offered her right hand:

"Jasminka."

"Leon," he whispered.

She leaned close to him and threw a glance at Siniša.

"We'll have more room this way," she said, leaned over the table, brushed her firm bosom against Leon's face and poured him a glass of whisky without asking.

Leon felt the softness of her thighs, under her skirt, which had ridden up considerably and exposed a section of bare skin above her garter stockings. The immediate proximity of her discreet perfume had no trouble overpowering the smoke of so many cigarettes. Leon quickly glanced at Siniša, who was looking at the black-haired girl like a snake looks at a frog. No, no, you're not getting away; I'm a hunter, I provide the experience and the money. This youngster is excited and confused, interestingly clumsy; but there's a gradual foreplay going on here, for everyone to see, the main show will of course play out in the hotel suite. He focused on the brunette next to him. She was more beautiful than the black-haired one, but she lacked the provocative, seductive audacity in her eyes, the audacity that speaks of the ability to indulge the highest requests, every last one of them, when expressed in the right way.

The boisterous evening sank deep into the night, more and more drinks were being brought to the table and were feverishly poured down throats; the conversation was increasingly proving the speed and decisiveness with which alcohol releases inhibited desires.

"Let's go!" Siniša ordered well after midnight and yelled to the waiter: "Come on, call us a taxi!"

The bouncer beckoned two large black limousines to drive in front of the entrance of the discotheque, and the drivers obligingly stepped out of their respective vehicles and opened their doors.

"Ladies first," Siniša exclaimed cunningly.

Jasminka and the brunette entered the first car, naturally quickly followed by Siniša and Bata. Siniša set things straight right away, turning to Leon with a sweet smile.

"You can bring over the other two girls, right," he ordered.

While paying for the short ride in front of the hotel, his fellow passengers joined the group and the entire vivacious company were already in the lift and on their way up.

"You're in for a rough night," the taxi driver grinned as Leon declined to take the change.

"We'll see," Leon murmured. He lit a cigarette, took a short walk in the cold air and then went to the lift.

Inside the suite, the atmosphere was peaking. The girls were already arranged on the armchairs and the couch. Drinks were laid out on the coffee table, the entire contents of the fridge. The golden heap Siniša acquired earlier in the day was still right there. Bata positioned himself on the couch between two girls, while Siniša was seriously moving in on Jasminka. She momentarily slipped out of his tight embrace and looked at Leon.

"Why are you late?" her eyes were asking, filled with a mixture of resentment and desire, and at the same time realisation that the beautiful thing that could have happened between them was not going to.

Siniša sensed the right moment to triumphantly display the way masters operate without restraint, in case anyone thinks they can mess with their plan. He got up and reached for the heavy Cartier chain, a work of art holding at least two hundred and fifty grams of gold. He raised it to display its luxurious gleam in the light from every lamp, and placed it around Jasminka's neck.

"Leon refused to wear it, so you're the one it shall adorn now!" he exclaimed.

The girls shrieked and Jasminka got goose bumps; hanging around her neck was the tuition for the acting academy, a heap of expensive clothes, a vacation or two in a splendid hotel...She blushed and practically melted into Siniša's arms. Siniša threw a bragging look over her neck in Leon's direction:

"Fuck it, son, money is everything!"

The other girls came even more alive, as there was more gold on the table and there was a chance some of it could go to them, also. Leon thought about Kristina for a moment, but right then one of the girls jumped up and surprised everyone with a loud, raised call:

"What are we doing, girls? We're not whores! Let's go home!"

None of the girls followed her in the momentary stunning silence, they just gave her a bunch of astonished looks. She waved her arms wildly, grabbed her purse and headed for the door. Bata, who felt just fine among the girls, didn't especially like Siniša's swaggering haughtiness, despite the fact that he didn't mind dealing with women once in a while, but his dislike was not strong enough to persuade him from participating when chance arose. He took his hand from under the beautiful brunette's skirt and waved to Leon:

"Come on, escort the lady to the reception desk, pay for her taxi and come back up."

Leon held the girl's light spring coat and opened the door for her. At that exact moment, the room service trolley arrived at the door, carrying drinks, a few bottles of champagne and a bottle of whisky. The multitude of glasses clanked against each other, creating an exciting atmosphere of anticipation. The girl snorted scornfully and went to the lift without saying goodbye. They descended to the ground floor in silence. There was no one in the lobby and also no taxi in front of the hotel.

"That's alright," she said, not even trying to conceal her anger, "I'll walk home. This will be my punishment. I was a bloody fool to hang out with you. God knows what got into me..."

Leon didn't like the idea of the girl walking off into the night by herself. Who knows where she lives, he thought, so he asked her to wait and went back to the reception desk. He rang the bell to summon the blond he had seen that morning and asked her to call a taxi.

"Good morning," the woman greeted him rather teasingly, "it'll be here in three minutes."

The vehicle arrived but it was not at all glamorous, of course. The people in need for a taxi in the wee morning hours are much different from those who drive around in one at the beginning of the night. Leon leaned in to the driver at the front window.

"Please, take her to..."

He turned to the girl and she mumbled an address which Leon could learn nothing from.

"How much?" he asked.

"I don't know," the taxi driver answered wearily, "I charge by the taximeter."

Leon thought for a moment and then got in next to the girl who was already in the back seat. They took off and the taximeter started ticking. They were silent for a long time.

"Thank you very much," she eventually said quietly, looking out the window into the increasingly light darkness, "I thought you were like that, too..."

"Like what?" Leon smiled and looked at her.

"Well, like," she answered calmly, "sex is all you want."

It wasn't entirely clear whether her eyes held resentment or slight provocation.

"Of course I like sex," Leon laughed out loud and his eyes met the driver's in the rear view mirror, "but not if it's forced. I have plenty of time. My friends, they have some ten years left, and then it's over for them. I can understand: first comes the prostate, then the impotence, they have middle-aged wives at home, and they prefer younger women, they want to revisit their youth. But you know what they say, that Venus drops and sex prolongs life..."

She interrupted him with her laughter.

"If that was so, we'd have brothels instead of hospitals."

Leon was pleasantly surprised by her wittiness. He realised that they were practically strangers that they ended up together entirely by chance, that they hadn't even introduced themselves.

"Leon," he offered his hand, "antique dealer and academy student."

"Nela," she replied, "medical student."

The cab took them past the last tram station and continued to the suburbs and from there on to the first village. They arrived in front of a two-story unplastered building with a broken wooden fence and a red Lada parked in front.

"Well," the taxi driver said and turned to the back seat. "Here we are."

The girl grabbed the door handle, then quickly turned back and gave Leon a hug.

"You're a good guy, thank you very much, bye."

Leon ran out of words, he wanted to say something, something polite and kind, but the girl already left the car and disappeared into the house. The driver looked at the entrance to the house in amazement for a while, and then at Leon for a while more.

"What's wrong with you, man, go after her, I can see you've got this," he said.

"Not now," Leon shook his head thoughtfully, "It just so happens that I'm the knight and you're my faithful horse who is about to deliver me back to my generals. They're waiting for me at the Esplanade."

The taxi driver mumbled something to himself and drove back. At the hotel, he quickly got out, paid the driver, passed the empty reception desk, went through the lobby and pressed the lift button.

There was no one in the anteroom of the suite, but the general disarray spoke of a night of debauchery. Items of women's and men's clothing were strewn all over the floor, interspersed with empty bottles and glasses, a few broken ones lay on the furniture, traces of spilt drink were stretching along the floor, ashtrays were brimming with cigarette butts and the air was thick with alcohol vapour, in addition almost shuddering under the heavy scent, a memory of passionate romping of roused bodies. The gold was gone from the table. Leon opened the door to the balcony wide and lit a cigarette. The stuffiness of the place was becoming almost bearable. He removed a black bra from the couch, along with Bata's tie, he shoved shiny black silk stockings off the table, just lying there like some looted trophy - Jasminka's? - he shuddered, he straightened the pillows, stretched over them and slept like a baby.

The sun awoke him, shining directly in his eyes through the curtains. He slowly recalled all the necessary information - where is he, why is he lying all stiff in the armchair, what happened, exactly - and got to his feet. He got the feeling that someone had already tidied up the majority of the mess, the glasses and the cigarette butts were gone, there were only black women's stockings, thrown across the table, like a reminder of the unbridled mess which preceded the provisional morning order.

He walked to Bata's door and listened. There was silence. He pressed the door handle with great caution, it gave silently, and looking through the crack he saw that Bata was gone. He stepped in. The bed was in complete disarray and a clear witness to the fact that Bata didn't go easy on the girls. Then he went to the room where Siniša slept and heard low snoring sounds. Is he alone already? Or isn't he? His empty stomach made itself known, so he decided there was no sense in looking for answers to questions which were none of his concern. He descended down the stairs, to get a morning workout, into the breakfast hall. He immediately saw Bata there, and a string of empty coffee cups in front of him. Bata was meticulously dressed, as usual, reading a newspaper. He lowered it and then put it down.

"Leon, my boy," he greeted him joyously, "come, sit down. How are you? I didn't want to wake you. When did you come back?"

His face showed not one trace of tiredness. You're alright, Leon thought to himself and said out loud:

"Around five. You were all probably asleep by then."

"Yes, yes," Bata nodded. "Those two young ladies of mine got tired pretty quickly."

And that was all. He held a firm belief that gallant gentlemen never spill the details of their accomplishments, because the ladies that gave themselves to their disposal deserve the necessary discretion.

Leon had his eggs sunny side up and also washed them down with a few cups of coffee. He needed them badly. They returned to the suite. Siniša was lounging in the armchair in his underwear, smoking. The gold chain hung around his neck. Jasminka was nowhere to be seen.

"Didn't you give the gold to the girl?" Leon asked in amazement.

Siniša averted his eyes to the ceiling.

"My God!" he exclaimed. "I'm not crazy to pay for a fuck with pure gold! You're too naive, son, there's a lot you'll have to learn about the traps of life."

"Well, well," Leon shuffled his feet, "but I suppose she didn't give it back voluntarily?"

"When we crawled out of bed," Siniša chuckled, explaining, "I took it off her and said: 'Well, my love, you've worn this long enough.' She almost flipped and ran out of the suite half naked. I didn't fall off a tree for her to trick me like this."

He laughed and slowly got Bata and Leon to join in, as they were looking incredulously at each other before. Then Bata checked his watch and said:

"It was fun while it lasted. And now, my dear boy, we're off to a great journey. You haven't forgotten about my silver bowl, have you? Work calls!"

We have a treasure here! Don't just stand there like a dummy

Leon bought a Quatrelle, formally known as Renault 4, to cater to his antiquarian needs. When the car first came to the market, it became the go-to vehicle for tradesmen and farmers, mainly because of its astonishingly spacious trunk; over time, when more solvent buyers veered toward cars designed along more modern lines, its awkward image came into fashion as a retro accessory for all kinds of strange characters. Leon's petroleum blue pal was able to fit even more sizeable pieces of furniture on the many field rides they made; it endured slowly crawling uphill and achieved stunning speed on a flat road.

On that late morning, Bata and Leon made remarkably good progress along the plain separating Zagreb and Belgrade. Truck drivers had obviously left the roads to have their first snack of the day, and the traffic police were saving their strength for later. Bata was nodding off in the passenger seat, occasionally looking out the window and again urging on with his eyes closed, let's go, let's go, we're in a hurry. Leon didn't take much persuading, he loved to drive fast. At the same time he kept wondering why exactly they had to go to Belgrade first, only to turn right back to Zagreb and Ljubljana. They knew everything there was to know about the silver bowl! It was a waste of time and gas, plus he was unable to reach Kristina by phone, to inform her about his delay. Bata met all of his questions with an almost reluctant answer:

"Calm down, son, calm down. I know what I'm doing. Shut up and learn."

Once they got to Belgrade and cruised off the main road onto the narrower streets of the city, Bata gave him directions and they quickly arrived to an apartment building in Obilićev venac in the city centre, where Bata and his family have been residing with his mother, temporarily, for three years now. Leon hardly brought the car to a halt when Bata already leaped out toward the entrance to the building. There he was met with a written note informing him that the lift was out of order. Bata got into a rage.

"Again? Why the hell do we even have a lift? It never works and the shitty janitor can't do the maintenance. To hell with everything...!"

They wheezed up to the fourth floor and, covered in sweat, entered the unlocked apartment. Enticing aromas were coming from the stove. Leon held the parcel from Zagreb in his hands. At the table in the living-room-turned-bedroom, a tall, grey-haired, scrawny, at first glance elegant lady played solitaire. She raised her head only slightly, peering over her spectacles.

"Where have you children been? Are you hungry?"

She then put her cards down and locked her eyes on Leon, almost unsurprised. Her door was always open to strangers and they were used to coming in without ringing the bell. And whoever came with her son Bata, was a friend of the family by default.

"Well, who might you be?"

"Mother, wait, don't ask, there's no time right now. This is my boy from Ljubljana, my assistant, we have to go to Germany quickly..." Bata almost yelled, ran past his mother to the far corner, opening and closing desk drawers under the window, "we'll be off in a minute!"

The apartment was small. A short foyer led from the building's hallway to the bathroom, and on to a room which featured a kitchen on the left, and a dining corner with a round table and two armchairs on the right, one of the armchairs converted to a single bed, the other to a double, and this room served as a temporary bedroom for Bata, his wife Mira, and their daughter Tamara; there was a chest of drawers in one of the corners, and a kitchen cupboard beside the longer wall; this room led straight to a small, separate bedroom where his mother slept. The place was crammed, creating the ideal atmosphere for a nervous breakdown. But his mother took this transience with superiority and calm. Bata, on the other hand, kept fleeing his wife's snarky comments, going out and hatching plans to move out and into their own place, to the house he was building but kept running out of money.

"Where are you going, you have only just arrived," the lady protested, put down her glasses, stacked her cards at the table's edge, got to her feet and stood next to Leon. Her movements were uncharacteristically lively for her age. She offered her hand.

"You're from Ljubljana, son? Would you like to eat? This troublemaker of mine won't let you have a breather, I know. Would you like some paprikash?"

Leon just stood there, in awe. The old lady had only just met him and yet she treated him as one of her own.

"Stop it, mother! Stop it with the paprikash. Make us some coffee, and we'll be on our way!" Bata rushed over from the other side of the room with a hefty book in his lap, sat down in a chair and started leafing through it.

"I couldn't wait to check this!"

The book was a thick German one, an encyclopaedia of sterling silver manufacturers' hallmarks. Bata leafed through it nervously, then finally stopped. He tapped his finger on a tiny drawing, almost hollering:

"I knew it, I knew it, I knew it!"

His mother and Leon looked at him in astonishment, taking a step closer. Bata pulled the parcel from Leon's hands and unwrapped it nervously. He leaned over the hallmark on the silver bowl with a magnifying glass, removed it and brought it closer again and again. His hands were trembling with excitement.

"We have a treasure here!" Bata quavered. "Look! The hallmark on my silver bowl belongs to Johann Andreas Thelot! He was the imperial supplier to the court of Catherine the Great. I suspected this, I knew it! This is it! Now I know what I have! Let's go, do you hear me, let's go to Frankfurt! Don't just stand there like a dummy!"

Leon leaned over, checked the hallmark and winced. He was right. This is it!

Bata's mother looked at them, surprised.

"What's this? What's this rush about, son? Shall we have some coffee? Would you like some cherry schnapps with it? Are you sure you don't want some paprikash, it's fresh and warm?"

"Stop it with the questions, woman, for God's sake! Make the coffee, pour the schnapps!" Bata ranted, turned back to the room, took two thousand Deutschmarks from a hidden drawer of the Biedermeier cabinet, stashed them in his inside pocket and sat back at the table.

His mother put the coffee on and pulled a small flask without any markings from the bottom drawer of the kitchen cupboard and put it on the table.

"Sit down, son, take your time and drink, we're people, after all," she turned to Leon, arranged three glasses and poured, "To luck!"

She was the first to raise her glass and down it in one go. Bata and Leon followed suit. They each had another shot with coffee.

"But you're driving!" Bata's mother exclaimed, staring at Leon, who silently replied with no more than a happy smile.

"Who cares about police!" Bata refuted, and he was already at the door.

"Hey, son! What do you want me to tell my daughter-in-law, when she comes home from work? And your daughter?" his mother called after him.

"Nothing!" Bata yelled from down the stairs. "Tell them I've gone to Germany! Where are you, Leon, let's go!"

Bata did all he could to get away from his temporary accommodation in his mother's house. He always managed to come up with a number of real and imaginary errands. The fact that he seemed unable to finish his building project ate him up, he ran out of money, the craftsmen not only refused to keep on working, but were now threatening him, his wife was sucking his blood with every word and every look, increasingly heightening accusations of his gambling, only his little daughter Tamara nursed his and her unhappiness with her hugs and gentleness... His wife was the last person he wished to see right now. He'd rather return quickly and put at least temporarily an end to this truly severe crisis with a bunch of money.

I need a man, my stud

Leon and Bata quickly got back in the car and sped off towards Ljubljana. Conversation was scarce along the way, as they were both engulfed in their respective dreams, relating the wealth they carried in the trunk. They made no unnecessary stops - only one, to get gas for the Quatrelle and a double espresso each - and arrived at Ljubljana just before the evening.

In the apartment, Kristina was busy preparing a meal for Šeri, who jumped to the door at the sound of the lock turning, and greeted Leon standing on her back legs. Her front paws almost reached his face. Bata pushed his way in from behind his back.

"Well, well," Leon stroked the dog, "there's my girl, there's my girl..."

Kristina chimed in from the kitchen.

"What about me, am I even here, or what?" she called decisively, not making it clear if she was for real or just feigning anger. She continued after emerging from the kitchen: "Where have you been? You leave for an afternoon and then you're gone for two days, no word from you, like you've never heard of a phone before, are we no longer an item, listen now..."

Leon blushed, he minded that she scolded him like this in front of Bata, who froze at the door, unsure and a little astonished. Like a proper master of the house, Leon pushed the dog away, walked over to Kristina, gave her a hug and shut her up with a kiss. What's all the fuss about? He went to Zagreb for her sake, for business, and then on to Belgrade; he's going to fix everything, he's going to make her happy, everything will be just fine, hey, won't you calm down, my woman! She was once again in his arms, beautiful, passionate, provocative, she made him lose his head completely, those girls from Zagreb were nothing, when he had what he desired most, the most he could possibly have... Kristina surrendered herself silently and promptly, she went all soft in his arms. After a series of long kisses, she pulled back, grabbed him by both ears and said passionately:

"You know I need a man, my stud..."

She paused for a moment, then smiled and added ambiguously, wide eyed:

"Maybe even two... I don't know how to be alone."

Leon once again shut her mouth with a kiss. He loved her lips, he loved everything about this woman, and was at the same time pursued by a morbid fear of whether he would be able to keep up with her high financial demands, too, staving off all the rich competitors circling around her. But now, Bata was here, and the big job, he'd get a substantial commission... He stepped back and pointed at the door.

"Look," he said, "Bata is here, I'm driving him to Germany, we need to finish a big job."

"Hey, Bata!" Kristina greeted him, feigning surprise, despite the fact that she had seen him enter earlier. She reached out her hand from afar, Bata immediately got hold of it and kissed it, "our gallant Bata!"

"At your service, beautiful lady, at your service," Bata chuckled. "Don't hold this against me, oh dear, I apologize, I always get confused in the presence of a beautiful woman, we're on first name basis, aren't we, don't hold it against me, in short, my *šegrt* here, so to speak, my *kalfa*, is taking me to Frankfurt. Something big is about to play out. He really needs to come along. My apologies, my apologies..."

He paused for a breath, then continued hurriedly:

"But what have you been doing, you're prettier than ever, there's no saying where we'd end up if it wasn't for my friend here, being in love with you."

"You're still so sleek and full of sweet lies," Kristina sucked up to him, smiling, "you make every woman feel like a goddess."

"Never mind the goddess, can I get some coffee, a strong one, and quickly, before we move on?" Bata added matter-of-factly and sat in a chair without waiting for an invitation, then continued to look around the antique furniture and paintings in gold frames which hung on the walls.

"Coffee? Oh, no, you should have Leon make it. He's better at... besides," she added, "it's about time you've made something big happen."

She turned on her heel and walked to the bedroom. Leon said nothing, made the coffee, poured Bata a large mug and followed Kristina.

She was sitting on the bed and angrily lifted her head.

Leon looked at her in surprise.

"What's this about? I don't hear from you, you get me all worried, and then you bring home an unannounced guest..., I don't like that!" she went at him hysterically after he closed the door behind him. "What's this about a *kalfa*, about a *šegrt*? What's he on about?"

Leon was equally displeased about the way Bata bombarded him with Serbian words for assistant and apprentice in front of Kristina, but it was clear to him that he was merely teasing him in the presence of his woman, just to show off.

"Oh, it's nothing," Leon responded swiftly, "he's just a bit confused, we're going to Frankfurt to sell a large and precious silver bowl which he had bought in Zagreb. We went to Belgrade to check the hallmark, and it's fantastic. There's plenty of money there, and part of it is going to me."

"Oh," Kristina calmed down immediately, "plenty of money? I hope so. When? I can't keep borrowing indefinitely...When do you expect you'll be back? Look here, more bills arrived in the mail...I can't live like this, from hand to mouth. I love you, but..."

He gave her another kiss, waved his open hand in front of him and assured her:

"Just a short while, just a little bit more, two days, maybe three, and we'll come out on top. Ok?"

"I hope so. I can't live without money, and you promised this wouldn't be a problem when you moved in with me. You gave me some the other day, but..."

He was struck unpleasantly by this. We're right back to the money, just like that? This never-ending story was being repeated over and over again, sometimes in lower, other times in louder tones. He swallowed hard, not hiding his disapproval. He gave her a very serious look and frowned slightly. She realised she had gone too far.

"Oh, come on, don't get mad, I had to remind you. You know I love you, but there's no way this is going to work without money. Do you really plan to go straight on? Aren't you tired, how will you...?" she realised there was no way she could express everything at once. She toned down her annoyance and again asked in a worried voice: "Are you sure you're not tired?"

"We have to go on immediately. I'm eager to see who Bata's working with in Germany, how he negotiates when it comes to high stakes; I want to get my cut quickly, everything will be different then. Bata doesn't speak German, and this is my chance..."

He hugged her again, he pulled her in tightly and kissed her forehead.

"This is about us, you know that. I phoned you from Zagreb, it was quite late at night, but you were not in," he remembered. "Where did you..."

"I didn't do anything," she promptly cut him off. "I was worried about you and I went to bed early. I didn't hear anything. I sleep at night."

She looked at him, wide-eyed, as if to say, what are you thinking, could it be that you don't trust me? Leon turned away, without saying a word, and started packing his suitcase with fresh underwear and socks, placing two shirts on top.

"How long will you be gone?" Kristina asked while watching him pack.

"I'm not sure," he responded, "As I told you, two days, maybe three...I'll call you if anything out of the ordinary happens. You'll stay home, right?"

"Maybe, unless we have to record something," she answered almost carelessly and returned back to the living room to keep Bata company.

Leon felt an unpleasant chill. Andraž, a very wealthy owner of a recording studio, was one of those men who tried hard to win Kristina over; he was married, which of course represented a certain obstacle, but the amount of money that came with him could prove a considerable mitigating circumstance.

After some reflection, he added a formal jacket to his suitcase, just in case. The solid Samsonite guaranteed that it wouldn't get wrinkled on the way. Then he brought his luggage back to the living room. Kristina and Bata were having the standard, non-aged Johnnie Walker.

"You could get some better whisky," Bata derided him. He enjoyed teasing him in front of Kristina.

"When I get a decent cut from this deal of yours, you'll get some decent whisky, too," Leon replied with a cross smile.

"Hold on, hold on," Bata chuckled, "you used to be a *šegrt*, now you are a *kalfa*, once you make a partner, you'll get the man's cut of the deal."

"Man's cut? That sounds brilliant," Kristina giggled. "What in the world is that?"

"A man's share," Leon went on to explain quickly.

"Is there such a thing as a woman's cut?" she asked. "Can I get something, too?"

"A woman's cut is the share given to insignificant intermediaries," Bata explained and continued his teasing, "and when Leon gets the man's cut, like the one partners get in business, I suppose everything will go to you anyway, right?"

Leon clenched his teeth again, raised his glass and said:

"Drink up now, as much as you planned, then I'm ready to go. Aren't we in a hurry, Bata?"

Bata sensed Kristina's constant covert toying with Leon, so he aimed to get the boy angry in order to act more decisively, despite clearly seeing that he was totally under the beautiful woman's spell and entirely blind to everything everyone else could read from their relationship. Leon emptied his glass and set it firmly back on the table, so much so that it cracked and fell apart. Kristina gave him a furious look, and Bata exclaimed:

"Well, that's good luck! We're sure to make a good deal on the bowl in Frankfurt!"

He finished his drink, too, and got up. A thought passed through Leon's mind, that this is the way special people act, the ones who couldn't care less about the entire world and are never thrown off track. They hide behind a mask which no one can see through, least of all the potential fears and mistakes hiding behind it. This is going to be me one day, he thought.

They bid farewell. Bata again "kissed the hand," while the kiss Kristina and Leon shared was swift and empty. I'm leaving my fortress unguarded, Leon thought, but quickly forced the image of the silver bowl in his mind, slowly melting it into thousand Deutschmark bills.

It's not about the coffee. It's about the system

It was already pitch-dark outside, but the line of cars waiting at the Ljubelj border crossing was very long and was moving up the steep hairpin bends at a snail's pace. Leon kept questioning whether he had hidden the silver bowl well enough beneath the seat. Bata kept silent in an attempt to hide the fact that he was becoming increasingly nervous. As they crawled into the vicinity of the customs checkpoint, they noticed that the customs officers were diligently checking every single vehicle. Leon looked at his watch and saw the hands pointed at just over nine. Although there were still some five cars in front of them, Leon left the line and stopped at a restaurant.

"What the hell are you doing?" Bata burst out nervously. "Are you crazy? What kind of madness has come over you? Where are we going to cross the border now?"

"Just chill. We'll have some coffee," Leon replied, getting out of the car.

"To hell with you and your coffee! I'm not about to have coffee now, what for?" Bata kept raging.

Leon lit a cigarette.

"It's not about the coffee, it's about the system, Bata," Leon said, stretched and checked whether the customs officers caught his manoeuvre. It didn't seem so. "The shift ends in half an hour. The guys leaving will have their minds at home already, those starting will still be pondering the day they had and their guards will be low. That's what this is about!"

The lovely waitress made their cappuccinos and poured each a glass of mineral water. They drank and waited. They noticed the line slowed down even more. This meant it was time for teams of officers to change shifts. They returned to their car, Leon backed up to the line of cars and started pushing his way into the queue. Two of the cars started honking like crazy, but Leon paid no heed. He pushed his way in almost exactly in front of the customs officer. He opened the driver's window and stuck out their red passports.

"What was this about?" the customs officer inquired. "Why didn't you drive down, to the end of the queue?"

"We started there and crawled all the way up here, but my

colleague here from Belgrade, wanted to get some real coffee and mineral water, before checking out Austria tomorrow and getting some grocery shopping done. I'm just the driver," Leon explained.

"I see," the customs officer nodded. "Do you have anything to declare, any foreign currency?"

At that moment, Bata realised that he was carrying two thousand Deutschmarks in his coat pocket, a fact which he completely forgot about, because he, too, was primarily concerned with the silver bowl and its hiding place.

"I have a hundred marks, just to get some food and presents for my children, and maybe a bottle of whisky in the duty-free store on my way back. Is that ok, officer?" he said in a very sheepish voice and gave the officer a pending look.

"Yes, and cigarettes..." the officer nodded, but Bata at once stood his ground.

"Oh, no you won't, I support our tobacco industry!"

He pulled a packet of domestic Drina cigarettes out of his pocket and triumphantly displayed it in his hand.

"Oh, I smoked these in the army, in Pirot, I served as a border guard there last year," the customs officer cheered up visibly, adding without hesitation, "Can I have one?"

"Of course, here you go, take two, save one for later," Bata nodded obligingly, extending his hand to offer the pack.

The customs officer did take two cigarettes, thanked them, smiled and waved them through. The man at the Austrian side of the border paid no attention to them, he just waved his hand, and as their nervousness died down, they descended along the road into the night.

You're throwing money out the window while I'm dying

Slowly it started to rain and the increasingly unpleasant drive through the mountains dragged on and on. The windscreen wipers kept tirelessly pushing off ever greater quantities of water pouring down from the sky. Every so often, the headlights of the oncoming cars annoyingly obstructed the view forward through the multitude of raindrops, which dispersed the light in all directions. There was no conversation and they reached road signs for Salzburg in silence close to midnight.

There, a trap awaited them. Bata was unable to resist, despite still fighting off the consequences of his unfortunate gambling episode a few years back. The old blood in his veins boiled.

"Let's take a breather," he suggested almost nonchalantly next to a giant casino billboard, glaringly calling for attention at the side of the road.

Leon understood what Bata meant by this and exited the highway without a comment. Not even ten minutes later they parked the car in the garage under the casino, designated for its customers; their Quatrelle was a noticeably crude intruder among luxurious limousines. They took the lift up to the hall, paid for their tickets and looked around. Luckily, they were both wearing jackets, this requirement was explicitly written in the house rules. Leon's jacket was indeed crumpled, but it passed the formal requirement. The casino spanned over two floors with giant glass walls, which provided a hedonistic view of the bright city lights and the dark outline of the mountains in its background. There were quite a few people at the tables: elegant ladies, draped in expensive jewellery, and the men, predominantly middle-aged, emanating wealth, as well as occasional slightly confused gamblers, with the fact that they were trying to catch a hold of a straw along which they could climb to a financially more secure side of life written all over their faces. There was the sound of clinking glasses, intermittent loud cheers and laughter, mixed with monotonous dance music.

Leon had been to this place once before with friends, and knew how the casino operated, as well as the kind of games it offered, of course. He reserved a sum of money which he decided to risk and perhaps lose, if it turned out that luck wasn't on his side.

Bata rushed to the cashier without hesitation, as if in a trance, and exchanged his money for gambling chips, then he proceeded to the roulette wheels and started playing at two at once. He stared at the monitors providing the lucky numbers of past spins for each individual wheel, and kept placing his bets. He didn't even register Leon anymore. Leon walked to the other end of the hall and looked around. There was only one group of players at the roulette wheels with two ladies present and his legs automatically took him over. One of them, older and with silver curly hair, was wearing a long, shiny silver evening gown, with glasses hanging on a silver chain around her neck, and she only bet on carefully selected numbers. She kept losing all the time. Opposite her there was a younger woman, early middle-aged with light brown hair, wearing a bright red dress with a plunging neckline reaching the edge of her breasts, which were boastfully traversed by a gorgeous, heavy necklace in white gold, and every time she lost a bet she caressed her necklace, swirled her long fingers and flashed her diamond encrusted gold watch. She must be bad at poker, Leon thought to himself, with mannerisms like this she would always give away her hand. She kept a glass of champagne by her side, slowly sipping it and constantly keeping the waiters busy, as they kept gallantly circling her. She was obviously a regular. When she won, she always gave the croupier one of her chips, and he quickly slid it through a slot at his side. She generally bet on three sets of numbers and she fared quite well. Leon started following her lead, placing the same bets, but with almost meagre chips in comparison to hers, of course. He was doing alright, he managed to pile up some money, a little over five thousand Schillings, but at the same time he noticed that his behaviour was starting to really get on the woman's nerves. He got up and headed over to Bata. Even from afar, it was clear to him from his gestures that he was on a losing streak, yet he continued to play with a feverish look in his eyes, going on and on and sinking further and further down. For this reason, he opted to avoid him for the moment and instead approached the Black Jack table.

He did well there, too; he played at the last two positions, which are the most important ones when playing against the croupier, as this allowed him to see which cards were already out, and decided on whether to draw additional cards based on the full and empty decks, trying to get a Black Jack or at least come as close as possible. He realised that he had won ten thousand Schillings already, so he quickly put a five thousand Schilling chip away in the inside pocket of his jacket, just in case, he said to himself. The men around him kept jointly winning against the house; the atmosphere was great and Leon's left side neighbour had twice ordered him a glass of whisky already, while the one on the right shoved a part of his earnings his way. At one point, the table controller interrupted the game and after a pause, a different croupier appeared at the table. He was obviously the grand master of his trade, as the cards, of which he of course brought a fresh pack, were flying around more audibly than visibly. The players at the table exchanged looks: they sent us their best one! Many a person would succumb to fear, get up from the table and leave, but the company of predominantly adept old hands were in such a vivacious mood by that time that the thought didn't even cross anyone's mind. In the new game, Leon was dealt two sevens, and he knocked for the croupier to hit him with another card. Another seven came flying his way: Black Jack! his fellow players applauded and started cheering: "Sekt, sekt!" Leon could have taken the money, one thousand and five hundred Schillings, but he instead ordered champagne and five glasses for all the players. He took the bottle from the waiter's hands and opened it himself. The pop and the joyous cheers attracted a group of busybodies from other tables. The men quickly lost the next two games to the house, but then their luck turned once more. At thirty thousand Schillings earned, Leon bid his farewell.

He looked for Bata and found him at the bar, sipping whisky and obviously nursing his gambling losses.

"What was all that commotion at your table about?" he immediately asked and motioned to the waiter for another round of free drinks. The entrance fee to the casino allowed the players to drink for free.

"I won and ordered some champagne," Leon answered and chuckled.

"How much did you pay for it?"

"One and a half grand. Schillings, of course," Leon explained and just kept smiling.

Bata jumped to his feet as if struck by invisible lightning and banged his fists against the bar:

"Are you nuts? It costs no more than seventy-five Deutschmarks at the store. You're throwing money out the window while I'm dying!"

Leon shrugged apathetically:

"This is how it's done here, Bata. You know this. Come on, let's head to Germany."

Bata emptied his glass ever so slowly and shook his head rather dejectedly:

"I'm not sure we can. I have no money. I blew it all."

Leon looked at him in surprise.

"What?"

At that exact moment, the woman in the red dress joined them, took a long golden cigarette holder out of her purse, and before either one of them could react, the waiter lit her cigarette. She gave Leon a meaningful look and said:

"Well, you did alright when you trailed me, didn't you? Once you left, I started losing. You took away my luck."

"What is she talking about?" Bata cut in, but Leon paid him no attention whatsoever.

"Are you coming with me?" the woman looked at him provocatively, puffing on her cigarette. "The night is still young."

She's not even forty, went through Leon's mind, he felt a slight tingle in his pants, but then flinched and shook his head:

"Thank you for your delightful invitation, beautiful madam, but my buddy and I have a long journey still ahead. We need to get to Brussels."

"Oh," she seemed surprised, "do they have casinos there, too?"

"I don't know," Leon replied, "we are art dealers. We have some business to attend to, and we need to be there by tomorrow morning."

"Interesting," the woman quickly summarized, reaching into her purse. She produced a golden clip boasting two impressive emeralds, took out a business card and offered it to Leon. "Iris Winkler. I'm an antiques and art collector, too. Sometimes I sell an occasional piece, when things fail to go my way, like today, for instance. I've just lost seven hundred thousand Schillings here. Give me a call sometime."

Leon blushed, because he didn't have a business card. He flat out lied:

"I apologize, I was in a rush when I left from home, and I forgot the case with my business cards on the table."

"Oh, well, you have mine, don't you?"

"What is she talking about?" Bata spoke again, and Leon once again ignored him.

"Goodbye then," the woman said gallantly, extending her hand.

Leon lightly touched his lips to her fingers, looked into her brown eyes, then she waved Bata goodbye, uttered a half audible *adieu*, turned around and left. Leon kept his eyes on her receding figure for some time, then he came around and placed four golden red gambling chips on the bar next to Bata's glass.

"By God!" Bata exclaimed, forgot all about the mysterious visitor in no time flat, and his eyes lit up, "we're not dead and buried after all! Way to go, son! It looks like someone's been luckier than me!"

Slightly tipsy from the whiskey, he then decided to heal his own wounds and open Leon's:

"Lucky at cards, unlucky in love, eh?"

Leon took this bitterly, he wanted to serve a gruff reply, but then decided to grin and bear it. Everything was fine, after all, he thought about Kristina and took the joke in his stride. It wasn't like her derisive talk about money meant the end of the world. He walked to the cashier without saying a word and exchanged his chips for money.

"We can move on now, I heard you wanted to sell something, and you were in quite a hurry, right?" he said to Bata with palpable anger in his voice and went towards the lift.

I am the only one who knows what needs to be said

Once in the car, Bata quickly dozed off, while Leon wildly put the pedal to the metal. The rain ceased to a drizzle. They crossed the Austrian-German border in no time, Bata didn't even wake up. By the time he opened his eyes, they were nearing Stuttgart; Leon stopped at a gas station to fill up. The dawn was breaking from the East and Bata looked around in surprise.

"Where are we? Did you drive the whole night? Are we almost there?" he was getting ahead of himself, as if feeling guilty for not chatting through the long journey to help Leon stay awake. "Do you want to get some coffee?"

"I'm not drinking this hogwash," Leon coldly turned him down.

"Are you hungry?"

Bata moved his head in weird circles, not indicating a yes or a no, he crawled out of the car and headed to the café. Inside, steam rose from the pots, filling the space with foul smelling fragrances, and they sat down at the only empty table. All around them, truck drivers were obviously hell-bent on sampling the famous local pork sausages with potato salad to see if they matched up to their international glory. They decided on the same menu, since the great number of dishes going out provided a solid guarantee that there was no stale food on the plates. Against his beliefs, Bata quenched his thirst with a jug of beer, while Leon drank two watered down coffees, not even trying to hide his distaste.

It was mid-morning when they reached Frankfurt. They left the highway and drove into the suburbs, slowly making their way to the centre. Numerous car dealerships proudly lined the road, and when they had to stop at a red light, they saw a sprawling Jaguar sign above huge glass walls showing off the latest models of prestigious, expensive vehicles. Leon caressed them with covetous looks.

"Eh, son, when I make a really good deal, I'm going to get myself one of those," Bata said. "And since I don't have a driver's licence, you'll be my chauffeur. Everyone will think that the car is yours, so it'll work out alright for you, too, won't it?"

Leon was awakened from his daydreaming by the sound of furious honking. The green light came on a while ago and he didn't drive off.

Following Bata's directions, he arrived at the Grey Swan, a small hotel where Bata always slept when in Frankfurt. The owner was from Serbia, of course, as even in Frankfurt Bata sought out people he could converse with in his native language to get most of things done. The boss was out and they received the key to their room from a young fellow, a student by the looks of it, working at the reception desk to earn some money. They went upstairs, where Leon clearly indicated his intention to finally drop down on a bed for a bit, but Bata stopped him.

"Not yet, there's one more thing we need to get done!"

They had left the silver bowl in their car, because it was neatly hidden and the car was parked in the interior yard parking lot, where the receptionist could see it at all times, and they headed on foot along the streets familiar to Bata. It took them over half an hour to arrive at a small store in the older district of the city. The store showed no signs of excellence. It was located in an old house, crammed between two more recently built office buildings. The anterior room where the customers came in was small and compact; a counter blocked the way to the back. Several silver items were displayed on the shelves, but they didn't even come close to revealing the true importance of the owner, who had put a concise sign over the door, *Frietzl: gold and silver, purchase and sale.*

They stopped and looked around.

Through the glass of the front door they could see that the shopkeeper was dealing with a customer; but it seemed that their negotiations were coming to an end. When the scrawny man in a hat, pulled down almost to his nose, and a slight limp walked out, leaning on his cane, they entered. A short, bald man with round glasses and thick lenses on his nose sat at a table, who must have turned fifty at least a decade ago, closed what looked to be a pretty worn out notebook, and took a good look at the two newcomers.

"What can I do for you, dear gentlemen?"

"The usual," Bata replied in robust Serbian, "the usual!"

"Oh," the shopkeeper Frietzl said delightedly, fixing his glasses, "my dear friend, Mr Bata, how are you, what's new?"

Then he looked at Leon.

"Mine froind aus Slovenien," Bata grinned.

Leon reached out his hand and introduced himself in English. Bata immediately cut in.

"Shut up. Only say what I tell you to, however crazy it may seem. You need to translate to the point, don't make any stuff up. I'm the only one who knows what needs to be said."

Leon nodded. He readily accepted his role of an apprentice, with no right to his own opinion, after all he was here to gradually acquire high levels of knowledge.

Frietzl inquired about their journey, Bata complained about the rain, Frietzl inquired about his family, and how the business was going, Bata nodded, affirming that there was an occasional find. Then he threw in the fact that Leon and him had brought with them a splendid piece, a silver bowl, one that several museums showed interest in, but one he had decided to nevertheless bring to him, to Frietzl first, after all, you can't overestimate the value of old friends. Frietzl nodded contentedly and they agreed to meet again the next day.

"Straight in the morning?" Frietzl suggested.

"Gut," Bata nodded.

After that, Bata and Leon took off into the still grey day. Bata unmistakingly led them to Hauptwache Square, next to the old guardhouse, and further down to an inn with a large board in front of the main entrance, promising leg of veal and pork, prepared in various ways.

"We should eat like proper people," he said, found a secluded booth, and as the waiter swiftly appeared holding two leather bound menus, Bata recited by heart the numbers signifying chosen dishes, concluding his order with a request and two raised fingers:

"Grosay beer."

A thick, black bread, seasoned with cumin, promptly arrived at their table, accompanied by a plate of diced onions, two roasted white sausages, and of course two bowls of potato salad. Separately, the waiter brought over a phalanx of different mustards, set on a slender wooden tray. They immediately dug in and emptied two pitchers of wheat ales each on the side. Somewhat satiated, they were presented with the main course, one that Bata dreamt of for the entire journey. They each got a roasted leg of veal, served on a wooden plate, doused in a delicious puddle of its own juice, coupled with an ample, equally famous semolina dumpling. The enticing bit of steam rising from the plates reinforced the expectations brought on by the almost debauched visual image.

"Here you go!" Bata exclaimed, "Crispy skin on the outside, soul-soft meat on the inside!"

He only paused his eating long enough to lift two fingers and order two more pitchers from the waiter who stopped at their table to inquire if everything was in order. The feast got the better of both of them, to the point where they didn't even feel like talking anymore. Leon settled the bill. They went back to their hotel, quickly dropped in their respective beds, and fell sound asleep, despite the fact that the evening was still young.

When they opened their eyes again, their watches co-ordinately read nine in the morning.

They followed the scent of fried eggs and descended to a small dining room. There was nothing special about the breakfast menu.

"Listen to me, son," Bata started, almost reluctantly taking a sip of his watery filtered coffee, "in this business you need to know how to keep your mouth shut, and you need to be able to wait. So don't turn up your nose when I ask you to only interpret what I say and not talk on your own accord. You need to have more patience, to wait, even if it's for ten days. Don't rush it, don't act like a broad. The other person is the one who must start the conversation, always, it's always them who have to call you. You need to be able to sit quietly in the silence, alone with your thoughts. Is this clear? This is your first lesson. Watch me and keep quiet. Alright?"

Leon nodded silently, chuckling to himself: Alright, I'll keep quiet. And right after this, he said to himself: We'll see how this ends.

"Now go to the car and get the bowl. I want to polish the exterior a bit," Bata asked and Leon obediently followed his order.

Have another whiskey! I need to think about this

They proceeded to drive to Frietzl's shop. The owner was already standing at the front door. He opened it himself, impatiently. They greeted each other and sat down at the table. Leon placed the heavy parcel on its centre. The merchant immediately began to unwrap it, sighing occasionally, and placed the bowl on the scales, which he took off a nearby shelf. The bowl weighed just over four kilograms. Then he lifted it up and inspected it in deadly silence, from every side, from above, from below...He reached for his magnifying glass and started checking the hallmarks. Then he got up, went into the adjacent room and came back with a book of hallmarks, exactly like Bata had done it back in Belgrade. He adjusted his glasses and traced his finger from one hallmark in the book to the next. No one even cleared their throat. Frietzl kept searching through the book, glancing at Bata several times. There was a palpable feeling that this was the real deal. After some time, Frietzl put down his magnifying glass and sighed: "Gut, gut." He started to turn the bowl in his hands again, finally fixing his gaze on the face of one of the nymphs on the brim. He moved on to inspect the fingers of the hand of another one, the fingernails were clearly visible. He looked up at Bata, rubbed together the thumb and forefinger of his right hand, and asked:

"How much?"

"Tell him that I'm not sure, I'll let him know tomorrow. I have to consult a professor from a museum first," Bata told Leon.

The merchant said nothing.

"Did you translate what I said?" Bata asked, and Leon nodded.

For a while, they stared at each other, glancing at the bowl at the same time. Frietzl then turned his back and walked to the wall containing a small safe, dating back to the end of the nineteenth century, a green one with a gilded frame. He opened it and took out a bunch of thousand Deutschmark notes.

"How much do you need for today?" he asked.

"Nothing, at the moment," Leon interpreted Bata's words, "I have enough to spend a week or so in the metropolis."

Without batting an eyelid, the merchant turned around and put his money back in the safe. Then he sat down at the table and weighed the bowl in his hands again.

"You can leave it here," he offered.

"I'm sorry, but I can't," Bata shook his head, "I told you, I am meeting a professor at a museum tomorrow. I need to learn the historic significance of the piece, then I'll be able to tell you the price."

Frietzl nodded silently and wrapped the bowl back up.

"So, tomorrow? When?" he asked.

"Shortly after three o'clock," Bata answered and they bid farewell.

As they walked down the street, Bata kept a straight face, he didn't even flinch. He was cold as ice. He walked along the pavement, immersed in his thoughts, silently, while Leon walked beside him, carrying the load. Suddenly, Bata stopped and said:

"You did well. Very well. Tomorrow is an important day."

When they reached their hotel, they placed the bowl back inside their car, and took a long walk around the city. They looked at display windows and went into every single bar they encountered along the way. Bata spent most of the time in front of jeweller's shops, looking for a silver bowl which would at least remotely resemble his. Leon was mostly drawn to kitchen accessories, knives in particular. They walked like this for over two hours, spending just as much time catching their breaths in various bars. They stopped at several benches they came upon in the parks. They didn't speak, each immersed in his own thoughts. Leon in particular didn't want to start a conversation, despite feeling the urge more than once. Together they spent half a day in silence, had a great number of different drinks, and before they went back to the hotel, Bata merely repeated what he had said earlier:

"Tomorrow is an important day."

It didn't start off great, as all the booze they'd had the previous day caught up to them.

"Wine for dinner means water for breakfast," Bata mumbled in the breakfast room at the end of the morning, swirling the brown liquid which was supposed to be coffee in his mouth. He put on a fresh shirt and a suit, which lost its creases in the bathroom steam, and added his famous tie in the colours of rotten sour cherries, as well as his equally famous tiepin. Leon got a fresh jacket from his suitcase.

"Direction museum!" Bata commanded.

The plan was obvious.

They took a simplified map of the city for tourists from the reception desk and off they went. On their way they stopped at Avdo bar, where Bata's friend Abdulah, an immigrant from Tuzla, made them some decent coffee, they exchanged a few usual nostalgic sentences with the owner, and went on.

"I'm going to check the silver section at the museum," Bata announced.

"Are you meeting the professor there...?" Leon asked.

Bata rolled his eyes to the sky, as if to say, what are you thinking, and they walked the rest of the way to the immense Baroque museum building in silence. Leon looked around the large entrance hall for a while, searching for rooms featuring applied art, and while he was busy drafting the order in which he would look at them, Bata was already gone. After a long walk through the halls which captivated him with splendid pieces of bourgeois ceramics, past large cases with tin pots and collections of a variety of pitchers, Leon found him in front of a large glass cabinet showcasing silverware. Bata even pulled up a chair from one of the corners to look at bowls similar to his, he sat down and struggled to read the inscriptions. Leon looked over his shoulder and saw that Bata focused on a large silver sugar bowl. Sugar was expensive in Baroque times and silversmiths manufactured correspondingly luxurious and ornate bowls for it.

At that moment, a warden came coughing from around the corner and continued toward them. He felt that the two visitors have been lingering in front of the glass case for an unusually long time.

"There must be something really interesting for you over here?" he asked politely, as he noticed they held nothing suspicious in their hands, as they would if they had bad intentions.

"We're looking at this piece displayed here, and we would like to know more about it," Leon explained in English.

"This is not my field, but I can get our curator of the department of silver for you," he offered kindly.

"That would be great!" Leon exclaimed, "That would be marvellous!"

He told Bata what the conversation was about.

"Excellent," Bata agreed. "But not one word about my bowl! We could be charged with smuggling art!"

After a while, a blond-haired man in his sixties descended down the staircase made of pink marble.

"Hans Peter," he introduced himself, "I'm the curator. What can I do for you?"

Leon explained that they were antique dealers from Yugoslavia, that he was an art student, and that they would like to learn more about the sugar bowl they were looking at: when exactly was it made, who manufactured it...Oh, Yugoslavia, the man sighed, the sea, the islands, the food...He took a key out of his pocket without hesitation, unlocked the glass case and took out the sugar bowl, held it for a bit and then handed it over to Leon. Bata gnashed his teeth:

"What did you say to him?"

He reached out his hands and practically ripped the item out of Leon's grasp. He inspected the sugar bowl up close, then got a magnifying glass out of his pocket and started checking the hallmarks. He realised that the sugar bowl was made by the same silversmith as his own bowl. He started asking questions and Leon interpreted them faithfully. The curator explained that the sugar bowl was a gift from the city's Jewish community to the German Keiser, and that the Keiser was generously credited by them. Since the rulers often settled their debts by simply deporting their creditors from the country, they, in fear of such a fate, generously gifted him the exquisite sugar bowl, filled with the finest sugar. They bought it from the silversmith for at least five thousand doubloons, double gold coins, which first appeared in mint houses in Spain at the start of the sixteenth century. As the curator placed the sugar bowl back in its case, Leon fleetingly asked him about the value such a piece might have today.

"I would say at least three hundred and fifty thousand Deutschmarks," the curator answered and locked the case.

Bata winced; this time he needed no translation. He gave Leon one of his "you-did-well-boy" looks. They thanked the curator and left. Back at the hotel, Leon picked up the silver load again and they were off to Frietzl's. Across the street from his shop they picked up the scent of real Italian coffee coming out of a small bar. They got two window seats and sipped their cappuccinos.

"Only say what I tell you to," Bata repeated his classic instruction, upon which they slowly and diagonally crossed the street.

Leon entered the store first and laid the parcel on the jeweller's table. They greeted each other. Frietzl started unwrapping the bowl, Bata leaned back in an armchair at the table, and Leon sat on a wooden chair, probably there for ordinary customers which the merchant was in a hurry to get rid of.

"So," he began once the bowl was fully unwrapped and mightily exhibited in the centre of the table, "did you reflect on it, what number are you thinking about, Mr. Bata?"

Bata seemed to be thinking this over for a bit, then fired:

"Two hundred thousand!"

He was never one to shy away from negotiating the price. He felt that the number was about right, according to what he had learned at the museum. Leon was pinned to the chair.

Frietzl sighed. The price surprised him. If he paid too much, he would make too little, but on the other hand he didn't want to let this beautiful piece slip away from him. He was not an infamous merchant, the place he chose for his shop was not in a prestigious part of the city. He liked to work covertly, like a master from the background, with access to the most important private collections of silver, gold, and precious stones. His nose infallibly led him to magnificent deals; he had expert knowledge of the best end buyers, and a network of good suppliers. Bata was often among them with his goods from the Balkans.

"I was thinking about a hundred," he said after slightly wrinkling up his forehead and fixing his glasses; his eyes never left Bata's face.

Nothing was going on there, it was as if a feeble gust of wind blew over Bata's completely frozen exterior. He kept his emotions very deep, guarded them, much in the same way as gold was guarded in the depths of Fort Knox. He knew he had won, he was in the wild throws of high profits he was about to make; now he only had to raise, raise...He shook his head gently. He didn't say a word, as the bowl on the table spoke, or rather screamed for itself.

"What do you say about one hundred and twenty?" the merchant spoke again.

And again, Bata said nothing. He looked impeccable: the hair, the beard, the necktie on his white shirt gave way to a blue bowtie, the calm look in his eyes revealed who was the complete master of the moment. Frietzl reached under the counter and brought out a bottle featuring a slightly torn label; it was red, with a black, hand written sign. A drink from the prohibition times, Bata realised immediately as an avid lover and connoisseur. The bottle was worth at least ten thousand Deutschmarks! He turned to Leon:

"He really wants our bowl; He brought in the big guns. We own him. Follow the conversation closely and translate precisely!"

The merchant set three ground glasses on the table, the low and wide ones which never slip out of your hand, even when you sweat. With a cork opener he pulled out the cork, without breaking it in the process. This meant that the whiskey was kept waiting for this moment, in a dry, safe place, to fulfill its destiny. It would fill the customers with special energy, endow them with fresh inspiration for cogent negotiations.

"It lost none of its colour; it's the same as the day it was brewed. Completely still on the outside, full of energy on the inside, just waiting to erupt with full force and flavour. Much like Bata. Calm on the outside, unquestionably a ball of fire on the inside," Leon thought to himself.

They raised their glasses and sniffed the wonderful aroma through their noses. This time, Bata didn't just down the drink quickly, as was his custom, but instead tasted it in the manner of a perfect connoisseur; he gave the impression of not actually drinking, but merely letting the whiskey vaporise in his mouth cavity, and in turn inhaling it. The unforgettable taste was somehow saving itself to a computer chip in his brain, where it would remain forever and ever. They almost forgot about the bowl on the table.

They could all use a break. Bata was the first to speak.

"I think our estimates differ too much, Mr Frietzl," he said. "You need to think carefully about this. Take your time. I can't sell this silver miracle to you at this price; I'd be practically gifting it for what you're offering. I can't do that. I hope you understand."

He got up.

"Don't go!" Frietzl jumped to his feet. "Have another whiskey, I need to think about this."

He poured another round. Bata raised his glass and started to look around the room, almost politely.

"I can give you one hundred and sixty thousand, and that's my final offer," Frietzl decided.

Leon could not believe his ears. In his wildest fantasies he got carried away no further than some one hundred and thirty thousand, and even this he thought of as a dreamlike number, and now here was Bata, saying no to an even greater amount of money. That's twenty times the price he paid in Zagreb! Bata shook his head.

"You'll have to try harder, my friend. In fact, I can help you a little. You can throw in some silver in the form of more modern artefacts."

Frietzl came to life. Bata often exchanged his goods for ordinary, broken silver and more contemporary silver items. They retreated to the room behind the counter. The place was brimming with stuff; beautiful antique silver artefacts, a multitude of "neo-products" fashioned after old models, trays, candlesticks, goblets, cutlery, desk watches..., all useful items. Bata calculated everything in his mind already. He needed to take products which the merchant bought per weight, he probably got them at around one tenth of a Deutschmark per gram.

"How much of this do you have?" he asked and waved his hand around the room.

"A quarter of a quintal, a bit over that," Frietzl replied. "You can have it all for fifty thousand Deutschmarks."

Bata stopped, drank the last few drops from his glass, and calmly suggested:

"This is what we'll do. I trust you, there'll be no weighing, you can give me the silver at half a Deutschmark per gram and we have a deal."

They returned to the counter, the merchant kept silent, calculating the deal on the table in his mind, while Bata again pointed to the ancient bottle. Frietzl poured him another glass, took out a piece of paper, noted down some calculations and said:

"My last offer is one hundred and fifty Deutschmarks, plus the broken silver you've seen in the workshop, by the kilo."

Bata immediately replied:

"One hundred and sixty thousand plus the broken silver, and we're done."

Frietzl also emptied his glass and leaned over the table, with a gesture of resignation.

"Alright, Mr Bata, we have a deal. And you buy us dinner."

"Fine," Bata confirmed, "but first let's finish this whiskey. My colleague Leon here will pack the silver in the meantime. I trust you have some cardboard boxes around, don't you? Oh, yes, and I'll need two receipts; one for our customs officers and another for my potential buyers."

"Of course," Frietzl nodded, he was used to Bata's way of handling things.

"I can give you one hundred thousand now, and the rest will be waiting for you in the morning at Herta's White Swan."

Bata sipped his whiskey while Leon packed the silver into cardboard boxes marked Chiquita Bananas. When they finished, a taxi, a large white Mercedes, took them and their merchandise back to the hotel. In their room, Leon opened one of the boxes and they went through the goods.

"I could easily sell this in Ljubljana for a Deutschmark per gram. I have a few customers..." Leon began.

"That won't do," Bata shook his head, halting him. "There's something else I have in my mind."

The dinner in an expensive restaurant in the centre of Frankfurt was over quickly, as Frietzl and Bata couldn't converse directly, and Leon didn't want to spoil his appetite with words. They bid farewell kindly, with talk of meeting again soon for some other lucrative deal.

When Bata and Leon shared a late breakfast the next day, they were approached by a young fellow carrying a thick envelope:

"Mr. Frietzl sent this for Mr. Bata..."

Bata took the rest of the money, went over the bills, nodded and signed a receipt.

"Let's move on now, to Belgrade!" he turned to Leon.

"I have an exam at my university in Ljubljana tomorrow..." Leon spoke up.

"Will you give it a rest with the university!" Bata waved him off. "You've learned more here in the past two days than you'll learn there in a hundred years."

Then he took ten thousand out of the envelope:

"Here, you get the woman's part, I added some extra for the gas and other expenses you've had these last few days."

Did the sabre hack like it was supposed to?

The drive back was benevolently monotonous. The weather was dry despite the clouds, and there was very little traffic. They enjoyed reminiscing about the deal they had made with Frietzl. In his mind, Bata saw himself settling his debts with his craftsmen, Leon's pocket felt contentedly warm: there was the fee from his first major deal with Bata, plus of course his earnings from the casino. Kristina can finally stop worrying now; occasional smaller earnings are giving way to big money, and she'll be able to cast away all doubt and surrender to their wild love, which offers luxurious pleasures to both of them. She will no longer confront him with stacks of bills or mention them reproachfully. They stopped twice; filled up the car, had some coffee and propped themselves up with sandwiches.

"What are you going to do with the money?" Leon asked, breaking a very long silence, when they started to descend down the hairpin bends of Ljubelj towards the evening. They crossed the border without any hassle; no one asked them anything, no one even checked their passports.

Bata looked at him in amazement, as if to ask what business of his that was, but then answered curtly:

"I'll pay for the work done on my house and invest in silver."

Leon almost let go of the wheel in surprise.

"In silver?" he gawked. "But we have a whole boot full of it."

Bata didn't say anything, but looked out of the window instead. He lit a cigarette and opened the passenger window, letting the smoke out and the cold air into the car.

"You'll see why, when the time is right," he murmured after a while.

Leon remembered the lessons on keeping quiet, so he drove on without asking another question. He turned off the main road in Šentvid, in the suburbs of Ljubljana, and drove towards Šmarna Gora. He explained his move before Bata could figure out what was going on:

"I'll make a quick stop at my parents' house. I haven't seen them in ages."

Bata realised there was no point in arguing. On the contrary, he looked forward to meeting them. He went on well with Leon's mother; a month ago, when he brought her a Lacković painting, following Leon's suggestion, for her fiftieth birthday, they had a great conversation and found a mutual understanding of business topics. Her weak spot were colourful works by naïve painters, featuring clumsy human figures. And every time they spoke, in person or over the phone, she asked him to take care of Leon, on account of him being young and reckless, and forgetting about his studies.

"Education is one thing, life is another," Bata always said. "Some experience is essential, so there is something to remember."

Bata was full of this type of pocket wisdom, which filled every atmosphere with joyous distraction; Leon's worried mother took to them with gratitude, despite not taking them too seriously.

"Are you coming or going?" she asked, happy and surprised, when they appeared at her door. As always, she appeared well kept, even in her own house, she never looked like a housewife. She managed a large sector in a pharmaceutical company and it seemed as if she was expected to look the part even in her free time. She gave Leon a hug, kissed him, shook Bata's hand and accompanied the handshake with three kisses on his cheeks.

"I'd like some coffee, mother," Leon grinned and remained standing next to the telephone in the foyer, while his mother and Bata moved on into a large living room, with walls buckling under paintings by Bahunek, Stolnik, Generalić junior, Magyar, Repnik, Kovanda, and others.

Leon immediately phoned Kristina, but the phone just kept ringing. Of course, she can't spend all of her time sitting home by the phone, he thought, she's probably in the process of producing some new music-fashion festival, that's what she talked about a few days ago. He tried to call several times more, waiting until the phone stopped ringing, and then he went to the living room, where a cup of coffee awaited him on the coffee table next to the armchairs.

"She's not home?" his mother asked in a somewhat scornful tone, and then answered her own question, "of course she's not."

She couldn't resist the temptation and looked at Bata while pouring him a glass of whiskey.

"Why don't you also tell him that this relationship with an older woman with a wild past doesn't have a future? Money is the only reason she's with Leon. She's let him in until she can find someone better, that is, wealthier. The boy should find himself a girl his own age..."

"Stop it, mother, we came by to say hello, to see how you're doing, how father is doing, I thought you'd be interested to know about our business, instead of this perpetual girlfriend story of yours. I can leave right now, you know," Leon harshly lost his temper. "Is there really nothing else you have to say to me?"

He was terribly annoyed because his mother started the conversation about his woman again in front of Bata, as Bata kept covertly teasing him about it since the very first time he met Kristina. But this time Bata merely laughed, put down his glass and smacked both of his hands against his knees.

"Oh, mother, don't, let him be. He needs to learn his lessons, our lectures are falling on deaf ears. Let me offer you some consolation: he's making great progress businesswise. We'll go far, him and me. You can take my word...Leave his women alone. Let him have his fun."

He raised his glass to the hostess, then to Leon and emptied it.

Leon's father had obviously left for a meeting just a while earlier, and it seemed there was no sense in waiting for him. Bata decided to spend the night at the Ilirija hotel, as he thought it unreasonable to arrive in Belgrade in the middle of the night; daytime was more appropriate for the deals he had planned with the silver he had bought. Besides, they could both use a rest. Leon dropped him off at the hotel and drove home. Kristina's car was not parked in front of their building. He took the stairs up to their apartment and found the dog gone, too. He took a shower, threw his dirty clothes in the laundry bin, and lay back in his armchair.

Where could she be? He pondered and tried to convince himself that she must be at work. Musicians are night creatures and she needed to adapt. He poured himself a drink and then got up, took the money out of the pocket of his jacket with a smile, placed two banknotes back inside, and threw the rest, a hefty sum of money, on the table in the middle of the room. This should explain his absence and put a smile on Kristina's face, naturally. His eyes were heavy and he went to bed. Before turning in he set his alarm clock, as he knew he would sleep well into the morning without it, when he and Bata were supposed to be far, far away by then, at least at Slavonski Brod.

After some time, he found himself in the casino, with the brunette in the red gown sitting next to him; she was leaning over him and her sumptuous bosom kept falling out of the deep neckline under her gold chain. Each time she threw her chips on the table, she leaned on him warmly and whispered in his ear: Are you coming with me? The night is still young. Then, suddenly, she threw her arms around him and started kissing him passionately on his mouth...Leon woke up in the arms of a completely naked Kristina, her hands searched demandingly all over his body, and her kisses moved from his mouth, to his neck, and lower..."

"My man, my man, my man," she kept whispering, "you're back..."

They made love as if they wanted to make up for the lost days, hysterically and immediately. They were together again, just the two of them, the rest of the world no longer existed.

"This is for all we missed," Leon wheezed as he laid flat on his back, gasping for air.

"No," Kristina shook her head, placing the upper half of her body over his chest, "this was for today."

Then they fell asleep.

In the morning, Leon carefully stole from the beloved naked body and got out of bed. Kristina slept soundly and didn't even budge as he left his place under the blanket. He kissed her tightly shut eyes and went into the bathroom. As he was putting on his clothes, he noticed that the money he had placed on the table the night before was gone. He laughed self-confidently, almost out-loud, petted Šeri who merely raised her head slightly under the table, and left. He didn't pack a suitcase, because he was certain that he'd be back soon.

Bata was already waiting for him at the hotel reception, smoking and drinking coffee. He got up the moment he laid his eyes on him, put his cigarette out in the ashtray, grabbed his suitcase and hurried to the car.

"Good morning, my hero!" he chuckled. "Did the sabre hack like it was supposed to? Everything alright?"

Leon merely laughed, boastfully and purposefully. He grabbed Bata's luggage, threw it on the back seat and ordered:

"Departure!"

If I may, dear madam, I'd like to ask you for this dusty little old notebook

They drove East and the sun glared ruthlessly in their eyes from the clear sky. Leon turned down both sun visors and put on his sunglasses. Bata sank back into silence, nodding off occasionally. Leon felt no need to wake him with unessential questions. The sky clouded over as they approached Novo mesto, and soon after annoying drizzle started coming down, making the road just barely wet and causing the cars to spray thin mud from under their wheels. The wipers spread the dirt all over the windscreen in fine layers, and Leon soon ran out of wiper fluid.

"We'll make a stop in Zagreb to rest a bit, right?" Leon asked. "Should we go check out that bookcase?"

Bata roused.

"By God!" he exclaimed. "I would straight out forget about it, you know? I can at least have a conversation now that I have the money."

He took a carefully folded piece of paper out of his wallet, containing the address the chef Karapandža had given him days prior at the Esplanade Hotel. Words under the address written on the paper read: display case - library, beautiful lady!

They drove through the centre of Zagreb and from there, asking a few passers-by for directions, to a single-storey building in Pantovčak, enclosed within an eye-high concrete fence. Spaces lined with cast iron ornaments afforded a view of a large, well-kept garden; the house had a white exterior, with corners and stucco painted yellow, decorated with some sort of white garlands over cassette windows. They rang the bell; there was an empty name box next to the doorbell.

"Who is it?" an aged woman's voice said.

Bata cursed under his breath; his friend had obviously tricked him with the promise of a beautiful lady.

"Mr. Karapandža sent me, we came for the bookcase which you're selling," he almost snarled.

There was a buzz at the door.

"Come in!"

A beautiful, well-groomed formal garden opened in front of them; waist high bushes spanned next to a concrete rim along the gravel road which led to the house, colourful flowers flourished in the background.

A magnolia tree in full bloom stood just off the house. They were met at the door by a woman in her early seventies, in very plain clothes:

"The lady said she'd meet you in the reception room. Come in!" She pointed to a tall door opposite the interior stone staircase, lined with iron railings featuring small gilded squares. There was a brass column with an open brass blossom standing at the top of the stairway, holding a chandelier made from multi-coloured glass. Exquisite art nouveau, Leon thought to himself and turned his eyes to the ceiling: the slightly darkened fresco in white foundation featured several fishermen casting nets, women picking grapes and carrying it away in baskets, children playing in a garden. The woman took them to a large room, furnished exclusively with art nouveau furniture, and sat them down in seats with chromium-plated framework, upholstered in cow hides with short hair. A large painting of dancing children by Eduard Kasparides, a great master of the art nouveau period from Vienna, hung on the principal wall opposite the window, the remaining walls lent their space to Babić, Becić, and Stančić; aristocratic dinnerware was displayed in glass cabinets. The woman, who disappeared unnoticed earlier, came back with two elongated glasses of lemonade. When they reached for them, a tall, elegant woman of forty with dark gold hair entered the room. Her modern two piece suit, almost entirely covering her neck, with a heavy golden broach fastening the collar, didn't match the overall art nouveau look. Bata got up, kissed her hand, and roared:

"Milorad Živković, at your service, beautiful lady!"

"Please, Mr. Živković, don't. Welcome to my home," she resisted politely and offered her hand to Leon, too, naturally not for him to kiss. She had a narrow and groomed hand, kept softly inside a white blouse, peering out of the sleeve, her nails were painted with a subtle transparent nail polish.

"Leon, from Ljubljana," he said.

The woman looked back to the older man.

"What can I do for you?"

"I got your esteemed address from my friend Stevo, he told me to come and have a look at a book case, a cabinet which you are selling," Bata explained and once again reached for his glass of lemonade.

"Oh, yes," the woman remembered, "of course; he had a change of heart and decided not to buy it. Alright. Let's have some lemonade, then we can take a look at it. We've had it since forever. My grandmother brought it from Vienna, she went to school there. The story goes that she had fallen in love with a member of the Habsburg family there, they both studied painting and literature. His family was against them marrying and it was a source of great sadness. He gave her the cabinet as a souvenir. My grandmother had passed and now we're not sure what to do with it."

"What a wonderful story," Bata said, giving their host an almost gentle look, then added with a sigh: "sooner or later, everything passes, doesn't it?"

A short while later, they went up the magnificent staircase to the first floor, and entered an elongated ladies' salon, where a bookcase positively beamed in golden brown walnut veneer with root pattern, among smaller pieces of art nouveau furniture. Without saying a word, Bata bent down and pushed it away from the wall. He checked the back and immediately located the signature of the master who had manufactured it. An exceptional piece, which must have cost a sinful amount of money at the time it was made. A few old books were kept on the front shelves, among them a relatively thick notebook in dark grey binding. Bata asked for the woman's permission to take a look at it; he noticed from the cover that it was a catalogue from an exhibition of French impressionists from 1939-1940. The first page of the book declared that this was a collection of paintings owned by Erich Šlomovič. The name sounded familiar to Bata. He turned to their hostess, catalogue in hand.

"And how much would you like for this exquisite cabinet, dear madam?"

"Oh," she sighed, "I'm so clumsy. Would you please be kind enough and call my lawyer? He's better at these things. He has my authorisation."

She took a business card from a before unnoticed small pocket of her tight fitting jacket. Bata clicked his heels, and, as if it was a matter of course, again reached for her hand to kiss, saying very politely:

"With your permission, of course, beautiful madam, at your service; I'll give him a call."

He put the business card in his pocket, still holding the catalogue in his other hand.

"If I may, dear madam, I'd like to ask you for this dusty little old notebook. It probably means nothing to you, and I'd love to take a look at it in peace," he waved the notebook politely.

"Of course, take it, take it," the woman replied.

"It was my pleasure," Bata took another bow, "we won't hold you any longer. Thank you so much for seeing us."

He put the little notebook - the catalogue of paintings owned by Erich Šlomovič - under his left arm and gallantly waved goodbye with his right one.

Leon also bowed slightly; it was clear who the boss was, which meant the woman didn't offer her hand but merely returned the curtesy with a slight nod. They descended down the stairs by themselves, went through the garden and to their car.

And what are you doing here, young man?

As they approached Belgrade, Bata ordered Leon to take the road to Pančevo, along the Danube River.

"Where are we going now?" Leon inquired, but Bata quickly stopped him: "You'll see. You've never been there before. It'll be interesting."

They drove over the Pančevo Bridge: it was wide, with two train tracks in the middle, and a traffic lane on each side. The road was riddled with deep holes, outright dangerous and providing speeding driver's ample chances to break an axle or lose a tire. Bata cursed the fact that nothing was being done to fix the roads in this cursed country, directing the course with the motions of his hand. They drove past a refinery and, once they reached Starčevo village, left the main road and continued down a back street. They ended up in a typical flat country settlement landscape: water filled gutters hemmed the road on both sides, bordered by tall fences separating individual houses from public property. Lime tree saplings lined the strip of grass between the road and the footpath in front of the houses.

"Here," Bata pointed, "stop right here. Wait for me in the car, don't go anywhere."

He then disappeared through a sagging oak wood double door into one of the courtyards. Leon sat in the car, patiently waiting for a while, but when the warm moisture started condensing on every window, he decided to step out. The sun was gradually tearing through the grey clouds, painting the entire landscape in a more pleasing way. He walked along the side of the road and watched chickens poking around the grass, as well as ducks and large white geese diving in the water in the ditch. Bata's angry voice brought him out of his enraptured observations of the bustle:

"I thought I told you to wait in the car? People around here don't like to let their neighbours see who's coming over to visit. Come on, pick up the other carton and follow me!"

He was holding a box of silver in his arms and moved through a small gate in the fence, holding it open for Leon with his foot. Leon picked up his load and locked the car. They entered a long courtyard which stretched far into the distance, and was lined on both sides with low-rise buildings with rather pointed roofs, which probably served as granaries, pigsties, barns, and henhouses in the past. The grass separating them was bright green and neatly mowed, it looked like someone was trying to grow an English style lawn in the middle of this plain. A doghouse stood on the inside of the large double door, and lying in front of it was a sizeable St. Bernard, which didn't seem to be bothered by the visitors. There was a willow wicker lounging set, freshly washed by the morning rain, in front of the main building. A stout man emerged from one of the houses, wearing an apron covering him from his shoulders to his feet. He was carrying a vessel reminiscent of a melting pot in his gloved hands; the pot indeed radiated as if it contained molten metal. Leon stopped in his tracks, astonished, but Bata was already hollering at him from the door to the building on the opposite side:

"Where are you? What are you staring for? Come in!"

He entered a large room through a thick security door - the strange coincidence of a heavy Jelovica door in the middle of a village in Vojvodina didn't escape him - and he put the carton of silver down on a large table, just as Bata had done before him. Bata immediately started taking items out of the boxes and unwrapping them.

"You just sit here, be quiet and don't ask any questions. Are we clear?" he said, pointing to a bench next to the table.

Leon sat down and wondered what was going on, what was this place that Bata had brought him to...He heard water being released from a toilet tank somewhere in the hallway, followed by the sound of hand washing, and then a man of about thirty-five walked over to the table. He had long brown hair, combed in what appeared to be a high parting, he had an oblong face and a fair, gentle complexion, and a distinctly aquiline nose reigned in the middle of it and under a prominently intellectual forehead. He held his chin high, as if he had decided to look down on the whole world. He gave off a very composed, almost aristocratic appearance, and there was a kind of a sly, shrewd look in his eyes. He was wearing a floor length white robe, much like an African kaftan at first glance.

"So, this is your man from Slovenia, the one that shows so much promise?" he turned to Bata, extending his hand to Leon at the same time. His unusually long fingers showed no signs of hard physical labour, although his palms were wide, almost shovel-like.

"How are things up North? Anything new? I haven't been there in ages. My name is Rista. Have you heard about me?"

Leon shook his head, but the man already turned his attention to the table, picking up various silver items, one after another.

"What sort of rubbish did you bring this time?" he asked Bata, then abruptly turned around and addressed Leon, as if they had known each other for eternity, but still unable to supress the provocative and evaluating look in his eyes:

"What do you make of this silver here?"

"Nothing in particular," Leon shrugged, "silver like any other, new, a German attempt at imitating classic."

He was surprised the man was asking him this. Was he testing him or merely paid him some attention, out of courtesy?

"Well, well," Rista smiled and snorted, "you trained him well, Bata. What are you studying?"

"Art history and painting, at the University."

"Oh, you'll be very useful to us once you graduate."

"If I graduate..." Leon mumbled.

"Oh, you better, don't mess it up. Bata has great plans for you, as far as I know; you need to graduate, you have to," Rista gave him a serious look. "I missed out on so much, I don't speak any foreign languages."

What Bata's plans did this strange man know about, that were unfamiliar to him, who was the subject of them?

"Let's not go on about this now, it's not important at the moment," Bata cut in roughly. "He doesn't know about my plans yet. I'll tell him when and if the time comes."

Rista went back to inspecting the silver on the table, speaking in a low voice, as if he was talking to Leon: Look at this, this could be a beautiful Baroque candlestick, oh, and this Renaissance sugar bowl, and these Napoleonic plates, hmm, will you look at this...

Leon kept quiet, as he was again unsure whether the unusual man was testing or teasing him; everything he was saying was complete nonsense, of course. Who could be senseless enough to historically age these relatively new products?

At that moment, Rista turned to the other door and yelled:

"Mijad, come here and get this stuff."

A short, round man appeared, he definitely didn't fit into the selected company; Leon thought he must have been around thirty. The trousers he wore were too short, the chequered shirt was coming out of the entire perimeter of his pants, the vest over the shirt was too tight and soiled, the eyes in his round head with short hair gave no promise of anything smart coming out of his mouth. He stared meekly at Rista.

"Take this stuff and weigh it. Write the weight down on a piece of paper and bring it to me."

The man nodded. Leon could see what looked like a workshop through the door he had left open after he came in. A few men were working on metal objects with small hammers, sharpening and polishing them, while two women kept rubbing something in their laps, and all of them wore goldsmith aprons.

"So, what did you think should become a Raguza?" Rista turned to Bata, who quickly brought his finger to his lips and then asked Leon to take a walk in the courtyard, or smoke a cigarette; he had noticed the way his inquisitive eyes followed Mijat to the workshop.

Leon was walking along the grass among the buildings and suddenly realised he could see a bunch of items which didn't exactly belong in a farmyard. One of the low-rise buildings, which particularly drew his attention, had a round wall, made entirely of old glass, standing on wooden brackets, you could see tiny air bubbles in the glass. He stepped closer and peered inside. As far as he could discern through the opaque glass, there were several easels inside, with a large canvas covered in vivid colours attached to the one positioned closest to him. He could see that it was an unfinished painting, something the artist was still working on, a peasant motif…But how in the world, at first glance, the painting looked like one of Milan Konjović's…No, no…that painter lived in Sombor! Could it be possible that he had another workshop over here? Was this a restoration studio? Leon thought to himself. The rest of the easels faced different directions so he couldn't see them properly, and when he moved further along the wall to get a better look, he felt a heavy hand land on his shoulder.

"And what might you doing here, young man?"

He turned around and saw a stature like the ones he was used to attributing to security guards in night clubs. The man's right hand was wrapped firmly around his left wrist.

"Nothing, just looking around a bit," Leon almost squealed, trying in vain to get out of the iron grip.

"There's nothing to see here. Get lost!"

He dragged him roughly to the door which Rista poked his head out from.

"I found this guy snooping around the yard," the strongman said, "what should I do with him?"

"Nothing," Rista replied quickly, "let him go, he's one of us."

The man gave a surprised look and let go of Leon's wrist, which bore the red markings of his mighty hand for quite a while longer, he spit and went away. Rista turned to Leon and offered him a shot of brandy. While he was gone, a transparent bottle found its way to the table.

"Have some, lad, this is mine, it's homemade."

"I could use some," Leon replied, trying to stave off the paleness which had settled firmly on his face, "I had a bit of a scare."

"You mustn't be too afraid if you want to make it in our business," Rista chuckled, "isn't that right, Bata. If he's going to work with us..."

"Leave him be," Bata waved his hand. "Drink up, son, we're done here. Let's go home."

They bid farewell. Leon and Bata got into their car and drove off.

That's very noble of you. It's one of the reasons I like you

The atmosphere back home in Obilićev venac was a happy one. Bata came back like a king, announcing that he and Leon had just returned from Germany, where business went well. The money was there: for expenses, for the house, for merry making! They would finally be able to move into their own place. Bata immediately sent his wife Mira to the nearby inn, famous for its roasted meat, to order a whole piglet on a spit, and to the winery for some wine, and he asked his daughter Tamara to go fetch the masons. Bata's mother started making *baklava* without saying a word. When this was taken care of, Bata sat down at his desk and started filling envelopes with money and writing names on them.

The word was soon out: Bata was settling his debts!

He sat at the table, waiting for visitors to show up. He set a bottle of Chivas in front of him, one that he had been saving for a special occasion. Before opening it he walked up to the cupboard one more time took a gold necklace from a secret drawer and put it in Leon's hand:

"I've already given you some money, son, and this here is for your woman. You'll get a bigger cut from our next deal, now I have to first take care of the people I've kept waiting for such a long time!"

Šotra was the first to appear, he was Bata's best man and his friend from college. He was the only one of his company to speak both English and French; he was a legendary stamp merchant and he did business all over Europe; he obviously had to speak foreign languages. He belonged to a group of Bata's friends who were antique dealers, book dealers and all sorts of other dealers; they were gradually taking over from post-war Belgrade merchants, who were getting on in years and were starting to show signs of negligence, which proved quite an aggravating circumstance in the modern times, sweeping the rug from under their feet. Štora was accompanied by Ljuba the "China," an antique dealer with a college degree in sinology and an expert in Chinese art, who was known to comment during cumbersome alcohol laden debates in the early morning hours:

"Boys, the future of art trade lies in counterfeits. What's the point in old paintings?"

"So, how was Germany? How much did you strip them for?" Šotra asked, raised his drink, toasted everyone with his eyes and elegantly emptied his glass in a single swig.

"What's the rush, my dear best man, let's empty this bottle first, we can talk later," Bata evaded the answer, then smiled and said, "It wasn't bad. A hundred and seventy thousand."

"Whoopee!" Šotra jumped to his feet. "What the heck did you bring?"

"A silver bowl, four thousand, five hundred and fifty grams, Augsburg, seventeenth century, imperial master," Bata explained.

"Whoopee!" Šotra winced again. "Did you get it from Rista?"

"No way! A true original, I'm telling you, I bought it in Zagreb. I didn't get it from Rista, I swear on my mother's and daughter's lives!" Bata asserted and drank up.

"If you say so," Šotra nodded. "And now, things being as they are, I'd like to ask you for the money you owe me, I could sure use it."

He paused, then threw in a cautious comment: "If you still have it, that is, if you didn't go chasing your luck again."

"No way, I swore off gambling," Bata shook his head and gave Leon a meaningful look, as if to say, our Salzburg casino thing never happened.

Leon kept listening and once again felt he had no idea what was going on. Every conversation he had listened to lately was filled with so many ambiguous sentences: the mysterious Rista, the tasks Bata had entrusted him with...It was obvious that everybody knew something, everybody but him. They accepted him in their midst, sure, but not as their equal, there was something he was missing, unable to pinpoint the exact meaning behind verbal clues. How could the precious bowl come from Rista? When it clearly came from Zagreb!

"Mira!" Bata turned to his wife, "take the envelope marked Šotra out of the drawer. Hop along, now, make my best man happy!"

Mira brought over the envelope. Šotra first weighed it in his hand and chuckled. Then he opened it and counted the money.

"You are actually settling your debt! I'm so happy for you, for the fact that you found your footing again...Oh, oh, oh, look at the interest! Bravo!" Šotra was unable to conceal both surprise and satisfaction.

There was a knock on the door, and Siniša the Heart walked in a moment later. He wore an elegant silk scarf wrapped around his neck.

"I heard..." he started.

"Here, take your envelope, count it, drink up, then speak," Bata ordered vehemently.

Siniša sat down, had his drink and peered inside his envelope.

"Well, well!" he exclaimed. "But this is..."

"Shut up," Bata stopped him, "I added a reward for your help in Zagreb. I couldn't do anything if it weren't for you. I haven't made this much in a long time. Thank you!"

Siniša nodded meaningfully, finished his drink and put the envelope in his pocket.

"That's very noble of you," he said, "and one of the reasons I like you."

There was no time left for more talk. They heard some noise coming from the hallway. The chief mason and the boys bringing the freshly roasted piglet arrived simultaneously. As they laid the deliciously roasted meat with the skin cut into tiny squares on the table, Bata handed the envelope containing the money he owed plus an advance over to the satisfied mason, and invited him to join the feast. The process of building his house on Šumatovaćka Street was back on.

More and more people came, some came to get their money, others for no apparent reason, other than they knew there would be food and drink aplenty, when Bata was merry and full of money; he knew no limits when it came to hedonistic craziness. He also knew no limits when it came to having no money at all; he would just sit at home and refuse to budge. But today was different, Mira kept sending for mountains of *chevapcici*, Bata's mother kept working at the stove, producing *baklava*, *zeljanica* savoury pies, *burek*...Eventually, the neighbours came over, as well, as the walls of the apartment building were unable to hold back the unstoppable rumble. The tiny apartment moaned and groaned, bursting at the seams. It looked like the celebration would never end.

"So, you achieved something big," Siniša mumbled with his mouth full. "Let's not stop here, right? This is a fine opportunity to take the cork out of that half a century old brandy I hear you've been keeping in the cellar. It's certainly the right occasion."

"Not yet," Bata shook his head, "we'll have to wait for that a while longer. I have a feeling that things are really going to take off now. I sense a great deal, a hundred times greater than this one, something's telling me..." Bata continued, enraptured, he kept drinking, happy about everything: the merry atmosphere at the table, the situation with the house finally moving along, the company of his friends. "I'll make even more money!"

"My God!" Mira lost her nerve, "don't overdo it. Don't get us in that position again, when we don't know what to cook for dinner, when no one will lend you money, not even for oil and bread, when the house waits unfinished..."

"Quiet, woman!" Bata hollered. "Go get some *chevapcici*, can't you see we're almost out..."

In the midst of all the racket, Leon left the company without anyone noticing and went into town. When he came back, no one would even register that he was gone for a while. He visited a few antique shops. He wanted to buy as many quality items as he could, invest some of the money he had earned, and enrich the resources available to him by re-selling the stuff in Ljubljana.

When he sat back down at Bata's table, the company was even larger, even merrier, people were practically walking over each other. The neighbours brought over a few additional chairs as there was nowhere to sit anymore. The atmosphere in the compact room was brimming with conversation and shouting, thick smoke and alcohol vapour, one could cut it with a knife and chuck it out the window in exchange for some fresh air. Leon realised that the wild revelry would leave Bata with a hangover which would require a long period of healing, and he saw no point in waiting. He decided to go back to Ljubljana. He pushed his way to Bata who was at first angry about his surprise decision, but soon relented indulgently, gave him a hug and kissed him three times.

"We're off to a good start, my son," he mumbled in Leon's ear. "Have a safe journey. Make your wild cat happy. And," he seemed to sober up for a moment, "remember that you'll be back on your way to Germany in a few days, to sell more of my silver. On your own, without me there! Until then, get some rest."

Leon stopped at the first gas station out of the city, filled up his car and focused on his driving. His arms and legs steered the Quatrelle almost automatically while he pondered what exactly it was that he had seen at the unusual estate in Vojvodina. A foundry? A restoration workshop? What exactly did the mysterious, strange Rista do? What was his connection to Bata, what were their plans? How come everyone knew about the "young Slovenian" and his role, while Bata only revealed it to him bit by bit? What would come from all of this? These thoughts were followed by a very prudent realisation that in the midst of all the unknowns his finances picked up considerably, that he had met a bunch of very interesting people, and that Bata had already placed a new business venture on his horizon. He pushed away all of his questions and instead looked forward to his own revelry, which was getting closer by the minute.

He arrived in Ljubljana in the middle of the night. He parked his car in front of his house and went up the stairs to the apartment, clutching the gold necklace in his hand. He walked quietly to the bedroom. Kristina was obviously sound asleep in their French canopy bed. He took off his clothes and got in the bed next to her. She lay naked under the covers: she hated nightgowns. Leon reached under her neck and fastened Bata's golden necklace around it. The cold metal and the movement of cushions awakened her. She opened her eyes. They momentarily reflected the dim light coming in from the street, as the curtains were not drawn.

"Oh, it's you," she whispered, "when did you come back? What have you brought me?"

She recoiled as he pressed against her. Her warm body shuddered, she got goose bumps.

"You're so cold," she hugged him tightly and excitedly, snuggling against him as if her body was made for his.

"This is just the beginning," he managed to say.

He slowly sank into her, trying in vain to decelerate his rapid thrusts.

"There's no rush," she sighed, sleepy, clinging to him even tighter.

Their desire soon became untameable. Joined together, they yearned for each other, demanding complete devotion, a passion of total oblivion. Leon was convinced that there were no lies between them, that she was playing no games, which he sensed at times when they were out among other people, walking down the street, or sitting in a bar; no, in bed, they were both supreme rulers of the world, and at the same time owned each other, to the very last atom.

They got up. Kristina walked to the mirror to admire her neck with the gold necklace, while Leon stepped in the shower, contrasting between cold and hot water to wash off the remnants of his long journey and breathlessness from rioting in their bed.

We're not going to shoot. Are we?

The days passed delightfully. They were becoming longer, hotter, it wasn't until late at night that the temperatures dropped down enough to enable people to breathe comfortably. Kristina worked with a young band; they were in the process of staging their first concert, putting the last touches on their first record, and tamely followed the directions given to them by the photographer and the graphic designer in charge of their poster. Leon visited his mother at work, providing her with the opportunity to once again reproach him with the slow progress of his studies and his pointless consorting with the wrong woman. He was ready to quickly disarm her when it came to the first issue. After quite a break, he started attending the university again, he was talking to his fellow students and even borrowed lecture notes from one of his more industrious female colleagues. His mother's secretary swiftly copied them for him. He was convinced he would pass the upcoming exam with flying colours. He didn't care to discuss the situation with Kristina; he refused to respond to any of his mother's comments, which of course angered her even more, but at the same time reassured her of the futileness of her efforts.

The discussion he had with his father was much easier. They spoke about business. His father liked the fact that his son was getting out of peddling at flea markets and getting on a higher level. Nevertheless, tiny warning signs began appearing in the background. Who were these people, exactly, the people his son had been hanging out with? Precious antiques, especially old paintings, were oftentimes shrouded in secretive veils which, once spread open, inevitably caused upholders of law and order to grumble. Did Leon reach slippery ground? If there are any issues, we'll deal with them when they arise, he said to himself, calmingly, only commenting out loud:

"I would hate for us to come under any police scrutiny. You're aware of this, aren't you?"

Leon merely smiled. He knew his father was well connected, with friends among the highest ranks of police officers. If anything did go wrong, he would be able to handle it. That's what friends are for, right? Besides, Bata was surely not so foolish as to push his fingers in the cogwheels of risky adventures. His crew dealt in grand style antique business and not crime, right? The first big deal he made with him brought him several interesting acquaintances and a big step closer to a financially carefree life.

"So, how are things, have you seen the Ulčars lately, how are they doing?" his father tried to lighten the slightly uptight mood.

"Yes, sure, everything's fine, they're kings of the flea market," Leon nodded, finished his coffee and bid farewell.

When he came home, he ran into Kristina at the door, she was late for a recording session. Her business suit was supposed to convey a serious attitude, but in reality everything about her screamed seductiveness, which made it hard to gather one's thoughts. Leon caught her in his arms and kissed her.

She wrestled away from him.

"You're going to ruin my make-up, and I'm so late," she resisted. "Wait until the evening. Would you like to go to the disco? We haven't been there in ages. I need to relax a bit. I won't be long," she said and she was already rushing down the stairs, opening her purse, taking out a hand mirror, fixing her lipstick and catching her balance in her stilettos. Petite clunks against the stone steps were gradually dying down towards the ground floor.

"Ha, disco!" Leon thought to himself. "I bet Ferkolj will be there with his latest enticing sticker-on. We haven't seen each other in a long time, I've been taking different paths lately. But sooner or later I'll have to face him and embark on a relationship of cold, yet calm silence. I guess he'll eventually come to terms with the fact that Kristina left him. It happens, there's nothing one can do about it, and perhaps time has already healed his wounds. I shouldn't have to hide from him for the rest of my life, should I? It's about time we were both able to pass each other peacefully in the street. Will he be sober or drunk, will he give me a hard time? What if he starts wielding axes again?"

His legs almost automatically led him to the wardrobe closet with drawers which were allotted to him by Kristina. He opened the bottom one and took out a parcel wrapped in linen, buried deep under his socks. He unwrapped it. It was a revolver, a Walter, which he got from Ulčar. He took it in his hands, weighing it, almost lovingly. He winced.

"We're not going to shoot," he shuddered. "Are we?"

He reached back in the drawer and took out a box of bullets. He placed two of them in the revolver, then put everything away, back under his socks. He sat in the armchair and absentmindedly started to leaf through the folder containing notes for his exam. He couldn't focus. He felt like he had good command of the subject, like even this one additional read-through was unnecessary. The room was nice and cool and the armchair was captivatingly soft. He struggled for a short while to keep his eyes open, but he couldn't do it. He soon dozed off and only woke up when it was already pitch-black outside, to the noise coming from the door.

"I'm already back!" Kristina yelled from the door. "We finished sooner than I thought."

She turned on the lights and stopped in her tracks in surprise.

"You're sleeping? In the armchair? And with the book...?"

Leon rubbed his eyes.

"I took a little nap," he tried to defend himself and quickly proceeded to question her, "how did it go, did you record everything, who was there?"

"Stop it with the questions, will you," Kristina said hurriedly, "I'm here now, everything was fine, get dressed, won't you, you promised, remember, I'm just going to take a shower and change my clothes..."

Leon felt as if she was tossing words around to swiftly avoid his question - who was there? - and the door to the bathroom already closed. He heard the hum of running water just a moment later. Leon was overcome with a slight tingling of anger, some sort of resistance; then determination seized him, yes, they need to go out right now, yes, to the largest disco, in front of all those people, so that they can see that Kristina is with him, that she is his, that he is worthy of her, even if there were to be a hundred Ferkoljs there, or a hundred owners of recording studios...He changed into a soft, light summer suit, and almost automatically attached his revolver to his belt, just hidden under the hem of his jacket. The tiny bump was hardly visible. Well, then, so be it, just to feel better, to give him some boisterous self-confidence. He was suddenly overcome by ebullient cheerfulness. Who could compete with him now?

Kristina slipped into a short, fluttering ivory dress, which seemed to only fleetingly stop on gorgeous womanly curves, slightly provocatively accentuated by the lines of her darker underwear. She knew how to drive a man crazy. Leon pulled her into his arms and passionately kissed her long, bare neck.

"Hold on," she purred while stroking his hair, "there'll be some dancing first, drinks later, and then..."

They drove over to Valentine, a disco located at the bottom of a hill, which invaded the edge of the largest city park; they struggled to find an available parking space in the lot, then entered the club. It was jam packed; a popular new turbo-folk band and a group of older, experienced musicians performing slightly nostalgic jazz tunes were taking turns on the stage. Dancers of both sexes crammed on the dance floor, moving to the music both in and somewhat out of rhythm. The bar itself was very crowded, as well. The entire room gave off the impression of a great number of people who came here to simply relax, abandoning their problems and etiquette in front of the door in order to surrender to superficial sensuousness without restraint. Prolonged kissing was common on the dance floor, while hands travelled along the paths of overt desire. The owner of the club approached them, pushed the drinkers at the end of the bar aside to make space for two glasses, and promised them to get them to the first available table. As the waiter poured them champagne, the owner leaned over to Leon and whispered in his ear: "Ferkolj is here. He has been alone and drinking a lot. Just so you know, right?"

The waiter had poured drinks countless times in the past for the threesome, which had now become a passionate pair plus a raging redundant third party, thanks to Leon and Kristina. Leon looked around the place, annoyed and attentive, but he couldn't locate Ferkolj. After emptying two glasses each, he and Kristina descended on the dance floor. Her bright dress and golden hair, pulled up high, all in sync with the right rhythm, practically transformed her into a dreamy mirage. They caught many a glance with their loud laughter to wild music, and gentle, soft hands in slow motion. Kristina and Leon moved in total harmony, enjoying their proximity. Her hand suddenly and fleetingly reached under his belly.

"Oh, my, what's this?" she asked naughtily, while her confident and joyous smile clearly provided the answer.

"Not much I can do about it," Leon replied in a hoarse voice, took her face in his hands, brought it closer and gave her a kiss, "I love you tremendously."

"That's right," she returned the kiss, "my man. Love me!" she commanded. "You know that I need a man," she added in playful provocation, "maybe even two."

Leon ignored the sting. He was here now, they were together now, he wasn't going anywhere, he was the master now. He kept pushing away the thought that this could one day change, he took Kristina's brisk comments as fuel to the fire of passionate expectations of everything the night was about to bring.

That's what led him to ignore his surroundings while they were dancing, relaxing and focusing too much on their wild embraces and kisses. After a while they were ready for a break and they made their way to the bar. Kristina ordered a shot of metaxa and promptly emptied the glass, as she was certain that the Greek cognac could indeed momentarily cool down her blood, while Leon had another double Four Roses bourbon.

"Another one?" the waiter asked, but even before Leon could answer, a shriek yell sounded in their immediate vicinity:

"If it isn't the newlyweds!"

Just a step away, leaning on the bar with one arm and barely managing to stay on his feet, there was Ferkolj, with a monstrously drunken grimace on his face, pointing in their direction with his free hand. He grabbed hold of a glass and it looked like he was going to hurl it right in Kristina's face.

"Whore!" he roared. People around them jumped back in surprise, creating a surprisingly large void despite the tight crowd and all the noise. "You whore, so this is it? You can't satisfy serious men, so you started picking on babies?!"

Leon twitched fiercely, clutched his fists and took a menacing step forward, but Kristina held him back, she hid her paleness under heaps of make-up and struck right back.

"Of course," she yelled, "babies happen to fulfil a real woman's needs much better than aging playboys!"

A few people roared with laughter. Ferkolj opened his mouth in surprise, astonished, he momentarily lost his voice, then lunged over to Kristina and grabbed her by the arm.

"What? You think you can..." he hollered, but then lost his train of thought.

A security guard jumped in, at first he just pushed Ferkolj to the side, and then embraced him tightly, securing both his arms, and took him to the other side of the club. Leon and Kristina exchanged glances.

"He's an idiot, what can you do," Kristina said.

"Mhm," Leon hissed through his clenched teeth.

He took deep breaths and his eyes darted around the place. He wanted nothing more than to jump right after Ferkolj, but he realised that having a fight in the club would lead to a great spectacle and uproarious slander all over town, indiscriminately falling on anyone's ears.

"Let's have another drink and then go home," he said, upset.

They were setting off. Once they got close to the exit, Ferkolj once again appeared as if out of nowhere. The security guard had obviously let him go, assured that he had calmed down.

"Hey," he called, "are you taking the baby home, to pee, and poop, and go to sleep? Do I get a kiss good-night?"

He grabbed Kristina's arm and pulled her in. Leon lost it. He leaped over to Ferkolj and aggressively pushed him away, making him stagger on his wobbly legs. Just a second later, he took his revolver from under his jacket, leaned over him, put the gun against his temple and screamed:

"Get lost, you scum! Right now! You'll be looking for your brain in every corner, if you don't!"

It seemed as nothing can stop him in his tremendous rage. Ferkolj immediately went white, his complexion was almost ashen, while Leon's face was flaming red and his hand holding the revolver trembled slightly. He felt his heart beating wildly in his head. The women close to them shrieked, a deadly silence came over the club at first, Kristina froze up, Ferkolj stopped dead in his tracks, his mouth opened. His eyes bulged in horror.

"I, I, I..." he started to stammer.

The owner of the bar hurried to their side and stood in front of Leon.

"For God's sake, Leon, don't do anything stupid. He's drunk, he doesn't know what he's doing," he tried to calm him down, pushing his hand up towards the ceiling. Ferkolj chuckled idiotically and started searching for something he could say.

"Get lost, you idiot!" Leon roared.

Ferkolj winced again, as he realized that Leon was indeed mad; he stood there in surprise for a few moments, then fitfully turned around and ran through the door. Leon kept shaking all over, still holding his revolver up in the air. The club owner then put his arm around him, took his hand and pointed it downwards.

"Give this to me, I'll put it away. If police come, I'll say you had a toy gun, and Ferkolj was drunk out of his mind," he said.

Leon swiftly let go of his gun, shook his head and straightened his jacket. People resumed their conversations, the band struck a dancing tune. Terror was replaced with awe in Kristina's wide open eyes.

"My man," she whispered, draped herself around his neck and kissed him passionately.

"Shall we?" she added, took his hand and gently manoeuvred him to their car.

Leon drove home in a bit of a daze. Did he really use his weapon as a threat? Will this idiot get the hint now and leave them in peace? They were silent the entire way, Kristina kept gently stroking the back of his neck and his hair. They walked up to their apartment in an embrace. Šeri was waiting on the other side of the door, Kristina shoved her away, grabbed Leon by the bulge in his pants and pushed him into their bedroom. She slammed the door shut with her foot, unbuckled Leon's belt and vigorously pulled down his pants. She pushed him to their bed and he fell flat on his back. She removed her fluttering garments with frenzied movements, sat on his face, shivering in excitement, leaned forward and sucked onto his almost rock-hard crotch.

"My man!" she squealed again. "I want to! I want to! I want to! My man!"

They released their tension, fiercely coiled around each other, erased the recent commotion at the club from their memories, and consumed every last bit of what kept them living together. The slumber they fell into afterwards might just stretch as far as the next day if it weren't for the phone which started to ring ferociously, which, in combination with the dog's unsure barking, got Leon to his feet at the first light of day.

Don't ask questions, learn with your eyes and keep your mouth shut

"Hello?" he mumbled in the receiver.

"Hey, my son, it's me, Bata. Are you asleep? Are you working? Have you managed to take on the difficult task?" words kept flying out of the earpiece.

"Is there an earthquake? A coup d'etat?" Leon fumed in response, trying to wake up, checking his watch. "What is this ruckus, first thing in the morning? What's going on?"

"No questions!" Bata commanded in his habitual tone of master ordering around his apprentice. "Get in your car right away and drive over here. I have the silver ready. I need to get it on its way! The money awaits."

Leon rubbed his bleary eyes.

"What silver, where to, why right away..." he pondered and slowly became all ears. He added out loud:

"Where to?"

Then he gathered his thoughts and started to resist:

"I can't, I'm taking Kristina to the seaside, finally, she's going to kill me..."

"Stop talking nonsense! The broad can wait another day, it's not like the world will come to an end if she has to keep her knees together for a while! This is serious business, do you hear me? Stop wasting time, I'm not going to explain it to you over the phone. Come over right away!" Bata ordered and hung up the phone.

Leon filled his lungs with air a few times, exhaling slowly. Back on the road again, and at this very moment, when he had already reserved a prestigious room in Portorož. There would be nothing better right now than to forget all about the last night's commotion in the disco! How can he explain this to Kristina?

But...a business with silver? What silver? Bata had never talked to him as harshly before, he wouldn't take no for an answer. And what was that about some money awaiting? Well, if it's about money, Kristina will probably understand. After all, if he set out right away, he could make it back by the middle of the night. What's one day, and they could sure use the earnings...He stood under the shower for the longest time, clearing his head completely. Bata sounded very decisive. And their recent silver business with Frietzl in Germany thoroughly shifted all kinds of attitudes. Are they about to embark on a similar endeavour? Well, what can you do, I'm off to Belgrade again, he concluded.

Kristina was sound asleep and he didn't have the heart to wake her, especially not in light of having to explain why their vacation would have to be postponed. He sat down and wrote her a message:

"I urgently needed to leave for Belgrade. Good business. I'll be back sometime tonight. You can go to Portorož by yourself, if you like, and wait for me there. I love you."

He filled the bowl with dry dog food and left.

The sun was in his eyes all the way to Zagreb, but the thought of a business which would bring him a large sum of money kept his foot happily on the pedal, all the way to the floor. On the plain leading to Belgrade he found himself dangerously overtaking other cars more than a few times, other drivers, mostly truckers, honked at him and flashed their headlights, but he was well aware of what his Quatrelle was capable of, which meant he stayed relatively safe and only playing with other people's nerves.

Bata was waiting for him in his mother's living room, holding a newspaper and chain smoking. He didn't even offer him coffee; he immediately got to his feet.

"You're good, son, this was fast. Fast action is required to grab double luck! Come on, let's go. We'll have coffee when we get there!"

"Where?" Leon asked after freeing himself from Bata's mother's embrace.

"My dear boy," she turned to Bata, "you're going to be the end of this kid from Ljubljana. You keep dragging him into your dubious business, when he should be studying. What's this all about? Let the man breathe, let him sit down for a moment, so I can talk to him a little!"

"Stop it, mother! He can breathe all he wants, and sit all he wants, too, but not right now. Let's go!" Bata bellowed somewhat nervously. "Let's go!"

"To Pančevo!" he commanded once in the car.

"To Rista?" Leon simultaneously asked and agreed.

The moment they were on their way, Bara turned in his passenger seat to face Leon.

"I have to tell you something straight away: you're going to witness some things you have never even dreamed about. I've made my decision: you're really going to be my second pair of eyes and hands. You'll learn the secrets of great masters. There are very few people who know about them and you're to keep it all to yourself. Not a word to anyone! No one! Not your father, or your mother, or, God forbid, Kristina! You're about to witness a miracle in real life," he kept explaining feverishly, clenching his palms into fists, flailing them about.

Leon almost physically felt the weight of layers of extraordinary, mysterious atmosphere coming down on him, and he couldn't fathom what in the world Bata was going on about. Was everything finally about to become clear?

"A miracle..." he repeated in astonishment.

"More than that! I've decided: you're finally becoming a part of our team, we'll live and we'll die together. Whatever you'll witness, whatever will happen at Rista, you need to accept it like it goes without saying. Don't ask questions, learn with your eyes and keep your mouth shut!"

Leon could hardly focus from all the excitement. He was trying to navigate safely among the potholes on the road. They finally arrived at Rista's house. This time, Bata jumped right out of the car and opened the double gates in the fence; Leon drove onto the grassy patch next to the lounging set. The noise of their car prompted Rista to come out of the house. He wore a long leather apron over the white shirt clinging to his back, sweat was running down his forehead, and he held a silver candlestick in his loosely gloved hands.

"Welcome, gentlemen," he smiled. "We'll be ready in just a moment. That's when your brain comes in, Bata, we'll need it. And it goes without saying," he turned to Leon, "your dexterity. I hope you have the guts Bata has been praising you for."

He offered Leon his elbow in place of a handshake, and only gave a nod to Bata. They entered the main room and from there went on into a large workshop. A number of various experts were standing or sitting around an extensive table - five of them all together, why, this is a small factory, Leon thought to himself - while three women were sitting at a long counter by the outwards facing window. The men kept polishing, cutting, forging, embellishing, and etching different silver items, and the women were obviously busy buffing them. A few pieces, seemingly finished, were lying on the centre of the table, and Bata immediately reached for a large candlestick. He kept turning it around in his hands, looking at it from every possible angle; then he brought a magnifying glass from his pocket and inspected each square centimetre. He was obviously looking for the hallmark. He motioned for Leon to follow his example and Leon got to work. He recognized some of the pieces as those he and Bata got from Frietzl. They were processed, but there were no hallmarks on them. Who would be foolish enough to take them off?

"Easy, son, easy," Bata smiled slowly. "Can't you see that these masters here have changed the present into past? Every piece we brought has been forged into something else. Surely you notice the difference in styles?"

"Every fool can notice that," Leon almost burst out, as he couldn't for the life of him comprehend what was going on. "But everything is shining and gleaming, all the contemporary items have suddenly turned to Baroque, Renaissance, Empire, yet there is no patina, and there are no hallmarks anywhere! No one is going to buy this!"

"Take it easy, easy, my boy," Bata kept reassuring him, "everything in its own time, these things aren't finished yet. Patina will be applied next. The grand master Rista has loads of patina; he lifted it off the pieces he had processed in the past. Now we will use electrolysis to transfer the patina onto our pieces, and no person in the world will even think of dating them to modern times."

Leon was left speechless, he ran his hand over his forehead.

"A mint of forgeries?" he suddenly realised. "It can't be?"

"Don't sound so surprised, son, we know what we're doing. This workshop of ours has been operating for five years now, producing some of the finest pieces of silver in the world. They are brilliant copies; no one can expose them as forgeries. They hold up to every expert's scrutiny. Now you can see all that is possible. This is an unparalleled secret. If someday you find yourself in a situation when somebody asks you for a practically non-existent piece, you can simply come here and produce it. With slight corrections by Rista the master genius, of course."

Bata looked at Rista, who stood up proudly and nodded.

"Ok then," Leon remembered, "but what about the hallmarks?

Where do you plan to get those?"

"Your head is in the right place, my boy," Bata looked at him happily, unable to conceal his pride in the fact that his apprentice was a quick learner. "It would show if we simply engraved the hallmarks. That's why," he proudly banged his chest, "we have every hallmark that has ever existed!"

Leon almost froze to the ground. What he just heard was downright impossible.

"Mijat!" Rista called. "Bring out the hallmarks!"

The round-faced Mijat, who had been listening to the conversation while working at the table, bent down and took a large wooden box out of a nearby cupboard. It looked like an old toolbox, the kind traditional typesetters used to have; it had a myriad of tiny crates, marked with letters and years. These crates held hallmarks, pinned to short steel rods.

"Here we go, Bata, which ones shall we imprint?" he grinned.

"Take it easy, Mijat, my friend," Bata grew serious. "Go back to your work. This is where I come in. I need to search my mind for original items I held in my hands in the past, and think about how to approach this. I need to figure out the years, decide on the styles, think carefully about the workshops. Come along, son, you can help me. You're part of our team now. You're one of us."

He pulled two chairs to the table and reached for a small silver jewellery box. In the crate labelled Raguza - ha, ha, the old Dubrovnik, Leon thought to himself - were just three hallmarks. Their markings denoted three different time periods, each covering around fifty years. The silver box was not special in any way, it could have been manufactured by many different masters. That's why Bata decided on a hallmark which was most common with silver items of this kind, a neutral and hardly noticeable one, found all over Europe. The item wasn't something that collectors in the market would fight for, but it could nevertheless bring a neat amount of money.

"Mile, come here!" Bata called. "You can imprint the hallmark on this little thing, and then you can return to your work."

An older man got up from the opposite end of the table. He wore a long grey moustache and a cap, he looked like he had just stepped out of a painting by Paja Jovanović. He held a medium sized hammer for processing copper in his hand. He picked up the steel rod with a hallmark on one end with his other hand.

"Where do you want it imprinted?" he asked.

"First place the box on the wooden base, and put a rag underneath. Then turn everything over; you'll place the hallmark under the rim, so it can't be seen right away... Hey, wait. You'll have to imprint it from the other side, just like a master would have done once he finished the box," Bata explained. "That's it, right here in the middle, and a bit to the side, so it looks like the master had imprinted it by the way, not reaching the same depth all around."

Mile stamped the hallmark, raised the box, inspected it and handed it over to Bata.

"Will this do?" he asked.

Bata immediately gave the box to Leon and said:

"You check it. Will it do?"

Leon picked up a magnifying glass, kept looking at the hallmark for ages, and then again at the whole box. The hallmark was perfectly stamped, as if it had been there for the last quarter of a century.

"It's fine," he said finally, "but what about the patina?"

"Don't worry, we'll get to that in a moment, young man," Mile smiled.

They went into the room next door. In there, a young woman was brushing silver items with phosphorous acid, or patina. She wore a long leather apron and was well protected, just in case she got some acid on her by accident. She took the jewellery box and started coating it. Bata interrupted her, instructing her to only use a thin layer, to make it look as if the box was buffed regularly, while the hallmark at the bottom should appear darker, and the edges somewhat green. At first, the box appeared even whiter. What in the world was she doing, getting rid of the tiny bit of patina which was already there?! Leon wondered silently. The coating had not dried entirely, when she started adding a grey-green and purple layer, fresh phosphorus acid. The box was beginning to take on exactly the kind of patina Bata required. The woman swiftly reached for a piece of cloth and created a tatty striped look on selected parts. Once the piece darkened, she started buffing it, leaving the edges dark. Finally, she took a tiny brush and applied dark green patina in several places. Leon stared at Bata.

"Yes," Bata nodded. "We used acid to take this green patina off some ancient Roman coins, and we're now using acid to replace it where we want it to go!"

The woman switched brushes and blackened the iron rods in miniscule hinges, additionally covering them with rust. She used the same patina to colour the hallmark, as well.

"There you go," she said. "Now we just have to dry it for a while in the oven, at one hundred degrees. The original will be ready in half an hour."

Bata nodded, indicating to Leon that it was time they returned to the main room. Once there, Bata inspected every item and selected the hallmarks which were to endow them with signs of renowned ancient workshops and appropriate age.

Leon sat by his side, mesmerised. Here, in the middle of the Pannonian Plain, he learned a lesson he had never even seen in the movies, let alone in restoration studios of prominent museums he had visited in the course of his studies. People just had no idea what was possible. He felt magnificent. He became part of a story, a special story, unparalleled in the entire world. He felt like he was about to burst, but he realised that silence was a promise he could not afford to break. Hello, world, here I come! he smiled to himself. He remembered the question Šotra asked Bata upon their happy return from Frietzl: Did you get it from Rista? - and he also remembered how Bata swore that he had bought it in Zagreb. That meant that Bata's best man knew about this, too.

"Everything will be ready by this evening," Rista brought him out of his contemplation. "We'll pack everything nicely and load it into your car. The girls will come over soon, to handle the paperwork, just in case cops show too much interest in your goods. You should already know the rest, or Bata will explain it to you. And now, sit down and have a drink. We've done a fine job."

He and Bata reclined in woven loungers in the yard; the mighty walnut tree provided the necessary shadow. One of the women from the workshop brought over a large pot of coffee and set it on the table. She was soon followed by Rista, carrying a three-litre fiasco.

"There's no hallmark," he chuckled, "but it's old. You can take my word for it. I'll join you later."

Bata grabbed the fiasco with his right hand, opened the cork and swung it over his raised elbow. He only drank brandy in his own house or when he visited his friends, just to make sure the drink was genuine. In bars, he only drank whiskey out of fear he could damage his digestion and liver with a miserable home-made discharge from some backwater brewery. He took two long swigs, weighing the fiasco a bit, as if to see if there was anything left, and then placed it on the table in front of Leon. His throat produced a sound, a deep belch, almost from the depths of his stomach.

"It's good, double distilled plum brandy," he commented, wiping his mouth with the back of his right palm. "We'll empty it by the evening. Rista has a few more barrels of this in the basement."

Leon took just one, shorter swig. He felt a pleasant burning in his throat, but he knew better than to follow his hosts' lead if he were to return to Ljubljana by midnight. There was no way he could keep up with them.

"So, what are the orders?" he sked. "Where should I take the silver treasures to?"

Bata gave him a serious look.

"Well, my son, my hero, this is where it begins. I've arranged a deal for some of the items with Frietzl, if there's anything left, you're off to Brussels. Of course now that you've become a partner, you'll get a man's share, which means we divide the profits. If you know of any buyers, be my guest. But don't even think of coming back with less than half a million! I hope this is clear."

He grabbed the fiasco again and drank. Leon kept silent, making feverish calculations in his head. If the silver, the raw material required for all these antiques, cost fifty thousand when they bought it from Frietzl, and the same amount has to be allotted for the pairs of working hands, this leaves four hundred thousand, divided by, ahem, divided by, well, ahem, divided by, well, Rista, and Bata, and myself. Divided by three! He almost blacked out and started shivering. Could this be for real?

Bata was cheering up.

"Calm down, my son. I need you to stay cool. After this we will embark on a new story, one never before witnessed in the whole world, more beautiful and better, one that will make this today look like small change, do you understand, small change! I sense something unbelievable. You just come back quickly with the money, alright? The money is the basis for everything! I need it for new investments!"

He took several additional swigs from the fiasco and purred contentedly.

After some time, Mijat appeared, asking Leon to open the boot of his car. Two cardboard boxes were carried from the house and loaded in his Quatrelle. Leon observed the action as if in a trance, all the while wondering if this was for real or could he be dreaming. A short while later, the woman who transferred patina to the silver beforehand emerged from the house and handed him an envelope. It contained two copies of a receipt, stating that the company Ristić and sons had issued twenty kilograms of silver items to Dota Company for commission sale, in accordance with the attached customs record, and that the purchase price, once the expenses were deducted, was to be transferred to the stated bank account in thirty days following the sale. The collection of goods was certified by the signature of Leon Sattler, authorised to do so by the company. Leon fiddled with the papers in astonishment.

"You look amazed? We're not kids, are we? This is your collateral," Rista laughed and went back to his workshop.

Leon turned to Bata, equally thrilled and unsure.

"But," he said, "all of these forgeries won't there be experts checking them for the buyers, there are tests, analyses, how in the...?"

"Our Rista is a genius, a natural talent. There isn't a thing he couldn't forge, and everything he does stands up to every test. This is of course a matter of money, but it's also about his self-importance and pride: I'm the best in the whole world, that's what he says. A silver bowl of his sat in an antique shop at London's Piccadilly for a whole month, fifteen kilos of silver; it was presented as a master piece out of Faberge's workshop. Every expert confirmed its authenticity. A Spanish museum bought a bowl once owned by the Knights of Malta, a piece dating back to the sixteenth century, which was, of course, Rista's work. I could go on for ages," Bata explained.

"But how, where did he study, where did he learn?" Leon kept asking, as he still felt like he was listening to a fairy-tale.

"He didn't," Bata shook his head, "he barely made it through high-school. He went on to the academy, but he never finished. He does read a lot, ha ha, well he's being read to, to be exact. He sits back in his chair and his lovers read to him...He's incredibly well-read. Plus, of course, he studies reproductions of antique works in detail, he knows everything by heart. You can ask him to draw Napoleon Bonaparte's goblet or Suleiman the Magnificent's sword, and he will draw every last detail. Our Rista really knows how to use his women, and don't even get me started on the cooking, ha ha!"

Leon was left speechless. After a while he came to.

"But...here, in the middle of this plain, so far away from everything, how can he know what to make, what can be sold?"

Bata chuckled as if to say, this is where I tried to get you.

"Naturally, Rista's dexterous hands need my clever mind. I can feel the market, I know what's in demand, so I organize things. Recently I've heard, for instance, of a Russian oligarch looking for a set of silver jewellery boxes with enamel coated tops; so I brought two experts in enamel drawing from Saint Petersburg, from the Hermitage, to be more exact, I added Rista, who is a master in silver, to the mix, and we produced it, and aged it," Bata explained, adding gravely, "now you know all of this, you're one of us. Do you realize who you're with, what you're going to do? You're about to become a rich man and a crook; if everything goes well, you'll make money, and pay a price if you talk about it. Rista won't budge from this place, he refuses to travel, he doesn't know how to sell. Behind this fence, he's his own state...This means he needs us just as much as we need him."

"I need to drink to this after all," Leon replied, in awe and conscious of the fact that everything was indeed possible. He took a swig from the fiasco and again immersed himself in his thoughts.

He felt like he was coming to a new breakthrough moment in his life. The first one happened last year, when he got himself into quite a challenge without even realising: he left his home and moved in with a woman he loved blindly, which almost caused a serious break with his parents. With this going on, his studies seemed to naturally fade into the background. But his parents were bound to come to terms with the facts sooner or later, especially when they will realise how much money he was making. And his studies? Well, he would graduate eventually, as this was part of basic hygiene, but it certainly wouldn't be his priority, as he would be well off. Kristina? He was never able to think clearly when it came to her, she'd bewitched him. Their worlds were quite different, they never had profound conversations, they were bound together by unstoppable attraction and passion. They spent some wild time together and then they were off living out their respective plans and desires. How much space was there left for the other on either side? When would the things they had in common run out? Would they? Would there come a time when Kristina showed him the door, just as she had invited him in, just as she had shown the door to Ferkolj? Leon kept pushing away this thought, but it kept lingering in the background and occasionally appeared unannounced right in front of him. He took solace in the thought that sex and occasional wads of banknotes thrown on the table should provide a sufficient solution to these issues. For the time being or forever? Would the ten-year-difference between them at one point become an issue? Was his mother right? What did Kristina make of this? She was surely very dedicated to her own work, which was selling beauty. And that was a field filled with smiling moguls who had already amassed their fortunes and could make her dreams come true without any delay. Well, he grinned, thinking about the wild nights, almost all of them. Besides, he, too, was about to start ascending the financial ladder. Bata took him in as one of his own. And it wasn't just words. He backed them with magnificent actions. Now I entered this world myself. I'm his partner now. There was a new, giant step, a new breakthrough. We'll see what time brings.

It was late afternoon when he left for Ljubljana. Bata stayed at Rista's; they embarked on the joint mission of emptying the fiasco of old plum brandy. They were ready to open another one, too, if need arose. The first half of the latest business deserved to be marked by a proper ceremony, including well wishes for its conclusion.

Leon turned into an exemplary driver. On one hand, he was dancing in the sky in his mind; pleasingly warm with the thought that the new business combination with Bata meant an end to all financial problems. He doubted anyone could match what he would be able to offer to Kristina from now on, or so he tried to persuade himself. On the other hand, he kept a firm grip on the steering wheel, as he knew that a long road like this one could drive a man crazy; it would be a shame to lose his concentration and spill the silver load all over the worn out asphalt, to the delight of strangers. That was why he kept driving slowly and steadily. Ha, a thought suddenly went through his mind. Where am I going to store the treasure? In the Quatrelle in front of the house? Behind the decrepit entrance door to the building? It's not like I'm going to set off to Germany right away. I need to go to the seaside, at least for a day or two, postponing it would cause Kristina too much disappointment. With Tone in the Dota, with his parents? This would raise too many unwanted and annoying questions, there would be too much to explain and nothing to say. Nope. Then he thought of the Ulčars. They lived in a large, very spacious house with iron crosses on their windows, they were interested in antiques; they were his friends, he could trust them. He would ring their bell, if they were still up, and asked them, just for a few days...

"Right, this should be the safest option. And no one will know anything!"

It was close to midnight when he reached the outskirts of Ljubljana and took a turn towards Polje. As tired as he was, he was pleased to see that the lights were still on at the Ulčars' house. He stopped the car in front of it and rang the doorbell. After quite some time, he heard a man's voice from the other side of the front door:

"Who is it?"

"It's me, papa Ulčar, Leon. I apologize, but I need your help urgently."

The key scratched the lock first, followed by the bolt, and Ulčar opened the door.

"Well, what's this about? Did you have an accident?" he asked worriedly.

He took off his glasses, holding a newspaper in his hand.

"No, not at all," Leon laughed, "I've just returned from Belgrade, I got some stuff there and I've nowhere to store it, so I was wondering..."

"Holy cow!" Ulčar acted upset. "He has nowhere to store his junk, so he's scaring honest folks in the middle of the night. Does it look like I operate a public storage house?"

He grinned, turned on the porch light, then the light in the stairway down to the basement, where he opened a door to a room.

"Here," he said, opening a large chest. "This should suffice, what do you think?"

Leon swiftly transferred both boxes into the basement. Ulčar closed the chest, handed one of the keys to Leon and pocketed the other.

"I hope you don't blow my house up," he mumbled, adding, "Shall we have a drink now?"

Leon quickly shook his head:

"Thank you so much, papa Ulčar, you're a life saver. I'm in a hurry to get home..."

"Oh," Ulčar flashed a cunning smile, "to that woman of yours... hmm, is your mother still upset about it? Why am I even asking, of course she is. Oh well, but you'll have to deal with this issue yourself, it's about time, don't you think?"

"Well, I guess..." Leon shrugged. "Thank you so much. I'm off!"

He drove back to the city.

Lights were on in his own house, as well, and he heard the sound of running water coming out of the bathroom. He checked the time, it was almost one in the morning, and he stopped in surprise. A shower, at this time of night? He sat down in his chair and crossed his legs on the coffee table. After some time, Kristina emerged, wrapped in a towel.

"Oh," she winced and seemed almost a bit scared while trying to hold on to the towel. "What are you doing here? You're back already?"

At first, Leon wanted to inquire about the reason for her late shower, but the sight tempted him, so he jumped up and pushed his hands under the towel. She resisted him slightly.

"So this is your idea? You disappear from the bed, leaving me a note, going God knows where, and I'm supposed to meekly wait for you? Like we weren't even living together? Should I look for another man?" the words kept flying out of her mouth.

Leon froze in astonishment; he wasn't entirely sure if she was joking or being serious. He swallowed his resentment. He was driving like crazy the entire day, entered a new chapter with Bata in order to get the money needed to lull them in luxury, and this was the reception he got. To be fair, she didn't know what had happened. He was too tired to explain all of it.

"Ok, alright, I apologize, but I'm here now. The moment you open your tired little eyes in the morning, we'll head off to the seaside. Ok?"

He thought he noticed red markings, mild abrasions on her naked body, especially on her neck, but he was too tired to pay attention to it.

Everyone wants white bread but no one wants to hoe the land

In a narrow hallway of a small one storey house in Belgrade's Banovo brdo, where the floor was playfully lit by sunrays coming through a small window, a phone rang, and just kept ringing and ringing. It rang impatiently, relentlessly and loudly. Whoever was calling was obviously certain that someone would pick up the phone sooner or later. Fane the Captain came staggering out of his bedroom. He was an antique dealer who had spread his collector's tentacles all over the countryside, looking for goods which he later personally sought more prominent buyers for in the city. Back in the day, he would tow containers along the Danube; but once he witnessed several of his colleagues getting on in years, it scared him, so he retired prematurely and settled on dry land. As a belated hippie in his forties, a long-haired bohemian, he now made a decent living dealing with antiques.

He was all crumpled up and unshaven. Who the hell was trying to get him out of bed after a drinking bout at his neighbour's house?

"Who is it?" he muttered, pissed, peering through the window into his orchard. The plum trees would bear well this year. The heavily laden branches stooped almost all the way to the ground.

"It's me, my good patron Fane, it's me, Gipsy," the voice on the other side hurtled, "I've got something for you."

"You must be out of your mind, you miserable man, it's not even ten o'clock, and you're waking me up in the middle of the night for God knows what nonsense. Leave me alone..."

"No, patron, no," Gipsy quickly went on, "this is important! You're interested in old papers and paint, and I've found heaps of them, for you, my patron, for you."

"Where did you find it, how did you find it?" Fane asked more calmly now, as he had come to terms with the fact that he would have to get up, pulling his slipping trousers up over his belly.

"In a basement, in a house back in town..."

"And I'm supposed to deal with this now?" Fane kept asking sullenly; he had awoken to the new day just enough to be able to turn on his dealer's tone of voice.

"The paper is very old, and the paints are old, still in their original packaging, my patron, I want to sell them to you," Gipsy was almost pleading by then.

"And what am I to do with this junk? Call the garbage collectors, why are you bothering me about it? I'm not a painter, what good are paints to me!"

"Oh, Fane, my patron, come on now, buy it, my children are starving, buy it, I beg you," Gipsy pleaded.

"Alright then, what do we have here?" Fane relented, still vehemently reluctant, as he started to ponder what could it be that the persistent Gipsy had found.

Gipsy, a man with thick curly black hair and undeterminable age, lived with his wife and kids in a construction shack which was left behind next to a nearby apartment building. His official job was caring for the neighbouring park, mowing the grass and cutting the shrubs, but in reality he was dealing in every possible way, for everyone to see, and always saw to it that he was left with some of the money. He regularly updated Fane with off the record information on old objects circulating around the neighbourhood. As a gipsy patron, Fane was sometimes brought a young gipsy girl to revive his lust for life. For this reason, he didn't mind listening to Gipsy when he called on him, despite his seeming anger, as many a times good stories came out of it.

"I'll come by with my car, and I don't want to get stuck in any potholes," he added.

Gipsy gave him directions and Fane slowly drove off in his Wartburg. At the beginning of a narrow alley which he had almost no difficulty finding, he caught sight of Gipsy from far away. He was waving and yelling, informing Fane that he had reserved a parking spot just for him, despite the fact that the alley was completely empty.

"Come, my patron, follow me!"

They went in through a fairly neglected entrance to an old two-storey house, and descended down the stairs into a dark, cool basement. The basement reeked of rotten apples, coal, decaying wood and dampness. Gipsy pushed open a low, grey-green door, already barely hanging on to the rusted hinges and scraping over the concrete floor. The room they entered was poorly lit by the light coming through the narrow windows located just under the top of the exterior wall; Gipsy flipped a switch and a lightbulb attached to a simple wire hanging from the ceiling started flickering.

Wooden shelves lined the walls and filled the space; they were stacked to the brim with different sized and labelled cardboard boxes; watercolours, crayons, oil paints, glasses filled with pigments in every colour, packets of glue, long lines of glass bottles were covered in thick dust, yet the drawing of a pelican was still clearly discernible on the labels, and items' serial numbers were cast in raised-relief on the bottom brims of the glass jars. Alarm bells started ringing in Fane's head, and his hunting pedlar's instinct came to life: attention, this is indeed old! And right after that: I wonder who would be interested in this.

"What have I told you, oh my patron, right, there's some good stuff for you here!" Gipsy sucked up to Fane, waiting for some signs of professional approval to appear on his face. "You'll buy it, won't you?"

Fane stepped further into the room and kept uncovering boxes and boxes of art supplies, all covered with decent layers of dust. He reached a deep cabinet at the far wall and opened it. He couldn't believe his eyes: packages and roles of the finest paper, some of it hand-made, carrying German, Swiss, Chinese and Italian markings, and of course a large parcel of paper labelled "Vevče paper mill," complete with a ribbon and seal of the monopoly of the Kingdom of Yugoslavia. As he started at the protective wrappers on the tall rolls, he uncovered several types of canvas, finely weaved, some already primed with gesso, made of rough sackcloth, manufactured with looms, out of linen and hemp; it was crazy, crazy, crazy. A giant warehouse of an art supply store, which no one had entered in decades. A miracle in a forgotten damp cellar. Fane momentarily got lost in his dreams. He was of course brought right back to reality by Gipsy, who kept talking and talking.

"Hey," Fane briskly interrupted him, "hold on. How much do you want for this heap of old junk?"

Gipsy leaped instantly:

"Give me ten thousand, my patron! This is just for you!"

"Have you lost your mind?" Fane shrieked. "You want ten grand for this rubbish? I'm not Rockefeller, man! Here, take a thousand, and off you go!"

Gipsy stammered:

"Don't, patron, I beg you, don't treat me so roughly, I'm a poor man, I have five kids at home, all crying, we don't have any food, patron, at least give me five thousand, so I can show my kids what a piglet tastes like, come on, my patron..."

"I can't," Fane was shaking his head. "All of this is old and useless. You won't get anyone pay a penny for this. Here, I'll give you two grand, but you have to haul it all nicely to Pera the Horse's yard in one hour, I'll give you the rest there. Are we clear?"

Gipsy nodded promptly. He had set the asking price wisely. He still had some left after the haggling. He was content, he had made a deal for that day. It would be enough to buy food, he would set some to the side for spirits and it would make Saljmira, who liked her drink, lively in bed.

"Thank you, Fane, you are a true gipsy patron!"

Fane the Captain, a gipsy patron, put on a face of a man spending too much money out of kindness, went out to get some fresh air, and then slowly drove off to Pera the Horse, while Gipsy quickly started to load the goods from the basement into his ancient Trabant.

Pera the Horse was at his house, drinking coffee and reading a newspaper. He started making fun the moment Fane the Captain appeared at his door.

"The times we live in! It's been seven days without any business. Do retired people have no need for money anymore? Someone should lower their pensions! Then you'd see them carrying stuff to Pera the Horse, enough stuff for at least two red horses. Alas, it seems nobody needs these banknotes!"

Pera the Horse swiftly demonstrated through his utterances where his nickname had come from. He liked Augustinčić's horse on the red banknote, a drawing of the Peace Monument sculpture (a woman riding a horse), the original version of which stood in front of the United Nations' building in New York. Hardly anyone knew what his real last name was.

"Stop the cussing, my friend, let me have some coffee, and I'll tell you the good deed that I've done for you," Fane interrupted him.

"You have?"

"I have."

"Speak up then!" Pera demanded.

"The stuff is already being brought to your yard! Make me some coffee if your wife is out of the house, so I can tell you all about the deal in peace," Fane asked in a friendly manner.

Pera disappeared into the kitchen and came back after a while with a pot of freshly made coffee. Fane took a sip and slowly started to recount the story that unfolded earlier in the morning.

"And where is this stuff now?" Pera asked with fire in his eyes, once Fane finished his story.

"I told you, my dear man, it's on its way to your yard, I've brought it right to your feet."

At that moment they heard the coughing sound of the loaded Trabant. An incredulous apparition rolled into the yard: an old eastern non-German car, almost buckling, but not quite, and on it, boxes, rolls, scrolls, loaded to three times the height of the vehicle...Gipsy was hardly visible at the steering wheel, as he was completely covered with stacks of paper. Only his black eyes shot joyous looks through the windscreen. He got out of the car with considerable difficulty.

"Fane, my patron, I wouldn't put up with such torment like this for anyone but you," Gipsy swore, straightened his back and beat the dust off his trousers.

Then he saw Pera.

"Good day, master Pera, make sure to open your eyes now, because you're about to see something you've never seen before in your life."

He started tossing the cargo out of his car.

"Will you stop, for heaven's sake!" Pera yelled, "you'll break everything, you ignorant gipsy spawn. Give it a rest! Leave it alone if you don't know how to handle it!"

Fane and Pera overtook the task of loading the boxes and rolls on old tables and chests strewn all over Pera's yard; they were careful not to cause more damage than was already done. Absolutely nothing went on the ground.

Gipsy happily grabbed the cup of coffee Fane had only started to drink from before and left on a table next to the front door; he sat on the steps, contentedly sipping the black potion, lit up a white Drina cigarette and murmured:

"Haha, I laboured before, now it's your turn, masters, put in some work while Gipsy takes pleasure in watching you."

Fane and Pera were out of breath when they finished the job, and Fane called:

"Uh-uh, Gipsy, you miserable human being, this is not all of it!

There was much more stuff down in that basement! Don't tell me you sold half of it to someone else?"

"No, no, my patron, I'll go right back there and load the rest. Just let me have my coffee in peace. Thank you, master Pera."

He jumped back into his Trabant. As Gipsy drove off, Pera quickly closed the gate.

"This is a miracle!" he cried, "it's impossible, all pre-war stuff, brushes, paints, canvases, sketchbook...Fane, this is pure gold. What do you intend to do with it?" he asked.

"I'm not sure yet. That's why I'm here," Fane explained. "Let's each pay for half of it, then sell it and split the profits."

"How much did you pay for this?"

"Oh, it was nothing, only fifty grand," Fane fired without hesitation. "I practically got it for free."

They shook hands and sat at the table. It was time to think about how to put the stuff into money. Who could be interested in this and who would be willing to fork over a decent amount of cash for it? Gipsy made two more rides.

The day soon took a turn which promised there would be no more need for complaining about lack of business.

Bata rattled the gate.

"What the hell are you hiding in there, Pera?" he yelled. "Open up. It's just me. The tax officers will be coming after you some other time!"

Bata was just finishing his afternoon stroll. He took a short nap at home after lunch, then set off to his favourite place. There was always a table for him on the terrace of the Majestic Hotel. The waiter quickly brought over a stack of newspapers, Turkish coffee and a glass of mineral water. They didn't even have to utter a word. Theirs was a ritual filled with silent understanding among men. Bata put on his gold framed Cartier glasses, though he really only needed them to get a more accurate look of the street, where all kinds of women ventured into the crowd as the afternoon heat started to wane. He liked pretending to read, while letting his eyes glide cheerfully along summer dresses which often revealed more than they kept hidden, and from time to time female sweat made the thin fabric of blouses or pants stick to their owners' curves, inspiring wanton thoughts with their alluring jiggle.

But today, Bata was not at ease with everything he had on offer. He had seemed quite indisposed for days. There was no word from the young Leon from Ljubljana, he hasn't been answering his phone, and Bata had no information on how the sale of precious silver antiques was going. It got even worse. There was no money coming in, although he needed it badly, some for his house and some for his deals. To be fair, the business somehow froze despite it being summer. There was nothing relevant on the table, no word of any decent bankruptcy which would force a wealthy family to sell off pieces of old furniture, paintings or other valuables in order to steer clear of it, all too familiar merchandise in antique shops was aging even further.

He finished his coffee, paid for it and headed off to Pera the Horse. He needed some conversation, some solace and to get away from the depressing atmosphere. When there is nothing going on, when there is no business and no money, it helps to visit a friend, sit together in silence for a while and stare into the distance. Maybe even have a drink. He walked to the entrance of the house and rang the bell. Nothing stirred on the other side of the door. He rang again, then knocked, nothing. It was weird. Pera the Horse never left his house. It was always other people who came to see him. Bata walked around the corner and banged on the side door. Again, nothing. He walked further still, to the back yard, and gawked: the permanently open gate in the tall wooden fence was closed. He kicked the gate, but it wouldn't budge. He found that even weirder. He took a step closer and peered into the yard through a crack. Uh-uh, there was Fane the Captain's Wartburg parked in the middle of some junk. So there was something going on! What were they up to?

Professional jealousy made the blood in his veins boil and he started banging on the door and yelling wildly.

"Open up, for God's sake, Horse, it's me, Bata!"

It was now Pera the Horse's turn to speak.

"Hold on, man, you're going to break my door down. What are you hollering about? Is the world coming to an end? Has the government collapsed?"

He opened the bolt and let Bata in the yard.

Bata was catching his breath and nursing his sore fist.

"No government ever collapses in this stupid country!" he answered and started ranting. "There are no Turks, no Germans invading anymore. Why are you hiding, what kind of a conspiracy have the two of you been plotting? What is it that Bata isn't supposed to know?"

"Calm down, have a seat, have some coffee. Fane and I were just talking about you. You couldn't come round at a better moment. Would you like it soft or sharp?" Pera asked, offering Bata some schnapps.

Bata kept mumbling for a bit and calmed down, but of course noticed immediately that the yard was filled with things uncharacteristic for the place: boxes of paints, inks, large rolls...hmm.

"Just pour, don't ask, you know I like it aged and sharp. But what's this, did you rob a store, what have you crammed your yard with?"

"Art stuff, old stuff, pre-war, paints and canvases," Pera hurried to explain, but Fane soon interrupted him:

"Well, Bata, you're the master. What shall we do with this? You should know how to turn this to cash."

Bata flinched and stopped dead in his tracks. He was suddenly struck with the memory of the catalogue of the Paris exhibition, the one he acquired while buying that old bookcase in Zagreb. He studied the catalogue carefully when he got back home and inquired about Šlomovič's art collection, which was partly lost during the war, supposedly because the train transporting it to Belgrade was bombed by German planes. He found himself instantly floating among the paintings presented in the catalogue. The paintings were of a similar age than the stuff he was looking at in the yard. God must have been thinking of him.

"Would you buy it?" Fane's voice brought him back to reality.

"Who in the world would be interested in some old paper and oil paints? The ones used today have a fast-drying effect. And no one is priming canvases with gesso anymore..." he began, as befits a good pedlar.

"Should we offer it to someone else then?" Fane pushed him deceptively. "You're not interested? What about restorers? You must know a lot of them abroad. You're the master when it comes to these things, everyone knows it."

"Oh, abroad, abroad. You think I should haul all of this to Amsterdam, pay the customs and crawl around the stores there with this in tow?" Bata started grumbling. "I should make next to nothing."

"What about if you offered it to Rista from Pančevo? He might know how to turn it into something useful," Pera suggested.

Bata instantly shivered. Of course, Rista could make wonders with this. And he will! But not on his own. I need to tell him how and what, I need to guide him. My hand will show him the way. I just need to get Fane and Pera out of this story as soon as possible!

"Something has just come to my mind," he said swiftly and lied, "I know a restorer back in Zagreb. I could ask him if he wants it. How much do you want for it?"

Pera and Fane exchanged looks. They hadn't had the time to discuss this. Fane struck out on his own.

"We were thinking about fifteen thousand," he said.

"Of what? Dinars?" Bata immediately turned back into his old cunning self.

"Don't be a fool!" Fane lost his temper. "You know exactly what of. Deutschmarks. You can pay us in Yen if you like."

"You're the fools, not I. Everyone wants white bread but no one wants to hoe the land. What a crazy country! Someone's hauled this in for you from God knows where, and you're selling it like it's pure gold. I'm supposed to toil all over and get left with a measly one hundred marks. No, thank you. I'll give you a grand and a half tomorrow, if that's fine with you, and another five hundred in a month, when I sell it," Bata proposed.

"That won't work, Bata, you know how much canvas goes for today," Fane picked up.

"Hell, no, not these old rags," Bata resisted.

At this point, Pera the Horse joined the conversation.

"What are you two idiots going crazy for?! Why are you insulting each other?! Let's talk like men. This is what I had in mind, Milorad, my friend, you can sell this for a good price, sure you'll have to put a lot of work in, but that is none of our business. It's also none of our business how much you'll make in the end. But we can't possibly let it go for less than seven thousand."

Bata realised he would have to give in a little, but at the same time he thought that nobody around here would be willing to pay more than three thousand for the lot.

"Three is my final offer!" he added loudly and firmly.

"Do you think we stole this, man?" Fane burst out almost angrily. "It's not like we haven't had any expenses. Five is our final price. Take it or leave it!"

He waved his hand as if to say, it's no use talking to you anymore.

"One thousand tomorrow, and the rest in a month, when I sell it," Bata said.

"No," Fane shook his head, "two thousand tomorrow, and the rest in a month's time."

They looked at each other in silence. Who would be the first to back down? Bata knew that he couldn't let the stuff go. A clear plan was beginning to take shape in his mind. He gave in with a deep sigh.

"It's a deal," he agreed to the offer, let out a groan and then steered to jollier things, "but first, Horse should get his famous plum schnapps out of his cabinet."

Pera nodded and went into the house. He came back with a bottle and two glasses. He filled them right up.

"What about you?" Bata asked.

"I drank all I was meant to in this life," Pera explained with a gloomy wrinkled face. "I'm having a dry spell."

"Here's to all of us!" Bata called and drank up.

You're a genius. Geeenius

They sat down at the table and talked, as befits old friends who can keep business out of a merry gathering of kindred spirits, always ready to share countless stories on every possible, mostly earthly, subject.

After a while, Pera the Horse asked:

"What are you going to do with all this stuff now? Do you want us to transport it somewhere for you?"

Bata had thought everything through in the meantime.

"No need, no need, I'll give my trucker a call, and he'll haul it to Zagreb. It's only right I take care of this myself," he shook his head.

He walked to the phone.

He knew that he would send everything to Rista in Pančevo. He knew that the premonitions he had been having for the last few days were starting to come true. He was about to embark on a business venture which would shake up the whole world. But no one could know about it, least of all where he was taking the goods he had purchased.

Not long after, a truck appeared in front of the house. It was an old, round-edged Mercedes. Šarec, the driver Bata had called, was very proud of the truck and kept turning down numerous offers by German old-timer enthusiasts. He was known to say, lovingly and self-confidently:

"They don't make them like this anymore. I'll put five million kilometres on it."

Šarec got his nickname after a Partisan horse from the Battle of Neretva film. He could take on every request, regardless of how doable or non-doable it was, transporting construction material, firewood, watermelons and coal; he helped people move.

They started loading the cargo onto the truck; it took them almost two hours to do it. They were dripping with sweat, as the thermometer hardly fell under thirty degrees Celsius, despite the fact that it was already getting dark. Pera the Horse chuckled, exhausted.

"This day is one for the history books. I've finally witnessed Bata working and getting dirty," he said.

Bata gave him a dubious glance.

"Don't even think of telling anyone that I was involved in physical labour. I'd be the laughingstock of the entire city!" he threatened decisively.

Amidst all of this, he told Šarec to wait for him with his truck at the crossroads for Pančevo, he'd meet him there in half an hour. For the other two men involved, he threw in a comment about hoping to get out of this business they had gotten him in alive, then walked back to the phone and called his regular taxi driver.

"Come pick me up, Whitey, before Pera the Horse and Fane the Captain get me completely drunk!"

Whitey got his nickname from his long white hair; he was tall and very thin, white skinned, almost an albino, a retired army officer who drove his friends around in his taxi, wherever it was they needed to go. He was always meticulously dressed; he never spoke before first thinking about it for some time. If he drove the way he spoke, Bata used to joke, even a snail would make it to wherever he was going and back quicker than him. As he drove up in his old Volvo, he stopped at the side of the road, waved and called:

"Hey, here I am!"

Bata bid farewell and climbed into the car. When already on the road, he explained to Whitey where he should take him; Šarec was already waiting for him at the roadside. There's a man worthy of his name, Bata thought to himself, always on time.

"Are you working?" Whitey called to Šarec through his driver's window. "I haven't seen you in ages!"

"Sure!" Šarec replied, turning on the engine. "We're not lazy like you taxi drivers are, we need to pile up some kilometres, and work while we're at it!"

"Follow us!" Bata waved.

When they reached Rista's estate, Bata swiftly jumped out of the car, widely opened the double gate to the yard and motioned to Šarec and Whitey to drive right in. He then carefully closed the gates after both vehicles. He suggested they should wait a while, have a smoke while they waited for him to return, and then went into the house.

The reception room was empty, so he went on to the workshop, filled with the usual noise. When he entered unannounced, everyone recoiled in astonishment and stopped what they were doing, but quickly resumed when Bata asked for Rista. One of the men grinned and said:

"He might be in the studio, or he might be sleeping."

He thought it fitting to add:

"The boss is sleeping, while we workers are working!"

"What the hell do you mean by this? It's been like this forever, for centuries. Just be glad you have work!" Bata reproached him. "Go and wake him!"

"I wouldn't, he might be sleeping, or he might be doing those things with his two angels," the man resisted, giving a sly smile and revealing his rotten teeth, while making the familiar gesture signifying what a man does with a woman.

Bata went to the bedroom and knocked.

"Who's banging? I thought I've told everyone that I'm busy. Leave me alone!" a voice came from the bedroom.

"It's me, Bata," Bata said loudly. "I apologize, but I need you, it's urgent."

"Wait for me in the kitchen, I only need a minute!"

Rista appeared, his hair was tussled and he was cranky, he had put on a white robe in a rush.

"What could be so important for you to interrupt me while fucking? I need more time, there are two of them I have to please, not like you people, who only have to deal with one at a time. And a third one is about to come over any time now. You better make sure I didn't get up for nothing!"

Two beautiful young blonds from the neighbourhood followed him out of the bedroom; at first glance, a lot of people would take them for twin sisters. But they weren't. Acquaintances called them Vesna number one and Vesna number two in order to tell them apart. They collectively and harmoniously took care of Rista's every need. Bata knew them and didn't pay much attention to them, but he felt it was only polite to utter an envious comment.

"Well, Rista, my friend, it seems you're living in paradise now. Once you face God, he'll undoubtedly deduct all of this from your heavenly residence," he remarked.

They went outside into the yard. Rista got a puzzled look on his face.

"What have you been up to? The other day you brought two boxes of silver, and now you came to collect the stuff with no less than a truck? Do you plan to rob me?" he wondered, genuinely displeased.

"Don't worry, Rista, my good man. I've brought you some really beautiful things. Take a look, and then tell me if you'd like to join me in business," Bata replied.

Rista watched in amazement, pulled back his hair, tightened his robe and slowly climbed onto the truck, while Bata faced both girls.

"Oh," he moaned, lost in his dreams, "what the three of us could do together if I was a bit younger. But since this dream will never come true, can I please ask you for some coffee, no sugar, I'm sure it'll be as sweet as you two."

"Oh, Mr. Milorad, thanks for the compliments. If we weren't in love with Rista, you'd be first on our list of candidates, you're the only real gentleman in the whole world," one of the girls said.

Rista jumped off the truck, almost breathless, flailing his hands about.

"Where did you dig up this stock, Bata, my friend, where did you find it? You're a genius. Geeenius!"

You must have gone mad. Go see some psychiatrists

Bata and Rista sat down each in their respective woven lounger in the garden in front of the house.

"Well, there's nothing one can't find, Rista, my good man," Bata began, shooting a reproachful look at the empty table in front of them. "These are the kind of things that require every ounce of brain power, and some serious work."

Rista asked the girls to bring over more coffee and a bottle, "my bottle," and two glasses. Then he turned to Šarec and Whitey.

"Take a walk to the bar at the end of the street, it's on me. I have some stuff I need to discuss with Bata. You could sit down and hang around, but you'd be bored."

He shifted his focus back to Bata, pointing to the truck.

"So, what now? What shall we do?"

Bata laughed and threw in perfidiously:

"So, the master is asking the apprentice, right? Is this how it's supposed to be? Don't tell me you don't know what it is you have in your yard?"

Rista pushed away the glasses and took a long swig right from the bottle. He crossed his legs, making the robe slip off his knees, and his sandals fall off his feet. Then he cleared his throat and started speaking, with some uncertainty.

"Hm, when I think of everything we organised in the past, what the workshop keeps casting and forging to follow your commands, I'd say you'll want more of my direct personal involvement; you'll probably require me to paint more. This is all a bit fast, but if you say we should be in business together, as far as I know you, you'd probably like..."

He thought about it some more, then looked seriously at Bata.

"Well, I reckon you're planning to produce a nice series of old Croatian painters, they fare quite well on the market, don't they? Dobrović, Bukovac, Medović, Crnčić, oh well, and a pre-war Lubarda to boot..., could this be it?"

He resolutely poured another copious portion of spirits down his throat, put the bottle back on the table with a thud, and gave Bata a searching look.

"Not bad," Bata said, "well done, master, your brain still works.

But if you took another look at the truck, you'd realise there's more material there than just for a measly ten paintings. Come on, think about it a little more, spread your wings, fly..."

"Ok, then, if we were to add the Slovenians, Jakopič, Sternen, Grohar, Stupica, and Mušič, of course, I read somewhere that one of his paintings was sold for over a million in Milan," Rista kept guessing.

Bata was smiling and shaking his head.

"That's all peanuts, master, peanuts, Rista, my friend, nothing but small change, make your mind work, won't you, think again. I know you can come up with something better. Reach out your hands, go for it, there are hundreds of millions right under your nose."

"You must have gone mad," Rista practically jumped to his feet, "go see a psychiatrist! A hundred million. It's not like you're Mimara."

"Calm down, Rista, my good man, calm down and have some more of whatever is in this bottle, just like I will," Bata said and took a very long gulp, followed by another one, "think about it some more."

The fragrance of brilliant peach schnapps had already enveloped the table, almost creating an air enclosure around the two men, it pushed away the nearby smell coming from the pigsties and the surrounding fields complete with ducks and geese. Rista silently drank from the bottle, several times, then cleared his throat, stared in front of him for a while and then roared:

"Are you fucking with me or are you being serious?"

"Now you're the Rista I know, my dear man, you are; I'm serious. I'm thinking what you won't say out loud," Bata beamed.

"So, what's this all about? What cunning plan do you have in mind?" Rista nevertheless asked, hesitating.

"Look, my dear artist, and wonder. Send your imagination to Paris, to Vienna and to Rome, yes, there, too, let it wander all the way to New York."

He took a small black and white catalogue out of his coat pocket and threw it on the table in front of Rista, the catalogue which had been burning a hole in his mind ever since the moment he came upon it in Zagreb. He had leafed through it a thousand times, pondering and thinking about it, looking for old newspaper articles over and over again, finding out that a part of the collection was most likely ruined, that a part of it disappeared mysteriously...And then he suddenly came upon a basement filled with old art supplies, canvases, oil pigments, brushes, paper...And now here we are! He was about to embark on a venture he anticipated and dreamed about! The truck was full of goods and the artist seemed in good spirits. The collection will reappear. The hidden Šlomovič treasure. Rediscovered! The world will be left speechless. The market for French impressionists and modernists will be taken by a storm. Our ears will hurt from all the clanking of money! Grand master Rista will paint, and I'll conjure up a story.

Rista gave him a surprised look, then started leafing through the catalogue.

"You don't mean..." he mumbled after a while.

"That's exactly what I mean!" Bata called.

Rista took another swig from the bottle, grabbed the catalogue and staggered into the house. He locked himself in his room, laid his feet on a coffee table in front of him and leaned back in an old armchair. He was known to spend hours upon hours there, whenever he fell into one of his drunken ponderings. No one was allowed to disturb him at times like this. He practically turned off his physical self, his heart beat slowed down to the point when his young lovers started screaming of fear and calling the doctor, when they saw him like this for the first time. But the doctor merely felt for his pulse, counted, listened, and shook his head.

"He's on a journey now, he'll be back once he's had enough," he finally concluded. "Leave him be."

Bata was familiar with these kinds of states. They were always triggered by a profound impulse. When Rista grabbed the catalogue and staggered into the house, Bata knew that the story had begun.

Rista suddenly found himself at the exhibition in Paris. The young Šlomovič took his hand and led him from one painting to the next. They were no longer black and white, like they were in the catalogue: now he saw them in colour. Look at this Modigliani, I got it from Vollard in exchange for a bunch of drawings by Picasso; I bought them because I couldn't afford to buy oils, and this Matisse, oh, that's quite a story...and Cezanne. There was so much I wanted to do! To build a large museum in my home city of Belgrade, but my train left for Dachau, and my paintings...I had never told anyone where I kept them. I'll find them, Rista replied, now that I have the pigments, now that I have the brushes, everything just like it used to be, I'll bring you back to life through paintings, a splash of wine will stain one of them here, I'll rub some cigarette ash onto another one, they'll float through the scent of young women, passionate or bought love affairs, debauchery and misery, in a hurry I'll dilute one of the paints with my spit...Šlomovič kept cutting in, there was the fire of a young, enthusiastic art collector in his voice, but he was fraught with doubt, oh, no, everything will be lost, the raging war will sweep all of it off the face of the earth...No, no, Rista resisted, it's not lost, I'll find it again, all of it! Rista spread his wings, he flew into a painter's nirvana, strolling along through a different time, taking his time to look at the paintings...

When he found himself in his worn-out armchair again, it was already pitch black, and he knew what kind of work he was about to embark on, and what the business Bata referred to was about.

He got up and walked out, barefoot, to thoroughly discuss the details with Bata, as he was the only one who could lead such an operation. A deceased and famous art collector's collection was about to be born. Every trace of his collection was gone. Could it be somewhere? Was it gone? It will exist now!

But it was night outside; he turned on the light and went to his bedroom, where his two beautiful companions were already asleep. There was no one in the workshop. He walked to the phone to give Bata a call. He looked at the time and shivered. Let's not bother him now, I'll contact him during the day. He went back to his armchair. He knew full well that he wouldn't be able to close his eyes until the morning, that he would be daydreaming instead, but this time fully conscious.

Once Rista retired to the house, Bata first ordered around the workers in the foundry, making them unload the truck and carefully stack everything in the shed next to the workshop before they left, he paid Šarec what he owed him and sent him on his way. He felt it would be a pity to leave what remained on the table in the warm evening, lest the drink in the bottle would get too warm, so he emptied it and decided to get some shuteye, a bit of a breather. In the meantime, he'd sort out the details: how is the collection going to appear, what kind of a story will narrate the miracle, how the collection will slowly, piece by piece, melt into money, who will be the one to start...Naturally, he'll have to throw enough money at Rista to keep him occupied with this and nothing else, to make him paint and draw exclusively, and to keep his mind off anything else. Damn it! The money! What the hell is young Leon doing with the silver? Has he sold it? Has he disappeared?

He fell asleep after this. When he woke up, he looked for Whitey. He found him sleeping in his car, in the corner of the yard, his legs dangling through one of the windows.

"Come on, let's go!" Bata nudged him.

Whitey slowly came to.

"What's the rush, man, can't you see that I'm sleeping!" Whitey barked.

"Oh, you can sleep at home. And so can I. Let's go!" Bata commanded.

They drove off. A new day was rising in the east and the city was awakening to its usual morning bustle.

Don't take me for a fool. I've come to get the money or the stuff

A phone rang in the room two-eighteen in the Palace Hotel in Portorož. Leon was just shaving, standing in the bathroom in his underwear, so he quickly picked up the receiver.

"I'm calling from the reception," a woman's voice rambled politely, "Mr. Sattler, there is a man here who is very adamant about being let to your room."

"Who's there, what does he want?" Leon asked quite angrily. The morning by the sea was pleasant, a gentle wind was coming into the room through light curtains from the balcony, Kristina was still asleep. The days provided such a nice break, and now this!

"Ačim Aćimović, he wants to see you, he's very persistent, I don't know what to..."

"Tell him to go to the breakfast room, order something to eat or drink, put it on my tab, I'll be down shortly," Leon interrupted her.

"What is it now?" he heard from the bedroom. "Can't we even afford three days of piece at the seaside?"

Kristina was stretching in bed, yawning and opening her eyes.

"I don't know, there's some guy named Aćimović who wants to speak to me. I'll go downstairs and check it out. You take your time and get ready, then we'll go out and get some toast and coffee. Alright?" Leon suggested while putting on his clothes.

The previous day he and Kristina went to Trieste, and he bought a few nice things for himself after a long time. He found a bright summer jacket, and a beautiful silver watch at Kavalar. He put on both and descended to the ground floor. He walked to the hotel's front entrance and looked around the garden, which was really more like a park, with a giant fountain and goldfish amidst the footpaths and greenery. He stretched and enjoyed the warmth of the summer morning. He rolled up the sleeve of his jacket to reveal the shine of the silver watch under his shirt. Then he went to the breakfast room. Hotel guests whom he had come familiar with in the past couple of days were sitting around the tables; several children were running among them, two waiters were standing quietly at the side, ready to assist anyone who needed anything. He looked around but couldn't find anyone who would evidently stand out from the group of almost aristocratic holiday makers. He stepped inside to the main dining room, which was almost completely empty. At the far end of the self-service bar, laden with all kinds of food, he saw a man in worn-out clothes, who didn't seem to fit in, although he almost feverishly stuffed his face with fried eggs from a yellow mountain, heaped up on a plate; he gave of a somewhat rough, dark vibe.

Leon approached him.

"Good morning," he greeted the man politely, "you must be waiting for me?"

The man looked up and stared at him. He had a piercing, uncomfortable look, there was something sharp and dangerous about him. Leon almost shivered.

"You're right, I've been looking for you," the man said coldly. "Bata sent me!"

Leon tried to diffuse the tension, forcing a smile.

"And what has Mr. Milorad been up to? How's he doing?"

"He's not in a good mood, not at all," the man replied harshly. "He sent me to collect the money for the merchandise you took from Belgrade a week ago."

Leon pricked up his ears. He was very uneasy. What was all of this? Why didn't he know anything about an unexpected visit from Bata's messenger? He decided to play dumb.

"What merchandise are you talking about? I didn't take anything from Belgrade."

This man is a troublemaker or a cop, maybe a mafia guy who has somehow learned about the silver, Leon thought to himself. It was all very suspicious. This was not among the standard procedures he and Bata agreed to previously. He suddenly realised that he was standing there, like a schoolboy facing a scolding teacher. So he reached for the chair at the nearby table, pulled it to the bar, sat down and tried to exude an impression of casual indifference.

The man said gruffly, with his mouth still full:

"Don't take me for a fool. I've come to get the money or the stuff. Are we clear?!"

He then hissed through his teeth:

"If you have a problem, you can make a call to Belgrade. Just don't play games with me! I'm not one to take to such jokes!"

He never even lifted his eyes, just kept stuffing himself, as if he had been starving for the last ten days. He practically oozed rough danger. He slammed his stout hand violently against the table and ordered, as if there was no question of who is who in this conversation: "Bring me some more bread!"

Leon got up and walked to the food counter as if in a trance. He was confused and unsure, almost frightened, and somehow couldn't find the strength to stand up to the stranger. He filled a basket with some bread rolls and returned.

"I don't have much time. Hurry! I drove all night. I need to be in Munich by evening. Hello! Where's the stuff?" the stranger ranted.

Threats were mounting in his eyes.

"I need to use the restroom," Leon replied quickly, got up, almost knocking over his chair, and walked to the reception.

He was overcome with an unfamiliar fear. What's going on, what's going on, what's going on, the thought resounded in his mind. He dictated Bata's phone number in Belgrade to the woman behind the desk and almost ran to the phone booth. The phone just kept ringing. Weird. He became worried. Did the police get involved? Was there something else going on? He felt like a rug was being pulled from under his feet. Where did this complete surprise come from? He needed to stall and get to Bata. He had to! The situation was far too serious.

He went back to the dining room.

"Did you make the phone call?" the stranger asked.

"No, I went to take a leak," Leon shook his head.

"Alright then, if that's called leaking now. What have you found out? I can't waste any more time with you. Give me the stuff!"

Leon sat back down at the table.

"I don't understand anything: who are you, what do you want, who sent you, what stuff are you talking about, and what have I got to do with this?"

"Don't monkey around!" the man hollered. "You know exactly what I want! And I told you I don't have much time. I need to move on right away. It's not like this is any of my business. I just have a job to do. And I'm going to do it! There's no question about it!"

He rose menacingly from his chair.

Leon almost instinctively sprung to his feet in fear and despair.

"And I have a job I agreed to with Bata!" he roared back.

"Whatever you want from me is none of my concern!"

He was done with being treated like a snot-nosed brat by this guy. The fear increased his strength. He yelled almost in self-defence.

"I won't lift a finger until I talk to him!"

"Alright," the stranger replied, once again coldly and calmly, with a scornful smile. "You can talk all you want. But don't take me for a fool. I'll be here waiting and I'm not leaving without the stuff!"

"I'm going up to my room," Leon said, "I'll call Belgrade."

He got up and left. All kinds of thoughts kept running through his mind, interspersed with fear and fury. What was this now? Bata handed over the silver to him, he entrusted him with the transport to Germany, with the instruction of who he was to sell the stuff to and how, it was all as clear as day. And he was to keep a large portion of the money. True, that was a week ago, but it was not like he didn't have his own commitments. He promised Kristina to take her to the seaside and that was that. The world wouldn't come to an end because of a couple of days.

He returned to his room. Kristina was again asleep. A wild night, Leon chuckled to himself and relaxed for a moment. Then he picked up the phone; the long wire enabled him to retreat with the phone to the balcony. He dialled the familiar number. He kept shuffling his feet nervously and nibbling his lips. After a long time Bata's mother answered the phone. She informed him that Bata was out, that he moved into his new house today. Leon gritted his teeth. What now? He told her to ask Bata to call his number in Ljubljana at three o'clock in the afternoon. Urgently. Urgently, urgently!

Kristina was awakened by the conversation.

"Who are you talking to? What's going on?"

"It's nothing," Leon came back inside. "I need to go to Ljubljana. Bata sent a man over to get the silver which I brought over the last time."

"What, aren't you supposed to go to Germany to sell it? You told me the other day..." she yawned.

"There's been a change of plan. Bata must have changed his mind. I don't understand. I don't know what's going on. I can't get him on the phone. He'll probably call me this afternoon, in Ljubljana," Leon explained, absorbed in thought.

"You mean I'll be alone again? Is the business more important to you than me?"

Leon sighed and grinded his teeth. Will you stop it, woman! I've got enough to worry about. Who the hell do you think I've gotten myself into this for? There's this dangerous guy downstairs, he's after me, and here you are, complaining again! He suddenly found himself surrounded by a strange insecurity, almost danger. What was going on, it was only yesterday that he dreamt and calculated what he'd do with his fat earnings. And now here came this shock! What happened to Bata, what was he going to do about Kristina? Two raging fires and him in the middle, burning up in total uncertainty.

"I'll be back by evening," he replied feverishly after some doubtful hesitation, but Kristina quickly cut him off:

"You better! Andraž is coming over in the evening, he wants to take us to dinner. We need to discuss some details about the recording sessions. Do you want me to go out with him by myself?"

Andraž! On top of it all! Leon shot a wild look and clenched his fists. Here she goes again with the recording sessions. Why does everything have to come crushing down on him on the same day? Will these insinuations ever end? He took a deep breath, sighed and kept silent. A giant wave of jealousy washed over his face once again. Andraž, the wealthy owner of a recording studio, who never went far away, who was always there, either in words or at Kristina's late-night shooting sessions, the seductive candidate. And now suddenly here as well, at the seaside, where they had spent the last few days alone, boisterously enjoying themselves. Would there ever be peace among the olive trees? He took another deep breath, calmed down some, and said with visibly forced excitement:

"That's nice. We'll have some fish. I'll be back for sure!"

He leaned over the bed, gave Kristina a fleeting kiss and waved to her from the door.

Down at the restaurant he explained to Bata's messenger that they needed to go back to Ljubljana, that he didn't have the habit of bringing all kinds of junk with him on holiday, that Bata wasn't answering his phone, and that he would probably contact him this afternoon.

"I don't know my way around Ljubljana. Are you planning on escaping me? I wouldn't recommend it," the stranger said menacingly.

"You can follow me to the city. I'll drive to my house, and you can wait for me at the Ilirija Hotel. You'll find it, don't worry. If everything goes well with Bata, I'll join you in the afternoon," Leon said and went to the garage.

"You better straighten everything out," the stranger grinned with an ambiguous smile.

The road to Ljubljana was fairly empty. No one felt like driving from the seaside in the midday heat.

Once home, Leon poured himself a drink and slumped on his couch. He turned on the telly and searched the channels until he found an old western starring Richard Widmark. The plot was pretty naive and made him laugh quite a few times. His phone rang just before three o'clock.

"What do you want?"

It was Bata, he sounded brisk and harsh.

"Hi, Bata," Leon purposefully ignored the unpleasant tone, "somebody I've never met before in my life has come to get the silver. Did you send him?"

"Yes."

Silence. Poisonous silence.

"What's this all about? Haven't we made a deal that I'm to go sell it in Frankfurt and Brussels?"

"Yes. Have you?"

More silence.

"Not yet, I had to take Kristina to the seaside, I promised her ages ago," Leon started explaining but Bata quickly interrupted him.

"Stop it. You had your chance and you blew it. I can't wait for you to go to work when you happen to not be busy entertaining your broad. I have my own plans, you know," he almost yelled.

"I thought I'd make some money," Leon started again.

"You lost that chance. Don't cry about it now. You're on your own!"

"Ok," Leon said, astonished and hurt, "I'll hand the silver over to that man. But who's going to cover my costs? I drove you to Belgrade, then to Pančevo, and the stuff all the way back, I had a fight with Kristina about it..."

"Shut up! I wanted you to be part of my team, I was going to give you loads of money, and you've been busy with things that are none of my business. Give the man the stuff and forget about your earnings. The interest far surpassed your costs in the week you waited to hit the road," the words kept poisonously flying out of the receiver.

"Alright," Leon said in amazement and offendedly ended the call.

Why is this happening to me, of all people? He felt surprised and insulted. Such a fuss over a few days? He couldn't explain the poison Bata had poured over him because of the delay.

He drove to Ulčars' house and loaded the boxes in his Quatrelle. Ulčar didn't ask any questions nor offered to comment. When he saw Leon's dark face he merely expressed a comradely wish that he would be alright. Leon thanked him and drove to the nearby forest. He selected two beautiful candlesticks from one of the boxes and hid them under the seat.

"I'm not going to work for nothing, and this messenger guy surely doesn't know how much of the stuff he should be getting," he reasoned with himself.

As soon as he entered the parking lot of the Ilirija Hotel, he saw a pretty muddy white Opel with Munich registration plates. The driver was dangling his legs from a barstool at the counter in the reception hall; he had a cup of coffee and a glass of brown Coca-Cola in front of him. There was probably something in it.

"You haven't fled," he grinned. "Pay for the drinks and give me the stuff. Have you settled everything? Was Bata pleased?"

They transferred the boxes into the Opel and the car sped off the yard after a wild start.

What now? Leon wondered. Was it all over? Would he run out of money again? Would he have to start looking for another business? Or should he focus on his studies? He got into his Quatrelle angrily, drove to the city and gave both candlesticks to Tone to sell. Then he headed toward the seaside.

Not a move on your own

Bata was furious, too. This snot-nosed brat from Ljubljana, the one he took with him to Frankfurt and showed him Rista's foundry, offered him a fabulous business opportunity, was now fooling around. Now, when he urgently needed the money to pay Rista to bite into this crazy job. He needed additional equipment, a bunch of stuff, special games, all kinds of stories, and none of that could be achieved without a significant amount of money. Money, which the marvellous silver pieces could provide. He had arranged everything with Frietzl in Frankfurt, and with Juncker in Brussels, as well. This couldn't be happening! And now he had to rush head-first into a deal with a special messenger, arrange for him to pick up the goods, transport it and sell it at wholesale price, albeit for money up front, to one of the Albanian masters of the German underground. Time was money in this case and a he was in a rush. We'll probably make up for the loss if we carry this new thing out correctly, but I need the money now. Right this moment!

It just so happened that Rista was totally invested in the new project, workwise and with all the zeal he could muster. He got down to business. He set up several easels and fixed old canvases on them. He studied reproductions in every book featuring old painters he owned, and he did it in detail. He'll need to get some more, as many as possible, he told himself. This was Bata's job. He painted on several canvases and pieces of paper simultaneously. He ran a test trial, and the old paints had retained all of their freshness. The pencils and coal blended smoothly with every type of paper. He had everything a painter could wish for. In just a few days, he painted a number of works by great masters in the formats as they were listed in Šlomovič's catalogue, then he went off in his own direction, following familiar motifs. He painted a reclining nude in one passionate stroke, as well as a number of black and white drawings for it.

"Marvellous!" Bata cried. "This is one of the most gorgeous Modigliani's I've ever seen!"

"Haha," Rista roared with laughter, "you've seen the real thing, too. Look a bit closer!"

Of course, the woman lying on the stretched out sofa was one of his beautiful lovers.

"Well done, master!" Bata called. "Just keep on working. My job now is to give everything a nice patina. There's a space in the attic of my new house where I'm going to set up a workshop, a lab, and I can do that there. The most important thing at the moment is that no one finds out about our collection. Especially not your friend Mijat, just in case he spills the beans. We're clear on this, right?"

Rista nodded contentedly and continued to show off the work he had done in the last few days with ostentatious confidence in his mastery.

Bata picked from all the pieces and put a few paintings and drawings in an old-school artist's portfolio, tying the ribbons at the top.

"You paint them and I'll prepare a plan for selling them. This needs to be a well thought-out, flawless, long-term operation, no playing solo," Bata explained. "Not a move on your own!"

"You paint and that's it," he repeated. "Is this clear?"

He called a taxi. Not Whitey, of course, as no one was to know about the secret operation he and Rista embarked upon. He told the random taxi driver who picked up the phone to drive him to Fane the Captain. Once there, he asked the boss without explaining too much to let him inside his old attic.

"You're going to fix my roof, or what?" Fane wondered, although he knew there was no point in asking questions if Bata had fixed his mind on something.

"I want to take a look at your wooden beams, to figure out what I need the carpenters to do at my place," Bata replied.

He climbed up the creaking steps to find himself under old beams and miscellaneous junk spread under them, carefully collecting decades old dust into an old box.

"Would you like some coffee?" Fane hollered from downstairs.

"Yours - always!" Bata yelled back and kept dusting.

When he was done he went down the steps and beat off the dirt and cobwebs which were stuck all over his body.

"You almost suffocated me up there," he chuckled, "so much stuff ended up in there."

"Well, well, you're right. I might get myself a mummy, while I'm at it. If you ever feel like it..." Fane chuckled right back at him.

They slowly drank their coffee and Bata went back to his house.

He untied the portfolio in his own attic and spread the forgeries over the floor.

"You're a master, Rista, excellent job!"

He picked out a Modigliani and a few drawings by Rodin. He set them on a table and started applying dust out of the box with a tiny brush. Once he felt the first phase was done, he put everything down on the floor. He cut out tiny potato stamps, like the ones he had seen in the catalogue of the Šlomovič collection and imprinted them in red and green ink on the backs of the works. He used an old pencil to copy various inventory numbers, adding different notes in coal, just as he had seen done on numerous paintings in museums around the world.

Throughout this, he was of course absorbed in thought: how could he get all of this on the market? Where would the first painting come from, the first out of many which were to follow, what would be its story? He thought about Leon often, the young student, the ambitious idealist, the guy who had proven his knowledge; he could...that was why I had chosen him...but what can you do, he was living his crazy years, influenced by women, he was indulging his other head too much, he already blew the first big solo job with the silver that Bata had offered him...What about Tone, the merchant from Ljubljana, he was known to assertively sell many a painting for big bucks, and he had connections abroad...It might be better to begin selling the paintings out there, abroad, someone had discovered one of the numerous Nazi hidden treasures...well, not exactly, all that was kept under the watchful eye of international institutions, that would not do...

No, he needed to start from below, at a flea market, with a total stranger, the story needed to sound crazy, yet believable...There was this man who inherited a run-down house somewhere in Vojvodina, an old bakery, perhaps, and he stumbled upon some bruised suitcases in the attic under a pile of old planks and other junk, wooden chests containing some weird paintings, drawings...So he took them to a professor or curator in Belgrade, someone who could know something about them, or maybe he just tried his luck at the flea market...

Fane the Captain! The thought suddenly struck his mind. He was right here under my nose, I was just at his house, and I never thought about him! Of course! Everyone, especially the gipsies, brought all kinds of stuff to Fane. After all, it was Gipsy who sold Fane the old canvases and pigments. That was where it all started! Exactly! It should continue from there, as well!

He remembered a drug addict who always used to scrounge for money at the corner of his street, giving out business cards which read "I'm a good person, call me if you need me," accompanied by a phone number. The addict had a brother who was one of the mafia bosses in London, so he was never short on drugs, but always short on money.

This could work, Bata thought, I just need to instruct him thoroughly from the very beginning, in order to make the story believable and convincingly acted out.

What kinds of misfortunes made you come and remember your mother?

He sat down by the phone.

He called the good person. He was in luck, the addict answered right away. Bata introduced himself and arranged to meet him in Lotos day bar. In addition to drinks, the bar offered women of all ages, who were always willing to make a little money even during the day. There was a stage with a dancing pole in the basement, featuring provocative dancing all the time, to the accompaniment of an out of tune piano.

When Bata arrived at the fixed time, the good person wasn't there yet, but he was instead immediately joined by one of the older ladies:

"Hello, handsome gentleman, will you buy me a drink?"

Bata dismissed her nervously:

"I don't have time to talk to you right now. Tell the waiter I'll pay for your drink, now get lost!"

"Oh my," the woman said in astonishment, "is this the way to treat old lady friends?" and she retreated, offended.

Bata nervously tapped his fingers on the table. He was about to start a great story, and the guy he planned to cunningly start it with was nowhere to be found. Over half an hour had passed before he walked to the phone, and it was in that moment that the emaciated long-haired man burst in the place.

"Sorry, there was this girl I couldn't shake off, she kept clinging to me, she won't leave me alone, until she gets another hit. Now she's asleep and I escaped," he kept apologizing.

"OK, OK, the important thing is that you're here now. We can't talk in here, let's go to my place!"

He put his arm around the guy's shoulders and they left, of course not to Bata's new home, but to the nearby apartment building where his mother lived. She was surprised to hear a key grind in the lock, and even more surprised when she saw Bata.

"Son? Is it you? What kinds of misfortunes made you come and remember your mother?" she asked reproachfully.

"It's nothing, mother, everything is fine. Listen, why don't you go over to your neighbour and have a little chat with her. I've got some serious business to take care of here," Bata dismissed her.

His mother merely shook her head and left the apartment.

"What's this about?" the guy wondered.

"Nothing," Bata shook his head and set the portfolio on the table. He took out two frameless canvases, "you're to take these to Fane the Captain. You got them from a friend who inherited a house in the middle of nowhere from his grandfather, and he found this in the attic."

Two paintings signed Pissaro and Renoir beamed on the table.

"And?" the good person asked. "Why don't you go there yourself?"

"Don't ask questions," Bata turned him down. "I know why and that's why I called you. If you do a good job, I'll make it worth your while, naturally."

"Alright, alright, I only asked," the good person mumbled.

"You're to agree to any price Fane offers, but don't sell them, give the stuff to him for commission sale, he is to pay you when he sells them," Bata explained.

"But why on commission? When money is everything," the guy wondered out loud.

"That's OK, but not right now," Bata answered in a calming tone, raising his hand, "if he doesn't make a good deal, I need both paintings back. Is this clear?"

"It's clear," the guy nodded. "Give me these, I'll go over to him right now."

Here we go, Bata thought to himself, I need to trust my luck. He rolled up the paintings and handed them to the guy. Let's see how this plays out.

Well, half a million, only half a million

It was already evening when Leon and Kristina returned from the seaside at the end of the week. Andraž never showed up for dinner and Leon kept silently convincing himself that maybe Kristina had merely been teasing and provoking him. She really did want more attention. Well then, he was going to keep on trying.

The very next morning he went to Dota, where Tone joyfully told him that he had sold both candlesticks.

"Good merchandise sells well," he chuckled. "Have you stumbled upon a silver mine?"

"There's this old lady in Zagreb, she has loads of stuff like this, and since I pay her more than others, I'm always welcome at her place," Leon smiled.

"Is that so, is that so," Tone nodded. "What's her name?"

"Silence is golden," Leon smirked. "You're a good merchant, Tone. Let's head over to the other side of the street and have some chilled champagne. It's my treat. And leave it to me to take care of the old lady."

They chatted about this and that, gossiped about passers-by a bit, and then Tone put on a slightly cunning facial expression, asking in a low voice:

"Listen. I hear that a Pissaro and a Renoir have become available in Belgrade. Do you know anything about it? You certainly should, since you have such excellent connections over there."

Leon shook his head.

"I have no idea. You know I've been away from the scene for a week. Plus, Bata's gotten a bit vexed."

Tone shook his head slightly, took another sip and said after a short reflection:

"I would sure appreciate it if you could enquire about it. Such pieces are always very interesting, and anyway, it's better to sell one big thing than a million small ones."

Leon looked at him unfeigned.

"Well, why don't you enquire about it yourself, if you're interested?" he asked.

"You know there's no way I could do that," Tone shook his head, displeased. "The moment I show some interest, the price doubles. You, on the other hand, could really turn something up. Are you planning to go down there anytime soon?"

Leon had indeed been thinking for the past few days about having to figure out what Bata's ill will was about. He found it odd, almost incredible, that he had been thrown out of the business they sort of started together, and in such a brutal manner. He wanted to talk to Bata face to face, and he was literally looking for a reason to head off to Belgrade. But, of course, every trip like that demanded time and money.

"Perhaps," he answered slowly, "if I were to get some chests to take to Pera the Horse. He's been constantly asking me for those."

"Well, look," Tone hastened. "I'd really appreciate it if you could find something out. In fact, I'd be prepared to cover your travel costs, if you happened to pick anything up. That's not all, if you get any good information, I'll make it worth your while. But you have to hurry, you know such items don't come along every day, don't you?"

"Kind words are like honey," Leon laughed and bid farewell. "I'll hurry up!"

He decided to act immediately.

He rented a van, as usual, and drove to Kristina's weekend house, which he occasionally used as a warehouse to store larger items, he took three chests he had intended to drive over to Belgrade for some time and dragged them over some planks he had placed on the floor, then stacked them in the van. The masters there were able to upgrade relatively simple chests from Dolenjska region with inlays and pretty metal finishes, instantly producing original bourgeois chests from the end of the previous century, the type especially popular with the Austrians.

Kristina and he executed a romantic dinner with a passionate ending, and he got in his van in the middle of the night and drove off. He loved to drive at night, because it always meant he would reach his destination in the morning with the whole day still ahead of him. Belgrade was the kind of a city where he could really take advantage of an early arrival. The night was warm, calm, there were countless stars in the sky, the conditions allowed for relatively safe driving.

He drove up to Pera the Horse at the break of dawn and parked in front of his house. He saw Pera through the downstairs window, sitting at the table and gobbling down some *burek*. He entered without knocking, greeting Pera from afar.

"Good morning, boss, you're up already?"

Pera was glad to see him.

"Good morning, young man! What are you doing here so early in the morning? Come, sit down, have some *burek*, it's still warm, here's some yoghurt and coffee, too. Did you drive through the night?"

They quickly engaged in conversation, and Leon carefully began probing while sipping the hot coffee.

"There are rumours in Ljubljana," he said, "about a Renoir coming to the market over here. Would you know anything about it?"

"Where did you get this from? A Renoir? Oh, come on. You're dealing in rummage sales and dreaming of French impressionists. Just stick to the flea market. Why Renoir all of the sudden?" Pera tried to calm him with a reproachful tone in his voice.

"It's nothing, really," Leon answered pretty convincingly, holding up his cup, "I have a buyer. And this buyer asked me to find the painting, if there indeed is one."

"Really? A buyer? Who could this be?" Pera wondered.

"Ha, ha," Leon burst out laughing, "I'd be crazy to tell you who it is, and let you go to him yourself, Pera, my friend."

Pera leaned back in his chair, calmly observed Leon for a while, then shrugged his shoulders, as if to say, what do I care:

"No, I've never seen this stuff, but Fane the Captain might know something about it. He always gets the news first-hand. But let's leave it now. Why don't you go through my stuff and see if there's anything you might be interested in, something I can trade in for your chests."

Leon walked around the warehouse, picking things out. There were loads of different pieces, from porcelain to rugs, bronze miniatures and crockery, interesting cargo to sell in Ljubljana, and it became clear to him that he should have no problems finding a swap. He therefore decided to stop at Fane the Captain, as well, just to find out if he actually knew anything about the two paintings.

The day was dawning. He drove through an alley and arrived to a hedge with a wooden fence behind it. The gate leading in was not so much a gate, but more a mesh of laths and wire. The house was just one step away. When he rang the bell, Fane's son appeared at the door.

"Father is still asleep," he said.

"Have a seat over here," he invited him to the kitchen. "I'll go wake him."

Fane appeared, hung over, spicing up his greeting with the usual sentence.

"What could be so urgent that you're waking me up in the middle of the night?"

He then turned to his son and asked him to make some coffee. He joined Leon at the table and continued to gradually come awake, yawning. At first he thought he'd put on a grumpy attitude, but then his face lit up. It crossed his mind that this guy from Ljubljana was just what the doctor ordered. He has been trying to figure out what to do with the paintings the good person had brought him for several days now, unsuccessfully. He had promised the boy ten thousand Deutschmarks, but had a feeling that his earnings could go up to hundreds of thousands, he was looking forward to making a huge amount of money. But no one budged in Belgrade. No one believed that the paintings weren't stolen... He was thinking about maybe going to Zagreb, perhaps even further. And now, there was Leon from Ljubljana at his doorstep.

"How's business in your country?" he asked, rubbing his eyes and yawning occasionally. "Any money coming in?"

"It's been so-so," Leon replied, looking for a way to enquire about the paintings.

"While we're on the subject, do you know of anyone who'd be interested in some older paintings? A bit on the expensive side? Anyone collecting things like that?" Fane continued absent-mindedly.

There it was! Leon heard the bells ring. Let's do this, then...

"I don't know," he said, "it depends who you're talking about, the Slovenians, the Croatians, impressionists, modernists, living, deceased...It all plays in. Do you have anything?"

"I could find something," Fane said, now fully awake. "But it's world class names."

"Austrians, Germans perhaps?" Leon kept guessing, careful not to seem too interested. At the same time, his heart was pounding. He didn't have to ask a single question. Good old Fane the Captain was bringing it all on his own.

"Let's say French. Let's say Renoir," Fane finally uttered.

"Oh, come on," Leon threw his hands up in the air, "not Renoir! There's no such thing in our parts! You can hardly find stuff like this in museums."

"And Pissaro," Fane continued.

"Let's give it a rest, please," Leon started to rant and rave. "We should be so lucky. What in the world are you talking about?! I've been in this business for years and I've never come across anything like that."

He let his hands rest tiredly in front of him.

Without saying a word, Fane got up, walked to his bedroom and came back with two pieces of cardboard. He placed them on the table with the back sides up, showing various markings, some in colour, as well as hallmarks and numbers.

"What if I said I have something like that?" Fane grinned proudly. "Would you have a buyer, or someone who could sell it?"

"I guess so, if it was something nice..."

Fane the Captain turned the cardboards over with a trembling voice.

"Well, watch and be amazed then. Pissaro and Renoir!" he nearly whispered.

Leon almost fell off his chair. It was immediately obvious that he was looking at works by the two masters, he had learned about them in school, the colours, the coatings and, of course, the signatures, the signatures which he had seen in countless books of reproductions, all of it messed with his feverish head. He felt his skin crawl. The things that Tone alluded to were right there in front of him! He was looking at, touching world masterpieces with his hands, with his own hands, for real.

The motif on the Pissaro painting was a forest of giant oak trees with a plain in the forefront, there was a tiny house with a red roof crouching in the right corner; green against the red, light and shadow. His gaze slipped right over to the Renoir. Of course, a girl with a hat, very bright, colourful and sweet, painted in mixed media, in watercolours, tempera, pastels, with oil colours on top. The signature in the bottom corner, Renoir, was legibly written out in reddish brown. He recognised the signature, naturally. He couldn't believe his eyes.

It was only then that he realised Fane had been observing him closely, judging his reaction and calculating the effect of the artworks displayed on his table.

"What do you think? Amazing, isn't it?"

"Amazing!" Leon exclaimed. "And I have a buyer for it! How much do you want for these two gems?"

"Well, half a million," Fane replied, "only half a million."

"Half a million? That's quite expensive," Leon retorted quickly. "Too expensive."

He inspected both paintings up close, then from the side, then the signatures, then the backs...

Everything seemed flawless! It was a dream!

But he needed to get his feet back on the ground.

"I know from catalogues that real oils on canvas have reached a million, but something like this would go for no more than a hundred thousand, maybe a hundred and twenty, and the Pissaro would probably reach no more than seventy," he pondered on. "And anyway, the final price can only be set by experts."

He twitched and asked:

"Where in the world did you get these?"

"I got them from a guy from Vojvodina, he found them in an abandoned attic, in an old wooden chest... Why do you want to know?" Fane asked.

"We need to know these things. Where do they come from, who had them before, we have to know that they're not stolen," Leon explained firmly. Then he proposed almost blatantly:

"Can I take them to my client?"

In a way, Fane felt like a great burden had been lifted from his shoulders; he would complete the job he had been unsuccessfully struggling with for a while, and he was stunned by the numbers at the same time.

"Of course," he nodded, "I trust you completely."

Leon was still trying to take in what had just happened. He had two of the world's masterpieces in his hands! He came over to snoop around for some information...and found a treasure. This would blow Tone's mind in Ljubljana! He had a fresh cup of coffee while Fane thoroughly wrapped the paintings up.

"I'll talk to you in a few days!" Leon assured him upon leaving.

He told Pera the Horse that he had gotten some old graphics at

Fane, unloaded the chests and picked up the goods he had selected to trade them for. He was practically walking on air, he turned down an invitation to a barbecue that evening at Skadarlija, citing his young wife as an excuse, and headed off to Ljubljana.

He thought about looking for Bata to make peace with him; he was eager to find out what had upset him so. That was the reason he went to Belgrade in the first place. But his ego swelled quickly on account of the parcel he had gotten from Fane. To hell with it, he said to himself, I couldn't care less about Bata, I couldn't care less about his silver. I have an altogether different treasure in my hands now, pure gold! I need to get home as soon as possible, I need to get to Tone, to the money."

He kept singing songs of combat and work the entire way, although off key, slapping his knees, waving to other drivers and praising his fate. The van would only go eighty kilometres per hour. Leon didn't feel like the drive was dragging on, although it went on and on, he was once again driving into a charming future. What a summer! After all: Bata wasn't all that! He can take his silver and his rude attitude and shove it! I can find better deals on my own, Leon mumbled half audibly several times over.

He arrived to Ljubljana late at night and parked the van in front of his apartment building. Kristina was out. He was fine with this, as he was awfully tired and at the same time crazy with happiness. He placed the precious parcel on top of the closet in the bedroom. He took a shower and fell on the bed.

I have solid connections at the Interpol section. The chief is a friend of mine

It was obvious that he badly needed some sleep; he woke up late in the morning. He gathered from the ruffled sheets next to him that Kristina must have come and gone in the meantime. Well, well, she'd be in for quite a story in the afternoon.

He placed the paintings in a large portfolio, protected them with some wrapping paper and drove to the Tabernakelj, to see Tone. He wasn't in his office, so he ordered a cup of coffee in a café across the street, intent on waiting for him. He was crumbling the biscuit which came with the hot beverage, observing pigeons which fought fiercely over every bite.

"Oh, you're back already?" Tone surprised him in the middle of his game. "That was quick. I guess this means you have some information on the Pissaro, right?"

"Heh, I have more than some information, I achieved more, a lot more, to be exact. I have the Pissaro right here in this portfolio. And not only that, there's also a lovely Renoir to boot," Leon grinned, pointing to the portfolio resting on the chair next to him.

"You're out of your mind," Tone bulged his eyes. "You're telling me that you have..."

He was left speechless, and Leon continued vehemently:

"Would you like me to show them to you? Do you want to look at them right here, in the street?"

He started untying the straps and slightly lifted one of the sides. The girl by Renoir appeared. Tone bent down and took a close peek. He swiftly shut the portfolio with his hand.

"Not here!" he snapped.

"What? It's not stolen," Leon kept chuckling.

"We don't know that," Tone whispered and turned to look around, "we haven't checked this yet. This could be dangerous. Wait for me here, I'm going to pop over to the office to let them know I have an errand in the city and I'll come back to work later. Also, I have to get the envelope with the money for the two candlesticks. Let's go to my place to discuss this."

Tone paid the bill and quickly ran to his office, while Leon tied the portfolio back up.

They proceeded along the Ljubljanica River, and once they reached the Karlovški Bridge, they went up a slight hill towards Križanke, where they entered a tall three-storey house with a remarkable entrance, built in the times of Napoleon. They climbed along the creaking worn-out wooden stairs to the second floor. Once there, Tone unlocked large triple wooden doors leading to a hallway of a beautiful bourgeois apartment, its walls covered with paintings. Tone immediately asked:

"Cognac, whiskey?"

"I'll have a whiskey, please, with three ice cubes," Leon responded while admiring the lavish living room interior. He sat at the large dining table, covered with a dark blue tablecloth with a somewhat obscured cashmere print. Tone brought over two glasses; there was some ice in one of them, and he poured whiskey over it. He chose cognac for himself.

"Cognac calms me down," he said almost apologetically.

Leon emptied the glass quickly, while Tone took a sip and then reached for the portfolio, placed it on the table and started undoing the straps.

"Shall we take a look, then," he said with trembling interest.

Both works were painted on cardboard, there were no frames, they were different, but they both exuded impressionist artistic vibes. Tone first reached for the girl by Renoir. Of course, Leon thought to himself, he knows which one is more famous and expensive. He examined it in detail, touching the cardboard, smelling it, stroking the surface, as if wanting to feel the structure and the colour scale of the painting with his fingertips. Then he got up, walked over to a bookshelf standing against one of the walls and laid a large Renoir monography on the table. He slowly leafed through it, lingering for a few moments on each and every reproduction, and at the same time turning his gaze every time to the painting on the table.

Leon was completely natural, relaxed, excited, almost cocky; his was a face of an honest young man, a merchant proud of his success, with nothing to hide.

"I think this is genuine, I think everything checks out," Tone said after a lengthy inspection and closed the book. "I still need to check that the painting isn't stolen. I have solid connections at the Interpol section.

The chief is a friend of mine," he added, as if that went without saying, and brought a phone from the shelf over to the table. He pulled a small booklet containing phone numbers from the inside pocket of his jacket.

"Of course," Leon thought, "these guys work hand in hand with the police. But that's none of my business. If there's a problem, it's Fane the Captain's responsibility."

Tone leafed through the booklet and dialled a number.

"I'd like to speak to Mr. Kafol, please," he said once he got through, adding right after, "alright, alright, I'll hold."

He winked at Leon, as if to say, everything will be just fine. He kept waiting, once again leafing through Renoir's monography. Something cracked in the receiver and Tone straightened himself in the chair.

"It's me, Tone, good afternoon, I would like to ask you about something. Could you find out if any paintings have been stolen lately, a Renoir, a girl with a hat, and a Pissaro, a forest landscape...You don't know anything about it? Well, could you look into it, please? Tomorrow? Excellent. I'm buying a bottle of cognac, the best one, of course."

Tone kept giving Leon thumbs up during the conversation, and once he hung up, he added, rather pleased:

"He hasn't heard anything. Everything seems alright for now. He'll let me know more tomorrow, just in case anyone reported the two paintings missing. Are you planning to leave them with me?"

Leon shook his head.

"I'm sorry, Tone, I can't do that," he said, "the paintings aren't mine, I didn't pay for them. It's not that I don't trust you, it's just too much of a responsibility for me."

"I understand," Tone nodded, "you managed to pull off a great thing, after all. I sent you to Belgrade to get some information, and you've come back with the paintings. That's great. Come over again, let's say mid-morning tomorrow, by then I should know what's going on."

They parted ways.

Back home, Kristina was preparing lunch and the dog was jumping around her.

"What's up then?" she asked when Leon appeared in the door. "Did you get the money for the candlesticks? I had to change the windows and doors of the weekend house, and I'm counting on you to pay for half of it."

Leon didn't say anything about the paintings he had brought back from Belgrade, he decided to tell her more about the great deal once it was done, instead of making a big announcement and facing possible criticism if something went sour.

"Of course," Leon concurred, hugged her and whispered in her ear with a smile, "You know I'm doing everything I need to do to make you happy."

He took the envelope Tone had given him out of his pocket. She ruffled his hair and leaned back.

"Well, well, aren't we cocky. You're self-confident, that's for sure," she gave him a side glance.

Leon kept on smiling.

"Shouldn't I be?" he asked half closing his eyes.

Kristina wriggled from his embrace, quickly turned back to the stove and joyfully called over her shoulder:

"If that's the case, sit down and eat my lunch, if you dare!"

Leon took a dewy bottle of Pinot Blanc from the fridge to have with spaghetti with chicken and peas cream sauce. They were in a great mood and chatted away while feeding chunks of meat to Šeri, who kept merrily wagging her tail, brilliantly mixing the air around the table. Once they were done, Kristina got up from the table and announced:

"You're doing the dishes today. I have to run, I have a recording session. No need to wait up for me. The deadline for the record is at the end of the week, and I'm not sure how long we'll be tonight."

She fluttered to the bathroom, and Leon rested his head in his hands. Will this never end? Why do quick comments have to eat at total bliss and trust, even when everything is perfect, when there's an atmosphere of joyful harmony? A recording session? Is Andraž going to be there? Oh well, he thought to himself, I'm seeing threats where there are none. Everything is fine, after all. Mind your own business, boy, he said to himself.

He took the thickest book on art history from a special pile next to the bookshelf. His professor at the academy was famous for demanding near encyclopaedic knowledge from his students, and, besides knowing everything himself, often poked almost cynical fun out of the confused candidates at his exams. Leon was so deeply immersed in the French impressionists that he didn't even register Kristina leaving. It was only minutes later that he sensed her perfume which filled the room.

Those guys at Sotheby's are annoying

The following day Tone greeted him with a smile, wider than Leon had ever witnessed. He was flailing about with his arms and his eyes beamed from behind the thick glass lenses. He quickly dragged him from the store and into a bar across the street.

"Interpol isn't looking for the paintings. They aren't stolen. We can move on!" he recited in a single breath. "How much do they want for them?"

Leon wasn't surprised by the news. He instinctively felt from the very beginning that everything would check out with the paintings, that these sorts of complications were out of question. They were inherited, after all.

"They wanted seven hundred thousand at first," he replied, "but I wouldn't go for it and we ended up at two hundred and forty thousand. A hundred and twenty thousand a piece. But there is one condition: they want to sell both paintings and they want to sell them immediately."

Tone sighed deeply and shrugged.

"I don't have that kind of money. I only have seventy thousand. I'd have to borrow the rest. But the interest right now is at ten percent, and if the deal were to take some time, the interest would eat up all the profits. We need to come up with something else."

He paused for a bit, as if thinking about it, then continued:

"I have this acquaintance in Munich, maybe he could help out. But first we need to take pictures of the paintings, not just some random pictures, we need to take them to a professional photographer, we need colour photos complete with a colour guide. This won't come cheap, either. The colours need to match, the brush strokes have to be visible. We'll need someone to assist the photographer, in order to cut down the costs. After that I'd personally take the photos to an auction house in Munich."

"I'll help the photographer, I'm interested in learning how it's done," Leon offered.

"Excellent," Tone was visibly pleased. "I thank you in advance!"

They agreed for Leon to take the paintings to a photographer that afternoon and to offer his assistance. Everything should start off swiftly enough. Leon was very curious to know who Tone's photographer was and how he approached his work. He felt he could learn something useful by the way, perhaps something which would come in handy at another time. Tone gave him the precise address and arranged the job over the phone.

The photographer was a man of few words. He walked Leon up and down his studio, had him move around heavy umbrellas and canvas walls used to reflect light, pass cables, set up stands. When he wiped the sweat off his forehead during the break, the photographer grinned as he apologized:

"Those guys at Sotheby's are annoying and I happen to know what kind of photos they want."

"Oh well," Leon thought to himself, "so this is about Sotheby's, not Munich, like Tone explained; wouldn't you know it, this guy, too, has been lying right from the start. I need to keep this in mind!"

Once he was finished with the photographer, Leon drove over to Ulčar. He felt that the chest in his basement was the most secure place for the paintings to wait for whatever fate had in store for them. Ulčar didn't ask any questions, he was just glad that he could help the boy; he liked him, he and his wife were childless, and he saw in Leon a young man who "will someday amount to something."

This is not a quick scam. It's not like throwing a rock and then running

Meanwhile, Bata spent his days on edge. His messenger to Germany hadn't returned with the money yet, the good person hadn't brought him any news about the paintings from Fane the Captain. The insecurity was killing him. He knew he needed to remain calm, that he had to wait, maybe as long as a couple of months, that he shouldn't lose his head; that was the first rule of the business he was in. Keep calm! The situation was eating him up nevertheless and he couldn't stand to remain in his house and focus on the work waiting for him in his attic. He had acquired a number of brilliant paintings and drawings by that time; but he couldn't move on until the story with the first two was finished! At the moment, he was reluctant even to visit Rista, because he would of course want to get paid immediately.

He ventured to his usual spot at the terrace of the Majestic hotel. There he would sip his coffee and *klekovača* brandy, perhaps leaf though a newspaper and of course check out the passers-by. This would get his mind off things a bit, free his thoughts. He didn't feel like visiting any of his acquaintances: Bata wasn't one to go to others, he was the one people came to!

He was having his third shot of brandy when Predrag known as Pedja the Book came walking by and waved at him from the sidewalk. Pedja was the most renowned bookseller in the city; his home and his bookstore looked like the national library and it was next to impossible to navigate through stacks of books filling every available space. He traded in old editions throughout Europe and he could answer any book-related question posed to him. No one knew his real surname. Everyone knew him only as Pedja the Book. He was a huge man; a tall, fat, good-natured giant. But when he held a book in his hand, he held it with such gentleness and love, as if it was the finest porcelain which the slightest of breezes could damage.

"What are you up to, Bata?" he called from afar. "Are you drinking out of boredom or joy, or, God forbid, sadness?"

"Nothing of the above, Pedja, my friend," Bata shook his head. "I'm just sitting here, looking. Beautiful women are passing by, my dear friend, and our time is running out. Stop for a while, have a drink with me!"

Pedja walked around the fence and took a seat. The chair almost wailed under his weight, after he and Bata spent an eternity shaking hands.

"So, how's business?" Pedja enquired after the waiter had brought him a tiny bottle of apple juice.

"There's nothing to brag about, really," Bata began, but Pedja immediately cut him off.

"What do you mean? I heard all about your deal in Germany, you've been settling your debts all over Serbia, your house is getting taller, you've gotten new merchandise. You were dripping silver, or am I mistaken?"

"True, true," Bata nodded, "but it wasn't easy at all. It's not like it was in the old days. The buyers have become picky, they have trouble paying."

"Well, well," Pedja wondered. "I haven't experienced any problems. Sales of old books at auctions have been going great; I'm actually running out of stock. You wouldn't know about any old prints, graphics...?"

"That was never my field of interest," Bata shook his head, "but I can ask around in Zagreb and Ljubljana."

A thought suddenly crossed his mind: Pedja might have some connections in antique bookshops, they get wealthy customers, maybe some of them would be interested in one of the paintings from his stash? He offered Pedja another drink. Pedja insisted that he hadn't been drinking alcohol for quite a while, so he ordered another juice.

"Listen," Bata leaned in closer, "Pedja, my good friend, you know everyone, would any of your customers be interested in buying a fine painting?"

"What kind of painting?" Pedja raised his head.

"Well, a fine one, a world-class one!" Bata said soundly.

Pedja shook his head in bewilderment, then flinched and asked in surprise, agitated, which was quite out of his character:

"What the hell is this? You're the third person who's been offering me paintings in the last few days! Has there been some kind of a flood or what?"

Bata dropped the newspaper from his hands.

"What are you saying? Who's been offering? What?" he cried impatiently.

"First Fane the Captain called me, you know, Pera the Horse's friend, then Rista from Pančevo called, and now you're asking me the same question. What is this, some kind of a joke?" Pedja was still upset.

"You've heard about the paintings by Renoir and Pissaro?" Bata sked. "There's been some talk about them, that's true. What else?"

"Yes," Pedja nodded. "Renoir and Pissaro. And Rista was offering me some southern fruit painted by Miro."

Bata finished his coffee, wiped his mouth and asked:

"Well, Pedja, my friend, that's life for you. But I'd still like to know: could you sell something like this?"

"I have no idea," Pedja shrugged, "I've never sold paintings in my life. But I'm going on a trip shortly, I need to go to London, I can ask around if you'd like."

He checked his watch and quickly got to his feet.

"I have to rush now, my friend. I need to close the store. My assistant wants to enjoy some night life!"

They bid farewell. Bata settled the bill, walked into the street and hailed a taxi:

"To Pančevo, my friend, take me to Pančevo!"

He was getting more and more irritated as they drove on. Bata was trying to think of what to say to the miserable Rista, he was trying to come up with a way to approach him. Any solo move could endanger his carefully thought out plan. Every detail of the plan was crucial. There were to be no mistakes. Those were the hard facts. On the other hand, of course, Rista was an artist, some things were simply beyond his understanding, and there was still no money coming in. Bata would certainly have to pay him something up front. But where was he to get the money? Of course, the money from the silver in Germany... Once it got here...He was again gripped by the anger he felt towards Leon: why didn't he venture to Germany right away, why did he have to stall! Thus he was forced to seek help elsewhere...But that was water under the bridge. Now he had to deal with Rista who started managing things on his own. He needed to be stopped at once. There were too many important things at hand! There was no room now for going solo! Only a choir could reach the grand finale. And he, Bata, only he must keep a tight grip on the baton.

The taxi driver followed his directions and drove him to Starčevo. Bata entered through the gate, walked up to Rista's house and knocked on the door. One of the young blonds opened the door.

"Oh," she was surprised, "it's you? You didn't call to say you were coming, we weren't expecting you..."

"I happened to be in the neighbourhood," Bata mumbled, "so I stopped by."

"Come in, come in, have a seat. Rista is resting. I'll get him right away."

The girl hurried down the hallway, there were sounds of talking and slamming doors. After a while Rista emerged from his bedroom, somewhat bleary-eyed and surprised.

"Bata? What are you doing here?" he asked.

He sat down at the opposite side of the table.

"We need to discuss something," Bata started off right away.

"We do? Did something get sold finally?"

"No, my dear Rista, nothing got sold. This is not a quick scam, it's not like throwing a rock and then running. It's a big and complicated operation and it comes with serious coordination and deep strategy. Without it, nothing will happen. If you're not going to cooperate, I'll have to go to Zagreb and find someone who can do a good job and stick to agreements," Bata said harshly.

Rista winced and opened his eyes wide.

"What do you mean, someone in Zagreb?" he asked in surprise. "Why are you talking like this to me, the master of all masters?"

"That's right!" Bata confirmed. "This is not about the master, it's about the con-artist. You double-crossed me. You broke the rule: you paint, I sell."

"Where did you get this from? I broke the rule?" Rista raised his voice.

"Of course you did. I didn't get it from anywhere. A painting came on the market, one that I haven't even seen before," Bata retorted angrily.

"What painting?" Rista wondered, growing more insecure by the minute. "Are you sure it was me who painted it?"

He turned to look around, fixing his gaze on the vineyard.

How could this be, he wondered, it's only been two days since I gave the painting to Pedja the Book, and Bata has already found out about it? I wanted to make some money on the side, since there's been none coming from Bata.

"That's what the agent you've given it to says," Bata stopped him, almost furious now, then continued, "Don't play me for a fool. You gave a painting to Pedja the Book, for him to sell it abroad. You had a good plan, but you forgot that our city of a million and a half residents is still a small one. Things get around."

He paused to catch his breath, then continued his angry rant.

"Why did you have to do that for? Can't you wait for six months, for everything to fall into the right place, so we can pull off the greatest scam after World War Two? You messed everything up right at the start. It's not been even ten days since I was here, I took twenty paintings, I explained everything again, you agreed, I planned everything carefully, to whom and when I am to give which painting, and you burn everything down in one single move, my time, my fat twenty thousand Deutschmarks, I've brought you a stack of monographs, and I'll bring you more, all you've put in was your work and already you're trying to fly solo!"

Rista slowly gathered his thoughts and decided to argue.

"Hold on, hold on, hold on! This is no ordinary work, this is my genius, my artistic genius...!"

"True, true, but it was me who came up with the genius idea, I'm going to make the genius deal, I brought you the material, I found the Šlomovič catalogue in Zagreb!" Bata hollered. "You're a genius alright, but you're nothing without me!"

He paused to let the words sink in.

Rista observed him, clenching his teeth and his fists, then took a few deep breaths and said, relatively calmly:

"Calm down, Bata, I haven't been working on anything because of these paintings, I put everything else on hold. I've been hiding from my own people. They think I've gone mad. I've been locking myself in my studio and no one is allowed in to see me. My two lionesses guard me furiously. They won't let anyone through the door. I can only work at night, under the lights, so no one catches me during the day."

He paused, certain that he had inserted a clear explanation into their conversation. Bata gave him a cold look and contradicted:

"Alright, Rista, but that's why we made an agreement, we're both sticking to our respective fields for the common good. And you stuck your foot in my part of the business."

Rista nodded wildly and bowed his head in mock repentance. His tussled long brown hair fell over his face. It was clear to him that they needed to make up and strike a deal.

"You're right. It's true. I'm sorry. I shouldn't have done it. I'm guilty. I wanted to make some money fast. How shall we handle this?"

Then he got up, grinned and asked:

"Are we going to have a gunfight?"

He brought a small German Liliput pistol out of his sleeve. It was designed for executions at close range.

"Oh dear," Bata jumped to his feet, "where did you get this? This is like Faberge to a regular egg! Give it here, let me take a look at it!"

The tension broke.

"Women!" Rista yelled, "Get us some brandy. It's time Bata and Rista get properly drunk. Isn't that right?"

He knew he had made a mistake. But they were about to settle it the way men do. It was lucky for him that he entrusted the painting to Pedja. Pedja was a professional. He would ask for the painting to be returned at once. No one would meddle with Bata and his plans!

A fiasco landed on the table, accompanied by two crystal shot glasses. No one counted how many times they filled them up and emptied them. At three o'clock in the morning they gave each other a friendly embrace and a kiss on the cheek, and Bata took a taxi home.

You're laughing, are you? Do you even know what this is?

Leon was strolling around the city. He suddenly felt the desire to talk to his father. He hadn't seen him in a long time; ever since he had moved in with Kristina they mostly spoke over the phone. But now, when he had just returned from Belgrade with two precious paintings, which would surely bring a nice income, he felt good. He felt he could be quite self-assured in conversation with his father. He thought that his father hadn't resented his moving away from home as much as his mother had, and besides, he had always been good at crunching numerical data and giving a realistic assessment of things.

He drove to Kolinska, a large company specialized in preparing light snacks and various drinks, where his father was known as manager Sattler. The gatekeeper at the entrance to the yard waved at him and lifted the barrier. He parked his car in the parking lot reserved for business partners next to the entrance to the main building and climbed the stairs to the first floor. He knocked on the door of the secretary's office and entered. There was no one in the room, so he went on to his father's office; the door was ajar, his father was not at his desk. He took a seat in an armchair and picked up a newspaper from a stack of papers. He hardly opened it when he heard voices and his father appeared a moment later.

"Oh, what an honour!" he exclaimed. "What a surprise! His majesty the son!"

He walked over to Leon and gave him a hug. He was a tall, balding man of athletic posture, with a charming ring of short grey hair around his head, and a few longer strands combed over his bald patch, with a clear gaze and strong arms. A man in his prime, some would say, even if he was preparing to turn sixty.

"We were just testing a new blend of coffee," he tried to apologize for his absence. "It's great. It'll be our new sales hit."

He walked back to the door and called:

"Milena, would you be so kind and bring us two cups of our new coffee blend!"

Then he sat behind his desk, quickly noticed that no new documents had been placed on it in the time of his absence, and focused his eyes on Leon. Leon felt that his gaze contained more than pure pleasure, but maybe also a hint of worry, perhaps even anger?

"Well, you big time art dealer, how's it going?"

"I've nothing to complain about," Leon smiled. "It's enough to make a living."

The secretary came in with the coffee. Leon quickly reached for his cup and had a sip. His father watched him intently.

"Bravo!" Leon exclaimed, smacking his lips like a true connoisseur. "It's really good. You're doing a great job!"

His father smiled, but then immediately grew serious again. He paused for a bit, as if trying to choose his words, waited for the secretary to close the door behind her, then started to speak in a calm manner.

"Son, a time is coming when you'll have to think hard about what you're doing. You're old enough. I'm not sure everything is going in the right direction."

Leon sighed.

"Not you, too, father. I moved in with Kristina, yes, I realise this is not ok with you two, but this was my decision, we're doing fine..."

"What do I care who you're chasing in bed, you'll stop eventually. This is not what I was talking about. It's about your business. I'll give it to you straight. An old friend came to see me, luckily he's a real friend, and he warned me about some stuff you've been doing."

"What have I been doing?" Leon wondered sincerely, quite stunned, as he was about to start bragging and now there was his father, striking an altogether different tune.

"Don't kid around with me, son! You know exactly what I'm talking about! The chief of Interpol for these parts came by, he's dealing with high crimes," his father continued. It was obvious it took great strength to keep his voice calm.

"High crime?" Leon asked again. "What's that got to do with me?"

"Quite a lot," his father replied, interlocking the fingers of his hands and placing them behind his head. Leon knew from experience that this gesture meant his father was not in a humorous mood. "They know about your trip to Germany, they know that you went to Belgrade and brought back two paintings by French impressionists...Should I continue or would you like to add something yourself?"

Leon sat there completely stunned and numb.

"Also, that the biggest criminal in all of Germany, originally from our parts, paid you a visit in Portorož? How many times did I tell you that this Bata of yours will play a good one on you one of these days? And of course I get none of this information from my own son, other people have to tell me about it," his father continued, staring through the window and stroking his chin with both thumbs. "And how do you think my co-workers feel about police coming to see me in my office?"

Leon gathered his thoughts. He began explaining, tentatively at first, but growing more determined with time, as if he was persuading and emboldening himself with his words:

"None of this is high crime, father. Bata sent a messenger to Portorož to pick up the silver I was supposed to take to Germany. I didn't know the man. It was quite understandable, although I didn't like it: it turned out that Bata wasn't able to wait till the end of my vacation and decided to speed things up. I got the paintings from Fane the Captain, who, as you know, is a legally registered antique dealer in Belgrade. I don't see what's the problem there."

He watched his father with genuine bewilderment in his eyes.

"Boy, you can't say it's nothing if it got Interpol to get involved. Why can't you stick to flea markets in Slovenia and Croatia? Why must you consort with criminals?" his father asked reproachfully, but obviously didn't expect an explanation, because he went right on, "If it's not a problem now, it's maybe going to become one. This can all turn to shit, the kind you can't even fathom. Do you realise that you and your friends might have bumped into one of the biggest unexplained secrets this country has, that those two paintings might be part of the Erich Šlomovič collection, which disappeared somewhere around here during the war? That a lot of people lost their lives because of it, including its owner, who ended up in Dachau?"

Leon remembered the name; of course, the catalogue from the beautiful woman's bookcase in Zagreb! Bata grabbed it quite rapaciously back then. A slight smile curled his lips. Fire shot out of his father's eyes.

"You're laughing, are you? Do you even know what this is? Hitler chased those paintings, well, Göring, to be exact, Tito chased after them, then Ranković...I hear some of them were found in Vojvodina. And now here you are, the great dealer, sticking your nose in state affairs. Come on, please!"

His father slapped both his hands on the table. Leon felt himself getting smaller. Not again! The moment a large deal appeared right under his nose, all he needed to do was reach for it, and bang! Everything comes tumbling down. Why is this happening to me? He gathered his thoughts and argued hesitantly.

"It may be as bad as you say it is. But my conscious is clear, I swear. I can't choose who's going to stop me in the street; Bata and I carried out a completely legitimate deal, with the exception of smuggling a single bowl across the border. Fane asked me in bright daylight if I could sell two paintings for him. It just so happens that I also sell paintings. Whether they belong to Šlomovič, or Blomović, or Janko Branko, I really don't care, as long as I get them from a store and sell them to someone who's interested in them," Leon slowly recovered from the surprise and started arguing defiantly. "I really don't see any crime here."

His father crossed his arms over his chest and rocked in his chair.

"Well, alright. I understand. It's obvious that there's a lot you don't know. But judging by what I was told, you're walking a fine line. Ignorance doesn't make it right. Because this stuff doesn't belong to, as you said yourself, Janko Branko, but probably comes from one hell of a dangerous source. You better be one hundred times sure before you reach into the lion's den, especially for someone else's sake," he said, then repeated, "that's what I'm saying, you're walking a fine line, my son!"

Leon was suddenly overcome by an emotion he had almost forgotten. What he saw before him was his father, who might indeed be yelling, but it was a father who cared for his son and was genuinely worried that his son was about to blow it all. God damn, father, I love you, that's what went through his mind.

"I wasn't aware of this," was all he could say, slightly shaken and with a lump in his throat.

"Well, now you know!"

Leon slowly started to get up from the armchair, when an unexpected question crossed his mind. How did Interpol find out about the two paintings? Why did the chief visit his father?

"Wait," he stopped suddenly and started thinking out loud. "Tone was the only person in Ljubljana who knew about the paintings. I never told him where I had gotten them from. That is, he doesn't know about Fane. He's the only one who could have told Interpol about me, and the chief, your friend, came snooping around to you, the father of the bearer of paintings. That means that they know nothing and they can do nothing."

He sat back down and drank his father's coffee, as well.

His father started thinking.

"I wouldn't count on that too much, if I were you," he said slowly and also stretched in his armchair. "This might be a very serious, big thing, and it might not be. We'll see. Now they'll follow you in every way they can. Watch out. And if I know what you're up to, I can at least counsel you if need be. Plus, there's a valuable lesson in this after all: you now know how this Tone guy operates and how much he is to be trusted."

They both got up. Leon walked to his father and embraced him.

"Thank you," he whispered. "Please let me know if there are any more news coming from the high circles."

"The same goes for you," his father replied. "Like I said, if I know, than I can help...You should stop by our house, too, it's not like it'll be the end of you if you have to listen to one of your mother's lectures from time to time. She knows how stubborn you are, but she also knows that you'll somehow do the right thing in the end."

His father patted him on the shoulder as a way to say goodbye. As he was leaving down the staircase, Leon was very determined to seriously think about what his father had told him. As he was getting into his car, he consoled himself with the fun thought that his father was maybe also pleased with him in some macabre way. After all, his son was to be no small-time flea-market thief, but at best a world-class criminal, the kind that you see in movies and read about in leading global newspapers.

How in the world? Nothing for a hundred years, and now three world class authors in one week

He drove back to town. He stopped once more at the Tabernakelj to find out if Tone had made any progress with the paintings. He wasn't in his office, so he went to take a look at the Artes Gallery. Just as he was about to grab the handle, the door opened and Pedja the Book came out. He struggled to get through the half open door.

"Oh," they both froze in surprise.

"What are you doing here?" Leon asked.

"I'm on my way to London, and I thought I'd check what's on the shelves over here," Pedja smiled. "I think I'm the only one who owns more books on art. Although," he checked himself, "these here are not as old."

He scratched his head, as if the thought had just crossed his mind, then continued:

"God must have sent you my way. You know about these things and I need to ask you: I have something good, something so good I'm not sure how to approach it. Would you know of anyone in Ljubljana who's interested in buying old paintings? I was told there was this Tone guy. Do you know him?"

Bells started ringing in Leon's head.

"Who told you that?" he asked, trying to seem uninterested, shoving his right hand in his pocket.

"Who, who, the one that gave the painting, don't you think?"

"What painting? By whom?" Leon could hardly curb his interest.

"Oh, well," Pedja nodded, "you I can tell. It's Miro."

I'm about to have a heart attack, Leon thought; first I get a lecture from my father, a serious warning, and now I'm in for a shock in the middle of the street.

"What Miro are you talking about, God damn?" he practically jumped. "What is going on? I got a Pissaro and a Renoir in Belgrade just last week, and here you are talking about a Miro."

Now it was Pedja's turn to gape.

"I don't know anything about the other two, you've surprised me with this information. There's no way I can take my painting on a flight to London, crossing three borders, but I have photos. If you like, you can offer it wherever you've taken the first two, and then let me know. I'll be back home in about a week."

He took a large envelope from his briefcase and produced two large colour photos. Leon immediately recognized Miro's brushstrokes. Pedja checked his watch.

"Well then, I guess I was really lucky that we crossed paths. I take it it's settled about the painting? Thank you. I have to run, there's a ride waiting at the hotel to take me to the airport. See you, my comrade in battle!"

They bid farewell. Leon was left standing in front of the entrance to the gallery, looking at the two photos. There was a storm unravelling in his head. Is this some kind of rude version of a hidden camera? Is he again dreaming about something which will never bear fruit? He turned around and headed back to the Tabernakelj. Tone is the only man for this kind of thing, despite all the deception coming out of his squinting eyes, while his brain is obviously capable of setting traps, as well.

Tone was now in his office, handling bills. When Leon showed him the photos of Miro's painting, we was shaken. He looked at them from every possible angle, turning them this way and that, unable to believe what had landed on his desk.

"How in the world? Nothing for a hundred years, and now three world class authors in one week. If the Miro is genuine, it's worth at least two million. Where did you get it?" he asked, obviously very excited as well; he was unable to take his eyes off the photographs.

"I'm not allowed to say, I promised the person who brought them to me. Anyway, we have agreed to keep these things strictly secret, haven't we?" Leon said.

Tone paused for a moment and suggestively lowered his head.

"Nonsense! Of course it's a secret, why would I want anyone to know about this?" he got agitated.

"As far as I know, you're not in the best position to talk about secrecy," Leon stopped him cynically.

"What's that supposed to mean?" Tone jumped to his feet.

"You wouldn't happen to know what the Interpol chief was doing at my father's, asking about the paintings by Pissaro and Renoir? I guess he heard about them through the grapevine, right? You're the one to preach secrecy to me. No, thank you, thank you very much!"

Tone puckered his lips, remained seated, then smiled. He wasn't prepared for this accusation.

"Well, what was I supposed to do? I needed to make sure that the stuff was clean; and I always get the chief of Interpol to find out. He's the best source," he retorted as if that was self-evident.

"And by doing so, you naturally had to tell him that you got the paintings from me? Couldn't you come up with some guy from the Czech Republic, or Hungary?" Leon ranted. "I'll be hardly able to sneeze from now on without two random passers-by calling 'Gesundheit'."

Tone laughed:

"Don't sneeze then, right?"

"Well, thank you," Leon muttered. His mind was still swarming with his father's warnings. "While we're at it: have you ever heard about some collection belonging to Erich Šlomovič? It's supposed to be some big thing, hundreds of paintings, mostly from Paris, which were supposed to have disappeared somewhere around these parts."

"Of course," Tone nodded, "there were a lot of rumours about it for a while, but then they died down. He was a Jew, he worked for Vollard, a gallery owner, he amassed a huge collection and was about to open a museum in Belgrade. But then the war came, and they both disappeared, Šlomovič and his collection. If there are any paintings from that source, the market will go haywire. What we have here could possibly be from that collection."

"Ok then, and what's going on with the Pissaro and the Renoir?" Leon interrupted him. "Have you made any progress?"

"No. There's too much talk about these paintings. It may indeed be my fault for letting Interpol in about it. That man from Germany won't answer my calls. And I can only pay thirty thousand for both of them," Tone answered reluctantly.

Leon flew into another rage.

"Are you kidding me? Thirty thousand! That can't be. They'll tell me to go to hell in Belgrade!"

"No, no, you're wrong. If there are more paintings where these two came from, they sent them first, to test the market. They need to get a clear picture, to see if there's any interest for them abroad. If they really belonged to a Jew, which I think they might, because we saw the markings AV, and S, and also the Star of David on the back, it's also dangerous. There are many organisations tracking these things," Tone explained, "it's a tough terrain to navigate."

"Ok then," Leon accepted his explanation and, in his mind, said goodbye to the handsome earnings he was looking forward to. "I'll make a call to Belgrade, but I can see now that this will amount to nothing. Do you think, the Miro also..."

"Oh, no, the Miro is another story altogether, completely different, I'll look into it... no Interpol, heh," Tone replied and winked. Leon didn't wink back.

He slowly walked to the phone booth in Novi Trg. It was becoming clearer to him with every step he took that the two paintings he was sure would bring him big money, were sliding out of his grasp. Nevertheless, he couldn't help but wonder: Was Fane the Captain a real dealer or just an intermediary? Was he in touch with the true source of paintings or did he get them accidentally? And Tone! Did he really have important connections abroad, did he have experience with paintings in this price range, or was it all just good-night stories? He'd never heard of Tone selling anything big to another country. There was a bunch of questions which puzzled him. And what about Bata? Did he really need to drive him away in such a rough manner over the silver? How would he handle a situation like this? Did he know about the paintings from Belgrade or not? Maybe he could swallow his pride and give him a call? Maybe he could. But first he had to deal with Fane.

The phone rang for a long time before he answered.

"If it isn't my Slovenian friend! Are you still alive? I thought you'd vanished. I've been anxiously waiting for some news from you for two weeks now, but there's been no letter, not even a postcard. I gave you some top merchandise, didn't I? What's up with that?"

He could tell from Fane's voice that he was really nervous and impatient.

"Well, Fane, my friend, this stuff is not something you can sell overnight," Leon began, but Fane immediately interrupted him.

"What do you mean, overnight, you've had the paintings for two weeks. Don't talk to me about haste!"

"I need at least two more weeks. One of my acquaintances is going to try to sell them in Germany, over here I have an offer of thirty thousand," Leon tried persuading him. He should know that he has been trying, but there's still no right answer for this deal.

"What the hell are you talking about? Two paintings by famous French guys and thirty...That's unbelievable. The owners over here will have my head, they refuse to wait any longer. Maybe it would be best if I returned them!"

"Don't be like this, Fane. We'll make nothing. Give me another couple of weeks."

"No way, you've had a couple of weeks already. I just can't," Fane rushed on, concluding harshly, "Well, I'm waiting for you. Bring them back. And hurry!"

Click! Click!

The line went dead. Nothing. Of course, it was clear there would be no deal for this kind of money. But he needed to cultivate decent relations with Fane, if nothing else for other possible deals. He'd have to go back to Belgrade. And what if...? Well, he'd have to enquire with those who knew everything. He'll try to reach Bata once he gets home. He'll swallow his pride, it's not like he didn't collaborate with Bata on his first big deal, why not try showing a sign of good will? What am I supposed to do? Making up would be the smart thing to do. At least it seems so. He couldn't achieve much from Ljubljana and over the phone. Bata could probably calm down his partners in Belgrade. Or perhaps he was behind it all, the great puppet master?

As he stepped out of the phone booth he bumped into Tone again.

"And?" he asked.

"And - what?" Leon wondered.

"Did you learn anything, would they be willing to sell it for this offer?" Tone kept digging.

Leon waved his hand, as if this was the most absurd thing he'd ever heard.

"Right. I told you so. They want the paintings back immediately. We've blown this chance," he shook his head, "this train has left the station, unfortunately."

Tone stared back at him with his covert, slightly appraising eyes, adding:

"Actually, I came running after you so we could discuss this thing a little further. I think there's really something going on in Belgrade, I feel it, something big must have come about, how else you would explain three monumental pieces emerging in just a week. We can't let this pass us by!"

His eyelids shot up and Leon was now facing a pretty excited Tone, afraid that the richly laden table will drive right by him. Well, not exactly a table, heaps of money was more like it...

"Well, and?" Leon repeated his question.

"You have some great connections in Belgrade, you got these two paintings, you were offered the third one, as well. So you should go back there, return the Pissaro and the Renoir, and there's no chance you won't find out where this all comes from. And once we have this information, we can do something about it. Maybe we can get something directly from the source," Tone explained.

"Oh, come on! How are you going to do anything about it if you can't even afford to buy these two paintings," Leon turned him down.

Tone took an exasperated breath, as if to say, you don't understand the first thing about this, man.

"Sure, I can't afford to buy two paintings. But if it turns out that there's more, something we could turn into millions, I'll easily pull in some investors. Do you get what I'm saying?"

This was immediately followed by another question:

"So, would you go back there? It's on me."

Leon thought about it. If it costs me nothing, I might as well go once more. This is something I can take time for. After all, I've been dabbling in almost-business and wallowing in almost-money for the whole time. And it's driving me crazy. I have to move forward! I need to catch a break. I should finally have some luck. The money is dwindling and there's none on the horizon. Kristina has kept quiet and is all smiles for now. But how long will this last?

"Well, if you think so..." he said.

"I do!" Tone swiftly nodded, producing two banknotes featuring a black German eagle from his pocket. "I guess this should cover it. If you're successful, we'll make another deal. Alright?"

Leon thought about it for a while, then consented hesitantly:

"I'll check if there are any tickets left for the flight tomorrow morning."

Is this what you want? Ha? Is this what you want?

He went to the city centre. At first he felt like arguing with himself for following Tone's orders just like this, but then he calmed down. It was not like it would cost him anything, he would actually make a decent amount, and at the same time this was his chance to pay Bata a visit and possibly bury the hatchet. It seemed Bata was only too good at moving in the circles devoid of guardian angels. On the other hand, the place was littered with banana peels one could slip on. I'll just swallow my pride and bow my head. Life is what it is. But I need to catch a break, I need to push through. Through hardships to the stars. Right now! He remembered it would be wise to get Bata a present, as a show of good will. Since he had just moved, there could be nothing better than some Velana curtains. He walked into the store adjacent to Nama and picked up some heavy, slightly gaudy curtains with a large flower print. The saleswoman wrapped them up for him in a tight travel roll.

When he was packing his suitcase back home, Kristina and Šeri just came back from their walk.

"Oh," she embraced him merrily, fighting for his attention with the bitch who was also jumping at him, "are you coming or going?"

He pulled her in tightly and gave her a long kiss.

"Yes," he nodded after a while, "there's some serious business up in the air and Tone is paying me to go back to Belgrade. I'll try to figure out what's going on with Bata, while I'm there. It would be sad for both of us to end it on a sour note. Together we can be winners!"

"There's always something up in the air with you," she smiled ambiguously and then asked, "When are you planning to leave?"

"Tomorrow morning, I'm catching a plane," Leon replied, adding an angry comment, "So I'll be up in the air, too. As long as I can get a ticket."

"Oh," Kristina said, ignoring his remark, filling Šeri's bowl with some food and quickly adding, "I have to go to a shooting again tonight and I don't know when I am back. You don't have to wait up for me."

"A shooting?" Leon winced. "Another one? Didn't you wrap things up the other night?" He paused, then added: "Will Andraž be there?"

Kristina straightened up and gave him an angry look. Her brows rose menacingly.

"Yes," she nodded, "yes, Andraž will be there. He owns the studio. Yes, he likes me. Yes, he's beautiful and rich. And when I get nothing from you, he lends me money. Money in exchange for nothing. But," her voice rose to yelling, "I'm with you, I love you, you're living with me, in my apartment, that's how we decided, and... and... I'm done with your jealousy. I have my own life, and you have yours. If that's so hard, why don't you put me on a leash, go everywhere with me, but I'll go everywhere with you, too. That's how things go. Is this what you want? Ha? Is this what you want?"

Her face got all red, and a vein bulged and throbbed in her neck, her beautiful neck. Leon was stunned by this outburst, he opened his arms and looked at her with wide, surprised eyes.

"What did I say?" he asked in mock playfulness. "I just asked, didn't I?"

"You did," Kristina nodded, "you just asked, you just asked. We both know what this is. Stop it. Stop it. Now!"

She was shaking.

The blush brought out her green, large, angry, slightly teary eyes, and the hair, which unravelled from her high do, made her charming look very exciting. The long fingers of both of her hands instantly formed sweet looking fists.

Leon hugged her again and pressed her to his body.

"I've stopped."

He was overcome with insuppressible desire. He leaned over to her ear and gently said:

"Could you spare ten minutes before you go to your recording session?"

"Robber," she screamed, grabbed him by the hair and hauled him to the bedroom. Šeri tried scratching at the door, but soon realised there was no point in keeping it up.

After a while, Kristina went in the shower, put on an evening dress and went to the studio, while Leon drove to Ulčar and took both paintings from his hiding place.

In the morning, when the alarm clock woke him up to go to the airport, Kristina wasn't back yet. We postponed the questions with passion, Leon thought, but probably just postponed.

Of course, you screwed the silver deal and pushed me in the gutter

Fane the Captain was waving his arms and disappointedly shaking his head.

"How in the world, my young Slovenian friend, were you not able to sell two superior paintings? You don't come across stuff like this every day, and you messed up like this?"

Leon took a taxi from the airport first thing in the morning and drove to his front yard.

"You wanted too much for them," Leon tried his best to lie with some conviction. "Even in Ljubljana people aren't capable of coming up with such sums of money on such a short notice. And besides," he quickly added, "everyone started coming up with these amazing paintings all of a sudden. I've just been offered another masterpiece in Belgrade."

Fane was visibly surprised.

"Who offered it, by God, who?"

"I'm not at liberty to say, I made a promise. I haven't told anyone about the Pissaro and the Renoir you offered, either. This is not something you talk about," Leon replied.

"I don't have any problem with it," Fane shook his head. "I've nothing to hide."

"Well, I do," Leon quickly added. "It's nobody's business. But of course I need to know the history of the painting. But this is another thing altogether."

"Too bad," Fane mumbled after thinking it through, wrinkling his forehead. He kept pushing his hair away from his eyes with nervous gestures. "Now I'll have to return the paintings and neither one of us will profit from them. Even worse, I might just lose a very interesting supplier. This is all turning out bad. I'm really disappointed."

"Well, it happens," Leon sighed and moved to get up. "I can see that you're so disappointed I'm not even getting a cup of coffee. Who would have thought?"

"Wait!" Fane leaped to his feet. "You've gotten me so upset I've forgotten all about it. Sit down, sit down, what's the rush?!"

He pushed Leon back in the chair and headed for the kitchen. A short while later a smell of coffee preceded the appearance of Fane holding a large tray in the doorway.

"Here, coffee and some sweets, something good for your stomach, I bet you didn't munch on those mouldy sandwiches they give out on the plane."

Leon grinned.

"Oh, my, the service by the waitresses in this joint is terrible," he exclaimed merrily, "but the coffee is damn good!"

They chatted some more about business which were more or less stagnant, about life which was passing on too quickly, and they both agreed on the fact that good coffee is essential for a successful day.

"I'll go check if Bata's had his first morning coffee yet," Leon slowly started to take his leave.

"Bata?" Fane asked in bewilderment. "I've heard the love you had was dwindling. Am I wrong?"

"Well, I couldn't say," Leon waved him off, "he got all upset over nothing, I want to see if he's calmed down by now."

"That's right, that's right," Fane nodded, "it's no use holding grudges. You need to make up. I know it's hard to take the first step, but after that everything gets better."

As they shook hands, Fane added calmingly:

"Bata is a good man. Give him the opportunity to back off honourably. It'll work out for both of you, you'll see."

Leon slowly headed toward the city centre. What was he to do? He didn't let Bata know that he was coming. What if he just walked over to his house? What kind of a reception would he get? What if Bata wasn't home? He was suddenly seized by insecurity and he was no longer sure he was doing the right thing. The best thing to do would be to first pay a visit to his mother, he thought: the nice grey-haired lady would surely know where her resentful son was hanging around and what he was up to.

The morning was evolving into a sunny day. It'll be hot again today, Leon thought. He needed to find shelter in some shaded garden. He reflected on the conversation he had had with Fane. Could it really be a coincidence that three exceptional paintings surfaced here almost at the same time? Was it possible that Fane the Captain and Pedja the Book weren't aware of each other's business? After all, the circle of people interested in these things was relatively small. Bata must know more about this for sure. There's no way a development like this would pass him unnoticed. He really needs to find him.

Slowly he arrived to the apartment building in Obilićev Venac, the one where Bata's mother resided. He took the stairs to the fourth floor. The elevator was again out of order. As he rang the bell, out of his breath, he heard her voice:

"Come in, it's open!"

Leon entered and locked the door behind him with a learned gesture.

He walked to the living room, calling out loud greetings from the hallway:

"Good afternoon, good afternoon, is anybody home?"

The lady was once again seated at the table, playing solitaire. The room was filled with a devastatingly alluring scent of bean stew.

"Oh, my son," the woman lifted her head, "welcome. You didn't call to say you were coming, but never mind, the pot is big enough to feed one more person."

She embraced him, kissed him and invited him to sit down.

"I'm not who you came to see, right? My Bata has been wandering about, chasing craftsmen; everyone was his friend till the moment he really needed them. Well, it seems things are about to wrap up, anyway. He moved and is running around. It just so happens that I'm making lunch for him today, and now he'll have a friend at the table, as well. Have a seat, take a breather. Tell me what's been going on in your parts. The bean stew will be done in the meantime."

She walked to the stove to check if everything was in order.

Leon wasn't sure what to say to all of this; he simply accepted the welcoming atmosphere and decided to wait: whatever happens, happens. The woman took a bottle of brandy from the cupboard and poured them each a shot. Then she took a different set of cards from a drawer and they played rummy. Leon couldn't help but notice that there was a lot less furniture in the apartment than usual. Of course, Bata must have moved some of it to his new house.

They haven't even finished the first game when there was some racket at the door, followed by a few nervous rings of the bell.

"This must be my neighbour," the hostess said, "she's a nice woman, you'll love to meet her. She usually comes round for coffee at this time of day."

She got up to open the door and Leon heard her voice:

"Oh, you're here already, son?"

"Well, it's nothing, I had some business in the neighbourhood, so I came right up; I can't live without your bean stew. The sooner, the better. No use waiting till noon. So, here I am."

Bata appeared in the door leading in from the kitchen and froze solid.

"What are you doing here?" he asked curtly, without offering a greeting, he merely stared harshly at Leon. Then he turned to his mother:

"What the hell are you two doing?"

"Hold on, my son, Leon is my guest, I invited him to have some bean stew. Everyone I care about is welcome in my home," the mother said, stroking Leon's hair. It was affection, not stubbornness that beamed from her eyes.

"Alright, alright," Bata nodded, "I didn't say anything, did I? I just wasn't expecting to find the boy here. How should I know where he's wandering around?"

He turned to Leon, coldly:

"It's been quite a while since we saw each other, hasn't it?"

"Yes," Leon replied, "you've gotten something against me."

Then he remembered Fane's advice and quickly added:

"It's true, I was a bit hesitant the other time, but..."

"Of course, you screwed the silver deal and pushed me in the gutter," Bata immediately ranted sombrely and walked to the table.

"But I didn't, you wanted me to drop everything and fire like a loaded gun, to follow your orders right away," Leon tried to find an excuse.

"Well, that's what I'm saying..."

"Hold on, children! What is this? I've never seen you bicker like this. What's wrong with you two? Bata, I've noticed you never mention him anymore, and he phoned here for you several times, despite the fact that you moved. Didn't you give him your new number?" his mother interrupted them with calming criticism.

"But he's not listening to me," Bata ranted on.

"Well, he's a grown man, not your busboy, he's practically family, and this is the way you treat him," the woman kept scolding him.

"Stop it mother, you're getting on my nerves," Bata waved her off, then turned to Leon, "you, traitor, you could have called first and let me know you were coming!" He looked at him reproachfully, but Leon could see the harshness waning in his eyes.

"Enough!" Bata's mother was angry now. "There is to be no quarrel in my house. You kiss and make up, that's the end of it! If either of you don't like this, the door is right there!"

"Look at this woman, showing the door to her own son," Bata mumbled and sat down. "Calm down. Bring us some bean stew!"

The mother placed two large plates in front of them, sliced the bread, brought in the pot and set in on a mat. Hot steam rose from the pot.

"Eat and stop your nagging!"

When Bata finished his first portion, he said:

"Shake my hand. I missed you."

Leon reached out his right hand.

"It's not like we're old men," Bata added, getting up, "get up, let's hug!"

Bata embraced and kissed him.

There's a scene straight out of The Godfather for you, Leon thought to himself, and the mother said in a stern tone:

"This is how I like you two, I hate to see you fighting. Friendship is the most important thing in the world!"

"Yes, mother," Bata nodded, "give me another portion!"

Then they emptied the bottle of brandy. The mother reproached Bata with drinking her booze now that he had moved to his own place, instead of bringing some over. Bata couldn't wait to talk to Leon alone, so he pulled him to the door, calling:

"I'll arrange the thing with the booze, mother. Thanks for the bean stew. You make the best bean stew in the whole world. But we have to run to the town now, to drink to our friendship properly!"

They said goodbye to Bata's mother and went across the street to the nearest joint called Parrot. They stuck to the bar like glue and ordered some drinks. Bata didn't hesitate to half whisperingly curse everything related to Leon he could think of, and ranting about business going on all the time, not only when someone felt like it, especially when the business in question was his business. If I told you to drive to Germany, you're to drive to Germany, and not try to get between some woman's legs, is this clear, he grabbed Leon by his ear. I have my own calculations and you're not supposed to ruin them. Drink, listen and be quiet. If you want to work for me, you need to do as I say. You can do your own thing when we agree that you can. Leon nodded, silently taking Bata's lead, one glass of whiskey at a time.

"This will be tough," Leon thought, "but it's just the way it is when two repenters agree to pick things up where they left them."

Modigliani, I'm holding a real Modigliani

Leon woke up with the first light. He lay in his bed, the sheets and bedding were clean; they smelled fresh. It took him some time to realize where he was. Bata's house, of course. He remembered the two of them calling for a taxi sometime during their night of drinking, and then he snapped. He got up with a headache and a terrible sensation in his stomach and ventured out of the room. In the hallway, he turned blindly in the faint light and luckily found the bathroom. He emptied his bladder and staggered back to his room.

When he woke again it was two in the afternoon. The smell of coffee and cigarette smoke was rising from the ground floor and through the open door to his room. This is probably what woke me, he thought to himself. He felt like throwing up. Awful. The boozing rampage led Bata and him through countless pubs and restaurants in the city, and they ended up in a discotheque. The amount of alcohol they consumed would probably be enough to kill a normal person, or at least trigger delirium tremens. He put on his clothes and went down the stairs.

Bata sat in the large living room, drinking coffee and smoking his Drina smokes.

"Did you sleep well? Sit down," he pointed to a nice Bidermeier chair. Behind him, there was a beautiful "the one? - yes!" bookcase from Zagreb.

For a while they kept quiet, observing each other. Leon could not for the life of him remember if they discussed paintings during their drinking spree or not. He decided to stay off the subject, just in case.

"We got drunk alright," said Bata while exhaling smoke, adding, "but what is most important is that things are like they were between us. What can we do, I'm full of myself and you're pretty much the same. We were born this way. But business is business."

He got up and put a large cup of coffee in front of Leon.

"Coffee, coffee," Leon smacked his lips and hastily made a few sips.

They looked at each other, appraising one another. Both of them were eager to start talking about the paintings, but Leon would like Bata to open the conversation, and Bata wanted to hear what Leon knew about the whole thing. They spoke about business, beautiful crockery, antique furniture; Leon praised the interior decor of the apartment and then remembered.

"Here, this package is for your wife. I see you don't have curtains on all of your windows. She might find it useful."

"Oh," Bata cheered up, "you are a true man, coming over with a present, despite our disagreements. I won't open it; I'll leave the pleasure to her."

Leon thought this would be a good moment to try a bit of spying.

"Did you hear something about some French impressionists for sale here in Belgrade? Do you know anything about it?"

"I did hear something, yes," Bata nodded cautiously.

"You wouldn't know where they might be, would you? I heard of some paintings being offered in Ljubljana, but the deal never went through. I might have a buyer," Leon said.

Bata gave him a more careful look:

"A buyer? This could be interesting."

"You could look around a bit, you can find out everything that goes on in Belgrade," Leon threw in. "I can't imagine how this could have slipped by you."

"It happens," shrugged Bata, "it happens."

After a short pause, he hastily asked:

"Did you go to see Fane Kapetan at all? He is connected to all sorts of people, from Gipsies to junkies to down-and-out old men, he does business with different questionable dudes," he felt his way. "Maybe he could tell you something."

Interesting, Leon thought to himself, Bata obviously knows nothing about this, and he has a nose for it. He knows where to look. Let him do the searching, he is the master, maybe there is a way for me to get to those paintings again.

Interesting, Bata thought to himself, Leon obviously knows nothing about this, and he has the nose for it. Let him search. Maybe he will get Fane to tell him the paintings were there, but they went back to the owner, who is of course unknown.

Isn't it incredible! Everything that happens in Ljubljana, somehow finds Leon. Even Pedja the Book confessed that it was Leon he offered Miro first, the one Rista was trying to peddle on his own.

There's nothing to be done. The boy is young and he's got talent.

I won't fight with him, I will include him back, like I was planning to from the very beginning. This is why I have chosen him in the first place. Ljubljana is an important starting point.

"I've heard some rumours that something came up in Vojvodina. Some old, long forgotten collection. A messed up junky inherited a house and there was this miraculous find in the attic. Everyone keeps whispering and hinting... we are all waiting... none knows anything for certain," he started again.

"This is something I would be quite interested in," Leon quickly came back to life. "I might be able to find a few buyers. This could be good money."

"Yes," Bata again nodded, puffing on his Drina, "this would be something. There is no business in the summer, everything is quiet, we are all suffocating in the heat. See," he flicked the ashes in a nice crystal ashtray, "stroll around the city for a bit, look around, ask around, wherever you know someone, and I'll go my way, I have some urgent business to take care of related to the house, I will visit my connections, and I'll see you again in the evening."

"Sure," Leon agreed, "I need to go to the agency to confirm my plane ticket; I haven't yet set the return flight."

"Wait, no need to hurry it," Bata suggested perhaps more firmly than necessary, twitched at his haste and added more slowly, "there will still be time for this. Who knows what information we will gather during the day. Also, you have to show the curtains to Mira..."

Leon left. He headed toward Skadarlija. He was certain that a good portion of roasted mixed meat would cure his upset stomach. Charcoal does wonders for indigestion, especially one drenched in alcohol, he thought to himself. On his way he went into Pedja the Book's bookstore.

As usual, the man sat in the middle of the book filled room, almost lovingly cradling a booklet with metal plates and buckles in his lap.

"And what are you doing here?" he greeted Leon joyfully, and pushed a book in his face, before he could even answer. "See, what the Hungarian book masters used to do?"

Leon nodded and quickly asked:

"You wouldn't have that painting here, the one you showed me pictures of? I would like to take a look at it."

"Oh, dear," Pedja winced, "I forgot to let you know. It's gone. The owner decided he wanted it back. I can understand him. I love books and haven't got the foggiest idea about paintings."

Leon gasped in disappointment he found unable to hide. Pedja at once noticed it and tried to soften the blow:

"What? You have too much money? Could you take care of it? I doubt it. The owner came up with some combination. Stop frowning, will you? You know how it is, now you have it, now you don't. Surely there's something around for you, don't you think? You've made it this far without Miro."

Leon was so upset he no longer felt like talking. He would now have to return to Tone with the bad news. He quickly bid goodbye. This is just awful! Big things are all around me, but when I reach out, they just fly away. He felt like a young brat, being teased with candy by older boys, only to be swiped away at the very last moment. Beginners have bitter starts, if they want to become masters. Oh well, maybe Bata will learn more.

As Leon went to the city and Bata was left alone, he slowly walked to the attic and locked himself in the big room. He took a file from the cabinet. There was a fat collection of oil paintings in it, ink, pencil and charcoal drawing, all of which he had brought over from Rista, once they smoothed the paper over. In the evenings and late into the nights, while his wife and daughter were asleep, he spent many days in perfect nocturnal silence, addressing his part of the business. He used dust to further age the masterpieces which were painted with old pigments on old canvases and paper by Rista, slapping their backs with tiny seals in different colours. He cut them from potatoes, dipped in bottles of old ink and made the impressions: AV for Ambrois Vollard, ES for Erich Šlomovič, a Star of David here and there, adding random numeral notes in pencil. Any attempt at investigation would show that every single component of the paintings was indeed old. He arranged all of them on the table and over the floor and observed them, absorbed in his own thoughts. He delighted in their immense beauty and of course artisan manufacture: layers of colour in different thickness, assertive, and again tiny brushstrokes, finger interventions, an occasional coffee or wine stain... Rista is a true grand master. He studied all the techniques well. He can brilliantly reproduce any painting he sets his mind to. He pondered his next step. Pissaro and Renoir came back, but he achieved his goal, the rumours were rife, the market shivered in anticipation, the birth of the story was neatly veiled in ambiguous mystery... Now is the time for him to make a decisive move and bring the events to a victorious conclusion. The world will flinch. He will catch millions!

He decided on a beautiful recumbent nude by Modigliani and a black and white ink drawing of a sitting female nude by Rodin. He observed them for a long time, wrapped them up in regular wrapping paper and placed them in his file. The rest he carefully put back in its place and went back down into the living room. He approached the phone. His connection quickly went through.

"What's up, my Whitey? See, your friend Bata's been thinking about you. You'll get good money to take me and Leon to Ljubljana at night, and then maybe even further. Is your Volvo still alive or was it crushed at some junkyard? How about you are you chasing a beautiful lady or would you prefer to get some work done?"

"Hey, Bata Batane, it must be hard times when I hear from you. I'm just supposed to let everything go and drive you around? The things I have to do to earn a piece of dry bread," Beli the taxi driver groaned.

"Is that a no, would you like me to find someone else?" Bata got fussy, playing angry.

"Slow down, slow down," Beli resisted, "I didn't say I won't do it, did I? Have I ever let you down? Is this how you're supposed to talk to me?"

Bata checked his watch.

"Ok, then. Look, I'm inviting you to dinner, you'll drive us to Raca in Boleč, an empty sack can't stand upright. We will fill ourselves with kajmak and new cheese, and get down a kilo of lamb or two, and drown the lot in Welschriesling. After that, Leon and I will take a nap and you will drive your horses up north. Is that ok? Pick us up at eight at my place. Ok?"

"Ok, Bata, my friend, ok. Now shut up, so I can get up and get my limo cleaned up. It will be as pure as my soul, it will glitter like the eyes of the beautiful woman you are about to pounce sooner or later. That's how we drivers are," Beli assured him.

Bata laughed and leaned back in his sofa. He immediately drifted off in contentment. He was woken up by his wife Mira. She returned home from work late afternoon and started clattering with pots and pans. A short, round brunette, a geology engineer, she forgot about the rough times in the cramped apartment of her otherwise very loving mother-in-law, and now spent all of her time in their new apartment dancing around the kitchen.

Not long after, Leon rang the doorbell.

"Look, wife, what my young Slovenian friend has brought for you," Bata immediately placed the parcel on the table.

Mira, who worked at the Institute for Geology in alternating shifts, inquisitively started untying the string and pulled out the curtains in no time. She shrieked in delight:

"Oh, my, these are just what I wanted, Bata, look..."

She spread the fabric over the table so she could take a look at the whole pattern, brought her hands together in delight and jumped over to Leon.

"My dear boy, how did you know, this is wonderful," she cried, hugging him.

Leon laughed merrily and even Bata made no attempt at hiding his joy.

"Let the man get a breather now," Bata tried to quiet his wife down and motioned Leon to follow him to the other room. He threw his paintings' file on the floor right there and then.

"My friend," he said seriously, "you disappointed me once, but that's in the past now. I decided to give you another chance. A chance bigger than anything you've ever dreamt of."

Leon came to life in tense excitement. He suspected Bata did not let an old grudge go for nothing.

"I admit," Bata continued, "I've known about the paintings from the start, the ones you asked me about. I have two of them myself. Some junky brought them to me, I've known him for a long time. He's got many more. He's the one who inherited the mysterious attic in a god forsaken village. I paid him for the two paintings on the spot and he promised to sell the others to me, too. He will ignore all other dealers. That's why I need the money, the kid is no fool. He dreams of big money. But I, or should I say we, can make even bigger money out of it. Catch my drift?"

Leon nearly froze solid. Of course, I knew it. Bata is aware of everything. Bata can get everything. Bata took me back in his business.

Bata rules. He was speechless.

Bata continued in a soft voice.

"I have two absolutely unreal pieces tight here in this file. I thought maybe we could take them to Ljubljana, you and I, see if we can make a good deal, maybe get the money for the other paintings together, and if not, we can go on to Munich. I know which doorbell to ring in Munich. But the first thing now is to do whatever it takes to get the money for this big deal quickly."

Leon still didn't fully register what was happening. The story kept repeating. Not only did he discover where the paintings were coming from, as Tone instructed him to do, there were two new ones here already. And he was again part of it. Will something finally play out right? Will there finally be big money for him, too?

"Beli will drive us. Keep the plane ticket for another time. A Volvo is quite a different story than your Quatrelle, isn't it?" Bata was already chuckling at the sight of the breathless Leon.

"Come on now," he said, "first we will have some dinner. And then off we go."

Bata chose this moment to flash a treacherous smile.

"What's up?" he asked. "Don't you want to know which paintings I'm carrying around in my file?"

He bent over, pulled the two parcels out and spread them open. Leon's eyes bulged; he could hardly keep his balance. He immediately recognised both the painting and the drawing, and he noticed the familiar signatures, as well: Modigliani, Rodin.

"This is unreal," he managed to utter and sank to his knees.

He checked the Modigliani canvas from every side, noticed every mark, felt it, caressed the recumbent woman and felt every beat of his excited heart in his ears. He literally felt his hairs standing up straight.

"Modigliani, I'm holding a real Modigliani!" went through his mind.

Then he checked the drawing; Rodin, as if the woman just wriggled out of the famous kiss.

"And," he almost stuttered, looking at Bata, "you bought this, you paid for this? That's millions!"

"The millions are still to come," Bata laughed. "I paid that poor fellow just a fraction of what you would have gotten for that silver deal if you hadn't screwed me up. But the rest of the paintings will cost us much more if we want buy them off him."

For a moment, Leon rested his head in his hands. He felt beads of sweat gather on his forehead, yet they had nothing to do with the hot evening on the other side of the windows.

"I can't believe this," he shook his head, collected his thoughts and said, "so we are taking this to Ljubljana?"

"Yes," Bata nodded and checked his watch again. "But most probably right on to Munich. Get ready. Beli is coming any moment now."

Indeed, the driver promptly rang the bell and they lost no time moving forward.

There are days when I hide my pain...

A vacant reserved table awaited at the restaurant. All the others were occupied and a hot summer atmosphere was brimming above them; it was converging with the smoke and the heat coming from the grill where several lambs were rotating on spits above the embers. The restaurant didn't have a regular garden; there was only a large roofed shack in the backyard, with multiple dining rooms with wide open double windows. Photos of famous guests who dined here in the past were on full display on the wall next to the entrance. Some were adorned with autographs.

Bata ordered some cheese and kaymak as an hors d'oeuvre, along with a bread basket full of fresh flat bread. But first, they prepared their digestive tracts with some herbal brandy, which the scrawny waiter brought over in three separate small flasks, without being asked to. This was immediately followed by a dewy pitcher of white wine, which landed in the middle of the table, along with cutlery. This was the normal house welcome. The waiter returned a moment later, carrying a tray of cheese.

"I don't care for wine," Whitey called amidst the general noise, adjusting his jacket, "there's a long journey still ahead, after all. Let's not waste any time. Aren't you in a hurry, Bata? I want to eat something first and just have a coffee later. A double, naturally!"

"Time spent on food and drink is never a waste," Bata replied, broke off some bread and spread a thick layer of kaymak over it. He then immediately turned his attention to the fresh cheese.

"You won't find better anywhere."

Leon wasn't shy about it, either.

The noise in the restaurant didn't die down even when musicians appeared at the door; the quintet was made up of the bass, the guitar, the violin, the clarinet and the accordion. The accordionist was also the singer. He spotted Bata, who was a regular there, and brought the music over to their table.

"There are days when I don't know what I'm to do..." the other musicians repeated after the accordionist.

"*There are days when I hide my pain...*" Bata sang along in a tight voice, raised his glass, proposed a toast and downed the drink. Then he took some banknotes which he had obviously prepared in advance from his shirt pocket and stuck them in between the creases of the accordion from above. The accordionist motioned with his head for the clarinettist to perform a solo part, put the money away in his pocket and took a slight bow.

"Well, my dear Slovenian friend, is there anything more beautiful in this world than a restaurant like this? Good food, music, and friends," Bata exclaimed enthusiastically, immediately answering his own question with: "No, there isn't! There's nothing more beautiful!"

Leon merely nodded with his mouth full, as he was already enjoying nibbling on supremely roasted ribs with the skin on top. Bata downed another glass of wine.

"Bata, don't, don't get drunk on us!" Whitey warned him. "There's a long journey ahead of us. Let's eat up and leave!"

Bata shook his head with a disapproving smile.

"Shut up, my dear Whitey. Your job is to drive. My job is to say when we're leaving, where we're going and what we're doing."

Whitey lowered his head and mumbled:

"Bata, Batane, we go to a bar to have some fun when we have the time for it, not when we need to get going. We should come here when it didn't matter when we start the next day."

At that moment, Bata reached for the meat as well. He forked out a piece of roasted thigh, bit into it, nodded and agreed while chewing.

"You're right, Whitey, my friend. But it wouldn't be right to offend the master who sweats over the fire for us. Let's eat! Do you like it?" he turned to Leon.

Leon enjoyed the excellent roast and watched the man with the dirty white apron, who manned the spits behind a large glass wall. The reason for the place being packed was obvious to him, as the eaters were constantly served with precious and freshly roasted portions; they were actually not really portions. Tables ordered meat by the kilo, two kilos...

When there was nothing more than a plate full of bones left in front of Bata, Whitey and Leon, and the wine pitcher was empty, Bata waved his hand and asked for the bill. After a while, a short, broad-shouldered, round-bellied man with a long black moustache appeared. He, too, was wearing an apron and a small cap on his head, wiping his sweaty forehead.

"Was everything alright, Bata?" he asked.

"You have to ask, dear boss? When Christ comes back to Earth, he'll forget all about the fish. He'll come to this place and take you under his wing. You'll feed the peoples for him, and there'll be no infidel with food like this, my friend!"

The innkeeper grinned. "Bata, Batane, my friend, you should be in politics, you are a master of fairy tales..."

"Stop it, boss, I don't take, I pay!" Bata interrupted him, got up, embraced him around the shoulders and took him away from the table. Not a moment later the waiter brought Whitey a large cup of black coffee. Bata returned after a while, and calmly faced Leon and Whitey:

"Are you done, gentlemen? I'd like to hit the road, if you don't mind."

The boss was waiting for them at the door, pointing at three shots of brandy placed on the bar.

"For the road," he said.

Bata turned to Whitey, explaining - "You really don't have to!" - immediately downed two tiny flasks and pushed the third one toward Leon. "For the road!"

Citizen of this state, shut up and open the trunk, as the competent authority of the state tells you to

They drove off.

Bata fell asleep on the passenger seat even before they reached Belgrade. Leon watched the city lights which they left behind. He felt good. The dinner was excellent, and they were driving towards an incredible business venture. Modigliani, Rodin, Bata added two Orthodox icons... nothing could go wrong now. He couldn't care less about Miro, Pissaro and Renoir that was all history, Bata was the master of his business. He had witnessed his approach when he dealt in silver with Frietzl; how was he going to handle the paintings at the Faber auction house? He was about to start a new chapter. He was starting to get drowsy, but felt a little bit of fear nonetheless. He didn't know Whitey all that well, he wasn't sure he could trust him to drive at night, especially after the large dinner and some alcohol. That's why he occasionally started a conversation, but they all dwindled shortly. Whitey was completely focused on the road, giving the impression that he was distracted by conversation.

Suddenly, Leon became fully awake and his eyes bulged. He saw a car wheel roll in the same direction, illuminated by their headlights.

"Will you look at this," he laughed, "what kind of magic is this?"

"What..." Whitey managed to open his mouth, and a moment later the car shook and started swerving, it tilted sideways and there was a fierce sound of metal grinding against the road. Whitey struggled to hold on to the steering wheel, breaking, swearing and manoeuvring, he somehow managed to stop the car, which only slightly slipped over the shoulder. Bata jumped up.

"What the hell are you doing?" he hollered at Whitey.

Whitey was almost spread over the steering wheel, he was shivering.

"We lost a first wheel while driving," Leon explained, upset. "Whitey saved our lives."

"What the hell is going on?" Bata kept ranting, increasingly awake. He opened his door and clambered out of the car. He immediately slipped and fell flat on his backside at the curb.

Whitey and Leon followed him out of the car. The engine was

still humming, the headlights pointed somewhere into the field. Whitey leaned on the hood of the car, trembling, shaking his head, as if he couldn't believe they all emerged out of this unscathed.

"You're a champ," Leon turned to him, quite pale and shaken, "we are born again."

Bata now came to.

"Are you insane, man?! You almost killed us all with this junk piece of a car!"

Whitey didn't say anything, while Leon started to explain in a conciliatory voice:

"Bata, don't, Whitey's manoeuver saved our lives..."

"He'll save us once he gets us out of this outback! People are expecting me tomorrow in Munich, and here I am, rotting away in the middle of nowhere," Bata kept raving as he was climbing out of the ditch.

He leaned against the car and looked around.

Whitey walked back a certain distance to place the warning triangle on the road, put the "taxi" light on the roof of the car, turned the daylight running lights on, and then started waving down passing cars to get someone to drive him to the nearest village where he could call a tow truck from. The very first passing truck stopped for him, sympathetically offering him a ride.

Both passengers from the broken vehicle now faced a long and excruciating wait in the hot night. Swarms of mosquitos rose from some marshes, rejoicing at the only two living beings far and wide. Bata kept cursing, Leon tried to console him, but none of them had the courage to go back and seek shelter in the car at the side of the road. Finally, they saw a light blinking in the distance, but it turned out their delight was premature.

A police car with flashing blue lights came whistling from the direction of Belgrade and stopped behind the Volvo. Two policemen jumped out of the vehicle.

"What happened?" the first one asked.

"We lost a wheel," Leon explained, wondering at the coincidence of police driving by in the middle of the night.

"Oh, my, for God's sake, you were lucky. Where are you headed?"

"To Ljubljana," Leon answered, counting on the officers' deep sympathy.

"To Ljubljana? By taxi? Well, well, if that isn't something. And what are you transporting? Come on, let's open the boot!" the younger and more decorated of the two officers ordered.

"Who the hell cares?" Bata flew off the handle, he was extremely agitated, yelling as he stepped closer. "We are citizens of this state, we pay taxes, we've just had an accident, and you want to know what we have in the boot. Can't you think of anything better?"

"Citizen of this state, shut up and open the trunk, as the competent authority of the state tells you to!" the older, heavier officer roared, making his cap jump on his head.

Leon raised his hand, signalling to Bata to calm down, walked to the boot and opened it. The officer unwrapped the paper off the first roll and looked at the icons, while the Modigliani appeared from the second one.

"Well, well, icons!" he exclaimed. "Whose is this?"

"Mine!" Bata hollered furiously.

He stepped closer and held on to the boot lid.

"Stop yelling," the officer interrupted him, "just answer the question, I asked you nicely. What about these doodles over here?"

"They're mine," Leon quickly replied as he wanted the officers to handle both of them equally. He wanted to take part of the blame, as well.

"Which one of you was driving?"

"No one!" Bata snarled.

The officers were stunned.

"The car drove itself, into the ditch, while you two were safe-guarding this stuff for the black market. Don't play games with me!" the younger officer seemed to be losing his nerves as well.

"No," Leon explained, "the taxi driver, he was driving, someone took him to get a tow truck and we're just stuck out here, waiting."

The blue angel lifted his cap, scratched his head and ordered after a short reflection:

"Come on, gather your stuff; we're taking you to our police station in Šabac, we'll have a little talk there!"

Just as he finished saying this, Whitey arrived at the scene with a tow truck, also with a flashing light.

"Here I am," he was waving from the booth. "We're saved!"

"Don't count on it!" Bata hollered. "These two faggots have invited Leon and me over to their place."

"Stop it, Bata, I'm begging you," Leon tried to silence him, then turned to both officers, "we have a meeting in Ljubljana, and we're going to miss it. That's why he's so nervous."

"Where we come from we call it being drunk," the older officer murmured, but luckily Bata didn't hear him.

"What about me?" Whitey crawled down from the booth and stood before the officers.

"You can go wherever you like," the officer answered. "These two are coming with us."

Bata and Leon transferred their luggage to the police car, a pretty run-down Zastava 101, and got into the back seats. Whitey helped load his car onto the practical tow truck and drove back, while his friends were taken into the other direction. Leon kept racking his brain, trying to figure out why things were happening as they were. Did the policemen really have nothing better to do in the hot night? Why did they focus on them? Were they allowed to seize passengers and their luggage just like that, off the road? What was going to happen to the paintings? Did Bata have some sort of receipt for them? Next to him, Bata first cursed the officers some more, then he turned on the state for paying fools to keep honest folk from doing their job, and he was just about to doze off again, when the car stopped in the police station's yard.

They got out and walked to an office. Every door and window were wide open, producing a draught which was the only thing making the place barely breathable. The older officer sat down at the typewriter, he told Bata and Leon to sit on two wobbly chairs on the opposite side of the table, while the younger officer stood by the side, determinedly asking questions. First name, last name, father's name, date of birth, address, where are you coming from, where are you going, what are you carrying, why...

The chronicler was busy searching for the right keys on the typewriter; the room echoed with infrequent punches. He tried to rescue his reputation by repeating the questions, as if he didn't hear them properly, what did you say, repeat the number, is that a street or an alley, and so on.

Leon kept wiping the sweat off his forehead the whole time, asking half way through the process:

"Why do you want to know all these things, what did we do, why have you brought us here?"

"Hold on, man," the younger officer interrupted him, "I'm the one asking questions here, and you two are answering them. Is this clear?"

He rose slightly on his toes to make his words sound more significant.

Then he sent both of them to wait in the hallway. It was his turn to sit behind the desk as he picked up the phone. The door was still open, so they could hear him yelling into the receiver:

"... Two very precious Orthodox icons, a drawing, looks nice, and a doodle, like something a child would make... aha, I understand, of course... we'll take care of it."

After a while he appeared in the hallway.

"Close the door the next time, so I don't have to listen to your nonsense," Bata greeted him, "art experts like you should be shot publicly!"

He sneered contemptuously, spit, but missed the spittoon. Leon quickly patted his knee, as if to ask him to calm down finally.

The officer stared right through him, he seemed somewhat tired, and announced dryly that the matter was closed. A curator from Belgrade's National Gallery was on his way to inspect the stuff. He checked his watch and said:

"I'll see you tomorrow morning at nine. Good night."

Bata and Leon exchanged glances. What did he mean, tomorrow? What were they to do now? That's your problem, the police officer responded and went back inside his office. Before disappearing he explained where they could find the only hotel in town. Sadly it turned out the fact that it was the only one, was a significant one. It was full, occupied by two women's volleyball teams training for some championship. It was just over three o'clock in the morning, so they went to a park to snooze the rest of the night away on a bench. They were just drifting to sleep when a familiar police officer woke them up. Come on, get up. You're not allowed to sleep in the park. The hotel is full, Leon explained. Fine, but you're not allowed to sleep here. Then arrest us and lock us up, Bata suggested. You're not under arrest that would be against the rules. Would you like me to curse your mother, your daughter and the rest of your family, and spit on the state while I'm at it, could you lock us up then? Don't try to straighten a bent cigarette, the officer ordered and left. They went back to the hotel. The nightporter took pity on them and let them sleep on the couch in the back of the reception room.

The next morning, they woke up hung over and sleep deprived and headed off to the police station. The curator, an older gentleman whose shirt was sticking to his round belly, was an hour late. He took off his sunglasses, put on some regular ones, took one look at the icons and immediately reproached the officers:

"This is nothing. It's a tourist souvenir. You made me come all the way down here for this?"

The officer took Bata's fierce look in stride and quickly pointed to the second roll. He removed the wrapping paper.

"Oh, my," the curator cried with a start after taking a good look at both paintings, "Modigliani, no less, and Rodin? This is an altogether different story. Are you going to Munich or coming from Munich? What have you done, rob the Louvre?"

He took off his glasses, wiped the sweat off them and bulged his eyes slightly.

"Oh, give it a rest," Leon meekly intervened, embarking on a story he had come up with during the troublesome night, "have you never been to the flea market in Novi Sad? There's a student there, he'll paint whatever you want for you."

The curator kept turning the painting this way and that, noticing the marks on the back side.

"Holy crap!" he cried. "This is Šlomovič!"

"I thought it was Modigliani?" the officer cut in. "It says so in the front..."

"Will you shut up, you idiot!" Bata lost his temper. "Were you born an idiot or did you receive special training for this job?"

"Let it go, let it go," the curator stopped him, turning to Leon with a very serious expression on his face, "flea market in Novi Sad, is that what you're saying?"

"Right," Leon nodded, "you'd probably have known about it long ago if I had stolen it from your gallery, wouldn't you?"

He continued, feigning great interest.

"What did you say, Šlomovič? What did you mean by that?"

"Yes, yes, something came to mind," the curator quickly responded and turned to the officer. "The two icons are worthless, but I need to take the painting and the drawing with me back to the gallery for further inspection."

"Wait a minute, what about me, you can't just take them from me?" Leon resisted.

"You shut up!" the officer interrupted him. "You're going to report to the central police station in Belgrade, and they'll tell you what happens. Don't you worry, if you've been stealing, you have your thing coming!"

They concluded by writing up a report about a confiscation of two artworks on July 3, 1984, which Leon received a copy of.

What the hell have you done this time?

The only taxi driver in town had his car at the repair shop, so Bata and Leon had to take the bus. The bus didn't drive along the main road, but instead took many local ones, stopping at practically every telegraph pole. The bus was boarded by women carrying chickens under their arms and baskets full of eggs, men with fiascos, school children and seasonal workers, someone occasionally unwrapped a spicy lunch, gassing their surroundings; the driver wasn't paying too much attention to bumps and potholes in the road, bags and boxes were on the brink of scattering from the shelves overhead, the atmosphere in the bus was stifling hot and so thick you could cut through it with a knife, despite the tiny windows being open. The bus from the movie *Who's Singin' over There* would surely be proclaimed this bus's younger brother if they both entered a beauty competition. Bata alternatively cursed police shit, Whitey and worthless imperialistic auto industry.

"You're staying with me until this mess is straightened out!" Bata instructed as they disembarked, worn-out and irritated onto the sun-baked central Belgrade bus station. "You're not to spend any money for hotels. Is that alright with you?"

Leon was lucky to be able to reach Kristina over the phone, just to let her know that he'd be staying a day or two longer than planned, because of business. She chirped back that it was fine, if that was the way it had to be, that she was recording all the time anyway. Leon clenched his teeth and concluded the conversation by promising her that he'd do everything to come back as soon as possible. He didn't go into details, only mentioned that Bata and him were back together, planning something big.

He couldn't know then that he'd be featured in the city tabloid's crime section the next day. The blown out of proportions, full page article in the paper cited him, although without a photograph and only identified by his initials, as the central figure of a possible sensational find. Could it be possible that they found leads to the famous Erich Šlomovič's collection of paintings, which disappeared in these parts during the Second World War? Could it be that the night-time car accident was about to unveil the secret everyone only whispered about up to now? Would the police and the experts, working hand in hand, manage to solve this puzzle?

Leon didn't so much as stick his nose out of Bata's house, he didn't even visit Fane the Captain or Pedja the Book, just so he wouldn't be found out by an accidental group of reporters by some strange coincidence. He hoped that the story which had erupted so suddenly would eventually die down, the way all yellow press stories tend to.

He phoned in to the central police station and let them know where he was staying. They told him not to leave town, to report regularly, every morning, by phone was ok for the time being.

"What do you mean, every morning?" Leon almost screamed. "What did I do? Why won't you let me go home?"

"All in due time," the inspector in charge informed him coldly, "all in due time."

In the evening, Leon also phoned home, to talk to his mother and his father, and his mother's frenzied response practically shot out of the receiver.

"What in God's name have you done this time? Police came to our place, they searched the entire house, I'm still not done cleaning after them! What's the matter with you, you miserable human being? If you plan on disgracing us like this, you might as well stay in Belgrade. What were you thinking, aren't you ashamed for everything you've put us through, where did you come from, anyway, is anything sacred to you, don't you ever think about us?"

The words came boiling out of her. She must have obviously dropped the receiver, because it was his father he heard next.

"Listen to me, this is again about Bata and his prized paintings! Didn't I tell you the other time..."

Leon suddenly realised what this was probably about, he realised that he needed to put an end to a conversation which was obviously going in the wrong direction.

"I'm sorry, father," he almost yelled into the receiver, "calm down, everything is squeaky clean, it's just that two local police officers from Upper Nowhere made a big fuss, for absolutely nothing. It's just a big misunderstanding! Everything will clear itself up! I didn't steal anything, it's all legal. I just had the bad luck to run into some idiots!"

"Do you think the Slovenian police officers rummaging through my house are idiots? Wait a moment..."

"They're not idiots. Idiots are the ones who cooked this up. Somebody here inherited the paintings, quite legally, and Bata and I are trying to get the rights to sell everything that was left in his grandfather's house. This has nothing to do with the police," Leon tried to persuade his father. "Everything will clear up, trust me! I don't even understand why they're making all this fuss."

"I hope for your sake that you're right," his father concluded in a calmer tone, "you can explain more when you come back," and he hung the phone.

This can't be, this can't be, this can't be, Leon kept saying to himself, why is all of this happening? What kind of screwed up fate is picking on me? How did a car crash which he was lucky to emerge unscathed from turn into this incomprehensible mess? Why must everything always come tumbling down straight on his head? Every bloody time!

Bata was seated next to him, listening, and he was conspicuously cool, sipping his coffee and smoking his Drina cigarette, gesturing with his hands to ease the tension.

"Of course," Leon resisted, "you were transporting two worthless Orthodox icons, while I'm suddenly a thief, operating the black market. And I volunteered as the owner of your stuff, too," he added hastily. "And what was it that the curator blabbered about Šlomovič? Do you understand what's going on?"

"Stop, calm down," Bata finally decided to dig out and reveal the blessing in disguise. "Everything is falling in the right place, my son. We're about to embark on the business of the century! Word suddenly started going around about a precious collection which reappeared: the Šlomovič collection, a collection which stirred imagination and was later slowly forgotten. This is a wonderful groundwork for the world to prick up its ears when stories re-emerge and everyone starts looking out for the paintings. And I'm the only one with access to them, or should I say, we are. Do you realise what kind of money we're talking about here?"

Leon looked at him in bewilderment but was unable to calm down. What money? What kind of big plan was Bata coming up with now?

"Bata, I beg you. The police think I'm the owner of the two paintings, that I'm the one who..."

"The one who...?" Bata continued. "The one who - what? Did you steal, did you kill, did you break into museums, did you rob a personal collection? Or did you merely get my back for the paintings which I obtained in an entirely legal manner? The kid offered, I took it and I paid. And he'll bring me more, once I wave some money in front of him. And you better be sure that I'll be waving some money in front of him, because we'll offer the dealers some superior paintings. They originate from a collection which the entire world is looking forward to. Here, have a seat, drink some coffee and just wait. Ours is a waiting business."

Again, Leon was at a loss to know what to do. Was he hearing what he thought he was hearing? Was Bata feeding him fairy tales just to keep him calm, or was there really something there? Actually... hm.

"You're not saying," he almost lost his footing as he hastily calculated, "that you purposely staged all of this, that you sawed up the screws, so that we'd lose a wheel, that you...?"

"Nope," Bata shook his head, "I'm not that smart. But those two miserable police officers from Šabac unwittingly cooked up a brilliant plot, one I could never have come up with by myself. A plot better than anything we could wish for. The paintings are in the papers and the whole city is talking about them. Especially the people who are important for us. And luckily this isn't going to end with just local rumours."

Unbelievable, Leon thought the things I have to learn still. To Bata, this whole circus is just grist for the mill which will help sell the paintings? How can he keep his cool and tamely wait with all of this going on?

The next morning, when Leon phoned in to report to the police inspector, he was greeted with a mysterious instruction:

"Come over, it's important."

The doorman of the central police station checked him over, asked to see his identification, wrote his name down in a thick book, pinned the "visitor" tag on him and explained the way to get to inspector Gagić. Naturally he announced his visit over the phone first.

"Look at you, what a young man," the inspector couldn't hide his surprise as he offered Leon a chair, "and what a story!"

The inspector was a tall man around sixty, with a large aquiline nose and long grey parted hair. There were leather patches on the elbows of his greenish brown chequered jacket, he wore flannel trousers and fine, brown round shoes. He looked like a gentleman who was about to light a pipe, take a walking cane from behind the closet and walk over to his retired friends for some whiskey and a game of tarok.

"So, I gather you're into art?" he asked, giving Leon an inquisitive look. His eyes revealed a calm business interest.

"I am," Leon said, "that's what I've been studying and I make an occasional deal on the side."

"And you're familiar with the scene around here, right?" the inspector nodded mildly.

"Of course," Leon confirmed, confident that there was no point in hiding anything, because the guys at the police knew that "I bring a chest or two, buy a rug, a silver candlestick, I rummage around for paintings..."

"And these two items," the inspector rose to his feet and took a large portfolio out of the closet, opened it and revealed the familiar painting signed Modigliani, and the drawing signed Rodin, "you bought them..."

"I did, my colleague Živković and I came across them at the flea market in Novi Sad. There's loads of students there, painting reproductions, for practice, and we liked these two..." Leon began.

The inspector interrupted him harshly, but with a smile:

"And the next thing you did was hail a taxi and drive to Ljubljana. With two doodles made by students? Did you want to sell them as originals? Come on, let's be serious. Cut the nonsense. We're done dealing with them over here. Both works were checked by our National Gallery, they have no evidence of them, there's nothing in police records about them being stolen. So they're your property. What's most important when it comes to the pedigree of the two paintings is that you have a clean record with the police in Ljubljana."

Leon choked.

"Excuse me, what was that?" he managed to utter.

"In other words, we're done with this. We have enough work as it is. So I'm giving you back the paintings, you can sign the receipt here, then report to inspector Kerin at the Ljubljana police station in three days' time. You are of course not allowed to dispose of them in the meantime," the inspector said, shoved a form in front of him to sign, wrapped the painting and the drawing back up, inserted them in the portfolio and handed it to him. "They know who you are and you don't have any serious record to speak of. They are looking forward to speaking to you, though. They took over the case and all the responsibility that comes with it; they can have it. They've been saying we don't have all the information here in Belgrade and that we should let them handle the case. That's fine. I have other things to do."

"So this is it?" Leon asked with surprise.

"Yes, this is it. As I said, inspector Kerin is expecting you."

"Alright," Leon said, put the portfolio under his arm and walked to the door.

"So long," he added.

"I prefer goodbye. I like it when things are done according to rules, so we don't have to get involved. I hope I don't see you again," the inspector said, giving the impression that he had shaken an unnecessary burden off his shoulders and that now he'd finally have his peace and time for his treasured errands again.

The business must go on regardless

Bata was nervously waiting for him back home. He had quite a pot of coffee on the table in front of him, which he eagerly filled his cup from, accompanied by an ashtray brimming with cigarette butts. Leon recounted the story, telling him that the Belgrade police would get off his case, they were handing him over to the police in Ljubljana.

Ha ha," Bata was visibly relieved, "We've done it."

"We've done what?" Leon stared.

"I was hoping we'd make it, but I wasn't totally sure," Bata said while a smile crept over his otherwise thoughtful expression. "Šutra's wife's godfather is the boss of the counter-intelligence service here. We had coffee yesterday. He let the police know that you were their man on a special mission and that they should leave you alone. That's why they flicked you over to Ljubljana; if there's any problem later on, their hands are clean."

"Their man? Me? I don't understand," Leon was getting increasingly bewildered.

"You don't have to. The main thing is that you can go home now. I'm sure you'll be able to handle everything once you're there," Bata mumbled, "Luckily I already know what we're going to do."

He poured Leon some coffee, it was almost cold, asked him to calm down and wait, he took the portfolio which Leon had brought back from the police station, and walked up the stairs to his room in the attic. After some time he returned and dropped another two artworks in front of Leon's feet: another Modigliani nude and another drawing by Rodin, the same authors with differently painted same motifs.

"Here, this is your cargo now!"

"Slow down, you're going to give me a heart attack!" Leon cried. He sank deep into the armchair and asked, completely flabbergasted: "Have you been doing magic or what? Do you keep a group of niggers in the attic, painting whatever you tell them to? New works by Modigliani and Rodin... How's that even possible?"

Bata lit another cigarette and answered in all seriousness.

"I apologize," he began, "I haven't told you everything. I bought four items from that boy: two Modigliani's and two Rodin's. I had to. It was his condition to promise not to speak a word of this, and to commit to selling whatever else he found in his attic to me and me alone. I don't know what else he has and how many works there are. But he trusts me, I used to help him out in the past and now I've given him a good scare, I told him he could lose his head if a word got out about the other paintings."

Leon was breathing heavily, trying to digest what he had just heard. He couldn't believe the way Bata was pulling his threads! He was obviously playing a big game. So it was true? Did he really come upon the Šlomovič collection? Was he really the one behind all of this? And why did Bata choose him, out of all people? He must have certainly expected him to do something that he himself wasn't able to, couldn't or wouldn't?

"And? What now?" Leon asked.

"Well, nothing," Bata continued. "You're going to take these two items and take them to your police. The paintings will of course differ from what they were made to expect. There'll be some fuss, but you have to insist that these are the paintings you've had all along, hint at the poor work police did over here," he was slowly thinking out loud. "Since you're a young man and you have no criminal history, and they'll have no hard evidence for anything, they'll decide to scold you and send you home sooner or later. But they won't be able to dispossess you of the paintings, because they won't match the ones that were checked here, and you'd be the one who had bought them. They're yours. Just keep repeating the fairy tale about the art student at the flea market. There are guys painting there after all, they'll paint whatever you want them to, and it's not like they can't play around with seals. What do you think?"

Leon listened in disbelief.

"But there's no way you can spread nonsense about things as priceless as these," he said doubtfully. At the same time, the idea sounded good to him; the police here wrote up a Modigliani and a Rodin, and he would come to Ljubljana with a Modigliani and a Rodin.

He was looking at the new paintings. He was turning them over in his hands, feeling them, wondering. What masterpieces!

In the meantime, Bata sipped his coffee and chuckled to himself. The new products by Rista are about to be shipped to Ljubljana, and he'll let Leon know what to do with them when the time is right. But first, the boy needs to get the police off his back.

"It could work!" Leon exclaimed. "Incredible masterpieces!"

"Yes," Bata nodded. "And with police as curious and sharp as yours, no one will be able to come up with information that this has ever been stolen. Because it hasn't! You bought the stuff for peanuts at a flea market and now it belongs to you. There's no law saying they can take it from you. If they're interested in buying, they should go to Novi Sad and order whatever their hearts desire. And they'll get it. But they should leave your stuff alone!"

Leon kept shaking his head.

"And what am I to do with these paintings then, once everything calms down, hopefully?" he asked.

"Don't worry, this is for me to figure out," Bata stopped him. "I'll let you know in a while where in Germany you're to take them and how much you'll get for them. For now, Whitey has ruined this deal for us with that crap of a car he owns," Bata explained harshly.

"Bata, don't," Leon resisted. "Whitey saved our lives. To lose a wheel while driving that fast and stay in one piece..."

"Shut up. That wouldn't have happened if his car had been in order. I had a great deal already arranged and I lost it. That's a fact. Staying in one piece or not."

"Well, luckily we did," Leon said. "I'm thankful to Whitey."

After a long pause, as he tried to get his thoughts straight, Leon decided that he should relieve himself and reveal his cards as well. After all, there were no more secrets between him and Bata.

"Pedja the Book offered me a painting by Miro just a few days ago, but today he told me that it was gone. Was that part of your plans as well?" he asked, still pretty puzzled.

Bata roared with laughter.

"Of course it was. It's nice of you to tell me. Now we both know everything. Miro went back to that kid, he's waiting for me to come with the money. That's settled," he confirmed.

Leon shook his head in wonder.

"So that's what this is."

"Yes, that's what this is," Bata nodded contentedly.

They spent another few moments in silence. Then Leon was struck with an idea.

"Did the same thing happen with Renoir and Pissaro?" he asked.

"Yes," Bata nodded as if that was self-evident.

Leon was shaken to his core. He then began to persuade himself, slowly, with a certain quiet intimate triumph that he had finally found himself at the beginning of the right thing with the right team. Finally. He had to endure a lot of surprises and tribulations to get here.

"Well," Bata broke the silence, "it's about time we cut the chit-chat. Go now, and check if there's a flight home tonight. The business must go on regardless."

Leon was still dizzy from everything that had happened and everything that filled his head. He went to the airline's office and confirmed his departure. There was plenty of room on the night flight to Ljubljana in the middle of the week.

Then he slowly descended back to Skadarlija and sat at a table in a remote corner of the Ima Dana Inn; he had a quick shot of homemade brandy to start, followed by a slow meal of roasted stuffed peppers. His brain was slowly and automatically shifting into a higher gear.

Let's say this was all true. Let's say that by the grace of God, some junky had inherited a treasure. Let's say that Bata accidentally knew the kid and that out of all of his options, the kid chose to bring some of the paintings to none other than Bata. Let's say that he wasn't aware of what he had in his hands, and that Bata was able to buy the paintings for nothing, but still a lot of money for the kid. That they were both going to keep doing good business in the future. Why then was Bata so happy after the unfortunate car crash? Did he really think that the articles in the papers were a good start to a big sale? Wasn't it possible that the articles would cause a stir in other, more important circles? Was he, Leon, going to be able to pull off the story quietly in Ljubljana? It was not like the police there wouldn't pay attention to such important paintings. As a matter of fact, they already had. What would Tone do, as he undoubtedly had a nose for these things and wanted to get something more from this story? After all, wasn't that why he had sent him to Belgrade for? There were a lot of questions.

As he chewed on the last chunks of a juicy smoked sausage, and a dry grilled pork chop, he was struck by another, probably fundamental question.

The story about the unexpected inheritance seemed good, alright.

As did the story of the discovery of a famous lost collection, that sounded great. But it was all too good to be true. What if someone had made this up and now wanted to get rich with forgeries? After all, there were lots of discoveries of paintings by old masters all over the world, mysterious rolls appearing from behind vestries, precious graphics found among waste paper, old icons by Rublev which almost ended up in the fire, as a basement of a run-down house of an Orthodox priest in Zvenigorod was being raided for firewood... Who could prove that the Modigliani, the Pissaro, the Rodin and whatever else came up were real? The buyers wouldn't be prepared to pay millions for paintings offering an interesting story instead of an expert's analysis!

"Good thinking, my son, congratulations!" Bata nodded, when they drank their farewell coffee at the Majestic hotel terrace later that afternoon, "Good thinking. Well, that's our next job. I haven't come up with a solution yet, but we'll have to. These first paintings are a trial run, they'll let us see if there's any interest in the market for them; since we don't have documentation, they'll be relatively cheap. But we can't go on without this step. I have a few ideas, but you should try to come up with something, too, son, that's why you're in school, isn't it?"

Your house was ransacked by default

He arranged to meet inspector Kerin for coffee at the Petriček confectionery, on the upper part where some steps led to from the ground floor. There were only a few tables there, usually frequented by romantic couples who couldn't think of a better place to meet. When Kerin and Leon arrived, the place was still empty. They knew each other from occasional and coincidental meetings at the Tabernakelj, visiting Tone. Leon lay his portfolio down on the floor.

"So," Kerin began, "you're still in the business of precious artworks? When we heard from our colleagues from Belgrade we asked them to leave the matter to us. We often have issues with this, but this time they were surprisingly accommodating. Did they give you a hard time?"

Inspector Kerin was nearing his retirement. His field was artwork theft, bootleg resale, finding the right owners; he often dealt with drug addicts. They would break into a ground floor window with a brick, took whatever they got their hands on first and ran around the first available corner, where they exchanged the loot for whatever kind of money they were offered. In the street, he kept his wavy brown hair hidden under a hat, and his body wrapped in a summer windbreaker. He was practically the ideal image of a person whom you didn't notice if you passed him in the street. And now a Modigliani and a Rodin suddenly landed in his moderately exciting life?

A waitress hurried up the steps and Leon ordered two cups of coffee. He lit a cigarette and answered:

"No, they didn't give me a hard time. I was in a traffic accident near Šabec and two stupid police officers thought they had caught a big fish. They made a big deal out of it, which amounted to nothing, and they dragged you in Ljubljana into it, as well. The National Gallery in Belgrade came to the conclusion that no one was missing the stuff available from the flea market in Novi Sad. That's about it. Oh, and," he winced, "I wasn't aware that I had you to thank for being allowed to return home. That was really nice of you."

"Alright, alright," Kerin smiled. "It was my pleasure. Tell me more."

"There's nothing to tell," Leon shrugged. "I haven't even made it home yet to see what part my mother and father played in all of this. Mother lectured me over the phone already. Why were you rummaging through her house again?"

Leon spoke calmly and indifferently, he even gradually persuaded himself into buying his own story. This resulted in him getting a bit reckless:

"So thank you, by the way, for dusting my mother's house!"

Kerin gave a forced laugh:

"Well, we just wanted to check if there was anything else from the flea market in Novi Sad at your house. You can understand our interest, right?"

"That's fine. Why don't you drive over to Novi Sad yourself, if you're so interested in flea markets? It's really beautiful there, the people are nice, the food is good," Leon added bitterly.

He knew the police had no real reasons for their inquisitiveness, a situation his mother was understandably furious with him at the moment.

The waitress brought over their coffee. Kerin gradually poured sugar into his cup, ignored the comments and said with certain exhaustion:

"Alright, then. Your house was ransacked by default. Why don't you show me the paintings?"

He took a large envelope from his briefcase, with Sattler written on it, and took out two photographs. Well, the photographs featured the works by Modigliani and Rodin, which Leon and Bata took with them to the unfortunate journey. Leon didn't bat an eyelid and opened his portfolio right there on the floor: a Modigliani and a Renoir.

"Wait a minute, wait," Kerin sprung up in anger, "this is not the same thing! Are you kidding me?"

Leon spread his hands in bewilderment.

"What do you mean it's not the same thing? Of course it is! I mean, I don't know what it is that you have. This is what I have. I've been carrying this around the whole time. Your snitches informed you about it right away. I got them a while ago in Belgrade, or more precisely, I and an acquaintance of mine bought them at the flea market and I'm going to sell them now in Ljubljana or somewhere else. What else could it be?"

Kerin looked at the photos, then at the paintings and again at the photos.

"You're playing me for a fool!" he said angrily. "I would strongly advise you against it!"

He had a fierce look in his eyes.

"What do you mean I'm playing you for a fool? Did I produce these photos or were they taken by your experts in Belgrade or even Šabec? What have I got to do with it? I couldn't care less who messed this up. I told you everything I know about the two works which I'm going to try to sell. And I obediently reported to you, just as you asked me to."

Kerin was obviously in a tough spot. Where did this go wrong?

"What business is that of yours, after all? This is a friendly private deal, and I hope to make a nice sum of money from it. Do you control all private transactions? Could it be possible that there is something fishy going on in state run institutions?" Leon kept chattering.

Kerin was silent, shaking his head in disbelief.

"And what do these kinds of things go for? How much do you expect to earn?" he asked after a long pause.

"The best price is the one you can get," Leon chuckled.

"Well, alright, thank you, I wasn't aware of this," Kerin mumbled angrily. He kept staring at the photos from his envelope for a while, then got up and said.

"Alright, then. You get to walk away this time. I'll check some more and keep an eye on this. Original paintings worth millions are more than just friendly private business. I actually don't care about what you have here, as we have no serious or reliable information. Do what you like. I hope everything turns out well and we don't have to meet again in a less friendly setting. You can pay for my coffee for starters."

He picked up his things furiously and left down the stairs.

"It will be my pleasure," Leon called after him, "are you sure you don't want some cake as well?"

He left right after Kerin, ran to his car and drove to Ulčar's place. The inspector probably hadn't made it to his office yet to arrange discreet observers to keep a "tail" on Leon. That's why Leon hastily made it to his "chest" where he deposited his portfolio and then drove off to visit his mother at work. He had already decided to try and convince her nicely. If you can't beat your opponent, invite him to join your team.

His mother was the head of the medicinal herbs department at the Ljubljana branch of Krka pharmaceutical giant. She was doing business with numerous partners around the world. As Leon appeared unannounced in his mother's secretary's office, she informed him that his mother was at a meeting which would last for at least another half an hour. He asked the secretary to tell his mother that he dropped by and that he would visit her at her house in the afternoon for some coffee.

"Late in the afternoon," he added.

"Wow, that's some protocol," the secretary smiled ambiguously, as if she was aware of his mother's opinion on Leon's life, "your dear mother might have a heart attack."

"Alright, give her some medication to take home then, please," Leon took an affectionate bow and left.

When he arrived at the family house at the foot of Šmarna gora Mountain later in the day, his mother and father had already been home for some time. There was a scent of homemade lunch coming from the kitchen: Wiener Schnitzel, baked potatoes and lettuce from the garden. Leon put two bottles of San Tomas Cabernet Sauvignon from the littoral region on the table.

"It's not exactly Teran, but I think you'll be pleased," Leon said to his father after giving his mother a hug and a kiss. Her flawless hairstyle with a slightly red hue made her look strict, she kept a very calm expression and he expected a couple of cold and toxic comments to come from her mouth.

"What kind of help do you need then?" she asked him right away. "I doubt you would honour us with your presence if you didn't need anything. What have you done this time? Are the police downstairs already or will they join us later, for coffee?"

"There's no rush, no rush," Leon shook his head, smiling uneasily. "I've just come over to tell you how I'm doing, and of course to let you know that I wasn't the reason why the voles searched your house."

"Don't remind me of that; I almost suffered a nervous breakdown. And our nosy neighbour had to witness the whole thing, as well. Do you really have no pity for your parents? I really can't understand why you needed to get involved with this," his mother reproached him, adding with an exaggerated shooting glance:

"I've calmed down a bit by now."

"Let's eat first," his father said. "We can talk later."

Leon thought his mother's Wiener Schnitzel was legendary, despite the fact that he often visited renowned restaurants. He cleaned everything his mother had prepared from the plate, even though the chunk of meat was quite substantial.

"Do they even feed you over there in Belgrade?" she finally smiled, happy that she still had her skills.

After lunch they sat in the armchairs and his father took a bottle of Curvoisier cognac from the liquor cabinet and opened it. He also produced the fancy cognac glasses with double bottoms.

"Well, cheers," he cradled his drink for a bit, then said, "now tell us everything from the beginning."

Leon felt like he had to seize the rare opportunity when they were all together and the atmosphere was warm and family-like; they were his closest people, he was their only son. He decided to tell them everything.

He spoke of Bata, how they sold the silver bowl with great profit, he spoke of Fane the Captain and the Pissaro and the Renoir, he told them how Tone acted, he told them about the traffic accident and the complications with the Modigliani and the Rodin in Šabec and Belgrade, and... well, he decided to explain the big story about the possible find.

Bata was contacted by this young man who found a treasure in a backwater house he had inherited. There were possibly tens of artworks by the greatest masters from the first half of the twentieth century there, we're talking many millions here. We suspect that this is the famous collection owned by Erich Šlomovič - "yes, the one you had mentioned, father." The whole world knows about it, the story was trending many years ago, but then it died down. This means all these paintings will now have to be turned to millions. It's an entirely legal affair. There happens to be this lucky guy who inherited it all. Leon got in on the job with Bata's help and he'll make a few millions himself. We have a number of contacts abroad, and we feel we'll be able to make everything run smoothly and in total discretion. The money he hopes to make will be enough to ensure him to live prosperously for the rest of his days, and there'll probably be enough left for his children, which are bound to come along sooner or later.

"So it's true," his father sighed deeply, "the Šlomovič collection."

"Yes," Leon nodded. "It seems so. And the police in Ljubljana got involved, thanks to Tone, no doubt, because he thought that what I brought to Ljubljana was stolen. But it's not. It's not! This has been made clear in Belgrade."

His mother was listening with her mouth agape.

"And when are these millions coming?" she asked practically.

Leon shrugged. The silence was filled with the ticking sound of the great clock in the bookcase standing across the room from the armchairs. He wasn't able to provide a quick answer to this very simple question. He decided to change course, adding after a short reflection:

"Actually, I think there's another detail here."

His mother smiled, almost scathingly:

"Well, I thought as much. And what is it?"

"There's a logical story, a history behind all these paintings. But there are no official documents. That means we have to find someone with a proper internationally recognized licence to say: yes, I have checked it, analysed it, this is an original Modigliani, the seal, the signature... This is the only way we can sell the paintings for what they're really worth," Leon explained.

"Ha!" his father explained. "That must cost a fortune. Experts like these are probably aware of their power to turn a piece of paper into something worth millions or not."

"Exactly," Leon nodded. "That's why we have to find someone reasonable. And I thought..."

He sipped his cognac and swirled it around his mouth.

"I thought that you two, being important business people, probably know some rich people around the world, who buy expensive paintings and probably have their own advisers. And could some of them possibly..."

He alternately shot a meaningful look at his mother and father.

"So this is it."

"So that's why you've come around, after you weren't contacting us for weeks, only sending police over to visit," his mother nodded, her eyes were saying that she understood everything.

"Yes," Leon nodded, "I just thought that we could come up with something together."

"You've presented us with quite a task, my son," his mother flinched, "perhaps you'll find this hard to believe, but not only do I love you and I forgive you every stupid thing imaginable, I might also have a solution for you."

Leon and his father exchanged glances.

"What kind of solution?" His father asked, surprised, while Leon was left speechless.

"It just so happens that you might have hit the jackpot, son," his mother laughed. "I have to check some things first, naturally, but I think I have someone you and your company will buckle under and bow your heads to."

"What are you saying?" his father asked again, and Leon thought it proper to continue to keep his mouth shut and wait.

"We're about to have our annual expatriate picnic. And I heard from an acquaintance of mine, I used to know him when I was younger, he's a bit older, but he used to be my neighbour back when we lived in the old house, France Benko. He emigrated to the west right after the war, and from there I think he moved to Australia, he hasn't dared to come back since."

At this point she turned to his father: "You communists eat people alive, you know that," and she continued, "well, he's the official adviser for art to the Australian government. I believe he has every title, licence and seal possible."

Leon bulged his eyes. He could not contain himself any longer.

"And now he's coming over here, to Slovenia, I mean?" he almost cried, sudden happiness practically shot out of his eyes.

"He is," his mother nodded, "and he's taking his wife to take a look at their homestead somewhere near the seaside. That's how it is. Would my dear son be happy with an expert like this?" she turned to Leon.

Leon walked around the table and embraced her.

"You saved my life," he almost sobbed, quickly adding, "again. This is the last missing piece of the puzzle. It's incredible. Is this even possible?"

"Obviously it is," his mother nodded. "All you can do now is pray that the plane doesn't crash."

"Let's drink to that," Leon sighed and looked at his father.

"Well, well," his father grinned, "so young and already an alcoholic."

"Not at all, father, it's just that this cognac of yours is delicious," Leon shook his head.

"Damn, what a coincidence," his father said, looking at his wife.

Nobody said anything for a while. They were each immersed in their individual experience of the unusual moment.

"While we're on the subject of money," his mother couldn't help herself, "how's that demanding lady of yours? Will you finally make enough for her?"

Leon felt the unpleasant sting, but he knew it wouldn't be smart to lose his temper, since his mother just pointed out a solution which would save him a lot of head scratching.

"There really will be plenty of money, enough for both of us," he merely confirmed. "We're going to have a pleasant, calm relationship."

"Do you know how you call a relationship where a woman only stays with a man for money? Why can't you find yourself..." his mother continued.

"Let's not get into this right now!" his father interrupted her.

I'm not having this. If you do this, I will leave with him right now

"I hear that you've been busy meeting the police" Tone chuckled, squinting at him. "Any news from the boys in Belgrade? What did you find out this time?"

They went to the Rotovž for a drink, catching an occasional breeze easing the summer heat in the shadow cast by the old building. Day was slowly turning into night. Clouds were gathering on the horizon and the atmosphere was heavy. It was obvious that a summer storm would develop soon. Leon was in fairly good spirit because of the news of the possible arrival of an international art expert.

"There are three things I want to tell you," he began with a decisive tone. He had decided to capitalise on his arguments. "But it all depends on your reaction to the first one. You're talking about police, and we both know that it was you who got them breathing behind my neck because of the two paintings I brought over on your behalf. And this circus just won't end. That doesn't feel good. I learned about a number of excellent additional paintings in Belgrade, but I'll only agree to talk to you on one condition; you have to swear not to blabber about them to your police friends. This is number one, and it can also be where we end this!"

Tone raised his head in bewilderment and straightened up in his chair. He wasn't used to seeing Leon like this. He understood this meant things were serious.

"A number of excellent paintings?" he asked.

"Right, the kind that blow your mind. So tell me now: can you stop yourself from running over to the cops? This business needs to be carried out in total secrecy, with loads of money and no talk whatsoever. Are you in?"

Tone laughed loudly.

"You want to know if I'm in? What is it exactly that you're asking?"

"Exactly what I asked, which is to say - no Interpol of yours!"

"Alright, alright. It's a deal. What are points two and three?"

Now it was Leon's turn to laugh.

"I knew it," he said. "So, number two: Bata can get ahold of over a dozen paintings, all of them first class: Modigliani, Renoir, Pissaro,

Matisse, Miro, Gaugin, Lautrec... the list goes on. There's this junky who inherited a run-down house in a backwater village in Vojvodina, and he dug out these paintings in the attic. There are clues pointing to them possibly originating from the Šlomovič collection. Bata has a hold on him, but the kid wants to be paid for the whole package in advance. He won't sell them piece by piece. No one knows about this yet. If we can get the money, the thing is ours, otherwise it will end up God knows where."

Tone squinted even more, leaned back in his chair, laid his hands on the table and called out: "Holy smokes!"

His exclamation contained everything: shock, surprise, joy and the thought of heaps of money.

"That's right," Leon nodded, "holy smokes!"

"Well, what's number three then?" Tone asked when he recovered a little.

"Number three is really essential: it seems I've managed to secure a renowned international expert with all necessary licences, which would be willing to write his expert opinion for all of this," Leon announced quite self-importantly, gesturing with fingers of both hands as if to say, it goes without saying, that's just who I am.

"Holy smokes!" Tone called out once again. "Holy smokes! You must be God or something! I can't believe it!"

"Fine, fine, you don't have to believe it right now," Leon said calmingly, "right now I just need to know if you're in, and of course, if you're able to invest."

Tone leaned forward and fired:

"For stuff like this, money won't be a problem. Providing, of course, the owner doesn't ask for too much and if the paintings are genuine, naturally."

"Let's not waste any more time: should I call Bata and ask him to arrange a meeting? So we can take a look at the stuff and come to an agreement, while we, that is you, arrive with a suitcase full of money? How much time do you need to come up with some serious advance?" Leon asked.

"Let's see," Tone said, thinking, "Give me three days. I need that much. My investors aren't exactly lining up, waiting every day for me to come up with something."

"Alright," Leon nodded, "that should be fine. I'll let Belgrade know."

There was a thunder in the distance; a sudden gush of wind blew through the square. First raindrops came falling down from the sky.

"So it's a deal?" Leon asked as he got up.

"It's a deal," Tone nodded and ran in the direction of his store.

Leon ran to his quatrelle, as well. He drove home. Kristina wasn't there. He sat in his armchair. The room was nice and cool. He started thinking. Things were really looking up now. Bata will get the paintings, Tone will bring the initial investment and he will provide the expert. But will he, really? He took his mother's story of her old school friend's homecoming as a fact. But will he be willing to participate? Does he really have an international licence? How much money will he want for his work? If he were to confirm the authenticity of twenty paintings, that could amount to quite a lot. But surely it would be a doable cost with paintings like these. Well, big money is about to start rolling in, finally. Once they deduct the costs, they'll start talking about thirds, there is no other way about it: Bata, Tone and I. Now I can let Kristina in on it a bit, to calm her down. She'll be able to hold on for money like this...

Kristina. There's not a moment when he's sure that she's completely and utterly his, except in moments of unbridled sex, when all their inhibitions disappear and they're overcome by a special kind of hunger for each other's body. Her hints, her long absences, and the recording sessions, and the wealthy Andraž... Where is she now, for instance? There was no message left anywhere, no phone call! It's night already, there's a storm outside, and she's not here...

He began to feel the shivers. A wild force made him spring to his feet, he rushed down the stairs, ran through the rain, jumped in his quatrelle and drove to the recording studio. The outside door was open, but not the inside one. He thumped on it. After a while, one of the sound technicians appeared and turned on the outdoor light.

"Is Kristina here?" Leon asked without even a greeting.

"She was," the technician said quite disinterested, "but she left earlier with the boss. Maybe they went to have dinner... I don't know when they'll be back."

Leon turned around, quickly left and got back into his car. To dinner. Oh, maybe they went to the castle? It was still pouring heavily. He drove up the hairpin bends of the castle hill, all the way to the entry ramp to the courtyard of the castle and ran to the restaurant. It was full. He looked around, noticing some acquaintances, but Kristina was nowhere to be seen. Drenched with rain he went back to his car. Something's going on, I can feel that something's going on! Jealousy was gnawing at him more and more. He spent some time driving aimlessly through the city. He stopped at a couple of the more popular bars he and Kristina used to visit frequently, and then drove to the Ilirija Hotel where he went to the bar. The atmosphere was smoky and boozy. He had a glass of whiskey and watched some of the dancers climbing all over their customers. Ha, a thought instantly crossed his mind, her weekend house! Why didn't he think of it before? He drove through the city and to the south, towards the edge of the forest. He could see from afar that there was no car parked in front of her house. He drove nearer regardless. There were no footprints of wet shoes on the doorstep. Just as he was turning around at the door, he saw wide tire marks and freshly trampled grass in the meadow. Did Andraž do this with his flashy vehicle? Did they not go inside the house but made love in the car instead? It made him see red. He drove recklessly back to the studio. The owner's four-wheel drive was parked in the lot. Leon smashed his fists at the outside door to the studio, which was now locked. He banged on the door, the rain washing off his fury. Of course, how could they hear me with all this sound proofing? He was overcome by a mixture of powerless despair and wild rage.

Furious, he drove home and ran up the stairs to the apartment. He turned on the light in the living room and opened the bedroom door. Kristina was lying in bed, giving the impression that she was sound asleep. He returned to the hallway and took off his wet shoes. Her own, also wet, were resting on the mat under the coat hanger. It was obvious that she had only returned home minutes ago.

Leon sat on the side of the bed and said, struggling to conceal his excitement:

"I think it would be fair if you stopped pretending like you were sleeping."

She didn't respond to this, so he shook her shoulder. She reacted like as if she was awakened from deep slumber.

"Oh, where have you been? I saw that you were home in the meantime, but then you disappeared. Where did you go?" she asked in a sleepy and somewhat reproachful voice, rubbing her eyes.

"I went to look for you at the studio, but of course you weren't there. 'She went somewhere with the boss,'" Leon pulled a face, "we don't know when they'll be back!"

"So, you're following me, you don't trust me," Kristina jumped up, then added in a calmer manner, "Andraž invited me to Cankarjev Dom to see a play, so I went. We got held up at the bar after it. He occasionally invites me to go somewhere with him, if you really like to know, you never do that. You'd prefer to keep me locked up at home."

It was crystal clear to Leon that she was lying right to his face and that she was trying to change the subject. His face distorted in a savage rage.

"And then you drove to your weekend house, probably to chat for a while, right?" Leon screamed, unable to contain himself any longer.

"What weekend house?" she asked somewhat surprised and blushed, as she could feel that Leon knew exactly what he was talking about.

Leon was clenching his fists, giving the impression that he was about to blow up. He gasped for breath, wiping his wet hair which was dripping rain down his face.

"Don't you lie to me again! You've been cheating on me with Andraž this whole time. Don't give me this Cankarjev Dom story. You've been cheating on me the entire time. Just like you used to cheat on Ferkolj, and now you're cheating on me! You drove to your weekend house, anywhere else you could be spotted by someone, and there in the back seat, you..."

He clenched his fists even tighter, shaking.

Kristina rose from the bed, she was very agitated, and she gave him a serious, almost reproachful look. She instantly realised acting ignorant was out of question now, that the time came when she needed to set thing straight, coldly. It wasn't the first time she found herself in such a position. She looked at him calmly, almost daringly. Her eyes filled with some kind of calculating wonder, as if she wanted to say, what's this all about, our relationship has been clear all along. Why are you making a fuss now? Haven't I been here for you, always, whenever you wanted me to?

"You know that I love you both, each in a different way," she explained very calmly, almost lovingly, but defiantly at the same time, "I won't choose sides, I won't choose between you two."

She stopped talking. Her words were left hanging in the air like a red hot sign.

"You got what you were looking for," her tightly pressed lips were saying.

Leon hardly visibly shook his head. Now we're here, finally and irreversibly. It was the first time she confirmed out loud and without beating about the bush what he had always suspected but convinced himself that it was all just teasing and games, because there was nothing normal about such a threesome.

"Well, you'll have to choose. I'm not playing this charade any longer!" he added harshly and then started screaming. "Do I need to explain to you that Andraž has a family, that he has children? That there's no way you can be involved in such travesty? Aren't I enough? When I'm not here I'm chasing money and bringing it to you. While you," he pulled another face, *"won't choose.* Should I go tell his wife about what you've been doing to her?"

Kristina lost her temper, hugging a pillow close to her.

"I'm not having this. If you do this, I will leave with him right now. Remember this!" she yelled.

They looked at each other fiercely. Leon was suddenly overcome with a strange relief. Things were said. There was to be no more dodging the issue.

"I know, alright," Leon responded calmly and offendedly, "you don't love me. I've felt it for some time. You've been spending more and more time with him. It's clear."

"Of course, when you're never home. I have no idea where you are. Plus, you haven't been contributing to the expenses lately. I'm on my own worrying about the money. That's not what we agreed. And when I find myself in a hard spot, Andraž gives me the money. Where else am I to get it?"

"What do you mean I haven't been contributing? The seaside hotel, the dresses, that's nothing to you?" Leon flew off the handle. "I've been chasing money this entire time, you've always gotten everything

I made. And besides, I'm finally on the verge of a really fantastic deal, one that will ensure we never have to worry about money again. Just a little bit, we have to wait just a little bit longer!"

Kristina sighed deeply, slapping her hands against her knees.

"Well, that's it, you see. It's always waiting and nothing ever comes of it. That's not enough for me," she said calmly, "that's not the lifestyle I'm used to. I'm really not that interested in student life."

"But you are interested in student fuck, aren't you?" Leon fired back at her.

He was unable to control himself again.

"I'm not getting down on that level," Kristina answered coldly.

"And I should just step back and watch the level you got down to with Andraž? No, thank you!" he practically exploded.

He got up, left the room and slammed the door; he felt like the whole building shook. He walked to the fridge and poured himself a full glass of whiskey. He felt like going back to the bedroom and hitting her. His blood was boiling. But he knew that would be a mistake, that he'd never see her again. Never again?! Impossible. Despite all the dirt, he still cared for her; he still wanted to be with her, whenever that would be possible. He had felt the distance slowly growing between them for some time, but he didn't want to admit it to himself. He was like the cat in a cartoon, jumping from the ship to the shore, but falling short, desperately clawing scratches into the hull of the boat, slipping into the ocean.

Anyway... where was he to go? Not home, that's for sure, as that would be akin to acknowledging defeat. His head was thumping. But she was agitated, as well. Maybe she's just saying this to make me angry. She must be. They'll talk about it tomorrow. Once he explains to her about the business on the horizon, everything will surely change. Everything will sort itself out. It always had in the past, even though the sparks sometimes flew between them. Yes, tomorrow is a new day.

Being a commoner, I would prefer a double whisky

He woke up into a bright, yet slightly cloudy morning. He looked at the clock: it was almost eleven. He rose from the armchair and went to the bedroom. Kristina was no longer there. He was all crumpled up and sweaty. He took a shower and shaved. He put on a light safari suit which he had recently bought in Trieste and put on some perfume. He wanted to make himself look better than he really felt. The fight he had had with Kristina troubled him, especially since she had admitted to everything in such an unfeigned manner. What was I even expecting from a woman, older than me, spoiled and always the centre of attention of wealthy suitors? That's alright, but we love each other; I know this can't go on forever, we will break down eventually and for good, but if we're together, as long as we're together, we're together, after all it was she who invited me to move in with her, we have amazing sex. Money hasn't been limitless, but that will change...

He walked to his beloved phone booth in Ambrož Square and phoned Bata. Bata was home as it was still early in the morning.

"Hello there, my boy, how are my precious Slovenian lads doing?" he was pleased to hear him. "Are we going to work or what? How did you handle the package?"

"Everything's fine. My police friends happily vowed to keep a closer eye on me from now on. I'll let you know when I'm coming over. As for what you were asking about, yes, we're on. Let me know when you arrange everything that we need. But give me three days first," Leon spoke, certain that Bata understood all the hints.

"Ok, nice. I'll take care of it. About the package, why don't you run to Munich, Mrs. Billinger would like to take you out for coffee, she'll be happy to give you seventy-five rolls? I've arranged everything," Bata roared merrily, completely turned on by Leon's message.

"And tell your mother to make some bean stew for me, the next time I come over," Leon added. "Did you manage to hang the curtains?"

"You've swept all my women off their feet, my darling Slovenian, there'll be no shortage of hugs when you appear at my door," Bata chuckled. "Well, talk to you soon then."

Bata's message was a good one. He was to deliver the paintings he had brought over from Belgrade to Mrs. Billinger at the Faber auction house, where he would get seventy-five thousand for the two of them. There, Kristina could get some more money right away, which should buy him some more time of peaceful or at least tolerable atmosphere. She probably didn't want to break up immediately either, she didn't want the war she hinted at yesterday. Then he phoned Ulčar and found him at his house. Leon asked him if he could bring over the stuff he kept in his chest, sometime in the evening. Ulčar said it would be his pleasure, he already had a dentist appointment planned, and would stop by on his way.

Leon spent some more time walking around the city; he wanted to be seen by as many people as possible. He was doing good and feeling good. He couldn't care less if someone from inspector Kerin's team was watching him from behind one of the corners. He was going to disappear in the middle of the night and be back in the middle of the next. He was walking home when he ran into Kristina, who was just coming back from taking the dog for a walk. She ran into his arms as if nothing had happened between them.

"Come," she invited him happily, "let's go somewhere?"

They got into the car, put the dog in a crate in the boot and drove to the castle. Sun was beginning to shine through the veil of clouds, they released the dog which started running merrily around, while they held hands like a couple freshly in love, walking along the tree-lined road. How idyllic, what a blatant lie, Leon thought to himself, the dirt I have to swallow and just forget. Everything is going smoothly, as long as I don't offer any resistance. He decided to top the good mood and the bright prospects for the future with some information about the big money coming in; he told her about the paintings and the prices they could reach. Naturally, he informed her that his cut would now exceed everything he had earned in the past. Kristina looked at him with big, loving eyes.

"Is this possible?" she sighed. "You're about to become the number one art dealer. We could go for a nice dinner tonight then, don't you think?" she asked. "We haven't been at the Šporn's for ages. What do you think?"

"Excellent," Leon said, sensing this was the ideal moment to break the news of the urgent journey Bata had instructed him to make. "I'll make a quick trip to Munich after. Again to get some money," he added quickly to stop any emerging bad temper.

"In the middle of the night?" she asked, gently leaning against him.

"After dessert," he laughed when he felt the pressure of her lovely body.

This woman is a witch, he thought. She's cheating on me, we both know it, and I love her madly despite all of this. He remembered Bata who once hinted about Kristina: love is the weirdest disease, my son. There's no known cure, but a miraculous recovery comes out of the blue. You'll see.

The Šporn was a renowned top restaurant in the outskirts of the city, complete with its own discotheque. The menu was full of substantial dishes, lacking any fancy concoctions, with pieces of delicious aged beef and brook trout the most prominent among them. One went there to eat well and a lot. A hired pianist was playing in the middle of the dining room every night.

The moment Kristina and Leon appeared through the door, the owner scurried over and greeted them theatrically; he kissed Kristina's hand and only fleetingly shook Leon's.

"Well, if it isn't Kristina and her young companion, nice, nice, welcome at our place again."

He sat them at a table opposite the kitchen. The pianist quickly came over and kissed Kristina's hand, as well.

"I haven't seen you in ages! I hope the young gentleman doesn't mind. What can I play for you?"

"You know, something from the old days," Kristina smiled.

The pianist sat down at his piano and started playing the tune from the movie Casablanca, bowing slightly. Kristina returned the gesture.

Leon was slightly annoyed with all the sucking-up, but at the same time he was pleased that the entire establishment was paying his woman so much attention, for every other guest to see. This made his male vanity swell, as well. But, a thought went through his mind, as it had so many times before, although he kept pushing it aside: a day will come when she sits in the lap of the wealthiest of all suitors, just as she chose the one who would provide the best and constant passion a year ago. Youth passes with time and he figured that money is becoming increasingly important to the spoiled woman. But for now, everything was mostly working well in their relationship. Let's forget about it. There's another beautiful evening ahead.

He ordered a beefsteak with green pepper, croquettes and lamb's lettuce. Kristina opted for trout, naturally. This was of course called for Rhine Riesling. He ordered a glass of Radgona sparkling wine.

The evening was wonderful. They ate, conversing gently, the room was filled with pleasant music. Old friends kept coming over to their table to greet Kristina, they sat down for a few minutes, proposing toasts, occasionally she ventured to another table. Every time some other man came over to fawn over her, Leon kept persuading himself that this was just her past. He was with her now. But a thin layer of jealousy started setting over him again. There were times when he wanted the ambiguous hints to stop.

He smoked a tiny cigar before the food came out.

When they finished their meal, the owner came over to check if everything was alright, expecting to receive adequate praise and then - on the house! - the waiter brought them two glasses of cognac. Leon's restricted rage exploded.

"Being a commoner, I would prefer a double whisky," he said, trying to force a smile.

In the meantime, a small group of people gathered around the pianist, both spontaneously and prompted by alcohol, singing along to familiar old tunes. Kristina joined them, as well. She was in a great mood, playful and sensual. Leon felt the skin on his back crawl. He got up, embraced her and took her to the discotheque in the adjacent room. They danced, touching gently and caressing each other they made it through a few slow songs, then ran back to the car without saying a word. It started raining again.

"I guess it will cool down a bit finally," Leon mumbled, caressing Kristina's knee with his right hand while driving, occasionally reaching upwards.

"What about people like me, who are always cold?" Kristina leaned against him and stroked his neck.

"People like that, I can help!" Leon laughed.

They hardly made it home before jumping feverishly into bed.

These are truly stunning pieces of art

The alarm went off as early as five o 'clock in the morning. Leon promptly turned it off and got up. He was driven by the thought of money he was about to receive in Germany for the Modigliani and the Rodin, at least temporarily keeping his woman satisfied in this department, too. He skilfully hid the paintings which papa Ulčar had brought him in an old basket the day before under his quatrelle's back seat cover. If all went well, he would reach his destination before noon.

The journey indeed passed without a problem and he had no trouble finding the auction house. It was closed to the public, but Leon rang the doorbell and when an old man's voice asked what he wanted, he answered that he had a meeting with Mrs. Billinger. Oh, the voice said and the sound at the door signalled that he could enter. He pushed the door open and walked into a vast room, leading to a wide and arched staircase. The Neo-Baroque building with painted and gilded moulding automatically instilled visitors with respect. There was a beautiful, hand-carved wooden counter awaiting them on the first floor. Leon stopped in front of it, laid down his portfolio and waited. Soon he heard the quick footsteps of high heels and a neatly dressed, pretty tall lady came down the stairs from the opposite direction. She was a well-kept woman of around forty, wearing a poppy-red suit, with light golden hair which brought out her blue eyes. She offered her hand in greeting.

"Agnesa Billinger, I'm the director," she said with a broad smile.

"Leon Sattler, I'm a student, just call me Leon," Leon returned the greeting.

"It's nice of you to drop by," the woman continued. "How's Mr. Bata doing? Still gallant and in good health, I hope?"

"Of course," Leon nodded and started to untie the straps on his portfolio. "He sends you these."

She followed the movements of his hands with interest, and once the portfolio opened, she reached in the envelope herself, taking out the Modigliani nude.

"Oh," she couldn't contain herself, her eyes beamed and her face betrayed the excitement she felt over the beautiful painting. "That's nice. Mr. Bata wasn't joking."

She looked at the canvas, feeling it, and finally turned it over. She spent some time studying the markings, nodded and placed the painting back without saying a word. She did the same thing with the Rodin's drawing.

"Well," she purred, "this is very nice, as well."

She then looked up from the artworks. Her eyes were gleaming with joy.

"Mr. Leon, where did Mr. Bata get these two gems? Why doesn't he just put them up for auction?" she asked. "These are truly stunning pieces of art."

Leon was unable to provide an answer to this question, but he did remember what Bata had instructed him, time and time again: shut up and wait, don't say too much.

"This is just what he decided this time. He might possibly come back with more," he replied, "and he might possibly want more then, too."

"Alright. In that case, we'll stick to the arrangement. Would you care to wait just a bit longer? Please, take a seat, perhaps in that armchair? I'll be right back," she said kindly and her high heels clinked back up the stairs.

Why did Bata choose this course of action? Why was he prepared to accept a low price for two such brilliant paintings right now, when he could have probably made significantly more at an auction a bit later? Was he really so pressed for money? Did he not want to be exposed? Was it possible that he had his own plans with the lucky heir? Well, if that was the case, I'm just the courier and there's nothing to think about. Bata knows what he's doing. He always has.

The high heels sounded once again from the stairs, but this time accompanied by the slight squeal of rubber soles. The beautiful woman was descending in the company of a small and fairly bald old man in a black robe, with black patches on the elbows, an ideal image of a fussy bureaucrat. He carried a briefcase in his right hand. When they reached the counter, he murmured a cold greeting, opened his briefcase and took out a large hard cover notebook and a pen, pointed to a line and asked Leon:

"Here, please, if you could sign!"

Leon could see that he was confirming the receipt of seventy-five thousand Deutschmarks. As the man was offering him the pen with his left hand, he took out a hefty white envelope with his right one. Leon signed, took the envelope and pushed his portfolio towards Billinger.

"There you go," she smiled, "we're done."

"Yes," Leon nodded.

"I'd very much like to meet you again soon and talk to you. Not in such a rush," she said, smiled sweetly and offered him her hand, "especially if you bring along something as nice again, right?"

"Yes," Leon nodded again, turned around and headed for the stairs. "You're going to let me out, I hope?"

"Just press the button next to the door," the little man explained, looking over his round glasses, attempting to conjure to his face something akin to a smile.

That's rich, Leon thought to himself, patting the heavily padded inside pocket of his leather jacket. The ability of a piece of paper to make a person feel warm and adopt a bright outlook, as long as it's nicely coloured and imprinted with a high enough number. He entered the first pub he encountered in the old city square and found a seat under the sunshade. He ordered a large beer and a sausage with sauerkraut. The chubby waitress in a summer blouse, with an overflowing bosom and short legs which ensured good stability even when carrying a dozen jugs of beer, brought his order over almost immediately. Groups of tourists were milling across the square in every direction, while the puppets representing musicians high up on the city hall played a tune signalling it was two o'clock in the afternoon.

"I did a good job," Leon said to himself and enjoyed another nice cold beer. He drank slowly and later ordered a double espresso, "I'll be home before midnight."

He settled the bill and walked to the nearby self-service shop. He bought some detergent, coffee and chocolate, so that the customs officer would take one look at the back seat of his car and clearly see what the driver was doing on the other side of the border.

Driving home on the highway was anything but strenuous. He set a casual traveling speed as he was in no rush to get anywhere. He was occasionally caught off guard as some roaring dragon made by the German automotive industry sped by his left side. He could visualise the wide river of gasoline flowing into the glorious carburettor of the wild car; while his quatrelle was a moderate drinker and at a moderate speed.

They would probably both make it to their respective destinations.

As the road started rising toward his home border crossing of Ljubelj, it started raining. The rain was coming down heavier and heavier. The windscreen wipers struggled to do their job, streams of water from the sky flowed down the screen. Leon carefully felt along the turns with his headlights, embarking on a true driver's rant in his head. Once he arrived at the customs house, he was over it. The officer on the Austrian side waved him through without even leaving his shelter. When he drove through the tunnel there was no one interested in him on the Slovenian side, either. Wouldn't you know, heavy rain can actually mean good weather!

It wasn't until he stepped out of the car in the yard in front of his apartment building that he felt the tiredness in his legs. He covered over eight hundred kilometres in a single day. But, he thought to himself, it was worth it. He felt the inside pocket of his jacket again. He took five one-thousand Deutschmark notes out of the envelope. He put one in his wallet and the rest in his pocket. Then he grabbed the bags full of groceries and slowly climbed up the stairs to the apartment.

There was a light on in the living room, Kristina was asleep in the armchair. The bitch ran to him, greeting him with happy tail wagging. Kristina opened her eyes and got up when he closed the door.

"Oh, you're back? See, I was waiting for you. I've been keeping a lasagna warm in the oven, I know how much you like it."

Leon dropped the bags of groceries, walked to her, hugged and kissed her.

"I wouldn't..." he managed to say, before she closed his mouth with another long kiss.

He wriggled from her arms, reached into his pocket and threw the money on the coffee table.

"A little something for the expenses," he said with a smile and gave her a sideways glance.

"Great," she said, took the money and added, "but it's not like you can't spend some time home as well, right? Will you stay with me for a while?"

"Yes," Leon nodded, "I'm knackered."

He went to the bathroom to take a shower. When he got back, draped in nothing but a bathrobe, a nicely served piece of lasagna was waiting for him on the kitchen table, with two glasses already filled with red wine.

"You can do it if you want to," he said, sat down at the table and pulled her close.

"I can," she said, kissing his hair. She sat across from him and watched him. With her hair slightly ruffled, wearing a robe and a warm look in her eyes, she was the charming image of devoted love.

Leon ate and drank up.

"I need to take a nap," he mumbled and left for the bedroom. He fell on the bed. He woke up once, in the middle of the night, and realised that Kristina was sleeping with her head on his chest, naked. He wasn't entirely aware whether he was awake or dreaming. When he woke again late in the morning, Kristina was no longer there. The collie was in her place, pressed against him and looking at him with eyes filled with total canine fidelity.

The eagle will land at noon tomorrow

Leon arrived at the Tabernakelj. There were several people inside the store and Tone greeted him formally, giving him the most business-like nod:

"Oh, good afternoon, Mr. Sattler. Have you come for that mirror? Please, come over to my office, I'll be right with you."

He then focused on an elderly couple interested in maiolicas.

Leon looked at him dumbfoundedly, but silently did as he was asked. When Tone joined him in the office some time later, he rushed to explain, as a way of apologizing:

"We can't discuss our business in front of others, not even in front of my own people. So I've sent you here, it's what I always do when important clients come over."

"He he," Leon smiled. "An important client, that sounds nice. You'll remember this, won't you?"

They sat down at a table.

"It seems I'll be able to get seven or eight hundred thousand for starters. The investors are quite eager. But we need to see the paintings before anything develops further. This is just too much money to play around with. That's clear, right? Do you know when we're going to meet by now?" Tone continued.

"I don't know, I wanted to check with you first. Now that I see you're ready, I'll give Bata a call," Leon responded. "And for that mirror you sent me in here for: you wouldn't happen to have any more of that whiskey in your closet?"

"I could check," Tone grinned, "since you asked nicely."

"Yes," Leon nodded, "I'm asking very nicely."

When they finished their drinks, Tone a bit less, Leon a bit more, Leon left to the phone booth at the central post office. No one answered the phone at Bata's house. He dialed his old number, at his mother's house. He heard a click in the receiver.

"Good day, auntie Zaga, this is Leon from Ljubljana."

"Oh, my son, are you coming to lunch? I have some paprikash," the old lady hurried merrily. "It's just hot enough."

"No, no, I'm calling you from Ljubljana. Is Bata maybe there?" Leon asked.

"He came over with this strange young man and asked me to go out. When I came back they were already gone, I don't know what it was all about, but this is how it always is with Bata."

"Well, if you see him, tell him that I've called. I'd like to hear from him," asked Leon. "Toward the evening."

"I will, my son, I will, if he happens to stop by again. And you come round, too, I have paprikash today, see?"

Leon said goodbye and then called his mother. She answered right away with a happy voice, not trying to hide her surprise.

"It's so nice to be a mother when your son needs something," she laughed. "As much as two phone calls in three days. What the heck is going on?"

"Oh, you know, first, I'm a son reporting to my beloved mother, and second, have you found out if this Benko guy is actually flying over from Australia?"

"Your beloved mother has indeed found out that this Benko guy will fly over from Australia," his mother kept laughing. "Will you ever call me again, now that you have this information?"

"You know I can't live without you," Leon confirmed.

He went home. He was starting to get slightly nervous. Things were beginning to fall into place. Now he needed to get to the paintings, see them, confirm that they were indeed part of the famous collection, as everyone hoped, and then prudently turn the paintings into money. Into big money, as works by great painters were always in high demand. Naturally, he needed to do this very discreetly, quietly, so that nothing fell on the wrong ears. He paced up and down the room, poured himself some whiskey by the way, as this always calmed him down, picked up a book, put it down, and struggled to keep himself from making another phone call. Time was running too slowly for him. He wondered if he should take another walk around the city again, but what if Bata called him in the meantime... Finally, the phone rang.

"The eagle will land at noon tomorrow," Bata said in a hushed tone as soon as he heard Leon's voice, "at my mother's place."

"Right, we'll take this into account," Leon replied. There was no need to say anything more. He put down the phone right after that. He practically flew down the stairs, jumping over two steps at once, and quickly drove over to the Tabernakelj. He probably missed every single traffic sign calling for well-mannered urban driving. Tone was just locking the store up.

"Tomorrow at noon!" Leon called victoriously from afar, running to the door. Tone immediately understood what he was saying.

"Alright," he said, his hand holding the keys was shaking a little and his glasses were slipping halfway down his nose, "my taxi driver is ready and waiting for my signal. Should we come over to pick you up?"

"Yes," Leon nodded, "six o'clock would be the best time. We need to have plenty of time. Will you bring everything necessary?"

"It goes without saying," Tone nodded. "Shall we meet at your corner? Look for the white Mercedes."

They parted ways. They were trying to keep from each other the great excitement that came over them. The biggest deal of their lives which would turn everything around was about to begin.

There are millions at stake and this is how you two act...

Bata was getting nervous in Belgrade, as well. In his attic-turned-art-studio, he kept checking the paintings he had brought from Rista over and over again, to make absolutely sure that no mistake sneaked up; he furnished them with seals, treated them with the proper finish and wrapped them in paper and covered it in dust he got from his vacuum cleaner, to make the wrapping appear befittingly old and neglected. They had gone over the story twice. It was of immense importance for the man to play his part right. He couldn't quite grasp why he was supposed to be doing all of this, but Bata had promised him good money if everything turned out well. He needed to project the image of a slightly capricious, confused, gluttonous drug addict, who wanted everything to be taken care of the right away, and was at the same time aware that he had great fortune at his disposal. He needed to scare some guys into thinking that he was about to give his fortune to someone else, unless they behaved properly. Bata gave him a portfolio of paintings and told him that he'd call him when the time came. He was supposed to come over, act nervous and difficult, asking for one million and promising to bring the paintings over later.

"No problem," he assured Bata for the third time, when he insisted on asking once again whether he truly understood what he needed to do. "I actually wanted to attend the acting academy, but they turned me down."

"If you do this properly, you'll get more than just an Oscar for your acting," Bata promised, nibbling his lips and at the same time persuading himself that everything would turn out fine.

So, tomorrow at noon.

Bata sent his mother to visit some friends again, asking her to stay out until the evening. His mother didn't ask any questions. When Bata got something into his head, it was best to just nod and keep quiet. She would probably go over to one of her friend's house and play cards.

At noon, when Leon and Tone were supposed to arrive at Obilićev venac, there was no sign of them. Half an hour later, the situation was the same. Bata made a nervous phone call to Ljubljana, but Kristina assured him that Leon had left early in the morning. He smoked a bunch of cigarettes, cursing under his breath and making another coffee. The good person was waiting in a nearby bar for Bata to call him, just as they agreed.

Finally, the doorbell rang.

"Where the hell have you been?" He almost yelled at Tone and Leon, practically dragging them inside. "You're forty-five minutes late! The guy is waiting for my call, and you're nowhere to be found. There are millions at stake, and this is how you two act! I really hope that he doesn't tell us to go..."

He didn't finish the sentence. They both knew what he meant.

"Roads are full of trucks," Tone said, adjusting the straps of the handbag hanging from his shoulder. He, too, was on edge. "It also seems every migrant worker was heading home. My driver can't perform miracles."

"It's over five hundred kilometres, Bata," Leon opened his arms reassuringly, "and the road is how it is. Don't panic, everyone knows how far it is. Your man must know it, too."

"My man is a very delicate person, he's not your average guy, we need to handle him very delicately," Bata explained, only intensifying the tension, "I don't know what he'll get in his head."

"Alright, let's not go on. Will you call this man already, so we can take a look at the merchandise," Tone interrupted. He combed his luxuriant hair with his hand and started cleaning his spectacles. Sweat gathered on the upper edges.

"I'll be fine," Bata said. "Do you have the money?"

"We don't," Tone shook his head. "I want to see the paintings first, then we can discuss money. We've brought enough for a decent advance."

Bata sprung to his feet.

"Have you gone mad? The man expects to get the money, and you don't have it. How do I tell him this?"

"I want to see the paintings first, then we can discuss money," Tone repeated determinedly, leaning against the back of a chair he stood next to. "I have the advance with me, if that's what we decide. Do you do business differently around here?"

"It's normal to check out the goods first," Bata nodded through his teeth. "But the man is nervous because this has been dragging on for such a long time, and he's expecting to get the money right away. This is a very unusual story we're a part of."

"That may be so," Tone shook his head, "but that won't work. Money is money and big money is big money. My investors have given me an advance, and they'll pay the rest later, when I know what we're talking about. That much should be clear."

An uncomfortable silence filled the room.

"Come on, now," Leon spoke, "are we going to just talk about it till tomorrow morning? Let Tone first see the paintings and we can discuss money afterwards. Seven hundred grand is not nothing. Bata, don't tell me you thought we'd bring that kind of money right over?"

"Well, since you took a taxi here, I thought you had the money with you," Bata replied and shrugged, giving the impression that he had accepted his fate.

"We can argue about this till kingdom come," Leon cut in again, then turned to Tone. "How much money have you got?"

"Forty thousand," Tone replied. "I can pay seventy-three in advance."

"Alright," said Leon. "That's quite a lot for starters. Bata, you think of something to make this advance slide. End of story."

Bata started pacing up and down the room, as if thinking about it, then he came to a stop and drummed with his fingers nervously on the table. He was obviously in a bad mood, and he ferociously lit a cigarette.

Everyone was silent.

It was Tone who put his foot down, the spectacles on his nose made a little jump, and he called furiously:

"What the hell is this? Have I come here for nothing? Call the man already! What the hell are you up to?"

Bata turned around and calmly, very hesitantly walked to the phone.

"So, you don't have the money... Have it your way. I'm not taking responsibility for this. Let's see what happens..."

He dialed a number. He must have waited for quite some time for someone to answer.

"There," Bata said, "I'm late, I apologize, there was a lot of traffic on the road."

He then went quiet, still holding the receiver in his hand.

"He hung up. I don't know what is going to happen now."

He went to the kitchen and made some coffee without saying a word. He returned with a plate holding three cups clattering on their respective saucers, as his hand was shaking slightly. He took a seat next to Leon, while Tone started putting on some mileage along the small room.

They were silent. The minutes dragged on unbearably.

Finally, the doorbell rang. Everyone flinched and Bata rushed to the door to open it.

"Bane, my friend, there you are... well, thank you," they heard.

A tall, thin man, almost a beanpole, walked in. He wore his brown hair in a ponytail, a few days' worth of beard sprawled down the cheeks of his face of indeterminable age, a colourful bandana was tied around his neck; he was dressed in tattered jeans and a leather vest over a yellow T-shirt with a smiley face on the front. His eyes with large bags under them strayed from one man to another. He was trying to determine who had the highest rank.

"This is Mr. Bane, we call him Good Person," Bata introduced him and then turned to him, "Good Person, these are two of my close acquaintances from Ljubljana, Mr. Tone, an antique dealer, and young Leon, who is indeed young, but has been dealing with antiques and art for a long time. Sit down, can I bring you something?"

"What I need is something you don't have," Good Person rejected him promptly and curtly.

"Have a seat, at least have some brandy with us," Bata insisted.

The newcomer sighed and cleared his throat.

"I have no use for your brandy, I haven't shot up anything in my days yet today, so I'm a bit nervous, if you know what I mean," he answered coldly. "What's up with our business now?"

"Hold on, hold on, we're here," Bata nodded in a reserved tone, "have a seat and calm down, show us the paintings. The gentlemen have been waiting for a long time."

"Wait!" Good Person called harshly, halting in the middle of the room, "do they even have the money? How many paintings are they buying?"

He acted like he was there in the room with no one but Bata, he didn't even acknowledge Tone's and Leon's presence. Tone jumped in.

"All of them," he said decisively, "all of them, as long as they're good."

"What now?" the man ranted. "Do you think my paintings aren't genuine? That they're rubbish? That I'm joking? What am I even doing here, Bata? You've brought two good-for-nothings. I'm off. I don't want to waste any more of my time."

"Hold it, hold it, Bane, these are honest people, they don't doubt the quality of the paintings, they'd just like to see them, to make sure that they're really here, to see if they like them, then we can discuss everything. That's how business always goes," Bata said in a calming voice.

Good Person turned to Tone. "Well, alright then. How many paintings do you want? These are not cheap paintings, I hope you realise that? Only world-class painters, the best."

"Where did you get them?" Leon asked, trying to calm the situation and at the same time hint at the need for some information to be included in the deal.

The man took a nervous turn, as if to say, why you are butting in for, I wasn't even talking to you. But he just waved his hands wearily and explained.

"I inherited a small estate from my grandfather's uncle, a stone's throw away from a village in Vojvodina. There's a bakery and I found these things in the attic."

"How many of them are there, sir?" Tone asked.

"Oh, I don't know, about a thousand, large and small, on canvas and on paper, happy and sad. You know, whenever I'm having cravings. I like to look at them, they make me forget all about the needle," the newcomer explained, almost completely calm now.

He looked at Tone with a thoughtful gaze. Tone swallowed hard. It was obvious he wasn't feeling comfortable.

He shot a glance at Leon, almost desperately. It wasn't until then that they both realised they were indeed dealing with a drug addict. Bata noticed their surprise and the reserved expressions on their faces, so he decided to interfere.

"Alright. And which paintings did you bring?"

"I didn't bring anything. What should I bring? I have no idea how many this gentleman intends to buy, and the student is penniless, I guess," Good Person responded.

Leon didn't say anything as it was clear that Bata and Tone were leading the game.

"I'll buy all of them if everything checks out," Tone confirmed again.

"Fine," Good Person nodded, seemingly pleased. "I'll bring over twenty of them, a few oils, a few watercolours, and some drawings. I'll be back in two hours sharp. You get the money ready in the meantime. Are we clear?"

He turned on his heel and walked to the door. Halfway he turned around and added, almost menacingly: "And no funny stuff, right?"

Bata walked him to the elevator. When he came back, he was visibly worried.

"Did you hear what he said, Tone, he wants to get the money as soon as we look at the paintings," he said.

Tone immediately replied gruffly:

"You failed to mention that we were dealing with a junky. It's impossible to do business with drug addicts. There's no way I'm showing my money in front of him. He might be armed and will take the money from us the moment he lays his eyes on it."

"Don't say that, Tone, there's no way, Good Person is the gentlest drug addict in Serbia, he wouldn't hurt a fly. He only flips out when something gets him riled up," Bata said. "Come, let's have a drink, let's calm down. Everything will turn out ok."

He took a bottle of Bisquit cognac out of the liquor cabinet, as well as a small fiasco of homemade brandy, which he always kept at hand, ever since his mother had scolded him for always drinking at her place and never bringing any liquor over.

"I'll have some brandy," Leon said right away, "I need it desperately."

Then he turned to Tone.

"Have some cognac, don't be so tense!"

"How am I supposed to not be tense, don't you see what we've gotten ourselves into," Tone kept shaking his head, warming the glass in his hand and started to pace around the table again. Nobody said anything. They were each immersed in their thoughts, playing out different scenarios with themselves as the protagonists.

Get out of my sight! You won't put your balls on the table

Leon stood by the window, looking out to the street. The traffic was impossible, total chaos, but everything somehow managed to function. Could it be a way of living here?

Minutes dragged on and the atmosphere was tense. Would the man return or wouldn't he, what would he bring, how would they solve the situation with the money?

The two hours eventually dragged by, as did an additional fifteen minutes.

"Just don't panic," said Leon. He was beginning to get amused by the sight of his nervous colleagues.

"Aren't you funny," Tone shivered and continued to pace around the table.

Finally, the doorbell rang once again. The sound of the door handle being pressed let them know that someone was trying to get in.

"It's him," Bata sighed, put his cigarette out in the ashtray and went to open the door.

Good Person entered carrying two parcels, which he deposited on the table. The three men waited for what would happen next.

"Well, open it, will you," the newcomer said nervously.

Leon and Tone approached the parcels in silence.

Good Person took a step back.

Bata went to the cupboard and brought over a knife. He cut the string and removed the wrapping paper. A handful of dust dispersed over the table. There was a layer of newspaper underneath. When he pushed it aside, the first painting appeared, a Renoir, a girl with a bouquet, mixed media on a medium sized cardboard. Greens and blues shaded into ochres and yellows, the little white dress exuded innocence. Leon took a deep breath and waited for Tone's reaction. He took the painting in his hands, turned it over, unable to hide his excitement. A Renoir, he held a Renoir once again! He handed the painting over to Leon. Leon was beaming, he felt like Indiana Jones when he finally found the treasure. Tone began to slowly and carefully arrange the rest of the paintings from the parcel on the table, blowing away the dust when necessary: Miro, Dali, Picasso, Mondrian... he and Leon stared at the images as if bewitched. How could this be?!

Their rapture was interrupted by Good Person's harsh voice:

"Where's the money? You've seen the paintings and it's clear that everything is in order! Let's see the money now!"

He gave Tone a glassy stare.

"Wait, I need to examine them carefully, this is not small change we're talking about," Tone said with a mixture of excitement, enthusiasm and attempted indifference. The paintings were too good for a classic haggling venture.

Good Person leaped up.

"What do you mean, it's not small change? Seven hundred thousand is nothing for these paintings, they are worth millions. Stop jabbering! Give me the money!"

Tone leaned against the table and looked at Bata.

"Tell him, Bata, tell him we can't do this just like that," he said and wiped his forehead. "This is a huge deal, it is, you know it, we can't arrange this in just a couple of seconds."

He paused to take off his glasses again and started cleaning them, although there was no need for this.

Bata stepped to the front.

"Alright, Bane, let the men look, while the two of us sit down and have some cognac, right, what do you say?" he proposed in a reconciliatory tone.

"They came a long way, they are ready to buy them, but they should check what it is that you have, right?"

"What are you blabbering about, Bata, you know I don't have the nerves for this. Give me the money and we're done. If not, I'll take the paintings to somebody else. I've had it with your muddling!"

Good Person stumped his feet and started looking toward the door.

"The money's here," Tone countered, pointing at his purse on the table.

"How can the money be in this small purse? There's no way you can fit a million Deutschmarks inside!" Good Person was almost screaming at the top of his voice, "I'm off!"

"How is it suddenly a million? We haven't set the price yet," Tone resisted, almost stammering. "We..."

"Shut up!" Good Person hollered. "The price is what I say it is, don't you get it, you demented idiot!"

Tone was totally caught off guard by the sudden outburst of coarseness, and at the same time gripped by fear of losing the deal. He grabbed the purse almost instinctively, took out the money and spread it out in a fan over the table. Banknotes, completely new, almost exuded the scent of fresh ink. Bata swallowed hard at the sight of the money, while Good Person cried insanely:

"You're fucking with me! That's not even enough for a single painting. What kind of bums have you dragged over here, Bata? Would you like me to kill you all on the spot?"

Bata mumbled:

"Well, man, this is just the advance, obviously."

"What am I going to do with an advance, you moron," Good Person screamed, "I want a million, do you get it, a million or nothing!"

He leaped over to the table and started wrapping up the paintings.

"Hold on, please," Tone begged him, with his hands raised in the air, "leave the paintings here, I need to check them thoroughly. You can have your money first thing tomorrow."

"Shut up," Good Person interrupted him, "no one was talking to you! You had your chance and you blew it. And you, Bata, you are nothing but a common con artist. Many have warned me about it, but I wouldn't believe them. You dragged over some pathetic rascals and you're all trying to swindle me. Shame on you! I'm carrying the paintings around the streets of Belgrade, risking my life, and these two bunglers don't have the money."

There was a dramatic pause. The mess was complete.

It was now Bata's turn to jump to his feet. He needed to perform the last dramatic twist. He started shaking furiously and clenching his fists. He turned to Tone and Leon and cried:

"You bloody riffraff!"

He took a deep breath and continued even more fiercely:

"You people from Ljubljana, you think that you rule the world! You came to do business without the money! You won't put your balls on the table! Get out of my sight! I've had it with you!"

His face went completely red as he pointed at the door.

Tone and Leon were in complete shock, momentarily freezing in surprise. What a circus! Was this really happening? Was Bata yelling at them? Was Bata kicking them out of his house? What was going on?

And they drove all the way from Ljubljana just for this...

Good Person swiftly picked up his belongings and ran out, Tone was hurriedly trying to stash the money back into his purse, while Leon came to and tried to catch Good Person to persuade him that he and Tone really were serious about buying the paintings. But the boy was too fast and he vanished around the corner of a neighbouring building. The apartment building where Bata's mother lived had two exits and Leon chose the wrong one.

Visibly shaken, he struggled to light a cigarette in the street, listened to his heart thumping and waited for Tone to come huffing after him.

"What was that all about?" he asked completely stricken and confused.

"I have no idea," Leon shrugged. "Let's go over there and have a drink."

They went to a bar across the street and collapsed onto a bench at the first available table. They didn't say anything for a while. Tone was very agitated.

"I don't understand," Leon spoke first, "why did you bring so little money. Everything is useless now. We'll probably never see those paintings again."

"Yes, I know," Tone nodded, his face pale, "that's what makes me furious. But I just couldn't get investors on my word only, how is that not clear? I had to see the paintings first, hadn't I? I need to think what to do now."

He ordered some cognac.

"That man is completely nuts; there was no way to talk to him. And why did Bata lose his temper at us like that? What's his problem?"

"I don't know," Leon shook his head, "I've never seen him like this. He probably lost it when he realised that the deal would amount to nothing."

"We can't just give up," Tone said slowly. "Go back to him and try to figure out what this means. What happened with Bata? Is this the way to scream at your business associates? He knows I always find the money for the right things. Remind him of this. Perhaps Bata will be able to bring that lunatic back, nevertheless. I'd prefer not to go. I'll wait for you here."

You were brilliant: strict and steadfast. You'll have them eating out of your hand now

Leon stared in front of him. As much as he tried to piece everything together in a meaningful narrative, he couldn't do it. They all invested so much in all of this, and it now ended with a crazy argument, or rather a misunderstanding. Was the beautiful story really crumbling again? He felt that it was really him alone, without Tone present, who could talk to Bata about it. Bata had reacted fiercely in the past, but he could also calm down pretty quickly.

He nodded, sat there a while longer, then left.

When he rang the bell, Bata opened the door instantly, as if only waiting for someone to return. He didn't seem furious at all.

"Hey," he said, "come in, son, quickly. Sit!"

Leon looked at him in bewilderment. Was this the same Bata who yelled at him just fifteen minutes ago?

"Listen," Bata began speaking without being prompted, "I'm sorry. I had to make a scene to let Bane think I was on his side. That was important, it was very important. On the other hand, I needed to release some tension, because Tone had really riled me up by showing up without the money. What the hell was he thinking?"

He stood up while talking and took a crystal bottle out of the cabinet.

"Let's first drink something to soothe our souls," he said and poured both of them a drink.

His hand was shaking and he spilt the drink. Leon laughed.

"Well, that's a different tune altogether," he nodded, gesturing that he would like another shot. He felt that the connection between him and Bata was still strong.

"Tone shit his pants," he started off in a friendly tone. "He's afraid that he blew the whole deal. My blood is still boiling, as well. He sent me over to see if there's any way you could bring Good Person back. Oh, and while we're on the subject of money," he grinned, relaxed, "this is from Mrs. Billinger in Munich..."

This was the first moment they were alone together, and it wasn't until now that he could settle this, without any witnesses present.

He took the envelope from his inside pocket.

"... Minus my five grand."

Bata greedily got hold of the envelope with both hands, his eyes filled with fire, unable to conceal his immense satisfaction.

"Oh, Mrs. Billinger," he said almost dreamily, "what a woman. Beautiful and rich. Did she give you a nice reception?"

"It was quite short, I was in a hurry. But she spoke very well of you, and she said," Leon said with an ambiguous smile on his face, "that she'd like to spend some more time with me the next time we meet."

"Alright, alright, we'll have to discuss this," Bata quickly concluded. "But now we have to resolve the troubling situation over here. This is our top priority for the moment. I hope Tone knows nothing about our beautiful lady and the money?"

"Of course he doesn't," Leon confirmed, "that was between us, it was only you and I."

"Your head really is in the right place, my son, we'll achieve great things together," Bata put the money in a side drawer of the cupboard without counting it first, covered it with a cloth napkin and returned, almost prancing, "you have no idea how important this money is to me right now."

His mood was increasingly good and he suddenly gave the impression that everything could be sorted out.

"Indeed," Leon said, "I'm glad that you got a decent amount. But let's get back to our business now. Will you be able to drag the junky back here? Don't tell me it's all over and done with? We drove here especially for this, we want to close the deal, I hope that's clear."

Bata thought about it, then shrugged a little.

"It's too bad we're off to such a bad start. Tone really messed up badly. I'm not sure what to do to remedy his provocation. There's so much at stake and the man shows up for the transaction without the money..."

It looked like he, too, could hardly believe what had happened.

He swiftly poured himself another drink.

"I'm sorry, Bata, but no one on earth would fork over so much money blindly, especially not Tone, since he has to borrow it when it comes to big business like this one," Leon defended him. "If it were you, you'd want to see the merchandise first, too, before reaching in your pocket."

"Alright," Bata nodded, "what happened, happened. Let's give it another try, especially if Tone still wants to make the deal. Listen, this is what we're going to do: I'll walk over to the joint where Bane usually hangs around, then I'll go see the dealer who sells him drugs. I'll think of something to bring him back, I'll be damned if I don't. You and Tone take a walk around the city and have some chevapcici somewhere, and we'll meet here, at my place in two hours. Agreed?"

"Of course," Leon said, "we'll do what you say, you know that. Just find Good Person! We can't lose these paintings in such a stupid way."

He went back to Tone to report the news. Tone was visibly relieved. They sat there for a while longer and then went strolling along Knez Mihajlov Street towards Kalemegdan, getting lost in the crowd which scurried along in both directions despite the heat. Leon especially enjoyed checking out sweaty summer dresses sticking to young women's beautiful curves in the sun. As his luck would have it, there was no shortage of them among the pedestrians. Tone was clutching his purse and thinking whether his negotiations with the investors back in Ljubljana would eventually make this deal happen or would the drugged out lunatic over here drive everything into oblivion.

Bata rushed to the Lotos bar. Good Person was drinking mineral water in the semi-darkness of the booth at the back, entertaining a drunken prostitute. When he saw Bata he waved at him merrily.

"How did I do?" he asked promptly.

"You were brilliant," Bata patted his shoulder. "I don't understand why you're not up there with the other film stars. Your acting was genius. You get the Oscar for the leading role! And you," he turned to the woman, "go to the bar and have a drink on me. We're not your customers at the moment."

The dancer turned up her nose and left.

Good Person grinned recklessly.

"Well, well," he shook his head, "I don't know about the Oscar, it was you who came up with all of it, you're the leading actor, you're the director and the screenplay writer and the producer, all in one, I can only get an award for supporting role."

"Right, let's discuss the second part now," Bata said. "The two

Slovenians are wandering around the city right now, be careful not to come across them when you leave. So, you were brilliant: strict and steadfast. You'll have them in the palm of your hand now."

"Heh, heh, that's me, you see. I didn't know I had it in me. What am I to do with these paintings now?" Good Person asked, pointing to the parcel under the table. "Should I come over again?"

"No, no," Bata shook his head, "I've come up with something better. You know what, go buy a Politika newspaper, spread it out and we'll tuck ten paintings in between the sheets of newspaper."

Bata chose the paintings.

"Then you're going to leave," Bata checked his watch, "at five o'clock down to the park in front of the Moskva Hotel, there's a bench over there, you'll hand the Politika to them and ask them to check what's inside. Then you're to say to them that they'll arrange everything with me, as I'm the only one you trust, and disappear. Do you understand? And be very nasty, of course. But first call me in about an hour and curse me out. I won't hold it against you, it's all part of the game."

"I get it," Good Person said, "I'll finish my drink and then I'll go."

Bata took what was left of the parcel and headed home. He sat there and waited. He was thinking whether he had planned everything right. He was certain that Good man would act his part two well, as he did great in the first one. When Tone and Leon returned, he met them with an unsure expression on his face.

"I couldn't find him anywhere," he reported with a tragic tone in his voice. "I went to every bar and left my phone number everywhere, asking that he should contact me urgently. I even went to his dealer; he told me that he hadn't been around yet today, but he was expecting him to show up shortly. I left my phone number with him, as well. I really tried to salvage this fucked up situation. You, Tone, you blew it big time. Yes, the boy is a drug addict and there's no way to know how he'll react. But we're the first ones who can get our hands on him. I hear there are tons and tons of paintings left in that attic. All we can do now is wait and hope for the best."

Tone sat down at the table and stared at the tablecloth. Leon was on to his second pack of cigarettes. He walked back to the window and stared outside. The apartment was luckily air conditioned and Leon's sweaty shirt, now pleasantly cool on his back, dried eventually. Bata sat at the opposite side of the table, leafing through an old newspaper. They had nothing to say to each other. Their fate was out of their hands. The three of them sporadically looked over to the phone, as if hoping to conjure up the redemptive phone call with their eyes. The flies circling the chandelier were buzzing loudly in the oppressive silence. Bata suddenly got up and started rummaging through his pockets.

"I'm out of cigarettes, I need to go across the road to buy some more," he said. "Mind the phone, will you."

Tone sighed and continued to stare at the tablecloth. Leon gestured with his hands that he needed another pack, too. Not long after Bata had left, the phone rang. Tone and Leon exchanged glances. Leon shrugged his shoulders. The insecurity of waiting for a phone call, and when it suddenly comes, you're not sure if you're allowed to answer or not, Leon waved his hand.

"Hello," he answered, adding quickly, "No, no, auntie Zaga, Bata will be back any moment now. We're working on something here... we'll be here for a while, yes... he'll call you, of course... I will, I will, don't worry..."

"Bata's mother," he said to Tone as a way of explaining, as he hung down the phone. "She wanted to know if it's alright for her to come home yet."

"My, what a circus," Tone mumbled.

"Did he call?" was the first thing Bata asked when he came back soon after with a fresh pack of cigarettes.

"No," Leon shook his head, "but your mother did."

"What the heck does she want," Bata ranted and walked over to the phone.

"Don't" Tone cried. "You mustn't keep the line occupied, in case the junky calls..."

"So, you're all pins and needles now, but you weren't thinking about it before. Why didn't you bring the money?" Bata resisted once more.

"Alright," Leon cut in, "we're all at fault and at the same time we're not at fault, who knew we would be dealing with a drug addict. We should stop giving each other a hard time about it. It will bring us nowhere."

"That's true."

Bata nodded and sat down at the table. He felt victorious inside, looking at two defeated Slovenians, two merchants who were ready for anything. Good Person would phone in about now and then the time would come for the final blow. The first part of the great Šlomovič operation would be finished.

Just as he lit another cigarette, the phone rang.

"It's him," Bata cried, "It's him. It has to be. Silence!"

He picked up the phone and nodded to them, yes, it's him.

The unintelligible yelling and piercing screaming coming from the receiver could be heard in every part of the room. Bata's face changed colours; he managed to fit in an occasional "yes, yes, of course... but I... oh, ok... as you say... well, alright..." and then put the phone down.

He kept standing for a minute, motionless, regaining his senses.

"What is it?" Tone came to.

"He cursed out my mother in more ways than I can count, damned me, told me where to go... but," his eyes beamed, "he agreed to bring the paintings over once more."

Tone and Leon exchanged glances. It wasn't completely clear the weight off whose shoulders was greater. Life was beginning anew. A kind of joy crept to their faces.

"But," Bata continued pleadingly, "don't ruin everything again! You have to do exactly what I say. He won't be coming over again, because he's afraid we'd set him up, call the police. He's paranoid. He wants you two to come down to the park in front of the Moskva Hotel. You're to wait for him there, at the bench next to a large bush, in one hour. He'll give you the paintings so you can take a look, then you're to bring them to me. He's holding me responsible for them. If you screw anything up, I'll have to pay for them, seven hundred thousand. If I don't, I'll have criminals from all over Yugoslavia and Europe on my back, every junky out there will be following me, I'm going to lose my house, me and my family will end up dead somewhere along the Danube. Do you understand?"

Again, there was deadly silence. Again, the only thing they could hear was the flies' buzzing. Tone stared into space; Leon was looking at Bata who leaned against a chair with his trembling hands. The story just entered another dimension.

"What are we going to do, Tone?" Leon asked. "Do we have the money in Ljubljana? If we don't, we'll fuck up Bata's life."

"Leave it to me to worry about the money," Tone reacted nervously, "don't interfere with things that are none of your business. You take care of your part of the job!"

Now it was Leon who lost his temper. All the tension accumulating through the day had gotten to him.

"I took care of my part of the job, the main part. I found the paintings, I brought you over here to look at them, and you did. Right? It seems it's your turn now!" he yelled. "The deal is hanging by a thread because of you, because of the money, because of your part of the job! Don't you tell me to mind my own business!"

He jerkily grabbed his empty glass and slurped out the last drops of drink.

"There's another thing, which I wanted to tell you about later. While you two have been collecting the money and already dividing the profits, I took care of the essential part. I found an art expert who is prepared to get involved only for us," Leon said and slammed his glass hard on the table.

"Alright, alright, don't you go flying off the handle, too," Tone flinched nervously while Bata pricked up his ears.

"What are you talking about, what expert? What's this all about?" he asked hastily.

"A top expert with an international licence," Leon said victoriously, "My mother helped me arrange it. He's going to confirm the authenticity of our stuff and based on his expertise we'll be able to make millions. We're nothing without the paperwork. And this guy, Good Person, he doesn't have it, he doesn't know the first thing about it. So this is part of our job. My job, gentlemen."

Leon's information came at the right moment. It was crystal clear that they needed to reach an agreement with Good Person, as the documents would put the final touch to the great deal. Bata and Tone silently mulled over in their heads what they had just heard. It was clear to them that this was a good thing.

"Where's he from?" Bata asked after a pause.

"He'll be flying over from Australia shortly," Leon said. He didn't want to say any more, as he already revealed more than he had intended to, and there were numerous details he hadn't worked through yet. At the moment, he only wanted to strengthen his position in the prospective project.

Bata nodded to himself thoughtfully.

"Well, alright, that's a very important aspect, but let's not go into it right now," Tone said after a while, returning to his old self, "first we need to get to the paintings. Is there anything else we need to be aware of about the drug addict in the park?"

"Not really," Bata said and checked his watch, his famous Patek Philippe, "just go there, do as he says and don't do anything stupid. Good Person will be there in fifteen minutes."

Tone and Leon had no trouble locating the bench and sat each on one side of it, as if they didn't even know each other. The sound of playing children resounded through the park, someone walked by occasionally, walking a dog, pensioners were breaking stale bread to feed the pigeons.

"They're taking us for fools over here," Tone said grimly when the time neared half past five. "If he's not here in ten minutes, we're going to get up, go to the garage and drive back to Ljubljana. This isn't good. I have a very bad feeling about this. I've never experienced a fuss like this."

"Tone, don't, everything will turn out fine. We need to have nerves of steel. Good Person might be secretly watching us from behind a bush, checking for a possible ambush," Leon tried to calm him down.

Some more time elapsed.

Suddenly they heard a rustle behind their backs and Good Person pushed through the green branches, holding an open newspaper in his hands. He offered it to Tone.

"Here you go, you can look all you like," he said, "pretend you're reading the newspaper. There are ten paintings stuck in there. After you're done, take everything to Bata. Go to the taxi stop, have one take you to the parliament, change taxis there, go to the train station and only then to Bata's place. He's responsible for the paintings now, you'll never see me again."

He disappeared at the other end of the park.

Tone opened the newspaper. Right away they saw Modigliani's Cariatide, a fantastic oil on cardboard. My God, that's worth at least twenty million, he thought. He didn't even bother to check further.

These kinds of things were not to take place in the street. He tucked the newspaper under his arm.

"This is insane," he murmured and gestured Leon to follow him.

They got up, went to get a taxi and followed every instruction Good Person gave them. They changed four taxis before they reached Bata's place. No one followed them.

The elevator was miraculously working and took them to the fourth floor. Bata was on edge, expecting them. He couldn't wipe the smile from the corners of his mouth.

He, too, should get an Oscar for directing the scam of the century!

Tone placed the Politika newspaper on the table and they turned the pages together.

"This Modigliani is truly exceptional," Tone repeated. He had never before held anything like this in his hands. "Fantastic!"

Leon lustfully took in every individual brushstroke with his eyes. He was beside himself. It happened!

Bata smiled. Every page brought another artwork by Rista, all conceived by him personally and aged at his house: Miro, Picasso, Matisse, Mondrian... Each artwork was better than the previous one.

They sat around the table in the atmosphere of enraptured victory.

"So, where's the money for the advance?" Bata asked.

"Take it yourself, it's in the white envelope," Tone pointed to his purse.

"Hold it," Bata raised his hand. "Now we have to talk about my position in this deal first. I procured the paintings, Tone, you took care of the advance, and Leon connected us. So, how are we going to handle this?"

"I don't get it," Tone said.

"Where's my profit?" Bata asked as if Tone was inquiring about something as clear as day.

"How much do you want?" Tone asked, looking at Bata like a hawk. Even the thick lenses of his spectacles were unable to conceal his cunning.

"I believe it's for you to say," Bata replied, "how much am I worth to you. You saw what kind of bollocks I had to pull to get our hands on the merchandise. And now I owe money to that lunatic. I guaranteed that he'd get paid. With my head, as you are aware."

"Don't worry," Tone waved him off, "the money is in Ljubljana."

"That's fine," Bata nodded, "so what's my cut?"

"Would you be willing to settle for two hundred thousand?" Tone asked quickly.

"You must be insane," Bata lost his temper, "just the Modigliani must be worth at least ten million, and you're offering me two hundred thousand. I beg your pardon!"

"Alright, five hundred, that's my final offer," Tone said. "Yes or no?"

"That won't do," Bata wouldn't go for it, "you're not being serious. I better just return the lot."

"No!" Tone cried, pressing the Modigliani to his chest, "that's not possible any more. These paintings are mine."

"They're not yours until you pay for them. I didn't even touch the advance," Bata resisted.

They looked at each other in silence, weighing each other up.

"Alright, how much do you want?" Tone asked.

"I want five million!" Bata fired.

"You're the one acting crazy now," Tone laughed, "completely crazy."

Bata looked at him furiously.

"I'm crazy? Me, who set this whole thing up?"

Leon was listening to them and he was getting fed up. They were like two strutting peacocks.

"That's enough," he called. "I've had it with your nonsense!"

They both flinched. In the heat of the argument they forgot Leon was even in the room with them.

"What do you want now?" Bata snarled.

"Me? I just want you two to include me in your plans, as well. You would never have even met if it wasn't for me, I've been busting my balls with this deal for three months now, and there's nothing in it for me, except for expenses. And, which is the most important thing in all of this, I arranged for the expert. So what do I get?"

"You're still young, you can wait," Bata tried to brush him off in a hurry, "besides, you're new to this trade. You get the woman's cut."

"And how much would that be in this case, gentlemen?" Leon asked crossly, looking from one man to the other.

"Two hundred thousand," Tone declared, "that's enough for you. That's the kind of money you could have only dreamed about with the business you were doing up to now."

"Fine," Leon agreed, "two hundred thousand is fine, but in that case I want a cut from the appraisals and a cut from the sale."

"Will you look at this boy?! You'd like a man's cut? Five hundred thousand is enough for you, and that's that. Will you take it or won't you?"

"I won't," Leon shook his head and walked over to the balcony. "I want half a million and a third of the sale."

Tone blinked repeatedly. It was clear to him that they needed to set their positions and shares of the profit straight, otherwise he wouldn't be able to take the paintings with him to Ljubljana. And the investors would be quick to open their wallets when they saw them. He brushed his hand over his face a few times, then said:

"I'd be willing to accept this, but under the following condition. Since I'll be the one procuring the money, I should get half of the profit from the sale, and you two get twenty-five percent each. Is that ok?"

Bata immediately acted offended:

"Tone, my little Tone, so I'm Leon's equal now, am I?"

"You're not," Tone turned him down. "I'm sure you'll get at least one hundred and fifty thousand from the junky."

"I might, and I might not," Bata shrugged. "But you have to realise that there are at least around a hundred paintings still there. And if you want me to save them for you, I want to get thirty, and Leon can have twenty. You, Tone, you can have half. I think that would be fair."

"Is that alright with you, Leon?" Tone asked.

"It's fine with me. But you two are covering the costs of organisation and the expert!"

"It's a deal," Bata and Tone replied simultaneously.

Bata checked his watch.

"Oh, how the time flies. I'm hungry. Let's go out to dinner. It's on me."

He grabbed Tone's purse and took out the white envelope.

Even God would do better to rest in this heat

Bata was pleased. Everything was going according to his plan. Leon brought him the money from the auction house in Munich for the first two paintings; Tone gave him the advance for the next ten. Now was the time to drive to Rista and pay out his first serious reward for the work he had already done. He tucked fifty thousand Deutschmarks in his purse and took a taxi to Pančevo.

Evening came and the setting sun shining at a narrow angle painted the landscape red, the Danube created wonderful works of art in its reflections under the bridge. Bata was rested. He expected unbridled debauchery upon Rista finally seeing a pile of money. The payday had the potential of dragging out. That's why he paid the taxi driver once they arrived at the fence of Bata's estate, let him go and entered the courtyard.

Here, too, the sunset scattered every shade of red over the trees, the grass and the buildings. Rista appeared at the entrance to the house, wearing a long white robe and tussled hair; he looked like a high priest of a red fiery deity in the scarlet lustre. Vesna number One and Vesna number Two were right behind him, and another young woman was following, a new one, a brunette, whom Bata had never seen before. They looked like some space religious procession. Rista was surprised.

He greeted him with both arms in the air.

"What's up, Bata? It's been ages since you came around. I was thinking about organising a hunt for you in your big city. Where did you disappear?"

"Take it easy, Rista, take it easy. You have never been good at waiting. You're not good at it now, either, you can't let what we sewed months ago grow," Bata spoke.

"That's exactly what I'm talking about, time is passing by and you're nowhere to be seen," Rista spread his arms like a father greeting his lost son.

"Come on," Bata came closer, "step away from the door, let me inside the house."

They embraced. Bata then looked around the place.

"Where is everybody? Where are your workers?" he asked.

"Where, where? I had to let them go, I had no money to pay

them," Rista explained with an aggrieved look on his face, "now I live with my women in solitude and poverty."

It was obvious that Bata would have to make an effort if he wanted to catch up with Rista in the amount of alcohol the boss had obviously consumed already.

"Very well, very well," Bata waved his hand, "let's sit so I can give you the good news."

"And that would be...?"

Bata pointed at his bag.

"Well, it's nothing special," he chuckled, "the postman came by."

Rista bulged his eyes and then started to express some joy.

"Are you trying to tell me that the pension has arrived?"

"Not all of it," Bata grinned, "just an advance. Here is fifty thousand Deutschmarks for you."

He released five rolls of blue German eagles out of his bag; they were all almost completely untouched hundred Deutschmark banknotes. Rista was stunned, he reached for them, shuffled them around a bit, then cried:

"Oh my, oh my, they're so pretty! So, payday has finally arrived? This calls for a good old Serbian custom, we need to get genuinely drunk! I'm off to the cellar. I need to bring out something special for the occasion! I have some old brandy left from my father, he maybe got it from his father, maybe even from his grandfather. Well, now's the occasion!"

He turned around and left, the first two women approached Bata while the third one took a step back. They kissed him warmly.

"Well, Mr Bata, you've brought joy to our house!"

They took two of the armchairs from the garden set in the courtyard and placed them under the trellis, spreading blankets over them; the men who were obviously about to embark on a long drinking bout, needed some soft seating. They went on to light colourful light bulbs which hung from strings amidst load-bearing beams, and the place was instantly graced with a magical touch.

Bata leaned back in his armchair. Rista came out of the house, carrying a fiasco holding at least fifteen litres.

"How much of the bloody brandy did you bring, Rista? Who's going to drink all of this?"

"You and me," Rista beamed, "and we'll let my angels have some, too."

He grabbed one of the women's breasts and buttocks with a hedonistic move.

"Do I get any of this, too?" Bata asked provokingly. He had always wondered how was it possible that a number of women always lived with Rista and yet there was no tension among them, let alone animosity.

"Where there's some for me, there's always some for you, as well," Rista replied. "But take it slowly, don't have all at once."

He turned to the woman pressing herself against him.

"Go and call Miško the Stamp Collector, tell him to bring over his music. We're going to have some fun tonight! And don't forget to tell the neighbours!"

Bata and Rista took turns drinking from the fiasco. Bata knew there would be no more thinking about business. Now was the time to drink, the madness was about to begin.

Miško the Stamp Collector was a merry member of a group of antique dealers from the town; he got his nickname from his affinity for stamps. He owned a huge collection, every stamp ever printed in Yugoslavia ever since the establishment of the monarchy, he was trading old ones and buying new ones all the time; but his heart was beating for Gipsy music, and whatever the happy occasion, he was the one to take one of the travelling groups from Skadarlija and bring it wherever duty called.

He entered Rista's courtyard in grand style. He kept his stout shoulders in a navy blue jacket with gold buttons, the creases on his trousers were ironed so sharp that one could cut a finger on them. He was holding two bottles of whiskey in his hands.

"Here, boss, I don't want you to run out of drink in the early morning hours!" he called, while Gipsy musicians were already entering from behind him and their trumpets roared with their anthem Djurdjevdan over the fence. People were getting up and applauding with arms up in the air. Any neighbours who hadn't been already there, were quick to arrive now. When Rista had a party, alcohol was flowing, ears were filled with music, women were feeling generous... Nothing was ever missing from his parties.

Rista was pouring the brandy into glasses, offering one of them to Miško right away.

"Excellent, Miško, you've brought the music..."

Miško, Rista and Bata downed their drinks in one go and slammed the empty glasses against the wall of the house.

"Give me some more!" Miško demanded. "I need to catch up with you two!"

He gulped down a few more shots.

The men took their chairs, drank and listened to the musicians.

"Hey," Rista then called to his women, "call some friends for my friends, we have to have everything today!"

They soon appeared, sparingly clothed and vivacious, they started dancing right away, first on their own, the dusk endowed them with fairylike appearance, and the men soon joined them. But their feet quickly grew tired from all the drinking and they staggered back to their chairs. They lustfully observed the women dancing alone, sitting in their laps from time to time and then evading them again. The curves in their reach and the alcohol roused them terribly.

Bata's eye caught Nataša, a brunette he had never before seen at Rista's. She kept dancing provocatively in front of him, her sun-kissed tan, inviting hands and long legs assuming positions full of promise aroused him. She didn't know Bata, either, but she heard that he was a cunning salesman, and a wealthy one, who always liked to substantially reward his mistresses.

The rambunctious party was going strong for quite some time, everything was overflowing with happiness. The heaven and the earth became one in this garden and untamed dancing, music, food, drink and merriment broke every known record.

The Gipsies were slowly getting tired, the double bass was no longer able to keep up with the rhythm, but the dancing women didn't seem to mind, they kept circling the men they chose like some magical beings. They were reaching for their bodies and expressing their desires without any restraint.

Rista then took one of his mistresses inside the house, to a chorus of luscious comments, his close neighbours gradually dispersed, several couples disappeared into appropriate little rooms around the outbuildings, garden niches and workshops; Miško the Stamp Collector had chosen a plump brunette and settled down in the guest room, Bata took Nataša to the living room.

When dawn started breaking at the east, Rista and Bata, once they managed to tear themselves away from their women, wobbled over to their armchairs under the trellis. They were totally knackered. All they could do until daylight came was drink in silence and snooze.

The morning sun woke them up, they had a good fill of the fresh coffee served by one of the women, and they slowly regained their senses. Rista was the one to start the conversation.

"This was a wild night, Bata, wasn't it wild?"

"It was," Bata agreed, "but that girl of yours, the one who was with me, she was even wilder. I don't think anyone could resist her. She is so beautiful, it's like she was made by Michelangelo, and very experienced! The things she did!"

Rista nodded in silence. Bata closed his eyes as if he was re-experiencing a dream. Then he winced and said:

"Let's not talk about this now, Rista, my friend. Things have started to unravel, as you can see. I need more good paintings now. What have you conjured up while I was away?"

Rista smiled proudly.

"A lot, Bata, Batane my friend, a lot. I have everything: from Picasso to Matisse, Loth and Kandinsky, there's Braque and Lautrec... A lot, truly a lot. I had some peace and I was able to work properly."

"Bravo," Bata applauded, "so you've been good!"

"I knew that you'd show up with the money sooner or later and that you'd want new stuff. So I made it, world-class, the way it's supposed to be. I get crazy in a way, when I work," Rista said.

"You are crazy, to tell you the truth," Bata nodded, "and if not crazy, at least not normal."

"No one is normal right now at this table," Rista roared with laughter. "Isn't that right, my friend?"

"You're right," Bata agreed, adding, "but let me now see the collection you have in your studio, let me take a look at all the famous works of art."

"Yes," Rista said again proudly, "the greatest in the world. Mine."

They walked to the studio, their knees still wobbling. Rista took a key from the chain around his neck and unlocked the door. They entered.

Bata saw long lines of paintings which were leaning against the walls of the studio. Five easels with large paintings were turned with their backs against the outside windows. Even the smallest one, one meter high and eighty centimetres across, a green abstract, was gleaming with shades ranging from extremely grassy green to bright lemony yellow-green and almost watery emerald green; when Bata looked at it long enough, he felt like he sensed nymphy figures, playing around by the water, draped in veils. The painting was signed above right: Picasso. It was a genuine signature, bright white with a touch of pink, a signature from before the war. The painting had already been aged, too. Bata smelled it and realised that it didn't give off any more scent of paint, but instead smelled like it had been wiped off with some special chemicals in a restoration workshop.

On the second easel, he saw a part of a pond and garden, complete with water lilies and aquatic grasses, as well as various flowers which stood out from the blue of the water and the green of the grasses and ferns. It was a stunning Monet. Bata rubbed his finger over the painting. The coarseness of the layers of paint felt hard, almost sharp. This must have been among the first paintings Rista finished, enough time must have elapsed. The Japanese wouldn't even try to negotiate the price, Bata thought.

There was a Kandinsky standing next to it. Colourful lines, from bright yellow to black, criss-crossed the white base, intersected by thin blue and pinkish ones. Squares and circles were lined in grey and red. It radiated some sort of extraordinary, regularly irregular geometry, akin to a disorder in the Universe. The painting could easily end up at one of the principal museums of Russian avant-garde. The easel next to it held a stylised male face, rich in its minimalism... Jawlensky, Bata guessed as the thought of great numbers went through his head.

The last easel held a beautiful art nouveau female nude. The elongated face exuded grace and elegance, the brown hair was very lascivious, the body was painted in a nice skin colour and the yellow background guilded this seductive woman. She was recumbent like a cat and Bata's mind involuntarily wandered off to the woman who diverted him the night before.

He was sure the forger had used her as a model. Rista brought him out of his daydreaming and the desire to repeat the night:

"You wouldn't happen to know this woman?"

Bata answered with a modest smile.

"If we continue our celebrations, we'll tell her to hold on to you today, as well," Rista promised, grinning.

They continued their inspection of the paintings. A bunch of sketches and watercolours by Rodin lay on the table in the corner, a few Renoir's were leaning against the wall, a number of works by Kandinsky were stacked in a separate line, Egon Shiele and Klimt were isolated from the others, there were Italian impressionists and Spanish modernists, paintings on canvas and cardboard, drawings and gouaches...

The immense number of artistic monographies on the world's leading painters had found their reverberation.

A normal man, an art lover, would lose his mind over this, but Bata, although excited, simply asked:

"Rista, my friend, how many pieces do you have?"

Rista fired without a moment's hesitation: "About two hundred, if you count the sketches over there in the corner."

Bata was dumbfounded.

"And who in God's name is going to sell all of them?" he asked, despite feeling like he already knew the answer.

"Who indeed, Bata, Batane my friend? Well, you, of course, you are a marketing marvel, it's obvious that you come from a family of merchants, although there might be a hint of a Herzegovian in you, as well..."

"Shut up, you miserable man, you know that I'm Serbian!"

"Oh, don't get angry, Bata, maybe there were some genes in the air and they influenced your mother, you know that Herzegovians are the best merchants, second only to the Jews, but since you're not one, there must have been some influence of the Herzegovian genes on your Serbian..."

Bata calmed down and shrugged.

"Well, alright. But give us some more of that brandy we had yesterday, so I can feel through the alcohol all the beauty you have amassed in your studio, so I can comprehend it and experience it," he said.

They walked out under the trellis, where Rista's lovers were already busy preparing a hearty breakfast. They didn't feel like eating so they started on the drink right away, chatting with the women. Miško the Stamp Collector was awakened by the noise and he came out of the guest room. He was carrying two heavy handguns.

"How can you start drinking without me?" he cried at first, then turned to Rista, "Where did you get these two beauties?"

He was waving a large nine-millimetre Mauser in his left hand, and a semi-automatic Luger with a long barrel in his right. He aimed both pistols at the well at the centre of the garden.

"Miško, don't," Rista jumped up, "they're loaded, stop it, we don't want any accidents! Don't play with fire, we're drunk!"

"You really think I can't handle a weapon?" Miško resisted, insulted. "I might be drunk, but not enough not to realise what I have in my hands."

Bata rose from the armchair and took the Mauser away from him.

"I always wanted something like this," he said, pointing at the nearby tractor, "plus a nine-millimetre Walther PPK with a silencer."

"If that's the case, you can have it, as a present. May it remind you of me!"

"Seriously?" Bata rejoiced. "Yes, it will remind me of you, always."

He then pointed to a nearby church belfry, gently stroking the pistol, as he had the brunette during the night. Miško then spoke:

"Bata gets a present, what about me?"

"I'm in a good mood today," Rista stretched, "you can have the Luger!"

"I won't forget it, thank you," Miško said joyfully and pointed his pistol at the belfry, too.

They all sat down at the table under the trellis and ate. The sun was already high up in the sky and warm, or rather hot rays were breaking their way through the grape leaves above their heads. The air was trembling and the high temperatures made the men begin to sweat.

"Bring some cold water and soft cloth, to cool us down a bit," Rista ordered and the young women swiftly returned with three buckets of water and white linen cloths. One of them attended to Rista, the other was putting cold compresses on Bata, the third on Miško's forehead and neck.

The men drank and theorized, there was no shortage of ideas and proposals, it was impossible to tell who was the smartest and who was the best, one of them suggested in passing, what if we took some shots, and Rista was instantly holding a handgun, as well, a large Browning holding fifteen rounds.

"Let me show you how to shoot," Bata said, got up and shot toward the church. A plume of smoke rose from the roof tiles of the belfry.

"You missed!" Miško cried; it was his turn to aim, his hand wasn't shaky at all, a shot rang out and the cross on top of the belfry spun around.

"Give it hell!" Rista revved.

"I'm not going to shoot at a cross," Bata refused. "I'd rather let God rest a bit in this heat, too. It's not like I didn't put a hole in every tin can and broke every bottle I aimed at the last time."

"That was then," Rista said, "and now is now."

"Well, alright, I'm going to take down the rooster from the roof of your studio," he suggested.

"Fine," Miško agreed, "hit the rooster."

Bata aimed, fired and the rooster turned to the north.

"You're good," Miško praised him, drank his brandy and smashed his glass against the wall. Rista and Bata followed suit.

"That's enough," Bata said, "It's time to have some food again!"

"What about women?" Miško asked, who liked to let his rooster run wild every time he got a chance. He had been married seven times and his friends teased him that he had married every woman he'd screwed.

"Why don't you take a breather," Rista waved him off, "wait for the evening, for dusk to fall, for the atmosphere to cool down a bit. We'll take care of everything then."

But it can't be possible, it can't be, how could it appear out of nowhere...

Leon and Tone slept all the way home in the comfort of the Mercedes. The tension and the uncertainty during the day, followed by a large dinner in the renowned inn Pri oraču had all taken their toll. Naturally, they were also comforted by the warm thought: they were carrying ten incredible paintings in the boot. If we manage to sell them well, the boot of the Mercedes will not be large enough to hold all the money, Leon thought to himself. The truth was better than any, even the most incredible dream.

As he was getting out of the car in front of his apartment building, extremely weary in the middle of the night, Tone tugged at his sleeve and said seriously: "There's only one job you need to take care of when it comes to our business: find out what's going on with the expert and when he's supposed to arrive. That's the key to our treasure."

Leon could hardly make it to the apartment, where he was met by a joyous and jumping Šeri. The noise awakened Kristina and she came out of their bed.

"And?" she asked him sleepily.

"Victory!" Leon cried and embraced her.

He was sure that the embrace would be everlasting.

Then he collapsed in the armchair, asked for a glass of ice cold mineral water and started telling her the story. It wasn't long before Kristina was completely awake, as Leon kept stringing all the details of the adventure, which, put together, formed the final message: I'm going to be rich now; we'll never have to argue about money again. The paintings were explosive, they would shake up the art market. He was careful to embellish his own role, without which Tone and Bata would be powerless. I'm going to bring in an art expert who will provide the final touch by confirming the authenticity of the paintings, my mother was the one who found him.

"Your mother?" Kristina pulled a face. "Your mother? So she's helping out her fugitive, expired-models-chasing son now, is she?"

Leon felt the unpleasant sting of this sudden nasty remark, as he'd been doing everything to overlook the extremely negative energy between the two women, in the vague hope that it would fade eventually.

Now, when he was about to erase the subject from the agenda by raking in a large share of the deal, he found Kristina's question totally absurd. So he just swallowed hard and replied curtly:

"Yes, my mother's been helping me, or should I say, she's been helping us."

Kristina paused as she immediately realised the foolishness of widening the trench she and Leon had somehow managed to step over without too many problems, one day at a time. Leon was finally winning. Oh, how she hoped he would. That is, we shall see.

"Great," she said, filling Leon's glass with some more mineral water. "Can we go to bed now?"

"Yes," Leon nodded, "I'm almost dead."

When he awoke at noon the next day, his body and soul felt excellent; a happy soul in a rich body, he told himself. He fixed himself up and phoned to let his mother know he was coming over.

"Just in time," his mother told him after greeting him, "I've just been writing a very important letter. I could use your help."

"Oh my, I'm going to be of help to my mother, the great boss," he grinned into the receiver and quickly got in his quatrelle.

As it turned out, his mother was answering a letter by France Benko from Australia, who again confirmed that he would come and that he was looking forward to meeting people in his homeland after so many years, and also that he'd be interested to learn more about the work his dear neighbour from his childhood years had mentioned.

"The man is a certified art expert for the Australian government in Canberra," his mother told him, adding suspiciously: "I hope you won't shove any hideous work in his hands."

Leon laughed.

"My dear and beloved mother, I won't make a fool of you. I spent the whole day yesterday running around Belgrade, and I had Tone with me, as well. We were entrusted ten capital paintings to sell, they have been forgotten for decades, collecting dust at a rural attic in the middle of Vojvodina. There's no doubt in our minds that they are authentic, but we need a certified expert with an international licence to confirm this," Leon almost boasted, "this is what your son is up to, this is what your schoolmate will deal with."

Leon's mother was caught a little bit off guard by his victorious tone of voice.

"And who are these great masters?"

Leon paused for a bit, then slowly started to name them: "Picasso, Kandinsky, Renoir, Matisse..."

His mother practically collapsed back in her chair.

"What did you say, what are you talking about?"

"Yes," Leon nodded happily, "you heard right!"

His mother just sat there, stunned, shaking her head in disbelief, looking at Leon in total surprise and whispering:

"But it can't be possible, it can't be, how could it appear out of nowhere... Is it possible that they're some weird reproductions? This can't possibly be true."

"Well, it is, and luckily Tone and I have gotten our hands on the whole thing. We reached a precise agreement with Bata about the profit, about who gets what, so there would be no fuss later on... There, mother, you didn't believe in my business, but it finally happened. I'll be sitting pretty for the rest of my life," Leon explained, feeling like a God making a brief stop in Ljubljana.

His mother struggled to get her head around the story. She was unable to calm down. Then she waved her hand.

"Have you put it in writing, and how does it look?" she asked, still pretty upset, but also with a touch of firm reality. "A lot of things can go wrong when it comes to money, much more than just relationships which seemed firm before. You know that, right?"

Leon ignored the familiar undertone and stated with self-assurance:

"We need each other, every one of us is crucial if we are to pull this off. We'd have to collaborate even if we fell out. Benko is my trump card, and I hope we can rein him in together. His expertise will be a crucial element for the buyers. Bata will make sure that the owner and first seller of the paintings doesn't go elsewhere, Tone will be the principal investor, and I'll have Benko in my pocket. That's the winning formula, it has to be."

His mother crossed her hands over her chest.

"Have you talked about this with your father?" she asked.

"No, not yet, I haven't had the time; I've come running over to you at the first flick of the finger. I'll go to him when we finish the letter," Leon smiled, suggesting, "so, shall we check if there is anything missing in your writing?"

They agreed that his mother should include the names of the artwork Benko was expected to appraise. Such an offer should shake any art expert to the core, Leon was sure of it. A lot of paintings, great names, a lot of expert opinions, great payment. Plus working in good old homeland, far from the crazy world. Could things get any better?

His mother took over the typing; she didn't want her kind and otherwise trustworthy secretary to feel any unnecessary temptation. When Leon read the letter, he felt it was almost too tactful and polite for his taste, but this was old school, naturally. He offered to take the letter to the post office himself, choosing every available delivery option: air mail, priority, express.

What will happen when the expert finally arrives? Leon kept thinking as he drove back to the city. Will the final little piece of the puzzle finally fall in its place and change everything, turn everything around? Is it his turn to forget about all the worries he has been plagued by until now? Will he and Kristina finally achieve a definite and complete reconciliation; will this put a stop to all the games? Will his dreams come true and he'll become an art dealer on the European, global stage? Will he forget all about his studies, as he will be able to get exceptional knowledge first-hand, in practice, through working with an internationally renowned expert?

He will arrange with his father and his mother to give up the upper floor of their house at the foot of Šmarna Gora Mountain, which he moved out of to live with Kristina, and turn it into a lab, like Benko described it in his letter, which could also serve as a place to spend the night. This would provide the man with total peace, they will give him everything he needs, everything will be done very discretely, and Leon will have complete control over him at the same time.

I used to be an ardent dissident back in the day

The highly anticipated day finally arrived.

Leon's mother and father drove to the airport in the morning to pick up Benko, who was supposed to arrive via Frankfurt, while Leon and Tone went to the Rotovž restaurant to arrange everything for lunch. They reserved a table and put together a menu after a lengthy discussion with the head chef. A man returning to his native country after so many years should taste all the delicacies of his homeland. After everything was settled, they just sat there, talked feverishly and drank a glass of Viljamovka brandy from Pleterje. Leon informed him that his parents wouldn't join them for lunch, as they didn't want to be involved in art business, they'd meet Benko for dinner at a later time.

"That's alright," Tone nodded, "it's a good thing that we have a large table. One needs more space with conversations like these."

An elderly couple appeared at the door at noon sharp, a gentleman of a shorter and fuller stature, with glasses and well over sixty, wearing a grey suit and a brown hat, and a lady with an almost exact same figure, only thinner, with permed blond hair and carrying a large black handbag under her arm. They were approached by the head waiter, and after a brief exchange he showed them to Leon and Tone's table. When they reached them, they both got up, introduced themselves, and the newcomers introduced themselves, as well.

"My name is France Benko, and this is my spouse, Francka," the gentleman said in a rather thin voice, smiling at Leon, "so you're the son of my childhood neighbour?"

They took their places around the table and were already attended to by the waiter. Tone took over the ordering process:

"First we'd like some Karst prosciutto and ham from Prekmurje, a bit of minced lard from Gorenjska and some butter from Bohinj, followed by veal ragout with žlikrof, and for the main course we'll have game, chamois roast in its own gravy, deer loin with pancetta and truffles, and a wild boar steak in cranberry gravy, with rolled dumplings from Prekmurje and Dolenjska on the side, naturally."

He looked victoriously at both guests, as if to say, "That'll do, right?" but Benko hastily cleared his throat and apologized, explaining that he and his wife would have to pass on the wonderful menu, as they were both vegetarians. Their life philosophy called for a different attitude toward all living beings, including animals; they were following the principles of Kabbalah. Tone got momentarily confused, and then ordered them a vegetable plate, as varied as possible, as well as a cheese plate. They chose charlotte cake from Štajerska region for desert, three types of sponge cake in vanilla and fruit cream.

They had some getting-acquainted conversation during the meal, they each revealed a little bit about themselves, and then Leon and Tone passingly outlined the expectations they had for Benko. He informed them that he was happy to see his homeland return to democracy, as he was forced to flee from Europe to Australia right after the war because he was not in line with the regime of the time. In Australia, he met a fellow Slovenian woman who eventually became his wife. He was received well over there and reached a high position in the government. Now he packed all of his working tools in a container which was about to arrive to Koper port shortly, so he could work over here.

They decided to have coffee at the Slon Cafe. His wife excused herself early as she had to arrange something at the Slovenian emigrant headquarters, while her husband enjoyed a short stroll after lunch. They sat down in the far corner of the largely empty cafe and effectively began their business talks.

"I have to tell you something right at the beginning," Benko started.

He wiped the bridge of his nose with the fingers of his right hand, as if the spectacles he wasn't even wearing at the moment were bothering him.

"I didn't want to discuss it in front of my wife. The situation with the container is not exactly as I told you: it has already arrived to Koper, but I received a hint that all of my equipment, including my papers and my seals have been confiscated because they need to check God knows what. I suspect they want to prevent me from working in Slovenia. I used to be an ardent dissident back in the day, fighting for democracy, my family lost a lot of assets and I was left with no other choice than to emigrate," he spoke, doling out meaningful looks.

A painful bit of history unexpectedly landed in the middle of a well-thought-out plan, which was something Leon and Tone really had no need to.

"Oh, come on, it must be some sort of misunderstanding. I'm sure it will sort itself out," Tone said calmingly.

"I can't work without my papers and seals," the man hurried on, "they're doing this on purpose, so I wouldn't go back home."

"Easy, easy," Tone tried to stop him, "we'll handle this. If it takes too long, I'll get you some personal seals, we can also prepare documents with your header. This won't be a problem."

Leon was surprised and remained silent for a bit, while Benko calmed down some and went on to explain:

"You have to know that international experts work with special paper, it's only manufactured in Switzerland and marked with a special code which is kept in professional records to prevent any misuse. That's a global standard."

"Don't worry," Tone said again, "I have a colleague who works with the Swiss papermakers, so what you're referring to shouldn't be a problem at all. Anything else?"

"Yes, for the first stage of the work I need infrared and ultraviolet lights; I use them to make check for any damage to the paintings, and maybe later to see if they have been retouched or altered in any other way. This plays a very important role in the price of the artwork," the man was getting fired up.

"If that's the toughest task..." Tone grinned.

"Excellent," Benko said, quite pleased now. "And when can I see the artworks we were talking about, are they available?"

"Of course," Leon and Tone fired simultaneously, and Tone continued:

"We have them here with us, in Ljubljana, you can see them right away."

"Oooh," Benko rejoiced, "that's excellent."

Leon spoke now, too, as he felt he should contribute to the solemnity of the event.

"We've heard nothing but nice things about you... What have you been doing up to now?" he asked.

"Oh, lots of things," Benko declared proudly, giving Leon a side glance which immediately reminded him of the glance in painter Stupica's eyes in the famous painting Self-portrait with a friend. "I worked for the Rijksmuseum in Amsterdam and for some wealthy collectors in Switzerland... I specialised in French and Italian impressionists, you see... and I also worked in Australia, naturally, where I completed a big restoration job in St. Patrick's Cathedral."

"Oh, good for you, good for you," Leon said with admiration. "So, when could you start working on our paintings?"

"If you don't mind," Benko suggested, "I'd like to take care of a few things in my homeland first, just to make sure I don't have to interrupt my work because of them later on. I'll have my lab at your dear mother's house, if I'm not mistaken," he turned to Leon, "which is really nice of her. Would it be ok with you if I started in a week's time?"

They shook hands. Benko bid farewell and left, while Leon and Tone remained seated. Their eyes were filled with positive mood. The missing piece of the puzzle to the final offer for the buyers was falling into place perfectly.

"Will you really be able to provide the equipment and accessories, everything that Benko needs?" Leon asked. "Benko mentioned that he uses over thirty different chemicals for his analysis..."

"It goes without saying..." Tone smiled confidently, "you have my word."

They each ordered a glass of Rhine Riesling, and Tone then began to list instructions:

"Since he'll be working at your house, I'm going to need you to report everything he does, the way he does it, what he needs; keep track of all the expenses, I'm going to finance everything: dinners, lunches, transport fees, any train or plain fares. I'll need that for the final balance sheet."

Look at you, mister big boss, ordering me about like I'm some bookkeeper. Am I a partner or a messenger? Leon thought to himself for a moment, but his mind quickly wandered off to other things, under the influence of the important meeting with Benko.

You own nothing. The stuff was bought by my investors

They first had some Turkish coffee, and then went into the room on the first floor of the house at the foot of Šmarna gora Mountain. There was a large improvised table standing on two trestles. Benko first covered it with some rolls of thick wrapping paper and then arranged all the paintings on the table. The sight was magnificent: bright colours employed by world-class masters, from Renoir and Modigliani to Miro and Picasso. Leon's mother and father, Tone and Leon stood silently by the window, observing the expert's moves almost solemnly and with interest. He seemed quite taken with the artworks, as he instantly became blind to everything else around him. Then he suddenly turned into a meticulous bureaucrat, he wrote down a number on the paper under each painting, the date of viewing - August 1984 - adding his seal and signature.

Benko claimed he hadn't yet managed to solve with the customs officers the fate of his container holding his papers and accessories, which he had sent over to Slovenia from Australia, so Tone arranged everything he needed. There were bottles of chemicals, special lights, brushes and dishes, various pieces of cloth, measuring tapes and weights, notebooks and pencils, and of course newly manufactured seals of the art expert in English, as well as numerous forms on special papers. All in all, it was a very respectable makeshift art expert's lab. Across the lab on the same floor, Leon's ex-room was rearranged into Benko's living quarters.

After a brief inspection, Benko decided to first analyse one of Renoir's paintings, a summer landscape. He spent a long time looking at the whole thing, then began turning it and inspecting it at different angles, then changed his spectacles and observed the details. He paid much attention to the markings on the back, as well. The room was filled with perfect silence, except for an occasional sigh and the rustling of paper on the table. Leon was nibbling his lips. Everything took quite some time. Finally, Benko turned to his audience.

"I think, at first glance, I'd say that the painting is from the correct period, painted in the style and technique employed by Renoir. I can confirm that what we have here is a genuine work by him. I can see this from the brushstrokes and the way the image is radiating its content.

The signature appears to be genuine, as well," he said and reached for a book featuring signatures of world-renowned artists, pointing his finger at Renoir's which entirely matched the signature on the painting in question. "I need to perform chemical and light analysis, of course, but I'm sure they will confirm my initial findings."

The atmosphere of reserved silence quickly turned into one of pleased joy. Leon beamed; in the first place because of the painting itself, and secondly also because his mother and his father were given an expert confirmation that their son was taking part in an important story. They stepped closer to congratulate him.

"Well," his father smiled, "you've reached the point you've been aspiring to your entire life. I wish you all the luck."

His mother embraced him; it looked like she was about to shed a tear, so she turned around and went downstairs to the apartment.

Tone immediately got into a scrupulous conversation with the expert. How are things to go on from here, how long will all the analyses take, when will the expert opinions be ready, and, since all of these will eventually have to be sold, does he as a renowned person in the international art collectors' field have any connections with gallery owners and final buyers, collectors around the world?

"Of course," Benko confirmed, "I can help you out with this in my humble capacity, for a small share of the profits, naturally."

"Naturally," Tone confirmed resolutely, "it goes without saying, that's what I had in mind."

Benko went on to explain that it would take him roughly two weeks to examine the paintings laid out on the table. He'd record his findings along the way, and then he would need at least another week or so to write detailed expert opinions. He turned to Leon.

"This kind of work demands concentration, a series of procedures need to be carried out in specific time frames. I can't start right away. I gather that you, Leon, are going to be my assistant" – I must be really young for him to jump to first name basis like this, Leon thought – "we're going to start first thing tomorrow morning. Please be here at eight o'clock, we'll have breakfast together and then go on to work. You should get yourself one of these white coats, as well. I need the right atmosphere to concentrate, and I've always had my assistants wear coats."

"I will," Leon agreed.

"You might find it superfluous or tedious, but you will get acquainted with some of the secrets involved in confirming authenticity and restoration of artworks. I should think you won't find them too interesting, but it's knowledge that you'll be able to use for the rest of your life. Not everyone is prepared to share it," he smiled.

They chatted some more and then Tone began to take his leave. He asked Leon to walk him out. He stopped once in front of the house, subconsciously raised his finger and said:

"Great, you'll be at his side all the time. You must be very careful, follow his every move, learn from him, you'll be able to learn much more than at any university; you'll be doing yourself the greatest favour of your life. Notice which chemicals he uses when checking for age and authenticity of materials and keep track of the way he works. I need you to report to me on everything in detail. When he goes back to Australia, you can keep doing this for me. You get what I'm saying, right?"

He got into his regular taxi and drove off.

Leon kept looking in the direction he left for a long time. Interesting, he thought, the way he takes it for granted that he's the one giving out orders. He wants to be the boss at all times, just like he is in his store. The guy really thinks I'm going to be his messenger. Did he forget about the deal they had made in Belgrade?

He went back into the house, where he found his mother, father and Benko having some tea in the living room.

"Tea's not for me," he grinned when they asked him to join them, "I'm going to take a stroll around the city, since I'll be working from morning to night in the next days. I'll leave you to discuss the good old days in peace."

Back home, Kristina was thrilled when he told her that the expert confirmed the authenticity of the paintings at first glance.

"So, when will you sell them?" she wanted to know.

Leon explained to her that this was not something they expected to happen right away, describing all the things that needed to take place first. In the end, they would also need to find reliable buyers.

"Mhm," Kristina merely mumbled and asked Leon to take Šeri out for a walk, because she needed some peace and quiet to prepare for her newest project, in order to make some money as soon as possible herself.

"Why don't we go together?" Leon suggested.

"Can't you see that I'm working?" she replied grumpily. "I let you attend to your business by yourself, too."

"Well, yes..." Leon simply remarked, before running down the stairs, accompanied by the bitch.

He was deeply immersed in his thoughts about the greatest deal of his life and didn't want any inessential remarks to get in his way. Supposedly inessential remarks.

The next morning he made a stop at a bakery in Šentvid to buy some fresh bread rolls. Benko was already sitting in the studio, reading the newspaper and drinking tea. He checked his watch.

"Being on time is a great virtue," he smiled, brushing his grey hair in place, although it was meticulously combed as it was. He combed it carefully over the bald spot on the top of his head. He had half a bread roll. He brushed the breadcrumbs carefully off the dining table.

"Ready?" he stood up.

They both put on their lab coats and approached the desk. Benko once again picked up Renoir's landscape. He observed it at different angles, mumbling all along and putting down some notes on the paper spread beneath the painting. Then he took a small notebook out of his pocket, leafed through it, mumbled some more and put down some more notes. He picked up a large magnifying glass and carefully inspected the painting, centimetre by centimetre. Every now and then he kept checking a catalogue of works by Renoir, in Dutch, which lay on the tiny shelf beneath the window. Leon was sitting at the desk across from him, observing him silently. After a couple of hours Benko took a deep breath, put down the magnifying glass and pen, and turned to Leon.

"Could I get a cup of tea?"

Leon went down to his parent's apartment and came back with a full teapot and a cup. In the meantime, Benko had placed a number of bottles containing chemicals together with some lab dishes over the desk.

"What now?" Leon asked.

"We're going to find out whether this is an oleograph which has been painted over. There are a number of copies of the same painting in the world, and they are made in a variety of ways. Oleography is one of them. Forgers take a high-resolution image of the original and later print this on a canvas or cardboard dating to the time the original was made. Then an expert forger would paint over the print with oils or watercolours and prepare it for ageing. Whenever possible, they would use old paints, but they are very expensive and hard to come by. So what they do is they often use newer paints and add to them some of the elements they used to contain in the past, like eggs or sheen, sometimes they even make pigments from natural minerals. Then the painting is dried, often in a regular kitchen oven. Once it acquires adequate patina, they cool it down with frozen newspaper and rub a heavy object over it, such as an old iron or flat stone, even a brick. The painting then needs to sit in a sunny spot, where it can spend several months. The sun fades the painting and adds the structure of dust which has collected and settled in the soft paint, giving the painting an authentic look."

Leon listened to him with his mouth wide open.

"First we're going to test the base of the painting with a mixture of acetone and ammonia," Benko continued.

He laid the painting on a soft cotton cloth. With a pipette, he added a few drops of ammonia and acetone to a dish and mixed them together. Then he applied a drop of the mixture on the edge of the painting. The smell of corrosive smoke filled the room. Benko observed this part through a magnifying glass. Leon was eager to have his turn and look through it himself. But Benko just kept looking, jotting down notes on the paper underneath the painting as he did so. Finally, he offered Leon the magnifying glass and said:

"Take a look and tell me if you can see anything on the part of the painting where we applied the tincture."

Leon eagerly got hold of the magnifying glass, carefully observed the marked part of the painting, but he couldn't notice anything.

"Should I be seeing something?" he asked disappointedly.

"Yes," Benko nodded, "the edge of the painting should rise and reveal the base underneath. But since it didn't," he made a short pause, keeping Leon in suspense for a few moments, and then grinned, "it's clear there was no stencil used and the painting was painted directly on the canvas."

"So this means," Leon winced, "that this is an original? That this is a real Renoir?"

"Almost," Benko confirmed. "Now we need to test it with infrared and ultraviolet lights."

They carried the painting to the bathroom, which was windowless. Leon wiped down the bathtub and placed a serving table inside. They turned off the lights and turned on the ultraviolet lamp. Benko checked to see if everything on the painting was done at the same time, or if something was applied later. The shadows and the dots fluoresced in the same way; all the brushstrokes and colours were of the same age!

"We got some new information on the painting we have been studying," Benko said.

"So it's genuine?" Leon asked again.

"Everything we have done so far speaks in favour of that," Benko nodded. "But I'd also like to look at an x-ray. This will allow me to confirm its authenticity beyond any doubt. This is our first painting and it will tell us a lot about the others, too.

They went back to the lab where Benko wrote down a number of additional comments on the piece of paper. Then he turned to Leon.

"I suppose Tone will be able to organise an x-ray in one of the hospitals over here. We could buy an infra light abroad, they are freely sold there," Benko added and then checked his watch again. "No wonder I'm feeling hungry. It's over noon already. Should we go somewhere for lunch?"

This caught Leon by surprise, as well. Time flew while they were working.

They drove to a nearby restaurant Pri Koširju. Benko again ordered a vegetable plate, while Leon opted for the daily special with a roast.

When they finished, Benko almost solemnly declared:

"We're going to spend a lot of time together. I'm France, you can call me by my first name."

Leon was caught a bit off guard, a little confused.

"I'm Leon," he offered his hand.

"Yes, I know," Benko grinned.

The surprises didn't end there, as Benko started to convince Leon quite seriously that he would have to lay off the meat and become a vegetarian, if he wanted to become a good art expert.

"That will be a tough one," Leon shook his head, "I'm a diehard carnivore. Why should I stop eating meat?"

Benko grew serious.

"Consuming meat weakens your vision and reception of cosmic knowledge through spiritual perception. Meat inhibits connection with higher entities which are all around us at all times," he explained.

Leon almost choked and his eyes betrayed complete lack of understanding of the idea Benko had just expressed, which the latter was quick to notice.

"Right," he checked himself, "I'll bring over some books on esoterica for you tomorrow."

Leon had to try hard to keep to himself the juicy remarks which were begging to fly out of his mouth.

Once they returned to the lab, France rearranged the paintings on the table a bit and asked Leon to gently rub them with a mild acetone solution to remove the surface dirt and dust.

"I have a few errands to attend to in the city today," he continued. "Can you give me a ride? I need to stop at the Theosophical society. I'll take a taxi back, ok?"

They drove off and Benko got out of the car at Nebotičnik, and Leon continued to the Tabernakelj to bring Tone up to date.

They immediately went across the street to the Rotovž, as Tone was careful not to let any of his co-workers accidentally pick up snippets of their conversation. When Leon informed that the authenticity of the Renoir painting was all but confirmed, the only thing left to do was the x-ray, he smiled happily, rubbing his hands in delight.

"Well then," he said, "we can slowly move on to selling them. I've never sold French impressionists before, and the ones we have are first-class, but I'm confident that we'll be able to establish the right connections. It's easier for us, we're part of Europe, the Serbs are from the Balkans and they have poor reputation."

He slowly sipped his cognac.

"I haven't sold anything like this, either, let alone own it," Leon began to speak, but Tone stopped him instantly.

"You own nothing," he said firmly, "the stuff was bought by my investors, I chipped in as well. You will take part in the profit, when we make it. The investors and their interest always come first. We need to be clear on this. After all, Bata has already made some profit; the only reason why we have him on our team is because he can provide the paintings. You'll just have to wait a bit."

"So," Leon became agitated, "I'm nothing but thin air! I, who have found the expert, I, who have brought you to these paintings? So this is suddenly nothing? Haven't we discussed our partnership and the division of profit back in Belgrade?"

"Fine, fine," Tone tried to calm him down, "but you're just too young for my financial partners to take you seriously, you haven't got enough mileage. Don't get upset. You'll get what's yours."

He took another sip and continued in a lighter tone.

"You know," he leaned over, almost touching his ears, "I'm very happy with you. You work well, you take good care of the old man, here, take this, it's two thousand Deutschmarks for expenses, spoil him, take him to candy stores if he doesn't like meat, help him with his work. This investment will yield a lot of money."

Leon pocketed the money, still moody.

"I almost forgot," he remembered, "France would like to take x-rays of the paintings, to check that as well. Can you arrange it?"

"Of course, that won't be a problem, one of my financial backers works at the University Medical Centre," Tone nodded. "Come back again tomorrow, when you're done, to report."

Leon finished his coffee. He got up to his feet and said goodbye.

He slowly went back home.

You're on your own, boy, he told himself. There's no partnership here, that was all just fairy tales. You're Tone's little nigger, who has to do what he's told, as long as there are any chores left to do. You can make suggestions. He'll reward you with some change. Think well about what you're going to do. You thought you were on top, and it turns out you're nothing but a side show. Don't let this great chance slip out of your hands. You have to think! Nothing like this will ever cross your path again.

He smiled. He remembered one of the first lessons Bata taught him.

"You always say - work hard! This means that you need to work hard with your hands if you want to make something. In our business, it's the other way around - think hard! Ideas about what to do are born in your head. There's a difference, heh, heh, between working hands and a thinking head. So remember, think hard!"

He decided he needed to talk to Bata and discreetly inquire about his take on the way things were developing. He was sure that their relationship was firm and honest, unlike the one he had with Tone, who could be kind one moment and secretive the next, even rough, when he felt that he had to be.

At home, he pulled the telephone wire to the balcony, sat down in an armchair and poured himself a glass of whiskey. Then he called Bata.

"Where the hell have you been, why haven't you called?" words came thundering out of the receiver. "What's going on? Has the expert checked the paintings? What did he say? Speak, will you, you miserable human being! I've been sitting here, glued to the phone, and all this time there's been no word from you!"

Laughter came over Leon, prompted in part by his nervousness and in part by his friend's rowdy mock venting.

"Everything's fine, Bata, stop," he placated him. "The expert and I didn't start working until today. We checked and cleaned the first painting."

"What do you mean - the first painting? Are you working or fucking around?!" Bata almost hollered.

"Slow down, Bata, slow down. First you have to do a physical check, then comes the chemistry, and the ultraviolet rays, then the cleaning and restoration, and then you have to write everything down... Don't you think I'd rather have this over and done with quickly? But it just takes time," Leon explained.

Bata paused, then continued in a reproachful tone:

"But why didn't you call me right away? Why have you been keeping me in suspense? And what does Tone have to say about it?"

Now it was Leon's turn to pause, but then he quickly let all his doubts out in the open.

"I think Tone would like to work on his own, he's been very mysterious, he wouldn't tell me anything, I suspect he's been looking around for potential buyers. He's not at all nice to talk to. He gave me some money for the expert and that's it."

"Heh, heh, just let him play solo, my son, don't worry about it. I paid good money for the initial paintings and Good Person has already brought over some more. Since Tone now knows the paintings are originals, he'll have to either pay a lot of money for them or include us as true partners in the entire deal, just as we discussed. Of course, Tone will try to go behind our backs. But it's not like we can't easily play the game without him," Bata reacted cold-bloodedly.

"What do you mean, without him? How will you deal with Good Person?" Leon asked.

"That's very simple," Bata explained. "Good Person got a huge payment for the first package and he'll be sitting pretty for six months at least. He gave me the next batch of paintings on commission. This means we don't need Tone and his financial backers. Don't you worry. I might come over to Ljubljana to see you."

Bata hung up. He was very pleased. Everything was going according to plan. The expert would provide the proper base for the big deal, he would provide documents confirming authenticity. If he confirmed the Renoir, he was bound to confirm all the rest, as well.

No. There are too many crooks and swindlers in this business all over the world

Leon was awoken by the sound of the telephone ringing. He answered it with much annoyance. Benko and he had been working intensely for the past couple of weeks. While the work was interesting, it was also tedious, and it was luckily nearing the end. Leon had already mastered every necessary procedure and Benko sometimes let him do a bit here or there by himself.

"Since when do you Slovenians sleep in like this?" he heard Bata's voice. Leon checked the time.

"It's only nine," he mumbled. "When I call you at noon, you act like it's the middle of the night. Well, why are you calling me?"

"Don't be angry, I was just joking. Can you pick me up at the airport?" Bata asked. "I can't just sit at home, waiting for you to deign to give me a call. It's been ten days since I last heard from you. Is this the way to treat your friends?"

"Come on, stop nagging. I'm working like a dog, helping Benko from morning till night. Of course, I'll come to the airport, you bet," Leon assured him. "When do you arrive?"

"I'm here already," Bata laughed, "at Brnik. I'll be waiting for you at the bar."

"At Brnik? Good grief, Bata, why didn't you let me know sooner?"

Leon washed himself quickly, put on some clothes and raced to the airport. The two friends immediately embraced and kissed.

"What's this all about? This spur of the moment thing," Leon asked.

"I just missed you, I guess. I stopped by, to see you, and to discuss business a bit," Bata explained as they were driving toward Ljubljana. "And to meet your famous art expert."

Once again he stayed at the Ilirija Hotel.

"I have to run," Leon said as they were filling out the application forms at the reception desk, "the expert is waiting for me. We have to work, you know, unlike some of us, who just stroll around."

Bata ignored the remark and asked:

"Can I go with you, I'd like to meet him?"

"Sure, why not?" Leon agreed.

They drove to Tacen and entered the house through the garage. France was sitting in the living room, reading a newspaper and having breakfast.

"You're late today," he turned to Leon.

"I apologize. I had to go to Brnik to pick up our colleague, Mr. Živković," Leon explained and introduced Bata.

"Milorad Živković," Bata said thunderously, "pleased to meet you, professor, at your service."

"France Benko," Benko introduced himself. "Are you in the same business as well, Mr. Živković?"

"I deal with antiques, yes," Bata nodded. "I mainly work with silver and jewellery. And you're an expert in art, I was led to believe?"

"That's what I've been told," Benko shrugged. "I've been working for the government of Australia for the last twenty years or so."

"Well done, professor, well done," Bata said with some admiration, "that sure is something."

"Well, a man has to find something to do in life," Benko replied humbly, then turned to Leon, "shall we go to work?"

"Excuse me," Bata said hurriedly, "I've never had the opportunity to witness this. Would you mind if I joined you? I'll be as silent as the grave, and just observe."

"Of course," Benko agreed, "I gather Mr. Anton, the owner of the paintings, wouldn't object, would he, Leon?"

Leon confirmed.

He went on to explain that Bata was the one who established the connection with the original owner, thus allowing Tone to even get to the precious paintings.

They moved up a floor. Bata's eyes bulged, as he exclaimed in admiration:

"Alright, this is a real lab! Bravo, bravo!"

Then he took a seat in one of the corners and went silent. Benko and Leon put on the white lab coats and went on to work on the next painting. It was a Chagall, Wedding on a village street. A young couple was flying off to the sky, on the ground, next to a church, an old goat with curled horns was watching them from below; the blue of the sky flowed into black, creating an atmosphere of the first wedding night. The bouquet in the bride's hands was made up of colourful flowers.

France inspected the painting, turning it every possible way, and then, as always, put a droplet of acetone on the edge and observed the reaction through his magnifying glass. There was no reaction. He contentedly mumbled something in his chin and jotted down some notes. Then the three of them went into the bathroom where Leon first exposed the painting to ultraviolet light, followed by infrared. Bata retreated against the wall, not to be in the way. France compared his findings to the x-ray.

"Everything is fine," he said after some time," it's all genuine, there's no retouching or later layering of paint or varnish. Leon, will you freshen it up with a soft cloth and a solution of acetone and water, there's no need for detailed cleaning. Then just put some protective coating on."

Leon nodded and Bata looked at him with awe.

"My, you've become quite a master, you've been a good student," he praised Leon, "hasn't he, professor, don't you think?"

"He has the feeling," Benko agreed while Leon silently began working.

"I won't bother you anymore," Bata said then. "Could you give me a lift to Tone, in the city? I'd like to have a chat with him."

"Excellent," Benko applauded at this, "I need to run some errands, as well. When we're finished with this painting, we can all go together."

Bata was silent during the ride, immersed in his own thoughts, chuckling to himself. Oh my, oh my, the experts! You have no idea, a poor sod like Rista and a poor sod like Bata have reduced you to rubble, like you wouldn't believe! What the heck did they teach you at those famous schools of yours?

Benko got out at the central post office in the city centre, Bata and Leon drove on. Tone was very surprised when Bata appeared in front of him.

"Tone, my little Tone, how have you been?" Bata shrieked, offering his hand.

"Good, I've been good. What are you doing in Ljubljana?" Tone asked, unable to hide his surprise.

"Oh, nothing, I've just come by to have a chat, to see what's been going on over here and what's been going on over at my place," Bata replied. "Let's go across the street, I'm thirsty."

As soon as the waiter at the Rotovž brought them their drinks, Tone asked: "Did Good Person contact you?"

"He did more than just contact me," Bata nodded gleefully. "He paid me a visit and took me to his attic somewhere on the dusty plain. I can't tell you where it is. But the main thing is that I saw the entire collection. It's a miracle, I tell you, a miracle. There are still over a hundred paintings there, different sizes, canvases, cardboards, stacks of drawings, paintings on wood, a miracle, I tell you, a miracle. Impressionists, expressionists, everyone... Schiele, Klimt, Braque... oh, and an occasional Picasso, as large as this door. The Picasso alone is worth twenty million..."

He began quietly enough, but his narrative quickly escalated to a fiery speech which left him breathless. Tone caught the excitement, he could barely stay seated, fidgeting on his chair, while Leon leaned back and turned on all of his senses. That's surely impossible!

"How much," Tone twitched, "how much does he want for everything?"

Bata put his hands in the air. He rocked in his chair, as if to say, well, that's a bit of a problem.

"Well, the sly fox won't sell everything. He's figured out by now that he's got enough money lying around in his attic to last him for years. He's willing to sell some twenty, thirty paintings at this point."

"Oh, ok, I get it," Tone leaped, "and how much does he want for them?"

"Two million Deutschmarks," Bata said, calmer now.

"What?" Tone asked with his eyes bulging, almost shrinking in his chair, "where should we get such a large amount of money?"

His enthusiasm fiddled down to despair.

"I don't know," Bata shrugged. "You could maybe quickly sell the ones you already have?"

"How?!" Tone got upset again, "the expertise is not finished yet!"

It was obvious that he was beside himself.

Leon spoke for the first time:

"We have just one more painting to run some additional tests on, and France only has two more expert opinions to write. This means we need another day, two at most. Luckily. I'm getting fed up with all of it. I have to shuffle paintings all the time, smelling the acetone instead of selling them. All my other businesses have come to a halt, as well."

"Well, that's better then," Tone's face slowly regained some satisfaction, "that would do."

He flatly ignored Leon's remarks.

"You know what, Tone," Bata quickly added as he noticed that Tone was giving Leon the cold shoulder, "I believe in the future Leon will be able to take care of the checking. He's been doing brilliantly."

"He could do the checking, of course, but he won't be able to write the expert opinions," Tone again added coldly, as if trying to push Leon down, to keep him in the lower class.

Leon was again hurt by this.

"Alright, then, we'll hurry up. I'll put together two initial packages for a couple of auction houses in Munich," Tone went on, all fired up once more. "For the one you said you know and another one. I'll contact some of my old acquaintances and let them know that you're coming, Leon. I can't put the paintings down in my name, as that would be a conflict of interest because of where I work."

"Fine," Leon nodded briefly, thinking to himself, "so if anything goes wrong, my name will be there in the documents; very cunning, Tone, my friend. I really am just a messenger to him."

"What about Benko, didn't he offer to help, as well? He's got connections all over the world," Bata chimed in eagerly. "I think we should employ all the channels."

"No," Tone refused right off the bat. "I need to personally test the ground first. And I'm going to do this with the people I know. There are too many crooks and swindlers in this business all over the world. And we should do it as quickly as possible, you're to hit the road next week, Leon. And you, Bata, you keep Good Person involved, tell him we're ready to move on. I have absolutely nothing against Benko, but we'll employ him a bit later. You did say there are still big, capital works waiting, didn't you, Bata? We have to feel the market first."

He got up, leaning against the table with both of his hands.

"If you don't mind, I need to get back to the shop," he declared. "You two can have another drink, it's on me."

When he was gone, Bata smiled.

"Awesome man, our Tone. But what if we make a step or two on our own, what do you think? Benko will soon have nothing more to do, and I have some paintings, which I got on commission from Good Person, I told you as much. Benko should check them, write the expertise, and then... we'll manage somehow, don't you think so, Leon? You've been to an auction house on my behalf once before, right?"

Leon was on edge. In the beginning, during the last few weeks, he saw himself in his mind as a grand art dealer, taking the paintings Tone would entrust him with all over Europe, from one auction house to another, paintings by the biggest artists, he'd be raking in huge amounts of money... but it was becoming obvious that Tone didn't see him as his equal, that he thought of him as some kind of an obedient servant... and now here came Bata with his own ideas, essentially doing the same, only without Tone... and here I am, sitting on two chairs... That's not what we agreed.

"I'm not sure," he said hesitantly, "you want to do business and bypass Tone?"

"Well, naturally, we need to have some protection. Do you think he's worried about us? True, we're in business with him, but this here is something else. I have some paintings, they're not his, he didn't put down a deposit, he didn't buy them, these paintings are my responsibility. That's clear. And besides, didn't you say that you think Tone has been working behind our backs that he's been trying to push you out? There's no way we can let our dear colleague to have all the trump cards in his hand."

Leon wasn't sure what to do. He needed to think all the relationships over. Why did everything get so tangled up all of a sudden? Was it impossible to play fair even among the three of them, when it came to money? Bata watched him, searchingly. Whatever was going on in that boy's head?

Leon feverishly clung to a convincing excuse, which came to his mind.

"Fine, but first I have to check with France if he'd be willing to do more work for us. I'm not even sure how long he's been planning to stay," he said.

"That's smart," Bata agreed. "Would you give me a ride back to the hotel? I'll spend the afternoon resting. The guy at the reception desk promised there would be a new programme at the bar in the evening, fresh girls, and you can check tomorrow about France and his time schedule. We could use some extra work on his part."

They embraced in front of the hotel and parted ways. Bata had invited him for a drink, but Leon excused himself, explaining that he had promised to be home on time for lunch; it was Kristina's day off and she wanted to pay special attention to him.

"I hope she has the night off, too," Bata chuckled, not knowing that his remark was not entirely off the mark.

Leon came home at the right moment: beef steaks with mushroom gravy, mashed potatoes and spinach just came to the end of their hot life on the stove and were transferred to the table.

"That's some kids' menu," he grinned, taking a bottle of white wine from the fridge, "will Pinot Blanc do?"

"Only if it's cool enough," Kristina replied. "As far as the food, you should taste it first and talk later."

Leon sat down at the table and Kristina pressed herself against him, generously filling his plate. Leon put his right arm around her waist, placed his head on her breasts and rubbed against them. She was unable to wriggle free.

"Alright, alright," she laughed, "but let's eat first. You can tell me how's business. Is there any money finally on the horizon?"

Leon uncorked the bottle of wine and poured them each a glass. They clinked. Then he began to tell her about everything. He made sure to focus on the part where he was to take some of the paintings to auction houses in Germany the next week. That meant real money was coming. Kristina asked him some questions about this and that, and Leon answered as if he were already priming the European market for the French impressionists and the rest of the famous bunch. He spoke confidently and enthusiastically, making himself believe right there, at his home table, that the moment he had been waiting for his entire life finally arrived.

Kristina was thrilled. She put away the dishes and proposed they should take Šeri out for a walk together.

"Even the Ancient Romans said that one needs to walk a thousand steps after a meal," she laughed.

"We can make it two thousand, as long as they take us to the most wonderful place of all," Leon laughed in turn, first looking at Kristina and pointing with his gaze to the bedroom door.

The old man is interested in business. He saw there was a ton of money involved

The next morning, when he arrived to Tacen, he was in a great mood, and Benko was not done shaving yet. His mother and father had already left. He arranged everything himself, so they could start checking the last painting, a small work by Mondrian, as soon as possible. He also brought a kettle of freshly made tea to the lab from the kitchen. He then put on his lab coat and sat down at the table.

"Well, hello," Benko greeted him, "that's some speed. Not that I don't understand, since we're going to finish today."

He started putting on his coat, as well.

"My colleague, Mr. Živković, that is, Bata, asked if you would maybe be willing to check a few more paintings, owned by him. He'd pay you himself but wouldn't like Tone to get word of this. Bata feels a bit embarrassed because he thinks you've only come over for Tone, and he doesn't want to cause any problems; he's been doing business with Tone for a number of years, you see. So, what do you say?"

"I've come here to work," Benko replied frankly. "If I see something nice, I'll be glad to check it."

"Excellent," Leon rejoiced. "Bata said he'd call me sometime this morning to see what you think."

They went on to work. Benko first carefully examined the painting, Leon performed the acetone and ammonia test, then he cleaned the painting... Mondrian's colourful square planes simply radiated on the desk. The phone rang just as they were checking the painting in the bathroom.

"That's some timing," Leon ranted. "Yes, of course, France will take a look at your paintings. I can't drive you around right now. Take a taxi and come over."

Leon started to clean the painting with a soft cloth, while France copied his notes on it onto the professional art expert's paper. At the end, he put down his signature and seal. The moment he finished, there was a bell at the door downstairs.

"I hope I'm not too late," Bata spoke loudly, "the taxi driver got lost and I had to guide him..."

"... and you got even more lost," Leon roared with laughter. "Well, come on, France is waiting for you."

They went upstairs to the lab, where they found Benko putting his notes in his black briefcase. He turned to Bata and offered him his hand.

"Have you brought anything beautiful, Mr. Živković?"

"I think so," Bata smiled, adding somewhat humbly, "but you'll be the judge of that, professor. That's why we need you, isn't that right?"

He put a portfolio on the desk and untied the straps. On top, there was a plastic bag containing a sketchbook with slightly curled edges. Leon opened it. An ink drawing of a large sailboat docked in a port was on the first page.

"Oh my!" Benko exclaimed. "Don't tell me you have a sketchbook of drawings by the famous Lyonel Pheininger?"

He started leafing through the book himself; all the black and white ink drawings featured maritime themes, mostly ships, sailboats, port infrastructure, bustle on the docks, various images of the sky and the ocean, the somewhat architectural quality of drawing endowed the images with volume, there was an occasional drawing with interventions in red or green ink. The date was meticulously recorded in the bottom corner of each drawing. Leon could practically smell the sea and hear the cries of sea gulls above it...

"This is fantastic," Leon murmured. "I've never heard of this artist before."

Benko carefully examined the entire sketchbook, felt the paper, sniffed it, again mumbling to himself in English, and finally nodded. Bata got ahead of himself:

"How much would you say this is worth, professor?"

Benko smiled.

"I can't tell you this at the moment," he said, "I'd have to ask around. Pfeininger reaches the highest prices in New York, because he spent most of his life living there, despite him being German. But I can also ask in London, where I know a lot of the gallery owners."

Leon then tackled the portfolio.

"What else have you brought?"

He took the first painting out of its paper wrapping. The red, black and yellow colours on canvas depicted some sort of Marsian. The colours alone left no doubt as to who was the author: the signature in the upper left corner read Miro.

"What do you think," Bata again asked, a bit impatient, "is this worth three hundred thousand?"

Benko frowned.

"I'm an expert for authenticity of art works, you know, evaluations are done by my colleagues."

"As far as I'm familiar with the conditions on the market, this could hardly go for more than one hundred and fifty thousand," Leon spoke.

Bata was unable to hide his disappointment.

"I thought it would be half a million at least," he said.

"Oh, dear," Benko almost took fright, "I hope you didn't pay as much. That would be really bad."

"Luckily, I didn't," Bata shook his head, "I have the option to give it back to the owner."

Leon unwrapped the second painting. A Picasso. A bathing suit on a rocky beach, oil on cardboard, of a size 40 by 60. The layered colours were quite glazy, indicating that this was one of the earlier works. Benko checked it and whistled to himself as enthusiasm rushed over him.

"Oh," he sighed, "this is something. This could reach two million; I just recently saw something similar, the owner whom I did the paperwork for, wanted a million and a half. What do you intend to do with this painting, Mr. Živković?"

"I was planning to sell it for as much as I can get," Bata confessed honestly. "Why do you ask?"

"Well, I know someone who would probably buy it," Benko replied and kept looking at the painting.

"So sell it, professor! I'm just a no-name guy from the Balkans, I can't sell it, but if we could get to someone with a good reputation in England, we could probably take care of it," Bata immediately came to life.

"Well, if you could deliver the painting to London for me, I could give it a try. It would be too much of a responsibility for me to take it over there myself," Benko explained and tiny unusual flames fired up in his eyes, as well. "But I can sell it."

"Wonderful," Bata nodded, "we'll take care of the transport, won't we, Leon? I guess we could take care of it."

Leon nodded, uncertain. He had never transported any paintings to London and he couldn't even imagine how they could do something like this now. But... two million? It was sure worth a try.

"If we come to an agreement on the sales and my part of the profit, I'll perform the expert analysis for free," Benko said, then checked his watch and said, surprised:

"Beautiful things always make me lose track of time. Can we go out for lunch? If I remember correctly, the local restaurants also offer some vegetable dishes?"

"Out of all the vegetables I like pork roast the best," Bata grinned. "There's a restaurant around here somewhere, I think, where I had superb cutlets."

"Right," Leon nodded, "sure, the Grad restaurant is only a short walk away."

During lunch they discussed Tone's paintings, which Benko had written expert opinions on; Bata tried to get as much information about them as possible: what were the expert's thoughts on the damage they sustained, whether the unprofessional storage conditions in the dusty attic had eaten away at them, how many similar works he had seen before... he of course finished with a proposal that Benko should inquire about the realistic price for the Pfeininger's book of drawings, as well as for the painting by Picasso. He didn't feel like wasting his energy on the Miro.

After the dessert they went their separate ways, but not before they agreed to meet again the next day after lunch, that time with Tone whom Benko would turn over all the documents on the checked paintings to. Bata again asked Benko not to mention any of the paintings he had seen that day. Benko decided to go for a short walk and Leon drove Bata back to his hotel.

"Are you at peace now?" Bata asked him while they were driving.

"What do you mean at peace, why would you ask me if I was at peace?" Leon wondered.

"You see, the old man is interested in business. His eyes beamed when he saw the Pfeininger and the Picasso. He saw there was a ton of money involved, and he'll gladly help us out. He also understood that we should leave Tone out of this."

I was sure they would find my stash and then half a million would go to hell

The following day Benko and Leon finished their work. Leon carefully wrapped up all the paintings, individually, and put them away. Before doing this, France went over his documentation once more, making an occasional check on the painting in question, made sure that the seals on the documents were clearly legible, that every evaluation was neatly concluded with his signature, he placed each expertise in its own separate folder, and then said, inhaling and exhaling loudly: "Well then. We're done here."

They drove over to the Rotovž where Bata was already reading the newspapers. He had Delo, Dnevnik and Večer lying on the table in front of him, while he was leafing through Mladina magazine. Immediately after they greeted each other, Bata smacked his lips loudly and shook his head:

"Horrible, the kids over here. The stuff they write?! This could never happen in Belgrade."

"Well, it's just who we are," Leon grinned proudly. "The children are our future."

Benko looked curiously from one, to the other, to Mladina magazine, and then simply said:

"I guess everything's different now. Democracy is taking hold around here. I had to run away because of things like these, many years ago. Now I'm here, in my home country, and I'm happy about the way things are going."

"Let's not talk politics now, right, professor, we're here for business," Bata said, folded the newspapers and pushed them to the edge of the table. "For business."

"Right!" Tone exclaimed when he crossed the street and overheard only the last couple of words. "For business!"

He sat down and joined them, ordered the waiter to bring over coffee for everyone, then stared at Benko: "So?"

Benko laid his black briefcase on the table and proudly slapped it.

"Everything is here," he said, "three weeks of hard work. But it was worth it!"

Tone reached for the briefcase, opened it and took out the first folder. He started to read, but then changed his mind.

"Brilliant. I'm going to read this later. All we have to do now is sell this," he exclaimed in extremely high spirits and looked at Leon. "I've already spoken to my people in Munich; there are two places who would immediately be willing to take a few paintings for an auction which is set to go on in ten days."

"My old connections are waiting, too," Leon said.

"Pardon me," Benko chimed in, "I happen to have access to some important galleries in London and I also know a few end buyers who might be interested. Maybe it would be better if I first offered the paintings to galleries specializing in certain artists. For instance, I have a friend who is an expert in Monet; I'm close with the Picasso specialist who sells mostly to the Japanese..."

The usually restrained man now came to life.

Tone took a sip of the cognac the waiter had brought him and shook his head.

"First we need to test the waters by selling them at auctions in Germany. No offence, France, but what we need now is to get to the money as quickly as possible, we need to pay back the investors, and we can't do business abroad with people we don't know."

"Fine, fine," Benko immediately pulled back. "Just so you know: I'm a citizen of the Commonwealth which gives me a more open access in many places, from Switzerland to England."

"Bata will soon deliver some more paintings, so we'll need the money for them quickly, and we'll also need more expert opinions. That's when we need you very much, France. Isn't that right, Bata? When can you bring them over?"

Bata listened to the conversation absent-mindedly, as he didn't understand everything, but he did understand this last bit, so he replied:

"In about a week, no problem. That is, if we have the money, of course."

He then checked the time and got up.

"I'm glad we're doing business together. We're doing great and I really think we'll all be happy in the end. It was nice meeting you, professor."

He shook Benko's hand and took a slight bow, gave Tone a nod and turned to Leon.

"I should get going, I have to get to Brnik. Will you give me a lift?"

"Of course," Leon nodded.

The rest of them got up, as well. Benko informed them that he would take a week to visit his wife's homestead in Primorska, but then he'd be happy to take on something new, whatever that was. Bata kept nodding, and Tone incidentally asked Leon to stop over at his place on his way back from the airport, to discuss his journey to Munich.

The plane for Belgrade wasn't delayed, so Bata and Leon had to say goodbye in a rush.

"We're going to win this thing, my son, don't worry!" Bata cried as he passed the police check and gave Leon a short wave.

"From your lips to a full cash-register," Leon sighed and drove back.

In the meantime, Tone arranged on his desk every expertise Benko had written and put together two packages based on his analyses: one for the Faber auction house, and another for the Grabner auction house, just as Leon had suggested.

"This is it!" he said seriously. "I wish you good luck when crossing the border and make a good deal with the merchants."

Leon sensed that things were starting to get real. It was minutes to midnight, just a little while longer and the money will come.

He knew he could not afford to make any mistakes during the transport of the paintings. So he drove over to the Španec, a bar on the other side of the city, where his good acquaintance Ljuba kept an office, or to be more exact, a table with a regular set of friends. Everyone in his close circle knew that he was smuggling cigarettes high up north, where they were subject to heavy taxation, and his truck with a double bottom could easily bring him up to a hundred thousand Deutschmarks per trip. This money, when shared properly, always ensured him a safe passage through the customs.

It was late afternoon when they sat down at a table in the corner of a bar.

"It's been ages since I last saw you," Ljuba slapped Leon's shoulder.

"I know, I've been busy with something, and now I need your help," Leon explained.

"Well, I'm all ears," Ljuba cheered up.

They slowly sipped their drinks and Leon explained that he'd like to get some paintings over the border, for a friend, they were worth around fifty thousand Deutschmarks, they'd probably reach a bit over that at auction, and he wouldn't like some overly enthusiastic customs officer to mess with his plans.

"When does your shift start?" he asked.

Ljuba smiled confidently, walked to the phone, talked for a long time and then returned smugly to the table.

"It's all taken care of," he informed Leon.

Then he went on to explain that he would need to accompany him over there in his own car, instructing Leon to follow him to the customs, driving right behind him and everything would be fine. They arranged when they should meet next to the restaurant before the border.

Leon carefully wrapped up each painting as usual, just in case, and put them into a hiding place he had prepared in the back seat. Even if the customs officers tried to feel under it, they couldn't feel anything.

He placed the documents pertaining to them in a briefcase which he negligently tossed on the passenger's seat, together with some newspapers.

He came to the border fifteen minutes before the customs officers changed shifts and he spotted the dark blue Golf with Sarajevo licence plates from afar. Ljuba observed a very safe protocol. He always crossed the border with a rented car; if anything went south and he got caught, they couldn't confiscate his vehicle. Leon drove up to him, honked the horn and they headed to the border together. When Ljuba reached the customs, the younger of the two officers took him over. After checking his papers he asked him to get out of the car, open the boot and also the hood. The officer rummaged through the booth a little while Ljuba stood at his side. Leon started to sweat and he tried to catch Ljuba's eye in order to get some sort of a signal to retreat. But there was none. Ljuba obediently stood at the side of the car, answered questions, nodded and shook his head. In the meantime, a queue of cars formed behind Leon's quatrelle, as well, and it became impossible for him to turn back, even if he wanted to. The customs officer waved his hand and Ljuba drove on. By the time Leon reached the policeman, he was quite pale and scared. He handed over his passport and was then approached by a customs officer, asking the usual questions - Where are you going? How much money do you have with you? Do you have anything to declare? - followed by the demands - Open your boot, open the hood, as well... In the meantime the policeman returned, asking for his driver's licence and registration. He checked chassis number against the registration he held in his hand, took a look at the licence plates...

"What's this, what are you doing?" Leon burst out in anger.

He has never before experienced such complications at the border, and now, when Ljuba was supposed to have arranged everything, he was subjected to a detailed inspection. He couldn't get his mind around what was happening. He was so nervous and scared and angry that he wanted to break the psychotic state he was in, even if that meant they'd take everything, lock him up...

"Drive to the side," the customs officer ordered, "and get out of the car!"

Leon did as he was told, almost tripping over while climbing from behind the steering wheel. The customs officer opened every door, searched around the booth, opened the glove compartment searching for documents, reached under both front seats, looked inside the briefcase laying in the passenger seat. He then straightened up and said coldly:

"Alright."

He moved on to the next car waiting in line.

"What about my passport and documents?" Leon asked quite crankily.

"That's for my colleague to decide," the customs officer retorted.

Leon began slamming the doors and the boot shut. Just as he tried do get back to the car, the policeman returned and handed over his passport.

"Everything's fine," he said and left.

Drenched in sweat and on the end of his rope, Leon drove off. Nobody even bothered to check him on the Austrian side of the border. He descended along the hairpin bends and stopped at a nearby inn, where he was supposed to meet Ljuba. He parked his car next to his in the parking lot.

Ljuba was sitting at a table, drinking beer and grinning from ear to ear.

"So, how did it go?"

Leon almost collapsed in a chair.

"Thank you, I guess. You really are a true friend. I thought I'd die there!"

Ljuba laughed even harder, struggling to get his words out:

"Did you get across safely or not?"

"Yes, I did, but..."

"There's no but about it, my men simply made some fuss, so the other customs and police officers noticed their meticulous approach. If the Austrians caught you, none of them could be held accountable for not checking you thoroughly," he explained through his laughter.

Leon looked at him with crossed eyes and wiped his forehead.

"I almost shit my pants, I was sure they would find my stash and then half a million would go to hell," he said.

"Oh my," Ljuba jumped, "it was fifty thousand when we last spoke."

"True, true," Leon nodded. "I'm counting on them making a bit more at the auction."

A waitress approached them and Ljuba ordered two more beers and three Carniola spiced pork sausages.

"Three sausages? Why?" Leon asked.

"The question is not why, but for whom. For this guy, for him..."

A young man joined them at the table, this time in plain clothes. Leon recognised the customs officer who had given him a hard time.

"Hello," he said, "I'm Martin. Ljuba asked us to give you a little scare. I can see that we did alright, didn't we?"

"Is this another one of your games?" the waitress laughed, still standing next to the table.

"That's just life," Ljuba laughed and slapped her behind.

What price would you set at the beginning, according to your own judgement

When Leon arrived to Munich, he first visited the Grabner auction house. Again, he was met by the director, Agnesa Billinger. He decided to begin his current mission with her, as he had met her before and was sure that he would do well. This would give him the confidence necessary to go to the Faber, where Tone had arranged a meeting for him.

Billinger shook his hand warmly and invited him to her office. It was no longer appropriate for her to dismiss him at the desk reserved for ordinary customers. Today she wore a blue suit by Escada fashion house, which matched her blue eyes perfectly. She had her hair pulled up, the same as the last time they met, and a necklace made of blue turquoise stones hung from her well-groomed neck. Her office was very modern, almost sterile in stark contrast to the ancient building. Thick binders were stacked high on both ends of the glass desk, and a leather folder was laid out on white fabric on the part of the desk in front of her chair.

Three large graphic works in silver frames were mounted on the central wall opposite the window. Leon was immediately drawn to them, as he had felt attracted to masterful drawings for as long as he could remember. Caravaggio's face of Bacchus and fruit was at one side, a series of portraits of a woman's face from girlish youth to old age on the other, an old man smelled a rose in a young woman's hands on the third; they were all exquisite etchings.

Leon stared at Mrs. Billinger in surprise.

"Masterpieces, aren't they?" she laughed. "They are by a Czech graphic artist Jiři Anderle. I can't hide my love for the Slavic. My colleague Gerd Köhrman from the Baukunst Gallery in Köln and I have decided to make a name for him in the West. We're doing well, I think. Ann Brauch from Chicago is selling his works brilliantly in the USA. Oh, of course, and a monograph of his works is about to come out in Ljubljana!"

"It's pure Dürer!" Leon exclaimed and sat at the desk.

"It is," Billinger confirmed, "but with a Slavic soul. I don't want to waste your time, what have you brought to me this time? I gather you have decided to put the works up for auction this time and not sell them immediately?"

Leon smiled, trying to infuse his gaze with a touch of overt flirtation.

"You couldn't waste my time if you wanted to, I consider it a gift," he said and opened the portfolio he had brought with him.

"Here you go."

He unfolded the wrapping paper and revealed luminous reds, blacks and yellows in a simple, almost childlike drawing.

"Oooh," Billinger purred in fascination, her eyes sparkling, "what a wonderful Miro. And on canvas, too. Where did you get this?"

"From a collection in Ljubljana," Leon responded swiftly. "The owners claim that it came from Paris. Here's the documentation prepared by an international art expert from Canberra, attesting its authenticity."

She turned the painting over and checked the seals on the edge. She inadvertently ran her finger over the AV and skilfully avoided the Star of David right next to it. Then she took a small magnifying glass attached to a gold chain from her desk drawer, checked the Miro signature and then the seals on the back.

She reached into the next wrapper without saying anything; Rodin, female nude, watercolours on paper. She checked this one carefully, as well, including the back side. She unwrapped the last piece in silence: Renoir, a girl with a toy, oil on cardboard. She gasped in awe and then carefully inspected the signs on the back sides with her magnifying glass: AV, ES, and stars of David.

"I have to ask you, because of these seals," she slowly went on, "where did you get this work?"

"The collector from Ljubljana said he got it from Serbia; several paintings were located there in the attic of an abandoned house."

Of course, Leon found it most inappropriate to discuss the remote village, the dusty attic of an old house, the unusual inheritance...

"According to the signs, they used to belong to a Jewish person; supposedly they are from a well-known collection owned by Ambrois Vallard and his secretary, Erich Šlomovič. The latter was a Jew from Belgrade. It would make sense," Leon explained.

The woman listened attentively.

"I looked into it a little bit; there are supposed to be several dozen of paintings, some of them were supposedly sold around the world on President Tito's behalf by a Croatian fellow, now naturalized German Mimara. He lives in a mansion by Wörthersee. He still speaks about it now and then. But my stuff comes from a different source."

"And," Mrs. Billinger asked, "Why have you decided to bring it to us?"

"That's no secret," Leon laughed. "For artists from our parts, Munich or Monakovo, as we used to call it, was the first artistic post in history. You must be aware that Anton Ažbe taught here, Kandinsky was his student, among others... and besides," he added in a sleek tone, "I just met you the other time and it seemed to me I'd be missing out if I didn't come to you."

"Alright, alright," she also laughed. "I can see that you're not only after money, you're fond of the art, as well?"

"I am," Leon confirmed, "I'm an art history student. But while we're on the subject of money, what price would you set for my things, and what kind of commission would you ask?"

"Do you have anything in mind?" she asked.

"I'd start with a hundred and fifty thousand for the Miro, eighty for the Renoir, and fifty thousand for the Rodin."

"No, no, Rodin is a great name, but this is just a watercolour, quite watered down; let's say twelve thousand, and we'll see where we go from there," she objected. "As far as the commission..." She picked up a small calculator, then a phone and spoke to someone in French, "since this is our first collaboration, we'll charge a twenty-eight percent brokerage auction commission."

She raised her eyes.

"I find that quite a lot," Leon objected. "I heard that the Faber auction house only takes seventeen percent."

"Why didn't you take your business there then?" Billinger swiftly retorted with both anger and politeness.

"It was the owner's decision," Leon quickly found an excuse. "Would you mind if I called him and let him know what we discussed?"

"Not at all," Billinger replied and pushed the telephone over to his side.

Tone picked right up and confirmed the deal. He sounded pleased with the set prices.

"Alright," Leon said, "you can go ahead and prepare the paperwork, dear madam."

In the meantime, Billinger went over the expert opinions.

"One more thing," she asked in astonishment, "where did you get the documentation written by an Australian expert? How did he find you?"

"Well, that's very simple," Leon smiled, "he belongs to our post-war diaspora; the Slovene diaspora in Australia is always ready to give a hand when it comes to culture."

"Is that so," she murmured.

She took some forms from her desk drawer and started filling them out. She crossed her flawless legs in comfortable blue shoes with a medium heel under the glass desk top and leaned forward. She reminded Leon of Kristina a lot; except that her face was a little bit sharper, more German-like. She was writing with a gold ballpoint pen. She raised her head unexpectedly and caught Leon looking at her appraisingly.

"Just give me another minute," she smiled, "I'm being as fast as I can."

Leon fidgeted in his chair uneasily. He felt like a kid who got caught peeking through a bathroom keyhole to catch a glimpse of his aunt.

When she finished, she shoved the paperwork over to Leon, pointing to where he was supposed to sign. Leon skimmed over the text of the document and quickly drew in a careless Sattler.

"And we're done," she said, got up and offered her hand, "I hope everything goes well at the auction. Maybe we could take off some more time at that point and go for a drink somewhere?"

"Of course, of course, I'd be glad to," Leon nodded, still somewhat excited, went to the door and when he reached it sent back a "goodbye."

He went to the parking lot where he had left his quatrelle, took the second package from its hiding place and headed for the Faber auction house. He was thinking about Mrs. Billinger and remembered the words Bata once said during one of their drinking bouts.

"Our business," he said, "is rife with beautiful women and great fraudsters. You need to be careful to always take the best from them."

"I have an idea when it comes to women, but I'm not sure what is the best I could get from a crook," Leon smiled to himself.

It started to drizzle. He walked on, sticking to the walls of the houses. He had plenty of time left before his next meeting, so he went to the first bar he came across and ordered some coffee. It was disgusting, of course, but it helped him kill the time and keep him out of the rain.

When he reached the Faber auction house after a while, he pressed the large brass door handle and pushed open the heavy wooden door. He entered a wide courtyard and saw a building overgrown with ivy at the far end, only windows peered brightly through it. The slanted red roof gleamed damply in the rain. Once he got there, an automated glass door opened in front of him. The hallway was fitted with gallery lighting and the walls were crammed with paintings: German, Italian and American modernists, abstract artists. There was a row of paintings by Lucio Fontana, his canvases with open cuts, followed by the graphic elegance of Hans Hartung's brushstrokes, and the colourful abstractions by Sam Francis.

"I hope Tone picked something appropriate for this place," he thought to himself, just then realising that he didn't even know what he was carrying.

He didn't have much time to dwell on this, as he was quickly approached by a tall man, he was probably already over seventy, wearing an army-style short haircut and a navy-blue suit. Leon was immediately inundated with memories of films featuring World War Two, namely the haughty Hitler's officers.

"Mr. Sattler?" he asked from afar. "My name is Albert Bauer. We were expecting you. Please, follow me."

Leon, who was wearing a leather jacket, unbuttoned blue shirt, corduroys and loafers, was struck with the same notion that overcame him while visiting Mrs. Billinger; he'd have to pay a lot more attention to his clothes the next time around. He suddenly realised the reason why Bata was always running around in elegant jackets and bow ties, and when he chose to wear a necktie, he pierced it with his famous tiepin. But one can't drive hundreds of kilometres in a tailcoat, he tried to console himself.

One look at Bauer's office almost floored him. The walls were covered in paintings, and several more were set on easels in front of them. They formed a fantastic whole: Kokoschka, Lempicka, Kandinsky, Javlinski, Klimt, Schiele, Mondrian, expressionists, cubists... There was a whole row of Kandinsky alone. Leon walked from painting to painting, forgetting what he was there for. So many treasures in a single room!

"Nice, isn't it?" Bauer brought him back to reality.

"Incredible," Leon almost moaned, "and the way everything is placed together, in fantastic balance, according to colours, styles... it's like you were selling a collage, a wonderful collage."

"I'm glad you like it," Bauer sounded pleased. "Mr. Tone informed us that you were going to bring over something exceptional. Can I take a look?"

Leon put the package down on a large Baroque table; the mahogany was polished to a shine, the tree rings almost disappeared in the light coming from the chandeliers, and naturally, beautiful golden patterns passed among them.

At the top of the package there was another watercolour by Rodin. Bauer picked it up in his hands and carefully examined it. After placing it back on the table, he asked:

"What else do we have?"

Leon removed the wrapping paper and handed him a Kandinsky; the painting was exceptional, colourful groups of lines on black background joined in sharp and elegant shapes.

"Higher school of geometrism," Bauer let out a sigh. "Marvellous. Kandinsky is my favourite painter."

"He studied here, in your city, with our Ažbe," Leon quickly added.

"Indeed, indeed," Bauer nodded, "professor Ažbe ran the Munich Academy, I remember stories about him. He supposedly spoke genuine Bavarian, without a hint of an accent. He provided shelter for many Slavic students. Slavic was modern at the time."

Leon unwrapped the final painting.

"Mondrian!" Bauer exclaimed. "Fantastic! Just look at the order beaming from this painting, the intensity of colours builds a balance of light and shadows. Unbelievable! My colleague from Ljubljana sure picked the right paintings for my soul. Bravo, bravo!"

He laid the painting on the table and invited Leon to sit down in an armchair next to his.

"These paintings are marvellous," he said. "I'd like to buy them myself, to be honest, before they go to auction. What's the price?"

"Didn't Tone tell you?" Leon asked.

"No, no, we agreed that I should take a look at them first and we would discuss the price later. But please, tell me where did these wonderful things come from? What are these markings on the backs?"

"They are the initials of the original owners," Leon responded.

"And they are?"

"The AV is a monogram of a renowned collector and patron Ambrois Vollard from Paris, and the ES stands for Erich Šlomovič, a Jew from Belgrade and the great collector's lover," Leon repeated the well-known story.

Bauer winced.

"How many more of these paintings are there available?" he continued with his questions.

"There is this man who had the incredible luck of inheriting an old bakery in some village in Vojvodina, and he found a bunch of paintings in the attic. These works here are part of that collection," Leon once again repeated a story he had told several times before.

The German's hands started trembling with excitement, but when he realised Leon had noticed this, he took them off the table and put them in his lap.

"And where did the owner sell them to?"

"He hasn't sold all of them yet. We bought twenty of them," Leon explained.

"What do you mean - bought?"

"I was the first person he had offered them to, by some strange coincidence, Mr. Bauer."

"And you offered them to Mr. Tone?"

"I did," Leon confirmed, "I didn't know anyone else."

Bauer leaned back in his armchair, brought his hands together as if in a prayer, brushing both index fingers over his lips. He was immersed in thought. Then he suddenly jumped up from the armchair, walked to the Biedermeier cabinet in one of the corners and took out a bottle of cognac and two crystal glasses.

"A good story," he said, "deserves a glass of good drink."

He poured them each a glass, they toasted, and drank slowly without saying a word. Leon was the one to break the hallowed silence.

"What price would you set at the beginning, according to your own judgement?"

The German thought about it some more and then said:

"We'd start at one hundred and eighty thousand for the Mondrian, Rodin could be thirty thousand, and Kandinsky three hundred thousand."

"Right," Leon nodded, "I think this should do, but you should still confirm this with Mr. Tone. What about the commission? I would think seventeen percent should be enough, after all, Mr. Tone is your regular customer."

"That's right, it's good that you have brought this up. Seventeen will be enough," Bauer nodded. "The auction will take place in ten days, let's hope it goes well. I'll immediately let you know the results, Mr. Sattler. Good luck to you."

He filled out a form confirming he received the paintings while saying this and handed it over to Leon. Leon folded it over and put it in his pocket.

"Good luck to you, too," he said and bid farewell.

It was getting dark outside. The city lights came on. He walked to his car. He didn't feel tired at all. I'll just go home. If I start to get sleepy, I'll stop at a parking lot by the road and take a little nap.

Is there something in the air here? Are they leaving me high and dry?

He came home just after midnight. Kristina's car wasn't in front of the building. She's probably at a recording session, he thought. He was too tired for jealousy at the moment. He collapsed onto the bed. When he woke up, it was almost morning. He felt a live act going on under his belly. At first he thought that his member stood to attention all on its own, which was not an uncommon occurrence in the morning, but he was wrong, it was passionate, hot, the blanket flew off him and he saw Kristina in the dusk, riding him wildly, grabbing his hips and erratically swaying her loose hair... he almost exploded and Kristina gradually slid onto his chest. He immediately fell sound asleep. When he awoke again late in the morning, he wasn't sure if he was dreaming or did it really happen, but the messy bed spoke for itself. Kristina was gone.

He cleaned himself up and went over to Tone to report on what went on at the auction houses. He walked slowly toward the Tabernakelj, but as he smelled the scent of freshly baked croissants coming from the diner in Vodnik Square he felt overwhelming hunger. He took a seat at the diner and immediately gobbled three of them, washing them down with two cappuccinos. It was grey outside: it wasn't clear if the weather was about to clear up or it would start to rain.

Tone took him across the street to the Rotovž without any delay.

"We have some inspections going on and I don't want anyone to see you," he began.

Leon flinched.

"What? Did someone get word of something?"

"No, no," Tone shook his head, "it's just routine checks, but it never hurts to be cautious. So, how did it go?"

"Everything went swell, first at the border and then at Grabner and Faber. The auctions will take place in ten days tops and we'll be notified of the results. I think you'll be pleased."

"Fine, fine," Tone commented almost by the way. "There's nothing for us to do now but wait. Listen, is France still staying at your house? I haven't heard from him, and I don't know what's up with that. Once Bata brings over new paintings, he'll have to start working on them right away."

"I don't know," Leon shook his head, "I came home this night and I haven't been to Tacen yet. Didn't he say he was going to Primorska?"

"Well, find out where he's at and let me know," Tone added quickly. "Excuse me, I need to go back, I need to see that nothing goes wrong."

He got up and left Leon to enjoy his coffee by himself.

"Hm," Leon thought, "he's in such a hurry, he doesn't feel the need to talk about the auction houses, although he certainly should, as they will surely be selling things through them in the future... and he doesn't know about France... Is there something in the air here? Are they onto something with Bata and leaving me high and dry?"

He was suddenly overcome with a strange sense of gloom. He had spent the last few months at the centre of a business which was supposed to be the biggest thing anyone could ever experience, and yet he was broke, he depleted whatever he had saved from his other deals, and Tone simply sped off, without even a serious conversation... Who could he count on, really? Alright, alright, just a little bit longer, something big was sure to happen at the auctions, the big money would start rolling in now... then again, Tone kept saying that the money would go to investors, first, then their interests... and my work means nothing, or what... perhaps I could get a hint or two from Bata...

He winced. Oh, come on. I'm probably just panicking for no reason. Bata always says you need to learn how to wait... Well, that's easier said than done!

But when he called his mother on the phone, she informed him that France had packed up his personal belongings and left. She didn't know where to, as he left when nobody was home. He left the key in the mailbox at the door.

Leon got in his car feverishly and drove to Primorska, to Dane, where his wife owned a house. He rang the doorbell, but nobody answered. When he walked around to the back of the house, he found France's wife sitting in a deckchair, knitting.

"Oh, no," she vivaciously shook her head and peered at him over her spectacles, "France's not here, he went to Vienna, and from there on to London. That's the deal you made, right? I don't know when to expect him back. He just goes off on his business and I wait. He comes when he comes. Would you like to have some coffee, Mr. Leon?"

Leon excused himself, saying that he had a lot more errands to run, and sped back to Ljubljana with a bad taste in his mouth.

"Ok, Tone must have sent him over to London to sell the Picasso, and now he's pretending not to know anything about it. He wants to push me out of the main business," Leon gritted his teeth.

Once home, he jumped over to the phone and called Bata. It was his daughter Tamara who picked up, but once Bata heard that it was Leon, he grabbed the receiver straight out of her hand.

"What's up?" he almost yelled impatiently.

"Everything's fine, I went to both auction houses," Leon started off.

"What are the starting prices?" Bata didn't wait for him to finish.

"I think they're alright," Leon said, "from seventy to a hundred and seventy thousand. I believe they will go up quite a bit."

"There you go, that's what I love about you," Bata calmed down delightedly.

"Did you happen to speak to Tone lately?" Leon inquired.

"No, not since the last time we saw each other," Bata answered, paused a bit and then asked, "why, is there a problem?"

"No problem, just asking," Leon mumbled. "What about France?"

"How the hell am I supposed to talk to him, I don't have his phone number," Bata was starting to fume, then asked sharply, "why are you asking me these weird questions, tell me the truth: is there a problem?"

Nervous silence filled the receiver.

"What did you say?" Bata insisted.

"Nothing, it's nothing," Leon mumbled again, "I might come over to Belgrade for a bit. I have to check if Pera the Horse and Fane the Captain have any new stuff, I ran out of everything, including money."

"Don't come," Bata stopped him. "I have to come to Ljubljana again. I have some business to attend to. I'll be in touch."

"So!" Leon shuddered as he put down the phone. He had some business to attend to. Could he and Tone really be doing something behind his back? Again, he felt that the two sly foxes wanted to pull a number on him.

He slowly started to put together the events of the past few months. He had been living a completely abnormal life. He moved in with a woman, without any regular income or any money set aside. He was going after big business, but he had nothing in his pocket. He had kept up a very sporadic contact with his parents, despite the fact that they were ready to help him at all times and backed this up with actions. He had been neglecting his previous partners from the flea market. He hadn't been showing up at the university. He was running around like crazy, first to Belgrade, then to Germany. And what did he have to show for it? He expected that the wide world would open up to him, that he would enter the highest level of selling art, start making big money, enter the big league... And where was he now? Still on the side lines, observing.

He could invest his time in daily tasks instead of just waiting around nervously...

He plucked up his courage and went to show his face at the university. His fellow students received him with astonishment, as he had been living his life detached from them, but they nevertheless provided notes from the lectures for him. He could at least pass an exam or two. He invested his time in his studies again, he spent a lot of time at home, cooking, Kristina and he were on good terms. She kept reminding him of her costs, dropping subtle hints, but she, too, gave the impression that she was comforted by the prospect of successful auctions. She was nervous because of the money up in the air and none on the table, but she kept herself in check. They tolerated the waiting during the day in some sort of excepting and superficial truce, and passionately embellished it during the nights.

Somewhere along those empty days he was again awakened by an early morning phone call from Bata. This time he wasn't calling from the airport but from the train station instead. He took a sleeper train so he could get a decent night's sleep for once, he explained. Leon went to pick him up.

"Let's go somewhere, we need to have a serious talk," Bata said after the initial embrace and kiss. "Let's find somewhere we can have some peace and quiet."

Leon pricked up his ears. Bata wanted to talk?

Once again, he thought about the Španec, a bar on the other side of the city, where it was impossible for Tone to run into them, even by accident. They sat at a table in the corner and ordered their coffees.

"So, what's going on?" Bata asked. "You're right here, with

everything under your nose."

"Nothing," Leon shook his head, "I'm waiting for the results of the auctions. They should be clear any day now."

"And what has France been doing?"

"I have no idea, it's been two weeks since I last saw him. I even went over to his place in Primorska, but he wasn't there. Supposedly he went to London, perhaps to revive his old connections. It's also possible that he and Tone are plotting something behind our backs," Leon added.

"I should think not," Bata frowned. "There's too much at stake, we're talking some serious money here, money for all of us."

"Bollocks," Leon lost his temper, "I bet you got a handsome share of the initial seven hundred thousand for the first set of paintings, while I've been working like a dog for months and I have nothing to show for it."

"Stop right there," Bata said, "don't tell this to me. You're on Tone's list."

"Right..."

In that moment Leon felt a thud on his shoulder. It was Ljuba.

Leon was happy to see him. But his friend immediately bellowed:

"Where have you been, man? Did everything go well the last time in Austria? You practically disappeared from the face of the Earth."

"Oh, it's nothing, I've been studying for an exam at the university and I forgot about the normal life," Leon tried to come up with an excuse.

"It's good that you see me as normal, but luckily I'm not, that would be way too boring," Ljuba interrupted him.

Bata burst into laughter.

"What are you laughing about?" Ljuba asked him unpleasantly.

"Oh, it's nothing," Bata replied, "I like the fact that you're not normal."

It was now Ljuba's turn to laugh.

"Have you got another delegation from Serbia?" he asked, turning back to Leon.

"Yes, this is my mentor and friend, famous Bata the Beard from Belgrade," Leon joined in the laughter.

"Oh my," Ljuba wondered, "and what is it that this triple B does in life?"

"We don't know each other well enough for me to tell you more, but for now let's just say that I'm dealing with everything possible and impossible," Bata chimed in.

"I like that," Ljuba commented, communicating joking interest with a nod of his head, "I find that people who deal in everything possible and impossible are always useful."

"By the way," Leon interrupted them, turning to Bata to explain the sudden and unexpected presence of the visitor at their table, "Ljuba helped me bring the paintings over the border the other time, when I took them to the auction houses; just so you know."

He gave Ljuba a side glance, indicating that they should leave out his special brand of humour regarding the customs officers for the moment.

"Oh, that's not something to sneeze at. Come, join us for a drink," Bata offered and Ljuba didn't hesitate to take the invitation.

Bata ordered three Viljamovka brandies right away, but Leon turned him down, saying that it was too early for him, so Bata immediately took over his share. Ljuba cleared his throat.

"What can I help you with?" he inquired as he felt there was a reason they asked him to join their conversation.

"Oh, it's nothing, apart from a few million Deutschmarks there's nothing we need," Bata said cheerfully, raising his hands up in the air.

"That's not impossible," Ljuba grinned, "as long as there's a perfect combination."

"We might just have the winning combination, but the question is if you could pull it off properly," Bata added, half-jokingly, and half seriously, giving Ljuba an appraising look.

"You never know in life. There's nothing I'm not interested in, except for drugs," Ljuba said, running his fingers over the rim of his empty glass.

"Well, Ljuba, if that's the case, what are your thoughts on the French impressionist Matisse? Would you happen to know of a good buyer who would be willing to make lots of money and an excellent investment at the same time?" Bata fired straight off.

Leon shuddered in surprise.

"Well, I know a few rich people," Ljuba answered, not at all disturbed. "How much do such things go for these days? Just so I know what we're talking about."

"It's a painting about the size of that window over there, and the price is unbelievably low, only eight hundred thousand Deutschmarks at the present moment."

"Boy, you're not kidding around, Bata," Ljuba said, leaned back in his chair and stared inquisitively at Leon.

Leon nodded.

"Abroad such a painting could reach anywhere from three to five million dollars," he said, "and the Japanese, they are the ones buying them, they're crazy about them."

"To hell! Where did you get this thing?" Ljuba asked. "It's not stolen, is it?"

"You won't believe it. It's a part of a forgotten inheritance from my parts. It's not stolen, don't worry. What do you think?" Bata wanted to know.

"I have a business partner who might be interested in something like this," Ljuba replied after giving it some thought. "He's an important tradesman, dealing in plastics."

"Really!" Bata exclaimed. "Gentlemen like that are full of money! And what is our candidate like? Is he reliable?"

"I have to admit that he's very greedy, almost rapacious, he's going to haggle like hell," Ljuba explained.

"There's not much room right now at this price," Bata continued. "If we want to make any money, we'll have to raise it to a million three hundred, and then we'll see what we can gain."

"And when could we see this painting?" Ljuba asked, shifting from cold calmness to solid interest. "We'd practically have to, after all."

"Well, if we're talking about a serious buyer, I could have the painting here tomorrow," Bata promised. "Sure."

"You're not playing, Bata," Ljuba commented, "That's pretty quick, considering it's not hot stuff."

"The thing is big and we need to react quickly. So you better get on to business, we don't want anyone to get ahead of us," Bata suggested. "That's just the world we live in."

"If you say quick, I'll make it quick," Ljuba said and got up. "I'll go check it right away. We'll meet here in one hour and I'll let you know if we have a buyer or not."

"I'm not moving anywhere," Bata promised, "I feel like drinking today."

Is this how you do businesses worth millions?

The minute Ljuba left, Leon lost his temper. How could Bata offer the Matisse to someone who didn't even deal with art? Besides, this was the kind of business Tone was bound to find out about. How would this affect their relationship? Bata calmly sipped his second Canadian Club and smiled mysteriously. This is our business, he said, Tone has nothing to do with it. And if the buyer is really interested in the painting, they'll want to know more about it. And the only one with more information is him, Bata, there's no way Ljuba can fly solo when it comes to the price and the money.

"He's an interesting fellow, this Ljuba of yours," Bata remarked, ordering another round of drinks.

Once again Leon realised that Bata was full of little tricks and that he really could keep learning from him all the time. Nevertheless, he felt uneasy about the conversation with Ljuba.

He frowned.

"Still, how could you start talking about Matisse with a total stranger, just like that? Is this how you do businesses worth millions?" he added to put a decent end to the myriad of questions plaguing his mind.

"He that doesn't ask will never get a bargain," Bata just kept smiling confidently.

When Ljuba returned they could see a pleased smile on his face, even through the cloud of cigarette smoke.

"The man is interested in the matter," he announced, "he doesn't have that kind of money though, but he would certainly like to learn more about it. He suggested that we should meet in the afternoon to talk things through in more detail. He's heard about French impressionists before, he knows that there's a good market for them, but the rest is all Greek to him."

"You did well, Ljuba," Bata nodded with admiration. "Sit down and listen."

He proceeded to tell him, like he had several people before, about a drug addict who inherited a run-down house, and about the collection owned by Erich Šlomovič, one that the entire world was anxiously waiting for, and about the fact that the ones who would come first would be served premium works for small bucks.

Leon didn't feel like listening to the same subject for the tenth time so he left them to their conversation, got up and walked over to the phone. It had been almost ten days and it was ok for him to inquire about the news now. He took his little black book where he kept the phone numbers from his pocket and called Mrs. Billinger. He was in luck, she answered right away.

"Oh, Mr. Leon," she called happily. "I have good news for you. Your paintings did wonderfully; the final price was over three times our estimate."

"That's great, dear madam, you have golden hands," Leon immediately started sucking up to her. "And what is the final total?"

"I can't tell you this right now, I have yet to deduct the commission and calculate the tax. Plus," she paused, "I'd rather tell you this in person, face to face."

"Of course," Leon agreed. "Did you have a specific time in mind?"

"Just a moment," she said, "let me check my calendar... Could you come over on Tuesday, next week?"

"Sure!" Leon exclaimed.

"I'll see you on Tuesday, then," she said and hung up.

Leon returned to the table in good spirits and cut right into the conversation.

"I have some great news! Our stuff was sold in Munich for three times the price."

He leaned against the table with both hands and started to laugh.

"Ha!" Bata cried, as well, and immediately turned to Ljuba. "You see, this is what our stuff is like. Even the Germans are fighting to get their hands on it!"

It didn't take him long to realise that he was hungry and he invited both of them to lunch: you pick a restaurant, I'll pick up the tab. They drove to the suburbs to the Pri lipi restaurant in Stožice and tackled giant Wiener schnitzels which certainly lived up to their fame. Ljuba suggested that they should meet his potential buyer as soon as possible. We said that we should work quickly, so let's get on with it. Bata nodded and asked for a ride back to his hotel.

"I need to make a phone call," he explained, "regarding the transport of the painting."

"Fine," Leon said, "I'll pick you up in about an hour and drive you over to the meeting. Where to, exactly?"

"The Dobro jutro bar," Ljuba said. "It's close to his quarters and Mlakar likes to meet there."

When Bata returned to the hotel, he immediately asked to get Pančevo on the line. The call went through quickly and he was soon enthralled with the business. The conversation was clear and decisive.

"Hello, Rista, my friend, have you been good, working? Have you managed to spend all that money I gave you the other time yet?" Bata started.

"You mean the change you gave me?" Rista stopped him in his tracks.

The tone of his friend's voice let Bata know right away that he'd have to work hard. So he immediately embarked on the story of money flowing in from the successful auctions that were held in Germany, and there were also other deals in the air... For instance, we've just got a chance to sell that Matisse... has the patina been applied yet? I have this guy over here, he's interested, and he has the money, should I send Whitey over, he could deliver you and the painting to Ljubljana, and then I can send you with the money back to your lionesses, you could do with a trip up north, you should get out of that boring plain of yours for a bit...

Once money was mentioned Rista softened up a bit.

"I don't know," he mumbled, "six hours is a lot..."

"You can take a nap, Whitey will drive gently, you know that, so why don't you grab that Matisse and come get the money that's waiting for you..." Bata insisted.

"Well, then..." Rista hesitated.

"That's the way I like you!" Bata called, "Whitey will fly over like a bird to get you, and then he'll bring you to Ljubljana. We'll even warm a bed for you over here if you want!"

Bata was pleased and went downstairs to the reception, where he was later picked up by Leon. He passed the time he had left by playing solitaire on the table in front of the bar. On the drive over to their meeting place, Leon again voiced his disquiet.

"If this man gets fired up and ends up buying the painting, there's no way Tone won't hear about it. And he's the one who invested money into this project. We don't know what his reaction will be."

The whole thing really troubled him. We've been operating behind Tone's back, even if he does deserve a lesson or two on the count of his stubbornness and the way he treats everyone like they work for him instead of acknowledging that they are equal partners.

"Let it go. Of course he's going to hear about it. But it's not his painting. He'll get a taste of the competition and it'll make him step up and work faster. Don't think about this too much. Let the experienced dealer handle this issue," Bata replied coolly.

Mlakar was an hour late for the meeting; Bata, Ljuba and Leon drank a litre of Radenska. He finally arrived, introduced himself and cited some urgent business that needed to be taken care of as an excuse. He was middle aged, wearing sporty clothes, grey haired and agile, his sharp gaze and powerful voice gave the impression that he was a businessman who comes, takes one look and wants to do the business he's interested in his own way. He had a hundred questions regarding the painting; it was obvious that he had no idea about art, but he was interested in every detail pertaining to the painting, especially the ownership and of course the price. Bata gave him the long version of the story of the unusual inheritance and the Šlomovič collection.

Mlakar was of course interested in the thing. They agreed to meet again next day, in the evening, to look at the painting and come to the final agreement. They all needed to think things over, after all. They dispersed quickly. Bata called Whitey from his hotel and explained all the necessary details.

Leon was still slightly bothered by the fact that Bata was playing his own game behind Tone's back. So he went back to the Tabernakelj the next morning, just to get a feel of what the atmosphere was like on the other end.

"Any news?" he asked after a brief greeting.

"Yes," Tone confirmed, "the Faber sold everything at several times the starting price. They need to deduct the tax and then Bauer will let me know how much money we have there."

"That's great," Leon was thrilled, "we'll finally make a good profit and get to some money."

"No," Tone shook his head, "the money goes to investors first."

"What do you mean?" Leon resisted, "I've been working for

months; have I been doing it for free? I should get something, don't you think?"

"First we pay off the debtors," Tone repeated coldly, with an air which wasn't open to objections.

Leon made sure to make his attitude known. He felt a sudden stubbornness which led him to keep the information about the message he had received from Mrs. Billinger to himself for the time being. Tone should first reveal the profit they made at his auction house, with "the Nazi," so he could make a comparison. And he wanted to find out how much would he get, naturally. He shook his head and pushed his cup away in anger. Tone looked at him, bewildered.

"Don't worry, when everything is paid for, you'll get as much as we agreed," he tried to calm him down a bit.

"And what should I do in the meantime, live on air?"

"And love," Tone added with a slightly cynical smile.

"I bet you know all about that," Leon replied gruffly. Tone had been living alone for years.

They didn't say anything for a while. The silence was unpleasant, there was nothing friendly about it.

"And where's France?" Leon broke the silence with a question, still frowning. "He's not in Dane, either, he left without saying goodbye... Has he called you by any chance?"

Tone glanced at him. He felt the moment was right.

"I might have sent him on a trip, to take care of some business for me."

Leon almost lost his marbles:

"Is that so? You didn't know anything about this last week, and now he's taking care of some business for you all of a sudden. Are we partners or not? What else have you been doing behind my back?"

Tone again said frigidly: "We are partners. But we have to be clear on who's in charge. That would be me. It's true that you organised some things, but the investors are the main part. Money rules the world. And that was my job."

Leon gasped furiously, grabbing the desk with both hands.

"Don't get upset about it, everything will be fine," Tone tried to stop him.

"And when is France due back?" Leon asked through his teeth.

"Next week, probably," Tone replied, got up and left.

Leon remained seated at the table. He realised nothing was working the way they had agreed. Tone and Bata were both playing their own games, and the one thing they had in common was that they didn't include him. Ha, it was a good thing that I kept my mouth shut on the subject of Billinger. I'll have to discuss money with her personally. If I don't take a piece of that pie, I'll never get anything. And I'll have no qualms about selling Matisse with Bata, that's for sure. I don't give a flying fuck about Tone in this case. Friends and money obviously really don't mix.

He drove to the Ilirija Hotel. Bata was playing solitaire again, drinking one coffee after another and chain smoking his white Drina cigarettes.

"Whitey and Rista are on their way, they're bringing the Matisse," he began instantly. "I hope everything works out fine. I've enquired about this Mlakar fellow; he really is very rich and a difficult negotiator. But," he grinned, "there's a doctor of negotiating sciences waiting for him at the other end."

He took a long drag on the cigarette, spit out tiny tobacco crumbs which stuck to his lips, and asked:

"So, how's Tone, did you see him?"

"I did," Leon confirmed. "He also got information that the auction was successful. All he has to do now is wait for the final tally."

He kept the news about France's journey to himself.

"There you go, my son, you need to have strong nerves in our business, you need to know how to wait. Patience is paramount. You'll never become a big art dealer without it."

Rista and Whitey arrived late in the afternoon. They all took turns kissing and shaking hands.

"How are you, Whitey, my friend, still alive?" Bata asked.

"Oh, Bata, Batane, I am. As long as I drive around you gentlemen, I'm at least making something. The day to day misery barely covers the cost of a piece of bread," Whitey answered, looking around the hotel lobby.

They all proceeded to go to the car to take a look at the painting. Whitey opened the boot and Rista slowly unwrapped several protective layers of paper. The painting was magnificent. Vivid colours in pink and blue hues were making a hippie impression. The painting was framed, in a true French style frame from impressionist times. Leon inadvertently let out a sigh of enthusiasm.

"What do you say, boy, did I do a good job?" Rista laughed.

Leon looked at him bemusedly: "I don't understand, what did you...?"

Bata swiftly kicked Rista's leg, brushed his finger over his lips, shook his head slightly and dragged Rista away. He whispered:

"I'm sorry, Bata, I had no idea that the boy doesn't know about this."

"Some things are better kept from young idealists. I think he's still too young and doesn't have enough experience to process our facts. You can see that his head is full of dreams on high art market. And he doesn't know that half of that market is filled with fakes," Bata spoke under his breath.

Leon walked over to them.

"What's going on behind my back again? It's the same as it was this morning at Tone's," he reproached them. He was again overcome with the feeling that something wasn't right but couldn't figure out what it was. Bata quickly changed the subject.

"What happened at Tone's?"

"Nothing, really, he just sent France to London on a special mission without letting anyone of us in on it," Leon said angrily.

"Right," Bata said curtly, "Leon, you are to stay in contact with him and pay attention. We'll get that fellow in check. Let's take another look at the Matisse now, it really is a masterpiece."

They went back.

The painting was marvellous. It was worth every Deutschmark, Leon thought to himself. Mlakar would surely love it, despite not knowing the first thing about art. Whitey wrapped the painting back up and they drove together to the Dobro jutro bar. The room was very noisy and filled with smoke, they could hardly find their way to a table in a remote corner. They pulled up a few more chairs.

Ljuba soon showed up. They introduced themselves and ordered coffee. There was no alcohol; everyone clearly expected a difficult conversation.

In his mind, Leon was going over what he thought he heard

about the painting. The strange disquiet which settled in him during his conversation with Tone was gradually getting stronger. It was like he was wandering around in fog, unable to clear it up. Something ambiguous had been going on the entire time, and he couldn't figure out what that was. He noticed Bata constantly looking at him from across the table, observing him, but Leon just stared defiantly in a non-existent point on the wall.

Mlakar was really late. Bata was checking his watch more and more frequently.

"Where could this marsh dweller be? If he's this sloppy when it comes to his business, he won't last long," he derided him, rolling his eyes.

"It's just the way he is," Ljuba said, "but he always manages to succeed. Do you want me to order you a whiskey, so you calm down?"

Bata declined.

"No, no, we all need to calm down," he ranted and waved the waitress over. "Bring us a bottle of Chivas."

"Don't get drunk," Leon tried to hold him back, "is there somewhere else you have to run?"

"I have to run to the next bottle," Bata declared.

At that moment, Mlakar finally appeared.

"I can see that you're celebrating. Have I missed anything?" he asked merrily, rubbing his hands together and looking over everyone in attendance.

"You know I always splurge when there are guests in the house," Ljuba replied.

Bata introduced Rista as the representative of the painting's owner; everyone that needed to be there was present.

"And where's the painting?" Mlakar sked, looking around the room.

"In the car," Bata replied. "It's just arrived."

"We're surely not going to look at it here," Mlakar suggested. "Let's go around the corner to my office. By the way, my colleague here is my attorney."

He pointed at a young man in a dark grey suit, wearing a yellow necktie. He was standing behind him like a shadow. He didn't utter one word.

"Fine," Bata said, "let's go. Leon, you keep Whitey company. There's still a lot left in the bottle."

Leon was unpleasantly hurt. He was excluded once again. It seemed all these gentlemen really did see him as a small-time dealer from the flea market, an art student, everything that had been going on for the last six months was indeed too good to be true. Well, at least I'm in on it, he tried to console himself. There's big business going on and I'm learning from professionals. A day will come when I'm included in the final stages of operations.

He and Whitey emptied the bottle and ordered a new one. They might as well pay us for waiting, Leon reasoned.

Over an hour later Ljuba and the two sellers returned. Rista and Bata looked pleased.

"How did it go?" Whitey enquired.

"It went well, Whitey, it went well. But that's none of your business. You are just the horse driving me," Rista interrupted him arrogantly.

Whitey looked at him in dismay and didn't try to conceal that he felt offended. Leon was unpleasantly surprised, as well, but Bata motioned him to stay calm, I'll tell you everything once we are left alone.

Ljuba poured drinks for everyone.

"Are we drinking to success or failure?" Leon asked.

"We'll see about that tomorrow, but I think our prospects are good," Bata said.

He gave Leon a telling look.

They drank up and Ljuba said good-bye. Whitey drove Rista and Leon gave Bata a lift. Once at the hotel, Whitey and Rista went straight to bed, as they were tired from the long journey and negotiations, while Bata and Leon went to the bar.

"I didn't want to say anything in front of Whitey, because it's none of his business," Bata began. "We're meeting the buyer here at the hotel, tomorrow at two o'clock."

"And, what do you think?" Leon asked impatiently. "Will he buy it or not?"

"I can't say for sure, but I think he's ours," Bata said.

"What do you mean - ours?" Leon wondered.

"Like I said, we have him in our pocket, he's eating out of our hand," Bata said, downing one glass of whiskey after another.

Once again, Leon had a bad feeling about it. He couldn't figure out why Bata would speak so insultingly about a man who was going to buy the Matisse, a painting worth millions. It's not like the buyer was an idiot, incompetent and stupid!

"What's going on, Bata? I don't understand anything anymore," he said.

But Bata just kept drinking and drinking.

"What don't you understand?" he asked with a rather drunken look in his eyes.

"Nothing: what Rista said about the painting, for instance," Leon began, "the insulting way you're speaking about the buyer..."

Bata's head fell on the table. He struggled to lift it back up.

"If you don't understand now, you will eventually," he mumbled incoherently. Then he went rambling on, something about Zagreb, and Pančevo, and Šlomovič, and money... he was more and more incoherent... he kept drinking and staring at his crystal glass...

Leon declared that he should be getting home now, but Bata didn't even register this. He had never seen Bata this drunk before. It was another question without an answer.

He stepped out into the fresh air and took some deep breaths.

He drove home, trying to piece all the details together in a logical picture. He couldn't do it. Maybe it was best to sleep it off. Tomorrow was a new day.

Will you kindly put away the money?

Still with mixed feelings, he drove to the Ilirija Hotel in the afternoon of the next day. The hotel bar and lobby were empty. He went to the reception desk.

"Mr. Živković isn't answering," the receptionist said when Leon asked him to call Bata's room. Rista and Whitey were nowhere to be found, either.

What could this be?

The receptionist informed him that they hadn't settled their bills yet. Leon sat down in an armchair and tried to figure out where they could have gone. In the middle of his thought process he was interrupted by Ljuba, who appeared in front of him, obviously in very good spirits.

"Oh, you're here already?" he asked.

"I've come a little bit early, just in case Bata has any questions. But there's no one here," Leon answered with slight surprise.

"Don't worry, they'll show up when they need something. Nobody who is about to collect a hundred and seventy thousand Deutschmarks just disappears," Ljuba affirmed convincingly and long-distance ordered a coffee from a waitress who watched him from the bar.

Leon shuddered. How did they get from eight hundred thousand to a hundred and seventy thousand? Leon thought even eight hundred thousand was far too low for a painting like this. But twenty percent of the asking price? That was madness.

"Where did you go?" Ljuba brought him back from his calculations when he noticed Leon's sickly pallor and astonishment.

"I just don't get it how they could come down to such a ridiculous price for such an exceptional painting," Leon kept shaking his head.

"Well, the gentlemen don't have connections all over Europe, and Mlakar can take care of this problem, right? Don't you worry, you'll get your share," Ljuba deliberated.

"My share?" Leon winced. "How much are you getting?"

"Ten percent, naturally. I guess you will get the same, they're your people, after all. If they start to fool around, I'll demand that you get your share, don't worry. Business is business," Ljuba went on overtly.

At that moment, Bata, Rista and Whitey appeared in the hotel lobby. Bata noticed Leon's bewildered look. He started waving to him from afar, explaining:

"We went to Bled, to catch some mountain air. And I had a craving for custard cake. Stop looking at me funny, is it a sin to go there, when we're here already?"

Leon couldn't help but laugh. Bata had a childlike passion for sweets!

They gathered around a table.

Mlakar arrived at two o'clock sharp. He brought with him his attorney, who clutched a thin Samsonite briefcase in his hands, Bata and Rista joined them at the next table. The aperitif bar was empty. The atmosphere was very formal and cinematic.

Rista turned to Whitey.

"Come on, Whitey, why don't you drive over to the gas station and wash your car? And don't be long, I'll be waiting for you."

Whitey got up without saying a word and left. Bata turned to Leon.

"Come join us, Leon, you also played a part in us getting together, making what is about to happen possible. Sit down with us."

Leon felt his heart sing. So, I'm finally one of them. It finally happened! He changed seats.

Mlakar turned to his attorney who started explaining dryly that he had put together a contract which they should now sign, as the buyer needed some insurance that everything was in order, that the painting wasn't stolen, for instance.

"Stolen?" Bata hit the roof. "Gentlemen, you must be joking. Get up, Rista, we're leaving, these gentlemen obviously don't know what they're buying."

"Calm down, take a seat," Mlakar said, "why do you have a problem with the contract?"

"I don't mind the contract, it's just that we don't have them in our business," Bata assured him.

"Well then," Mlakar added serenely, as if he had anticipated the situation to develop as it had, "if you don't want to sign the contract, I'd be willing to pay eighty thousand. This is advice I received from my attorney and I'm going to follow it."

They were all looking at each other in silence.

Ljuba was the first to speak: "That won't do. We talked about one hundred and seventy thousand yesterday and now we're down to eighty all of a sudden. That's no way to do business. These are my friends, Mlakar, and I won't let you treat them like this."

Bata and Rista exchanged glances.

"Alright," Bata said almost inaudibly, "this is what we're going to do. We can agree to a hundred and ten thousand, and you pay out Mr. Ljuba's reward. If that's ok with you, we have a deal."

"It's a deal," Mlakar said.

The attorney leaned in to speak, but Mlakar pushed him back. He gestured to the briefcase with his head. The attorney took out an envelope and started counting a thousand Deutschmark banknotes. He stopped when he reached a hundred and ten and inserted the stack of money in a different envelope. Then he counted an additional eleven brown banknotes and handed them over to Ljuba.

"Is everything in order?" Mlakar raised his head. "And where is the painting?"

"In the taxi. We need to wait for the driver to come back," Ljuba explained.

"I don't have much time. I have some partners waiting for me at my office. You collect it and bring it over to me," Mlakar turned to Ljuba and got up.

"Gentlemen," he said, "if you come across another thing like this, don't hesitate to contact me."

He left in the company of his attorney, without shaking anyone's hand.

Rista raised his hands in the air and applauded.

"Good job, Bata, you're a real master when it comes to doing business with idiots."

Ljuba gave him a surprised look: "Business with idiots? What do you mean?"

"Well, like this, without the papers."

"Oh, what are you going on about," Bata rejected him. "I always do business without any papers. Let them chase the papers around Europe. Getting papers in order is a risky and costly business, especially for us Yugoslavs."

Leon sat silently in his armchair. He was there the whole time, but he didn't understand anything. Bata sold the painting at an unreasonable price: he first offered it for eight hundred thousand, which was about a tenth of its market value; then he negotiated twenty percent of that price and finally settled for just one percent of a normal market value. What was wrong with him? Even stolen paintings went for two to five percent of the estimated value on the market, and Bata was throwing away this exquisite Matisse with a confirmed pedigree for peanuts, practically. And Rista was happy about it?! He found that odd and unreasonable. This story was completely crazy!

He swallowed hard, pushing aside the main questions for a moment, gathered his thoughts and asked:

"So what's up with my commission?"

"You practically did nothing," Bata shook his head carelessly. "All you did was introduce me to this man who became my great friend today."

He pointed to Ljuba, who quickly raised his hand in return.

"Oh, no, you don't become a friend of mine this quick, you don't gain my trust with a single deal and one commission. It takes years of affection, shared risks and good stories."

"Don't get angry, Ljuba, you're right, we only accomplished a single deal together, but I believe we're on the right path," Bata nodded.

"What I'd like to see now is the share that goes to my friend Leon here, as it seems you are about to leave him out," Ljuba said, giving Leon a meaningful look.

Bata rocked in his chair and started to explain, as if he'd reflected on this:

"Well, not everything is about money, I'm giving him important life lessons, aren't I, Rista? You know what I'm talking about. You've learned a lot from us in this time, my dear Leon, and you'll learn a lot more," he looked at Leon. "It's true that you've done us a lot of favours, but you're still a long way away from acquiring the mastery needed to become a part of a well-tuned team. You are entitled to the women's cut, of course."

"He threw three thousand on the table in front of Leon.

"What? Three thousand?" Leon objected loudly, flabbergasted. "I connected you with these people, I brought an international expert, I took the risk and took the paintings to auctions... and now I get the women's cut! So I'm nothing but a beginner, an apprentice!"

Bata stared at him coldly. He's just like Tone, Leon thought. Unfortunately, he's like Tone.

"Slow down, my son. This was all my idea and coming up with it was the hardest part. I suppose you realise as much," he said.

Rista came to life then, when he saw Leon getting angry and upset. He quickly intervened.

"Listen, Bata, if that's all you're willing to pay him, I'm going to give him four grand out of my share," he said.

Bata jumped in the air.

"My, my, are these some new connections? That's no good, Leon, my friend, you're never supposed to have more than one leader. You have to have one teacher, always, to guide you and keep you on the right track and dole out knowledge in doses you can handle. But alright. You can decide to go with me or others. You can take the three thousand you are entitled to or choose seven and have two teachers from tomorrow on."

Leon felt that Bata was setting up a tricky position for him. Bata was a master dealer. He had already learned a lot from him and he could learn a lot more. He quickly went over everything they had done together in his head, swallowed hard and said disappointedly: "Fine, I'll take the three thousand, and let my knowledge soar."

Bata laughed smugly at Rista and said:

"Do you see now, what's loyalty, what's real learning? Leon made the right choice. Money's not everything."

It was Ljuba's turn to speak, after listening to their quarrelling with wonder and interest, looking from one to the other.

"If I were you, Leon, I'd take money from both of them, they both need you. If they didn't you'd be at the carwash with the taxi driver."

Leon smiled, as he forgot all about Whitey who just entered through the door and immediately asked: "Are you finished dividing the money? Have you left anything for me?"

"Here, you get three thousand," Bata handed the money to him. "You should get one, but Leon renounced his share."

Whitey had a puzzled look on his face, but his past experience had taught him that it was best not to ask any questions in this company, so he took the money. He and Ljuba went to their cars to transfer the painting.

"There, we're done," Bata exclaimed, snapping his fingers.

They kissed some more and then Whitey and Rista headed home while Ljuba drove off to Mlakar.

"And now," Bata said solemnly, patting Leon's shoulder, "we can toast to your graduation."

"What graduation?" Leon asked grumpily. He was in a very bad mood. He had expected to get a larger commission, and now this.

"You graduated from loyalty, modesty and respect for your teacher. This marks a great victory in your life. It's clear you're not going to renounce your friend over money. You are now my partner and we share everything down the middle. Waiter, bring us a bottle of Dom Perignon!" Bata called, quite at ease.

He reached in his pocket and counted forty five thousand on the table in front of Leon.

Leon couldn't comprehend what was happening. He couldn't believe his own ears, nor his own eyes. What was this all of a sudden? One moment he was thrown into desperate sadness, and the next into confused happiness. Tears started streaming down his face and releasing all the tension, insecurity and doubts which he had amassed lately. He was unable to stop. He cried like a baby, and sniffled uncontrollably. What had just happened!

Bata was moved, as well, Leon's disposition didn't leave him cold.

"This is too much," Leon uttered with a stiff voice.

"No, it's not. You've proven yourself worthy of being my partner," Bata shook his head.

He continued: "You know, my son, money's not everything. Money comes and goes, but true friends are hard to come by."

He raised his glass.

"To you."

He stared at Leon for a long time, then added, evidently moved: "If I ever had a son, I'd want him to be like you."

All the boundaries came down.

They had a few more glasses. Leon wiped his tears with a napkin he took from the table and ordered another bottle. A stack of thousand Deutschmark notes was still lying there in front of them.

A waiter came over.

"Will you kindly put away the money," he asked seriously as he brought over another bottle, "otherwise I might think it's a tip."

Leon laughed and put the banknotes away. At first, he wanted to spill out all of his doubts, all of the questions which had been bothering him, he wanted to clarify everything that he found uncomprehendable with the selling of the Matisse. But Bata gave him a friendly pat on the shoulder, raised his glass to him, the money in his bulging pocket felt nice and warm, he felt like he and Bata were going through some very special moments together, so he pushed the questions he had far away. They drank and chatted. They could discuss all the weird issues at some other time.

Then Bata went to his room to get his suitcase, as the hands on the large wall clock relentlessly pushed forward. Leon drove him to the airport. He was fighting off sweet fatigue and pushing away his doubts. The sudden sum of money which he hadn't expected was a good argument in favour of friendly silence. Once under the jutting roof of the airport building, they embraced each other warmly for a long time.

"Talk to you soon!" Bata said by the way when leaving through the glass door, just before it closed.

"Talk to you soon!" Leon confirmed.

It started to rain.

When Leon came home that evening, Kristina was sitting in the dark living room. He turned on the light and looked at her in surprise.

"I've been thinking about us," she said slowly. "We can't go on like this. You're running around with those Serbs of yours, I never know where you are, the toilet is leaking, I can't afford a plumber, the fridge is empty, I'm behind with my rent..."

She was looking out the window.

Leon, who came home victorious and bubbling over with confidence in his work, was again flooded with a strange feeling of doubt, which he only briefly shed during his drinking bout with Bata. He sat on the edge of the armchair and took the stack of money from his pocket.

"There you are, from my Serbs," he said quietly.

She silently took the money and put it away in a drawer of the bookcase, without even counting it. Then she came back, there was no sparkle in her eyes, she took Leon's hand and led him to the bedroom. Raindrops were hitting the windows louder and louder.

Leon suddenly realised that he was actually paying for sex.

This is really not enough. I want nineteen million

In the morning, Leon got a call from his mother, informing him that France reappeared during the night. He was still asleep when she left for work.

Leon rushed to his car. A severe storm caused immediate traffic jam so he had to drive quite slowly, which only exacerbated his curiosity. He parked in the parking lot in front of his parents' house and sprinted to the front door, without an umbrella. France was having his tea and reading a newspaper, as if there was nothing unusual about him being here one day, then disappearing without a word and suddenly appearing again.

"Oh," he greeted him kindly, "Leon, how are you?"

Leon didn't know what to say. He couldn't make out whether France was joking or he really didn't understand the scope of the questions he triggered with his disappearance.

"I'm fine." he said finally. "And you?"

France laughed merrily.

"I have wonderful news. As you know, Mr. Anton sent me to London to get in touch with some of my old friends. I'm bursting at the seams. The green Picasso immediately caught someone's eye and if we agree, my friend is willing to pay twelve million dollars for it."

France beamed as he felt that he had just delivered the news of the decade.

"What?!" Leon shrieked. "Twelve million?"

He couldn't see straight. A wave of jaunty gaiety overcame him. With that kind of money, Tone could pay back his investors, buy new paintings from Good Person and divide a huge profit among the rest of them. I'd get at least a million and a half, he quickly calculated. For one single painting! We finally won! Not just for the time being, I'll be taken care of for the rest of my life. And well taken care of at that!

France noticed Leon's excitement and just kept going:

"The other paintings I told them about could sell for good money, as well. Rumours about the Šlomovič collection are already spreading around London and every gallery owner is certain that the new paintings will greatly increase the buyers' interest and give the market a boost."

"What about Bata's Pfeininger?" Leon remembered.

"Sold!" France added victoriously. "Providing he would accept an offer of six hundred thousand dollars."

"This is crazy, this is crazy!" Leon mumbled, as the most beautiful images ran through his mind: his share from all the profits, he as a great gallery owner in Paris, London, the French Riviera, a waiter under the parasols on the beach, a casino in Nice, a large Bentley, vacations in exotic countries, endless celebrations in Belgrade, Kristina, finally forever pleased, draped in gold necklaces...

"Does Tone know yet?" he remembered.

"No," France shook his head, "I came back in the middle of the night and I haven't got a chance to phone him yet. Do you want to go over together?"

"Of course, hurry up!" Leon yelled. He lost all self-control. Every expectation he had kept hidden, all the compulsive tranquillity, every wish, everything came together in boisterous rumbling.

"Let's go, let's go, let's go!"

While France was getting dressed, Leon decided to give Mrs. Billinger another call. Days of torture were coming to an end, giving way to days of payment. Perhaps she'd had the time to deduct the taxes and the commission and could tell him how much money was waiting for him over there.

Again, she answered the phone right away.

"Oh," she said, "Mr. Leon, I was expecting you on Tuesday, that's what we said, didn't we?"

"Yes, of course," Leon brimmed with excitement, "but I wanted to ask you nevertheless, how large a suitcase I should bring for the money. You probably know what my share is by now?"

"Of course," she said. "Nine hundred and seventy thousand. Is this ok with you?"

"I will gladly accept anything coming from you," Leon roared.

"I can hear from your voice that you are thrilled," she tried to continue, but Leon interrupted her.

"I apologize, but we have a big family celebration going on here, and it made me think of you," he lied.

"Oh, that's really nice," she exclaimed now, as well. "I'll see you on Tuesday, then!"

Leon hung up the phone. He couldn't believe any of this. So I'm finally full of money!

France came back from his room wearing a raincoat, a hat and a typical English black umbrella.

"Shall we?" he asked, observing Leon's happy expression with great content.

They drove off into the storm. Leon kept his eyes carefully on the road and felt like he was drowning in good news. He wondered how Tone would react to this. And Bata, of course, he needed to contact Bata as soon as possible, right after he and France were done with Tone.

He found an available parking spot under a horse chestnut and they ventured outside into the wind and rain. They struggled to avoid the gusts which could easily invert their umbrellas. By the time they reached the Tabernakelj, they were dripping with rain.

"Hello," Tone greeted them as they appeared in the door to his office, then turned to France, "welcome to the rain. Have you brought it back with you from England?"

"Perhaps we should go across the street for some tea," France suggested calmly, "the air is better there and the walls don't have as many ears."

"You're right, I could use some tea in this cold rainy weather," Tone nodded, sensing right away that there was more to the talk about the air.

When they got to the Rotovž, they took a remote table.

"Your mood seemed to improve," Tone looked at Leon. "You were quite bothered and grim the other time."

"I have reasons for both," Leon nodded. "France is the reason why I'm in good spirits."

"Well, let's hear it," Tone smiled. "I'm all ears. What is it then? Was there any interest for Picasso? And the rest?"

France took some time to give his words the proper weight, then said victoriously:

"A collector, a friend of mine and an end buyer, offered twelve million dollars for the Picasso."

Leon stared at Tone, as well, as he didn't want to miss the pleasure of seeing his reaction. He wanted to witness his face finally breaking into joyous smiles. Him being floored. Him wiping his spectacles. France's message was a bombshell. But Tone didn't even bat an eyelid.

He was silent for a while, as if he was thinking about something, and then he said coldly:

"That's not enough. I can't sell a top Picasso painting from his best period for that much. I checked some data from the global market and I know that it's worth twenty-four million. You're offering half of that. I could understand if the offer came from a re-seller. But the end buyer has to pay much more. No. This won't work. This is really not enough. I want nineteen million."

France froze with his mouth open. Leon bulged his eyes in shock.

"But that's an excellent offer," he charged defiantly, unable to control himself. "You can pay off the investors and we'll have a ton of money left. We could get more paintings from Good Person. The auctions will rake in a lot of money, as well..."

"No they won't," Tone shook his head. "I only got seven hundred and fifty thousand from the Faber. Do you know what the situation is with the Grabner yet?"

Leon felt his world crumbling under his feet. All these millions are not enough for Tone? That can't be. He's playing! He's joking! He's testing them! No normal human being would react like this. He answered swiftly.

"There's eight hundred and fifty thousand at the Grabner. We can do a lot with this money and we'll still have a lot left," he almost nagged. "We can grab everything in one go, everything that kid still has in Belgrade. Don't you see this?"

Tone shook his head again.

"That's not enough," he concluded coldly, as if he was discussing something insignificant, and not playing around with heaps of money. "We obviously started out too low with both auction houses."

"But you were the one who confirmed the prices," Leon burst out, "I even called you from there."

"Well, I just didn't have enough information. If I were there, I'd appraise the situation differently and I wouldn't allow them to take advantage of me. This is excellent stuff we're selling, and it calls for top prices," Tone insisted.

France and Leon kept staring at him. How could this be happening! They were waiting for Tone to break into laughter, slap his knees and tell them he was just playing a joke on them.

"I think," France started to speak again, "that the offer made by my friend from London is a fantastic one. Out there no one is waiting for guys from the Balkans to make such a big deal."

"No," Tone insisted. "It's not enough. Nineteen million is my final price."

France cleared his throat.

"Think about this again, Mr. Anton. Twelve million is a lot, truly a lot of money. And we could pull everything through quietly and without a hitch. There's no rush. Sleep on it, think this through. I'm going to come over tomorrow to ask you again."

"There's no need. Nineteen is my final price. I won't change my mind."

The news which was supposed to derail the entire world fell flat on the table. Tone acted like he was waving away an annoying gnat which happened to fly by.

Leon couldn't listen to this any longer.

"For God's sake, Tone, you paid a few hundred grand for this painting and now twelve million is not enough for you?" he asked with a horrified face, struggling to restrain himself from starting to jump in the air and smash his hand against the table.

"Yes, it's not enough."

Then, as if all the astonishment was not enough, either, and he was tired of the senseless conversation, he added: "I can see you're going to be of no use to me and I'll have to take over the selling myself. You are of no help whatsoever. If you have no better news, I'll be heading back to the Tabernakelj. I have serious work to do over there," he said frigidly.

He got up and left.

France and Leon were left sitting at the table, completely stricken. There were no words to express how they felt.

"This was bad," France said after a while and shuddered.

"I'm going to go see my friends at the Theosophical society, that'll calm me down. I'll see you later at your dear mother's house," he said quietly.

He, too, got up and walked out into the rain.

Am I still on the team?

Leon sat there for a while longer, then drove to the bridge crossing the Sava River in Tacen. Even as a kid, he had a secret spot there where he used to sit, throwing stones in the river and thinking.

Tone was turning into a total disaster. Whatever was going through his mind? What kind of plans could he be hatching? No normal person would turn down an offer like this. It would change everything. The enormous business would acquire the necessary financial backing and they could take everything as slow and prudent as they needed. A single painting would make them all rich! Could it be that Tone was onto something ineffably big, unbeknownst to everyone, so that the twelve million, which translated into at least a ten million profit, didn't mean anything to him? How could he disregard everything anyone else thought? So the story about their partnership was void. All the deals they made were off. Fortunately, I decided to keep a hundred and twenty thousand from Billinger for myself. Otherwise I'd again be left with nothing. I just hope nothing goes wrong there, as well. I need to hurry over to the beautiful lady!"

He sat by the water for quite some time. He felt like just staying there forever. It's peaceful here, and everyone I deal with in the city is a scatterbrain.

The evening came. He drove to his parents' house. They were sitting in the living room with France, having tea. His father also had a glass of cognac in front of him. He embraced Leon and shook his head.

"I can't believe it," his father said. "This man must be crazy. Even our colleague France here can't understand what this Tone guy is doing."

France explained a little about the gallery market in London, he talked about what else he could help Tone sell. But with an irrational head like his, he thought it would be better to just leave everything alone. No serious person would drag his name through the gutter like this. Providing expert service was one thing, but human greed was something completely different.

Leon didn't feel like talking. He sat in their company for a while, but then said goodbye, clearly ill-disposed, and headed home.

He was the one sitting in the armchair now, waiting in the dark.

Kristina came back from her recording session, she was in a very good mood, she turned on the light and fluttered around the apartment. It took her some time to stop in front of him and ask:

"Is anything wrong? You seem a bit down."

She sat opposite from him. Leon slowly retold the story about France, Picasso, and Tone.

"Well, that's antique dealers for you," she said quite carelessly and inconsiderately, "one is weirder than the next. You'll probably have to find something smarter to do with your life. First there's this constant waiting, and then nothing happens, I don't like it either."

Leon couldn't understand the logic about her disregarding millions with such haste and ease. Did she understand what he had just told her? Did she even listen? Did she have a different plan?

She got up, raced around the apartment and informed him that she only came home to eat something and to feed Šeri, and then she had to go back to the studio.

"Don't wait up for me," she called as she walked through the door.

Leon merely nodded in silence. He couldn't be more miserable. Once again, he didn't understand anything.

Why was Tone doing what he was doing? Twelve million dollars were not enough? And on the other hand - Bata. How could he sell such a beautiful Matisse for mere change? It was true that he gave Leon, for the first time ever, a nice sum of money. But what was behind all of it? He felt like a tiny grain being crushed under giant millstones. Who could explain all of this to him?

And now Kristina! Lately she's been paying even less attention to his work. She accepted the nice earnings from the Matisse somewhat coldly; she just took the money, without saying anything. In all likelihood, a very nice share from the auction will come his way next, but it will be stolen, not a deserved share among friends, the way it was supposed to be. The amount should suffice for at least a year of exquisite life even for a spoiled woman. But will it?

Nevertheless, what were these hot and cold repetitions about?

It was finally becoming clear that the friendly business story which Bata, Tone and he started in Belgrade was coming to pieces. He could understand somehow if he was the one who had ruined it, but there was also France, an international expert, he of all people knew what he was saying. And Tone didn't hear him. Why? Could it be possible that he wanted to double cross both of them now, when everything was so nicely taken care of, and continue to sell everything by himself?

He was brought back to reality by the sound of the phone ringing. Bata! The man had some incredible intuition. He always appeared at just the right moment.

"What's up?"

"France came back. He said he can sell your Pfeininger for six hundred thousand dollars, if that's ok with you," Leon said sarcastically, only later realising that Bata didn't do anything to cause his disappointment.

"That's wonderful," Bata rejoiced, ignoring the tone of Leon's voice. "What about the other stuff?"

"Tone went crazy," Leon spilled the beans, "he refuses to sell the Picasso for twelve million, and he thinks the money from the auctions is not enough, either... well, that's what's new!"

"Cool down," Bata quickly said. "I'm coming over. Pick me up at the airport tomorrow. I've been having bad premonitions. I'm going to have a talk with France."

Bata, my friend, Leon thought to himself. He never loses his head. He always makes a decision as soon as he needs to.

He had some whiskey, set his alarm clock and went to bed. In the morning, as the alarm went off, Kristina briefly opened her eyes at the ringing sound, looked at him - you're off again? - rolled over and fell back to sleep.

The plane from Belgrade arrived on time. Bata appeared at the exit, holding a thick folder.

"What's that?" Leon asked.

"If Tone is planning on selling by himself, we're going to hire France by ourselves, as well," Bata grinned, gave Leon a hug and kissed him three times. "Let's have some of this disgusting airport coffee, then we can go over and talk to him."

He was in great spirits and his cheerfulness was contagious. Tone paid for the Picasso himself, which is to say, he put up the money, so he's free to do with it what he likes. Let him, and may he choke on it, the greedy bastard. But I have a heap of other paintings, Bata chuckled, and France will break a happy sweat, turning them to big money over in London. Let's go!

They drove to the house at the foothill of Šmarna gora. Leon's mother came to the door, wearing a bathrobe and a very makeshift hairdo.

"I have a cold, so I stayed home," she explained as by way of an apology.

"Is France still asleep?" Leon asked.

"What do you mean? Haven't you heard? He packed all of his things in boxes yesterday, they're waiting up in the lab, and as far as I know he took a taxi late in the evening and drove to his wife in Dane, at least I think so. I believe he met Tone once more before he left," his mother told them. "He said he left a message for you upstairs. I didn't read it."

"Well, that's something," Leon exclaimed, he and Bata entered and walked up the stairs to the lab.

Everything was clean and tidy there, there was no trace of what he and France had been doing there for the past several weeks. A number of taped cardboard boxes were stacked in the centre of the room, one of them clearly contained personal items. A large envelope was laid on top of it, marked "Leon."

Leon opened it and started reading:

"Dear Leon, I went back to see Anton once again late in the afternoon, to have a serious conversation with him. Sadly, we were unable to find any mutual ground. He stuck with his decision despite all my suggestions. He paid my fee for the work I had done here. He was very gentlemanly. I have to admit that I expected us to become partners in business and I would be able to sell a lot, from London to New York, from Zürich to Frankfurt. Regretfully, he turned me down. I'm extremely disappointed. I want to thank you for the pleasant experience of working together. Would you be so kind and drive these boxes to Dane, when it's convenient for you, my wife and I will probably stay there until the winter. All the best, France"

Leon stared at the piece of paper in astonishment.

"What's going on, son?" Bata wanted to know. "Where's France?"

"End of story," Leon said, shaken to the core. "Tone paid France out. France is no longer on our team. Read it."

Bata couldn't understand everything, but he did realise what had happened.

"It is what it is," he said, "we need to take a different course now. Let's drive over to see the professor, and check things out in person."

They loaded the boxes in the car. Leon leaned against it and tried to think things through. He thought that he should try and figure out what Tone exactly was up to himself. After all it was he, Leon, who arranged France's cooperation, and now Tone dismissed him on his own, without letting anyone in on his decision. He went back inside the house and called Tabernakelj. Tone answered right away.

"Hi," he said, when he recognized Leon's voice.

"What's been going on with France? My mother informed me that he packed his things and was probably leaving for Dane. You wouldn't know anything about this, would you?" Leon asked careful not to sound agitated.

"Well, sure, we don't need him anymore. He restored the paintings, wrote the expertise... keeping him around would only lead to more expenses. Well, I might as well tell you, so you'll know it, too: I paid him for everything he had done for us, a hundred and ten thousand Deutschmarks. I also let him know that he's welcome to work for us in the future, if he wants to and if we need his services," Tone explained, paused for a bit and continued, "you know how it is, everything's got to end sometime."

Leon got the hint and asked:

"Am I still on the team?"

A cold gust dashed from the receiver.

"Yes, for now," Tone answered harshly, "but I have to let you know that I've heard about the deal you are arranging with Mlakar, and I'm not happy about it, of course. I hate it when things are being done behind my back."

Leon quickly resisted.

"I didn't offer Mlakar anything and I also didn't sell him anything. This deal was made by Bata and his people."

"That may be, but you were the one who secured the connection," Tone insisted.

"No, I didn't. I've never worked with Mlakar in my life," Leon stood his ground.

"I couldn't care less about that, but you'll have to decide whether you're going to work with Belgrade or with me. It's as simple as that! Just pick a team."

"If you insist," Leon took a harsher tone now as well, "I'll pick the team which plays more fairly."

"That would be my team," Tone laughed, but Leon eschewed an answer, played ignorant and asked:

"Where's France now?"

"He is where he is. That's none of my business anymore."

With this, the conversation came to an end. Leon went out and found Bata smoking next to his car, absorbed in thought and looking at the mountains in the distance.

"You were right," Leon reported, "Tone disbanded the team, he paid France a hundred and ten thousand and let him go. He found out about the deal with Mlakar and got on my case about it. I have a very bad feeling about this. I don't know what his intentions are."

"Don't worry son," Bata said, took another drag and flicked the butt of his cigarette into a nearby puddle. "Every disease has a cure. As long as there's people, there's money."

The village of Dane basked in the autumn sun, but a strong bora wind made everyone go inside, unless they had some urgent business to take care of out in the open. They found France at home.

"Oh, gentlemen!" he was happy to see them. "What an honour, and how quickly you've come! Come in, you too, Mr. Živković, come in. Our house may be humble, but it's warm."

They sat on sturdy wooden chairs.

"Why the sour expression on your face, professor? What ails you? Has the wind got to you?" Bata started.

Benko looked at him with a sad look.

"You're joking, Mr. Živković, you're joking, but indeed, I'm sad, even more, disappointed. I expected to become a part of a great story, but this is obviously not going to happen. Anton decided to market the paintings and everything else himself, but if he plans to continue in his apparent greedy fashion, I expect he won't do well," France said somewhat resigned.

"But why do you worry about that, professor?" Bata asked frankly.

"I think it's a shame, I have really good connections which could help us sell, but now this will amount to nothing," France explained.

"Besides," he added, "I could have made a nice profit myself."

"Come on, it's not the end of the world, professor. Go, Leon, go to the car and fetch that folder I've brought," Bata suggested.

"What for?" Leon wanted to know.

"You'll see. Don't ask!"

Leon brought the thick folder and laid it on the table. Without saying a word, Bata undid the straps and started taking out smaller folders.

"What do you make of this, professor?"

He began unwrapping the packages, revealing oils on canvas and cardboard, signed Matisse, Modigliani, Cezanne, Picasso, Klee, Kokoschka, there were drawings by Rodin...

Leon had to grab hold of his chair to take in the latest surprise.

"Would you be able to sell these in London, professor?" Bata enquired.

France instantly turned professional, he asked Leon to bring over the cardboard box taped with a green strip, opened it and took out a few bottles. He picked out Cezanne's painting of Sainte-Victoire Mountain, laid it on the table and began the procedures which Leon knew in detail by then. Once he was finished, he took off his glasses and looked over the other paintings.

"Well, professor, what do you think?" Bata asked.

"A beautiful Cezanne, hardly any damage," France said, his face lighting up. "So...?"

"Yes," Bata nodded, "would you sell these things over in that London of yours?"

"Benko beamed for a moment, but then stopped himself.

"Mr. Bata, what you have here is a wealth worth millions; at first glance I'd say six or seven million pounds. But how can I be sure that you'll accept the prices I'm offered? Did you feel six hundred thousand was enough for the Pfeininger sketch book, that's what I told Leon? I don't want to experience another disappointment, like I did with Anton."

"Let's not talk about Tone, this is our thing," Bata continued cheerfully. "No offence, professor, Leon, but wouldn't it be better if we went to a good inn or something, to discuss this properly, like men?"

Leon was again in shock. Yesterday the catastrophe with Tone, today the immense surprise with Bata. Calm down, nerves. You'll need to become nerves of steel in this business, with these people.

"I don't know this part of my homeland very well, so I'd prefer to go to Snežnik castle, if that's alright with you," he said.

"Fine," Benko said, "they cater wonderfully to us vegetarians there, as well."

They got into the quatrelle and drove off.

Snežnik castle appeared magnificent in the autumn sunlight. They ascended the stairs and looked around the restaurant, fitted out with old furniture. A waiter in old fashioned attire appeared and led them to one of the solid wooden tables. They came early, there were no other guests there yet. The room had a warm and calming vibe to it. Bata and Leon at once ordered a Viljamovka brandy each, while France opted for elderflower cordial, a homemade house drink. They looked at the finely decorated menu and naturally picked a vegetable plate for France and a roast leg of veal for Bata and Leon.

"You really never eat anything proper, professor?" Bata grinned. "Are you on diet all the time or is it because you owe it to some special divinity?"

It seemed like Benko couldn't wait for a chance to start explaining his life principles to Bata. Leon was already familiar with all of this, as during their time in the lab, France often offered a thought or two on why this was important in their line of work. He was quite interested to see how Bata would take to all of this. France was all fired up and hardly stopped for long enough to get a bite into his mouth. He spoke of the occultism, of his realisations and of his involvement in various organisations supporting his world view. Bata listened to him, naturally, but his thoughts were elsewhere.

When they were done with dessert, France mysteriously leaned forward and said:

"Strictly between us: I'm a member of a Masonic lodge and I hold a very high rank in the occult section. I was wondering, considering our good collaboration, to recommend that you get accepted. I can recommend you when I go to Paris, and provided everyone who needs to confirm this agrees, you could drive to Vienna to get initiated."

He looked victoriously at each of them respectively, as if to say, look, there's more I can do for you than inspect paintings, because I care for you as men.

"Unbelievable," Bata was first to come to, "I heard about the Freemasons many times in the past, I also heard about all the people from our country who were members, but to think that I..."

He shook his head doubtfully and went on:

"What would I have to do? What would change for me? What would I gain from it all?"

"I'm sure you're familiar with the basic principles and you already follow them without even knowing it: knowledge, beauty, power. You'd keep on living the way you are now. But the brotherhood would take care of you. Everything goes on almost invisibly, there's no commotion on the outside, but all of a sudden you'd be the one who got the job among equal offers, you'd never again have to deal with con artists, you could occasionally join a meeting of some wonderful people..." France explained quite convincingly, only minimally reinforcing his words by leaning his hands slightly against the table. He conjured up an impression of a small conspiracy, despite the fact that there was no one else present in the dining room.

"Ha!" Bata winced. "I, a Freemason? Can you imagine that, Leon?"

Leon was embarrassed. Although France did drop a hint here and there while they were working together, Leon never reacted to it, sometimes he even deliberately pretended not to hear what he had said.

He smiled.

"Well, if you think so," he began, adding after a short reflection, "I'm going to read a book or two about it first."

"You're right," Bata agreed, rearranging the cutlery on the table in front of him. "Let's first discuss what we came here for. So, professor, you think you could sell my stuff over in London."

"Without a doubt," France confirmed once more. "If your head isn't up in the clouds, as is the case with our Mr. Anton, and you could accept six or seven million pounds, I can confirm this right now: yes, I could sell it."

Everyone went silent, they just kept looking at each other. France was again the first to speak, asking calmly:

"And I want to make it clear from the start: what would be my share?"

Bata promptly answered:

"We would divide the profit three ways: to you, Leon and me. That goes without saying!"

France practically swelled in his chair and smiled broadly.

"That's truly very gentlemanly of you, Mr. Živković, it goes way beyond normal intermediary commission. I'll be glad to get on it. What do you think about it, Leon?"

Leon was stuck in his mind, trying to scramble from under the heap of money which appeared unexpectedly on the horizon and was now really about to come crushing down on him. All he could say was:

"Yes, of course, that would be fine."

Bata rushed on.

"So, I'm going to leave the paintings with you. If there's any problem, Leon will help you transfer them to London. And, of course, feel free to sell my Pfeininger sketch book, the price we agreed to is fine. So, do we have a deal? Let's see the hands!"

They put their right hands on the table, as if they were setting on to victory. France, whose hand was on the very bottom, pulled it out and asked in astonishment:

"This is it? We gave our word and this is it?"

"Naturally, professor, we are all honest people at this table, covert Freemasons, if you will, and by all means gentlemen," Bata laughed. "Since you're not drinking, Professor France, I'll finish up by having a Viljamovka brandy on your behalf."

Then he got up, went to settle the bill and they drove off into the night. Benko got out in Dane, while Bata and Leon went on to Ljubljana. Bata soon drifted off and Leon struggled to stay awake. At one point he was brought to full attention by blinking lights and a honking horn of a trailer truck, and he hardly avoided it. Leon stopped at a gas station. He got out of the car, lit a cigarette and walked around in the cold air.

"It takes so little, and everything's gone," he shuddered.

He entered the gas station and took two cups of coffee from the machine. Bata was sound asleep, so Leon drank both of them.

When he arrived to the Ilirija Hotel, he woke Bata up. He got out of the car, all groggy. Leon lamented that all the events and road trips lately had drained all of his energy, besides, he'd been having more problems lately at home, so he would like to sleep in the morning instead of taking Bata to the airport. Bata ensured him that it wasn't a problem and he would take a taxi.

They embraced.

"See," Bata smiled tiredly, "the grey-haired men will bring us money now, since Tone didn't want to."

At home, the shepherd dog greeted him happily. Leon filled her bowl with dog food, went to the bedroom and closed the door behind him. Kristina wasn't there.

"Oh," he said almost out loud, "I'm so fed up with her games. She'll really have to make up her mind now. Money won't be an issue any longer."

He thought about the agreement they had made at Snežnik castle but was too tired to play all of it over in his head again.

And what do you plan to do with this money?

On Monday evening, Kristina was getting ready to leave for another recording session. Leon lost it and started yelling that he'd had enough. He was about to go on the road in the middle of the night and the money he was going to bring back should last any normal woman almost a lifetime, and even Kristina should be able to survive at least a few years on it. This prompted Kristina to go off, as well, so I'm not normal, she screamed, and what about you, you've been bringing in nothing but small change for the entire time since we were together, we're constantly waiting for some big money, but it's always just empty words, the big money never comes, she has to beg and humiliate herself in front of Andraž... The bitch retreated to one of the corners, whining in fear. They heard someone banging on the ceiling from above, the chandelier swayed.

No one screams at me in my own apartment... I'll scream when I feel like it and where I feel like it.

There was another bang on the ceiling.

Kristina went to the bathroom, slamming the door behind her. She emerged after a while, looking captivating, she ran across the room to the front door and left without saying another word. Leon poured some more whiskey in his glass, threw in some ice and laid back in the armchair. In his mind, he went over all the moments that made him suspicious, the hints and the actions, and the conversation when she first started seriously talking about the wealthy Andraž, and all the caresses which seemed to point to a positive outcome, and then more fights, ups and downs, doubts and hopes...

He was about to receive some really big money from Billinger, and that moment would provide an opportunity for him and Kristina to put their cards on the table. He would have a really strong hand now. The time they'd spent together was filled with every sort of thing, but mostly wild sex. Nevertheless, that was not all there was to it. A decent relationship between a man and a woman was much more than just that... She would finally have to decide what it was that she wanted, and she would have to start acting accordingly. No buts about it.

He didn't go to bed. He set the alarm clock right there, beside the armchair. He was going to leave in the middle of the night in order to arrive to Munich early in the morning. He felt pleasant excitement at the thought of meeting Billinger again. Would she really take some time to have a drink with him? He put a clean shirt, a tux, three bow ties in different colours and black crocodile skin shoes in his suitcase. This time around, she would meet *Herr* Leon in his best version.

The drive to Munich went off without a hitch.

He parked in his usual parking spot close in the vicinity of the auction house. He took his suitcase to a nearby restaurant where he changed his clothes. He tied the black bowtie around his neck and put the other two in his pocket. Once he got a look at her, he might change it depending on the colour of her outfit. His mind was filled with rollicking thoughts. He's going to invite her for some champagne, that's for sure. You choose the place, I'll pick up the tab...

He finished his coffee and walked to the already familiar gate of the Grabner Auction House. He pressed the doorbell without hesitation. Nothing happened. He rang the bell a few more times, and his defiant effort was finally met with a cranky man's voice. There are no office hours today, the voice crackled dryly over the wiring. I understand, but I have a meeting with Madam Director Billinger, Leon explained resolutely. That can't be, she's in a meeting with her shareholders at the moment. Leon felt breathless. Before he could say anything else, he heard a scratch next to the doorbell. He pressed it once more. Will you tell her, he began, that it's Mr. Leon, I've been driving from Ljubljana for six hours. She told me to come, he explained rashly. Alright, wait a moment. Fifteen minutes must have passed. The door opened and Leon was met by the short black man who handed him the money the other time.

"Please, follow me," he said formally and led the way, waddling up the stairs. He showed him to a small room next to the reception desk.

"Madam Director Billinger apologizes. She didn't think you'd come this early. Your money is ready. Would you care to count it?"

He took ten one hundred thousand packets from the safe, tore one open, took out thirty banknotes and pushed the rest toward Leon.

"There," he said, "take it, please."

Leon put the stacks silently in his suitcase. The black bowtie was the right choice for this coxcomb, he thought to himself. The man offered him a document to sign, stating that he had received the money, adding dryly:

"Madam Director Billinger kindly invites you to come back at five o'clock, if you're still in town."

He gave him a searching look.

Leon thanked him, ignored the invitation, got up and left. Even going down the stairs he felt the added weight in his suitcase.

"Imagine what will happen when France calls us over to London," he chuckled to himself and then thought with a sting of regret, "beautiful Mrs. Billinger, till next time then. I suppose we'll collaborate again. There's no way I'm waiting till five."

He didn't change back. He got in his car as he was, in his tux, and drove toward Ljubljana. The thought of spilling the money on Tone's table spurred him on. Minus one hundred and twenty thousand, of course, which he had moved to his pocket. He earned it, after all. The possibility of having his suitcase searched at the border never even crossed his mind. And even if that happened, he had the receipt...

When he went through the Ljubelj border crossing, he was met by customs officer Martin on the Slovenian side. There was no way he could forget his face after the stunt they pulled off with Ljuba. What a lucky coincidence!

"Look at you, all fine and in black in this old banger, where did you go?" he wanted to know.

"Oh, it was nothing," Leon waved his hand, "I went to a funeral."

"Oh dear," Martin reacted and signalled him to drive on.

Leon spent the entire drive immersed in his thoughts and he finally decided to stop at his parents' house. They should see the heap of money, they should realise that not all was lost, they should see that their son was in the right business. He saw his father's car parked in front of the house, which meant that he was home, and this cheered Leon up in particular. His mother was doing the dishes as they were just done with dinner, and she asked if he wanted some barley stew.

"I'd love some," Leon exclaimed and placed his suitcase next to the table.

"How have things been going lately?" his father asked. "Did Tone come to his senses? Did you reach a deal with Benko?"

Leon adored his mother's stew and quickly gobbled up half of what she had put on his plate, then he paused.

"It seems that Tone doesn't care about anything we have agreed to, or rather wants to make every decision by himself, and whatever happens, happens. Bata and I think this is madness. But Bata luckily acquired more paintings which France will sell for us in London. Tone can take his silliness and shove it, Bata and I will get our money regardless," Leon explained, laughing.

"I hope you do," his mother spoke from the kitchen. "Considering everything you've been doing it's about time you make some money."

Leon cleaned the plate.

"About the money," he said, "you might be interested to see this."

He placed the suitcase on the table, opened it and started taking parcels of thousand Deutschmark banknotes from under his clothes. His mother let out a muffled cry, his father whistled.

"That's almost a million," Leon said proudly, grinning like the Cheshire cat, "this is from my first auction. I get twenty percent."

He took one parcel from the heap and counted twenty additional thousand from another. He placed the rest of the money back in his suitcase. His mother and father looked at each other, then at Leon and then at the money.

"I'll be damned," his father came to. "That's something. It's yours? And it's all perfectly legal? We're not going to start seeing dodgy gun-carrying characters sneaking around our house?"

Leon shook his head.

"Everything's fine, father. Here's the receipt confirming the paintings were sold at the auction. If you took out that cognac then you're keeping in the cabinet that would really loosen my tongue right now."

They sat in the armchairs.

Leon began with the story of Good Person and the crazy exchange of paintings in Belgrade, going on to describe how France checked them and wrote the expert opinions, how Tone chose which paintings were to go for auction and how Leon transferred them across the border with the help of his friend. He also let them in on Tone's peculiar behaviour, especially his care for the investors and his careless attitude to everyone else, and then he frankly admitted that he lied to Tone about the amount they had made at the auction and took a hundred and twenty thousand for himself, as he wasn't sure what idea Tone would come up with when it came to dividing the profit. His mother and father listened astonished to his recount of the story.

"And what do you plan to do with this money?" his father asked.

"You could buy an apartment," his mother jumped in without hesitation, but his father looked at her, signalling her to stop.

"That's not what I have in mind right now," his father explained. "That's a lot of money. You can't," he checked his watch, "drive around with it just like that. Leave it here, I'll put it in the safe, come back for it tomorrow and deliver it to Tone. Probably not to the store, ask him what he'd like."

Leon thought about this and nodded. He put twenty thousand in his pocket and left the rest on the table.

"You're right, father," he said. "I'll leave my hundred thousand with you, as well. Perhaps you can advise me what to do with it."

"That's never happened before," his father laughed. "Thank you for your confidence."

They continued to sip the cognac and Leon told his parents all about the deals they had made with France. Heavy millions were in the air. We won. It was close to midnight when Leon finally drove off.

When he got home, he was once more greeted only by Šeri. He took a shower and climbed into bed. He didn't even want to think about the fact that the space next to him was again empty. It was close to morning when he heard Kristina open the bedroom door. He pretended to be asleep. He felt way too tired to embark on what would probably turn out a difficult conversation. When he woke up late in the morning, he made quite a noise while getting up, but this time it was Kristina who pretended to sleep. He was making coffee when the telephone rang. It was France, letting him know that he had made it safely to Vienna, "with all our stuff," and that he was heading off to London.

"Excellent," Leon said, "let me know when you get there."

Then he gave Tone a call, informing him that he had returned from Munich during the night. Tone instructed him to come over to his house in the afternoon.

"How much should I keep for myself?" Leon asked.

"I'll tell you later; you know, the investors come first," Tone once again turned him down coldly.

"I'm nothing but thin air," Leon said and hung up.

Leon arranged with his father to get the money ready, as he would come over soon after lunch. His father was home, preparing to leave on a business trip, going over an investment study for a renovation of an industrial complex.

"Keep the one hundred thousand with you, like we said," Leon chuckled, "I don't own a safe."

The conversation Leon and Tone had in his luxurious apartment in the afternoon was not at all pleasant. Tone took the money and gave Leon five thousand. Leon practically leaped in the air.

"This is less than one percent of everything we made, far from the quarter we agreed to back in Belgrade," he said furiously.

"You haven't been listening," Tone interrupted him calmly. "We said we would divide the money after expenses. This here is for your expenses. Don't tell me it's too little! I've been saying the whole time that the investors have to come first, this is serious business, plus I paid off France out of my own pocket."

"Yes, but you weren't willing to earn ten million on Picasso alone, which France had sold for you. Otherwise everyone would be happy right now," the words flew spontaneously from his mouth.

"Not everyone, I wouldn't be happy," Tone shook his head. "The Picasso is worth twenty-four million, twelve million is peanuts for a painting like this. Don't lecture me on things you know nothing about."

"While we're on the subject," Leon asked irately, "when do you expect Bata and I will see any money at all?"

"When I personally manage to sell something. You are of no use to me," Tone said and started to put the money away into a box he had prepared earlier on the table.

"You better sell something soon then. Neither my quatrelle nor I can live on thin air. It's about time I made something, too. You wouldn't be in this business if it weren't for me, remember? I've told you this once before. And give my regards to your investors. You're obviously only about the money, and nothing else."

He got up and headed for the door.

"Such are the times we live in," Tone said and locked the door behind him.

Leon headed home to tell Kristina what happened in Munich. He entered and as usual, the bitch ran to meet him. Kristina was at the table, rummaging through her make-up case.

"Why are you looking at me like that?" she asked.

"I'm waiting for you to have a minute; I wanted to tell you how everything went in Germany," Leon boasted, carelessly throwing fifteen thousand on the table.

Kristina looked at the money, her hand reached out for it, but stopped mid-way and returned to the case. She stared at him with great seriousness.

"Before you tell me anything," she said, "there's something I need to tell you. I think it's about time. I've had enough of this strange way of living. I love you, Leon, you know that I do, and I don't want us to fight. In the time we spent together -" oh my, past tense, Leon thought in astonishment - "we had some very good times, we supported each other, we were both busy doing our own things. You were away an awful lot, big money was around the corner every step of the way, but it sadly just never arrived. I was getting really tired by all of that. I needed to find a different solution. But, as we both know, I'm much older than you, I want a high standard, I want the best life. I can't afford to wait any more, unlike," she gasped a little, "unlike you."

Leon looked at her, amazed; he felt his stomach churn.

"We haven't discussed this. Things were getting along somehow and we never stopped to realise where we are and what is it that we really want. Let's try to have an earnest conversation, let's talk right now," she said, "it's what we both deserve."

She paused and looked away. Leon didn't say anything, either. Suddenly he found himself floating in uncertain uneasiness once again. What was this all of a sudden?

"Fine," went through his head, "I was madly in love with her, I left everything and went with her, I gave her absolutely everything I had made during our time together, I embarked on all sorts of businesses like a madman, just to please her, I let so many of my relationships go sour, and now she wants to have an earnest conversation... I might just lose my sanity."

He felt like his blood was boiling right into his head, from every little part of his body. He went off the rails in a second. He couldn't even think anymore.

"Who is it?" he burst out violently.

"What - who is it?" Kristina asked, blushing.

Leon struck both of his hands, rolled in fists, against the table.

"Stop jabbering," he started to pull faces, "I love you, let's talk, we deserve this... bollocks. Is it Andraž, or perhaps someone new, even richer, who won't put up with your double-faced act, being together a little, and then not, who won't live in a tolerant threesome?" he hollered. He was spewing up anger and resentment.

Kristina looked at him, not saying anything.

"I really don't want to talk to you like this," she said after a long silence.

"And you have to tell me this now, unexpected and sleek, when I finally got my hands on really big money, at the auction in Germany, which I spent six months working for..." Leon kept screaming.

"Stop," Kristina said, raising her hand, "I'm no longer interested, whether it's a million, ten or one hundred million... I'm not interested anymore. I really can't do this any longer. We're not going to live together anymore."

She seemed relieved. She said it.

Leon swallowed hard, took deep breaths and tried to calm himself down.

"So, it's Andraž. He finally got you in his bed, or should I say his wallet," he added cynically.

"Leon, don't make a fool of yourself, take this like a man. It would be the proper thing to do."

"You want to talk to me about what's proper? Oh please," Leon frowned offendedly. "So when was it the first time he...?"

Kristina looked him straight in the eye - he thought he could see tears welling up in hers - then she said, stricken: "Leon, Leon, I met Andraž when you were not even around yet. We made plans together, where we were going to live, and how, but then you came along, like a shooting star, you swept me completely off my feet, I couldn't see anyone but you, just you, only you... I was crazy. But Andraž never backed down, he always remained somewhere close, he helped me out, he offered a shoulder when I needed one. While you were running around chasing your deals, a moment came when I realised that this was not going to work. You're young, I'll be old soon... and Andraž is getting a divorce, he and his wife agreed- So, now you know."

Leon shuddered.

"Now, now, now... when we're crossing the finishing line," he almost wept.

"You're crossing the finishing line, Leon, and I'm crossing the finishing line," Kristina shook her head. "It's just not the same line."

I have to do everything myself

Bata was at home, sitting in his favourite armchair in the salon. He tried to come up with possible directions to steer the great story to, which had obviously entered the grand and final phase. The grey-haired professor in London was about to secure the biggest money he'd ever seen in his life. Everything will change. He will finish building his house, furnish it with exquisite things, he will buy a pub for his wife to run, so she will no longer have to toil away in that accounting job of hers, he will buy a rock house somewhere in Dalmatia, where he will be able to spend his old age shamelessly keeping his bones warm in the sun, he will send Tamara away to school, somewhere in Europe...

Nine months have passed since he discovered the catalogue to the Šlomovič exhibit, and just as much from the moment a treasure in the form of old art materials landed in his lap at Pera the Horse's house. Ever since then, the brilliant Rista has been following his instructions, painting, painting... It is time to start thinking about how this is all going to end. It is the last moment to steer the plan soberly toward a good outcome. When millions come thundering over from London, something which France will take care of, he will give Rista a lot of money and take everything he has amassed in his studio in the meantime. For the time being, Rista is all fired up and in top form, making miracles happen with his unbelievable energy and imagination, his paintings are often better than the originals. But... sooner or later this will come to a halt and his appetite is bound to increase once he gets a taste of the big money. Greed knows no bounds. Every art dealer is now aware of the fact that the Šlomovič collection appeared somewhere in Vojvodina, and they are fishing for information, looking, snooping, and sooner or later Rista might hand over one of the paintings to someone who won't know how to market it, and then suddenly a five thousand Deutschmark Cezanne will appear in Amsterdam or Frankfurt, everyone will prick up their ears, this will lead to some serious search and investigation, the dominos will start to fall... He needs to act fast, and make as much money as possible before this happens, and when Leon, and most of all Tone who invested a lot of money in this, find out what this was all about... Well, actually, he only brought the paintings over, all in good faith, naturally, he never said anything, the prices were set according to the expert opinion of a renowned expert, after all it was the two of them who procured them, they dragged the professor all the way from Australia, he, Bata is not at fault... We're going to think this through later. My first concern at the moment is to get the money from London... But something is off, it's been a while since there was any news from over there..."

He couldn't stay home any longer. He took a taxi to his favourite spot, a table at the Majestic Hotel. It was cold outside, so he ventured in and looked around the room. There were mostly retired people sitting at the tables and drinking coffee, reminiscing and saving the world, which had obviously been heading straight to hell from the moment they let go of the reins.

"Hey, Bata, come sit over here," Pedja the Book called him from a table next to the display case with cakes. He waved to point to a chair next to him. A very refined looking, middle aged man was sitting next to him, wearing a grey suit and a necktie, he was smiling cordially.

Bata approached them.

"Look, Bata, this is a friend of mine from school, Mr. Kostić, he used to work as our cultural attaché in Australia for five years, now he's packing his bags to go back. We were discussing books, and you can tell him something about paintings," Pedja hastened.

"Well, I guess I can join you for a little bit, I have a meeting..." Bata spoke, as he never liked to give the impression that he didn't know what to do with himself.

Bata and Kostić shook hands, and while Bata was arranging his chair, he nodded towards the waiter "espresso, double, no sugar."

The three men started chatting informally about how the situation in the country had changed in the last years, that Australia was not as far as it once used to be, that more and more migrants were returning back home...

"Ha," Bata remembered, "colleague Kostić, did you happen to come across professor France Benko during your time as a cultural attaché, he used to work for the Australian government."

"Oh, sure, sure, that was a very well-known story, of course I've heard of him," Kostić nodded, smiled and lowered his head to his chest a couple of times, "the gentleman in question supposedly vanished into thin air, and at least as far as Australia is concerned, this scandalous affair is now closed."

Bata almost choked. He cleared his throat and forced a smile.

"Thank goodness other countries have scandals, as well; it would be a shame if we were the only ones who had to deal with such things. I'm curious, what was that all about?"

"The man was just greedy, that's all. He started out as a restoration specialist in one of the museums, he was good at his job, there's no doubt about that, he used to work in prominent cathedrals, and that was his springboard, he was invited to join the government institutions. He acquired a licence to produce expert opinions on the authenticity of art works for the government. Australia is a young country in this respect and many galleries are doing their best to acquire famous works of art in order to attract more visitors. Well, it turned out the man even painted under assumed names himself and gave the government seal of approval to several works which were later recognized as forgeries. There was a tremendous circus. I know everyone then tried their best to keep the scandal under wraps, even museums and galleries, in order to avoid getting a bad reputation. As far as Benko, the last I heard he left the country voluntarily, as he could even face deportation, being an immigrant," Kostić explained.

"Funny thing," Bata said, giving the impression of polite interest in the story.

He finished his coffee, excused himself, saying that he never even intended to sit at the coffee house, he was only looking for someone, he said good-bye and left.

When he got back to the street, he hailed a taxi and quickly returned to his house.

"Oh, you grey-haired little professor, you, you Free mason, *expert*... I've met many a crook in my life, but I've never been duped like this before," he thought. "What a story!"

He swiftly poured a glass of homemade brandy and made him himself another coffee. He was alone in the house and had the peace and quiet to think about what he was to do with the news which turned all of his plans upside down. Or did it?

He called Leon in Ljubljana. The phone just kept ringing and ringing, but nobody answered.

Next he phoned Tone. This time he was in luck.

"Tone, my friend, how have you been? Have you sold anything yet?" Bata began. "This is Belgrade calling."

"I can hear, I can hear," Tone replied. "Well, I've been trying, I've been trying. I'm moving along slowly, but there's still no result."

"I thought you had a better plan in your mind, since you didn't want the professor to help you out with his millions," Bata continued. He was pretty certain that Tone might already know something of France's history, if he had been offering paintings with his expertise over Europe. But Tone just continued calmly.

"I have to do everything myself, as usual," he went on. "The investors were getting on my case, so I've pawned most of the paintings in banks over here, just to be able to pay them out. The bankers play hard, but they are nevertheless more reasonable than the greedy private collectors. That's just how it is, you know, you always end up alone in hard times, and as soon as there's profit there's also company."

"Well, my dear Tone, why don't you just pull the plug, let France sell the Picasso for you," Bata hastened, "you can make up for any lost profit with the other paintings."

"Don't you try to persuade me as well, Bata; there's no way I can let good stuff go at half the price, I can't ruin my name like this. And as far as France is concerned," he continued after a short pause, "I haven't heard from him in quite a while. I don't know where he is. But never mind, we're done dealing with him, as you know."

"Well, fine then, Tone, my friend, you just keep on working, save yourself, save us all," Bata said good-bye.

Well, Tone obviously didn't know anything about France.

He called Leon again. Again, nothing.

Cursing, he remembered Leon's parents. He embarked on a lengthy persuasive mission over the phone with the employees at the post office, and after much toil and trouble, he got his hands on the Sattler's phone number in Tacen. Nobody was answering the phone there, either. Bata gritted his teeth. He thought feverishly about his next step, but he couldn't come up with anything even remotely sensible.

"Just sit and wait, that's the gist of our business," he remembered the sentence he had tried to install into Leon's head so many times before.

He really set himself to tackle the bottle of homemade brandy.

In the meantime, he kept calling Leon and his parents respectively. Finally, Kristina answered the phone.

"Hello, beautiful lady, could you get your beau on the phone, I need to talk to him urgently," he said merrily, convinced that he was halfway through solving the problem.

"He's not here, Bata, he's not here," Kristina started to speak.

"Oh, the miserable man, leaving such unprotected treasure at home alone. Whatever is he thinking? He shouldn't be doing this," Bata said in mock agitation, then added coldly, "will you please tell him to call me. It's urgent."

"You know, Bata, Leon and I..." Kristina began, but then suddenly felt like it wouldn't be right for her to talk about this, so she stopped herself, "yes, of course, I'll tell him, as soon as I see him. I have to hang up now; I need to take the dog out for a walk..."

"My, my, where has this world got to," Bata lamented, "beautiful women are taking out the dogs, and the heroes are nowhere to be found. It's just plain wrong."

He laughed and hung up.

In the evening, he called Leon's parents once more.

"Oh, Mr. Bata," Leon's mother was pleased to hear his voice. "How are you? You know, I've been honoured by the presence of my dear son, he's come over to dinner."

"Sons never forget that their mothers make the best food," Bata hurried cordially, adding, "could you get him on the phone for me then, please, before he rolls on the sofa with a full stomach and dozes off."

"Listen, my son," Bata began as soon as Leon greeted him, "I'm a bit nervous. Have you heard from the professor at all? Has he finally left a message? I have a bad feeling about this. It's been dragging on for too long. Could you go over to Dane and check if his wife's still there? Perhaps she knows something?"

Leon felt an unfamiliar fear in Bata's voice. This wasn't the Bata he knew.

"What is it? Is something wrong?" he asked with much surprise.

"I don't think so, or should I say, I hope not," Bata replied with uncertainty, "go on, drive over there, and let me know. On a second thought, you might come over to Belgrade again, just to talk about things, and I could show you what my house looks like now."

Leon was confused by Bata's tone of voice.

"What is it Bata? Tell me. What's wrong?" he pressed him, concerned.

"Well, I'm not sure. It might be nothing. My mind might just be haunted by these strange fears. Just check on the professor, and get back to me," Bata concluded.

That was strange, Leon thought, what could he be worried about? It was true that France hadn't contacted them in a while, but so what, this kind of business took time. Bata was always the first to point this out. His mother saw the strange look on her sons face and asked:

"What is it? Is something wrong?"

Leon winced, trying hard to smile: "No, no, nothing out of the ordinary. He wants me to come over to Belgrade for a bit, to see his new house. It's almost finished now."

He thought it was for the best that he and Bata kept their conversation short. He should urgently explain the situation with Kristina to him, but even his parents weren't aware of it yet. Actually, no one was aware of it yet. After Kristina had so nonchalantly dumped him, or should he say, informed him that they were to be no longer living together; they sort of agreed to stay roommates for a while; Leon had nowhere to go and going back to his parents' house was the last thing he wanted. Let's give it some more time, perhaps we might... He moved to the couch in her living room, they ran into each other now and then, living their lives peacefully, independent of each other... Nothing changed, actually, except for the sex, there was no more of that. Leon was gripped by wild desire from time to time, but Kristina showed absolutely no sign, not even the slightest hint of interest for what she used to be so unbelievably attracted to. Obviously she was helping herself elsewhere...

Bright and early the next day Leon drove to Dane. There was no answer when he rang the bell at the front door of the beautiful Karst house. He went through the yard, noticed that the door of the woodshed had been bolted, as well, the well covered, there were no tools lying around. He walked over to the back of the house. Everything seemed neatly prepared for winter. The shutters on the windows were closed. It took some dexterity to lift and pry open the ones on the window to the main room; he peered inside, but as far as he could see the place had been packed up for a long time to come. He walked to the neighbours, asking if they had any information of Benkos' whereabouts, but nobody knew anything, it had been a while since they saw anyone hanging around the house...

He drove to the Tabernakelj with a strange premonition and looked for Tone.

"What is this, you're getting on my case now, too?" Tone greeted him reluctantly.

"What case, what for? Who's been getting on your case?"

"Well, Bata, he's been calling and asking when I'm going to sell something. And he asked me about France. I don't care about France, we're done with him. If we happen to need his services again, I'll contact him," Tone went on.

"Where will you contact him? Do you have an address?" Leon asked carelessly.

"I don't," Tone shook his head. "If nothing else works, I'll look for him in Dane. I guess someone there should know something."

"Have you sold anything yet?" Leon asked, changing the subject to make it clear to Tone why he came by again.

"I haven't, I haven't. If I did, I'd let you know, you know that."

"I sure hope so," Leon nodded. "Why don't you want to get France to do it?"

"Will you give it a rest with France! Has he been trying to turn you against me or what? I'm going to sell by myself, the way I know how and the way I feel it should be done. I put in the money and it's my decision to make. How many times do I have to tell you this?" Tone was becoming increasingly irritated.

"Sure, sure, I should mind my own business. I intend to, I have to make a living somehow, don't I? It'll clearly be a long time till I see any money from you," Leon said, not trying to conceal his bad temper, and left.

So, Leon thought to himself, Tone has no news about France. So what's eating Bata?

In the end, I was duped by that deceitful professor of yours

He made the rash decision to inquire about flights for Belgrade at Kompas shop on Titova Street, and he bought a ticket for that very same evening.

"Here I come," he phoned Bata.

"Here I come to the airport to pick you up," Bata confirmed in delight. He and Beli waited for him at Surčin.

"Welcome, young man," Beli greeted him cheerfully. "Did you come to give me another piece of the profit from the new business, by any chance?" He laughed at the memory of their last meeting, the Matisse transaction.

Leon managed a sour frown. The thought of that strange deal with Mlakar still weighed heavily on him.

"It would only be fitting for you to drive the boy free of charge wherever he wants to go" Bata joined in the laughter, gave Leon a hug and kissed him three times. "But first, we are going straight to my Šumatovačka."

In the car Leon could sense there was something troubling Bata, something he would never share with Beli there. He always tried to solve problems one on one, with the person in question. Once they got to the house, they all received a loud greeting from Mira, who cooked a delicious paprikash for the guests. The fragrance filled every room. Bata immediately poured schnapps in shot glasses, they sat at the table and discussed everything under the sun. At one point he whispered to Leon that they would discuss serious business later, not in front of Mira.

"Well, Belče, my man," Bata said when they finished their meal, "I know you have to work. We've fed you; we've quenched your thirst, now you are ready to hit the renowned streets of Belgrade. They will never come to life without you." Beli got up.

"Thank you, good people, I'd starve if it weren't for you," he laughed, turning to Mira, "it was finger-licking good. If you ever have any leftovers, I'm here for you." At that moment, Bata turned to Mira, too.

"This was delicious, my wife. You deserve a break. Now is the time for you to go over to the neighbour and find out what's new."

"Bata, my love, I know full well you're about to discuss things that are not meant for me to hear," Mira said. "But I'm not going anywhere. Don't usher me out of my house, I waited for it for too long. I'll be far away in the kitchen, banging pots and pans, not paying attention to your conversation. Be careful, Leon, lest Bata gets you too drunk." She gathered the dishes and retreated.

"What is it, Bata, what's bothering you?" Leon asked right off the bat, as it was all he could do to keep his mouth shut throughout dinner.

"My son, this damned old piece of shit, this damned liar and crook, dirty bastard, I've never experienced anything like it. I can't believe it. It's a disaster! This is the end of our story," Bata blurted out immediately and started flailing about with his arms. Leon flinched at the sudden scene, almost startled; he couldn't put two and two together, he didn't know what this was, what it was about, he just observed with eyes wide open and looked at Bata in dismay.

"Bata, you miserable man, what on earth are you talking about, who is a liar, who is a crook? What happened?" Bata jumped in his armchair, hitting his knee against the coffee table, dangerously rocking the bottle of schnapps.

"This damn Benko of yours, whom you brought to my house!" he was practically spewing his words. "He was deported from Australia, and we took to his crap like bees to honey!"

"Hold on, hold on, what the heck are you talking about?" Leon almost stuttered, growing pale.

"I'm talking about the dirty yuppie, world champion in deception, the villainous blabbermouth, who played us like we were kids, the professorial scum, he stole our paintings and vanished," Bata bellowed, while Leon kept leaning further in, making sure he heard right, even though Bata practically screamed every single word.

"What the...?" he was lost for words, yet he managed to keep his focus. "What are you talking about, who said what to you, what proof do you have of all this?"

Bata was literally trembling in evident fury.

"Well, listen, my son, and be amazed!"

Bata took a long gulp right out of the bottle and slowly related everything he learned the day before at a chance coffee meeting in Majestic hotel. He tried speaking calmly, there were moments when he seemed on the brink of exploding, but he managed to retract and calm down. Leon listened, baffled, and kept sinking deeper and deeper into his armchair. He felt like a chance guest in a perfect piece of theatre of the absurd. Surely, this couldn't be.

"Hold on," he slowly gathered his thoughts and came to, "France told us that he had sent all of his documents, all his business stuff from Australia in a container, like normal, that they were held temporarily by our police, because he was a dissident, because he had fled right after the war..."

"Oh, come on, give me a break with your Slovenian jokes about dissidents who fled here right after the war because of their fight for democracy! It's unbelievable how you people buy into these sort of fairy tales, falling for everyone who wants to be a hero in hindsight. This France of yours just told you what you all wanted to hear, this is clear as day! And now he's going to take us for all we've got! He took the paintings and vanished!"

Leon cringed. He tried to contradict but was left out of breath.

"But he knew the business, he wrote expert opinions, it's not like I..."

Everything went black before his eyes. He felt like he was losing blood, from his legs somewhere, he felt completely weightless... His knees buckled and he fell to the floor, face forward. After a while he felt light pats on the left and right sides of his face, splashes of water, and as he opened his eyes he saw Bata, worried, and obviously posing some questions.

What has just happened, he thought.

"Wake up, my son, are you alright?" he then heard Bata's voice, and saw Mira appear in the door, scared, stuffing her hand in front of her mouth. "Wake up!"

Leon shook his head, got up on all fours and dragged himself back to his chair with difficulty.

"What happened?" he whispered.

"You must have fainted; I thought you had a stroke, but I guess it'll wait for a better opportunity," Bata said, dabbing his forehead with a handkerchief. "Here, have a glass of water, and then some more schnapps, that'll make you better."

"France, a con artist..." Leon started stammering. "I didn't..."

He once again ran out of words.

"Leave it, don't worry about that crook now! Tell me, are you ok, my son, come on, drink up, calm down," Bata rushed.

He was obviously much relieved to see Leon conscious again, with his eyes open. They sat in silence for some time. They needed to digest what had just happened. Leon kept shaking his head, flashing back in time in his mind: how they came upon France in the first place, how they welcomed him, how convincingly he spoke of the confiscated container, how well he got on with the work... did he really just arrange traps with prices for things he was supposedly willing to sell for us... or did he... maybe he's just going to keep the paintings safe for a while, until things blow over... is there any point in looking for him, in compromising him, well, and what's going to happen to the things I gave up for auction...

"What are you thinking about, my son?" Bata asked, concerned. "How are you feeling?"

Leon closed his eyes again. Oh, dear Bata! He's asking about my health when he should be livid over the fraud. Fraud? Is this even possible? Despite everything... it probably can't be true. It might have really happened in Australia. But now France made a fresh start, he was about to turn a new leaf in Europe. We were his excellent opportunity. Of course, it's terrible to fall, but what's important is to get back up! Why would France be an exception? Why would he rob us when he can make money with us? He might still call... How terrible... Bata is probably right: if we haven't heard from him in this long, he must be a thief! He played us and vanished.

"I'm fine, Bata, I'm fine. This thing with France, it was a big shock for me. For him to play us like this? I hope you believe me when I tell you that I had no idea about this," he said slowly.

"Of course I believe you, Leon, my son. There are so many things you know nothing about," Bata smiled, "even things that were right under your nose."

Leon lifted up his head and focused his gaze.

"What do I know nothing about? Are you going to tell me?"

"I am," Bata said. "I am, time has come. There is no point in keeping silent. Now that everything has come crashing down, it's only right that you should know this, too. Everything we have been doing with the Erich Šlomovič collection was a scam."

"I don't get it," Leon shook his head, again not able to understand. Another disastrous news after the story about France? "Erich Šlomovič is a scam. How exactly?"

"Šlomovič is not a scam. The story about his paintings is a lie," Bata quickly delivered.

"How?" Leon still couldn't comprehend. "Where did the paintings come from, if they weren't Šlomovič's?"

Bata leaned back, he seemed to be choosing the right words in order to tell it as straight and as simple and clear as possible.

"We made the story about Šlomovič's collection up and forged the paintings," he said. "Do you understand now?"

Leon laughed.

"My dear Bata, of course I understand. All the Modigliani's, and the Picasso's, and Rodin's, and everything else, they were all forged? What are you talking about? I was there, remember, when the Good man brought them down from his attic! The paintings were perfect, France even checked them, I saw it with my own eyes, with every chemical and light possible, he wrote expert opinions, every auction house accepted them without objections, Tone paid you a nice sum..." He just kept on laughing and staring at Bata in utter disbelief. What was he blabbering about?

"...and you are now talking about forgeries. You want me to believe that you forged the great masters, here, in the Balkans? And in such numbers? Come on. Stop kidding me. Even kids wouldn't buy this."

It was now Bata's turn to crack a smile.

"It's so nice to listen to you, my son," he said. "How beautifully naive you are. This was the magic of it, to involve you in the deal, young and enthusiastic as you are. You never question how it came that we expressed a desire for something and I delivered just the thing shortly after? Someone said Modigliani, and a Modigliani appeared, when there was interest in Renoir, we got it... Think Leon, my son!"

Leon was left speechless.

"But how did..." he uttered.

"Rista," Bata answered shortly. "Our Rista is a genius. You saw what he can do with silver. When a group of Gipsies found a stash of old painting supplies, in some cellar, not an attic, in some cellar in the middle of Belgrade, not in some remote village, and I came upon the Šlomovič catalogue at that pretty woman's place in Zagreb, and studied it, it was then that the whole narrative was born. I led and Rista painted. This is how it was. We produced beautiful, flawless forgeries! And on top of all, in the end, I was duped by that deceitful professor of yours."

"This isn't true," Leon whispered, "if I hadn't already, I should collapse now. Is this really possible?"

"It seems so," Bata said calmly.

Leon thought to himself that it should take him at least a week to process everything. Two completely crazy stories: France and forgeries. And himself, in the middle. He sat in his armchair, again he felt like parts of him were missing, only his brain firing off from multitude of new data, earth shattering data. Once again he closed his eyes and watched a movie detailing everything that had transpired since he chanced upon Bata last spring at the conservatory of Ilirija hotel, becoming his "apprentice," as Bata used to call him all the time, followed by the mysterious foundry, and the eccentric Rista's studio... Crazy!

"Hey," Bata snapped him out of it, "let's get back to life. Let's forget the paintings. How is your beautiful lady? I'm sure you promised her millions. What happens now?"

"Nothing," Leon was short.

"What do you mean - nothing?"

"She dumped me. She left with some rich old man," Leon explained bitterly. "She traded an old man in for me, we had a blast all the time we spent together and now she traded me in for another old man. I keep telling myself that this had to happen, I kind of sensed it would all the time, but I kept hoping that big money would somehow glue her to me for ever... Indeed, she's ten years my senior, but..."

He pondered whether he should say more but was abruptly stopped by Bata.

"Oh," he laughed merrily, as if he breathed a sigh of relief after so many terrible stories, "this is the first piece of food news I've had all day. Kristina was not a woman for you, my son, you know that, right? She must have given everyone she met a hard... ha-ha, time. She must have been one hell of a woman from the waist down, I like the kind myself, but only for a short time; what she wore on her neck was not worth much, though. But even women like her one day face the calendar and stare back in time. Then even they stop thinking of sex as their main priority."

He paused for a bit and then continued, in a gentle manner:

"You did manage to get some money off of those unfortunate paintings, I hope you still have it. Find yourself a nice young woman your own age and make some babies. Have a family. It's time!"

Then he leaped with joy.

"This calls for a serious celebration. Aha," he kept grinning, "we'll send that old man a thank you note and the best bottle of whiskey you can find. Chivas Regal would hardly cut it!"

Would you mind if I took down the painting so I can check the back?

Many prophets predicted the world would come to an end at the dawn of the year 2000. Leon and Bata, still friends and partners in small operations, Leon in the company of his wife and Bata with his new wife Svetlana, were off to Vienna to celebrate the New Year, at the invitation of Miško the Philatelist. In case everything bites the dust, including us, naturally, we shall bite in majestic style befitting people of significance. They arrived a day early, wandered around the city, stopping for a genuine Turkish coffee at Faruk the Bosnian's, among other places. He had run an antique shop and gallery in the very centre of Vienna for thirty years.

"Are there any decent offers in the city?" Bata asked, as per usual. Faruk lamented the present times and lauded the past.

"Oh," he remembered while pouring the second round of coffee, "you two are dealing in old paintings, aren't you? There is this one rich lady, a good customer of mine. She asked me the other day if I could help her sell a painting, supposedly a very expensive one. I don't know much about these things. She would like to renovate a castle house outside Salzburg and needs the money."

"Oops," Leon picked up, "that kind of thing costs quite a lot."

"Why don't we check it out?" Bata asked. "It won't cost us anything. We can send our ladies shopping in the meantime. I doubt they would mind."

The two women nodded in agreement and the men headed past St. Stephen's Church, towards the Opera House.

"This is no poor neighbourhood," Bata said as they entered a mighty old building right next to Sacher hotel and started climbing the stairs. Faruk rang the bell and recited into the intercom that he came with the two colleagues, as he had announced earlier.

Sometime later, a tall, slender, brown-haired lady in her fifties opened the door. Leon immediately noticed her necklace made in white gold, spreading itself out over the still interesting hills under the elegant neckline. A pretty tailored red dress hinted at a well-preserved body.

"Damn," Leon commented without thinking and Bata gave him an astonished look.

"Good day, gentlemen," the lady smiled at them and turned to Leon. "Iris Winkler, I guess you've remembered me. I recognised you right away, too, despite the fact that you are now dying your hair silver."

"What is she talking about?" Bata asked.

"Oh, Bata, my friend," Leon smiled. "We met this lady at a gambling house in Salzburg, when we took that silver pot to Frietzl in Frankfurt."

Bata bowed, grabbed the woman's hand and kissed her fingers.

"Milorad Živković, at your service," he said in hard Serbian.

"I don't understand," the lady smiled and Leon explained that this is a classical greeting performed by gentlemen from Belgrade.

"I would like to sell a painting, one that I know is very valuable. But my dear Mister Faruk can't advise me as to where I should turn. I suppose you will know what to do. Follow me, please."

She took them through a spacious salon, exquisitely furnished with antique pieces, and opened the door to a smaller room, most likely a study. Above a pretty Biedermeier table there was hanging... an image of a beautiful brunette from Rista's collection. A beautiful Modigliani.

Bata and Leon exchanged glances. Leon was the first to find his footing.

"Would you mind if I took down the painting so I can check the back?"

"Of course not," the lady agreed.

Everyone was solemnly silent. Faruk was delighted because he provided his client with two experts who knew their field. Leon took down the painting and placed it on the table, back side up. There were clear markings at the edge, reading: AV, ES. A bit further down there was an imprint of a Star of David and, still lower, "Zagreb 1939," written in pencil.

"So," Leon began.

"One moment, of course, just a moment," the lady stepped in, opened the drawer and brought out a thin file. "The documentation."

Leon quickly scanned the paperwork in English. It concluded with a stamp and signature: France Benko, Expert, United Nations Office, New York, 1989. Above it was the final conclusion, written in block letters and numbers: estimated value - eighteen million dollars.

Bata understood all of it, without needing any translation. He cleared his throat, turned to Leon and spoke in a somewhat hoarse voice: "Translate, my son. Tell her that this thing is out of our range. The best thing for this lady would be to try and sell it in New York."

Leon hung the painting back up.

Leon and Bata declined Mrs. Winkler's invitation for a drink with the excuse that their ladies were waiting for them with cake at Amadeus coffee house.

"Another time, then," the lady said, "Thank you very much for your advice."

They bid farewell. Outside, on the always busy Kärntner Strasse, Bata paused, turned to Leon with a smile, and said:

"It seems the world isn't going to end yet after all."

www.ingramcontent.com/pod-product-compliance
Lightning Source LLC
Chambersburg PA
CBHW071016240526
45469CB00006BD/1946